Driving Complexity in Economic Development

Diego Gomez • Sebastian Aparicio
David Urbano
Editors

Driving Complexity in Economic Development

The Role of Institutions, Entrepreneurship, and Innovation

palgrave
macmillan

Editors
Diego Gomez
Fundación ECSIM
Medellin, Colombia

David Urbano
Department of Business
Universitat Autonoma de Barcelona
Cerdanyola del Vallès, Barcelona, Spain

Centre for Entrepreneurship and Social Innovation Research (CREIS)
Universitat Autònoma de Barcelona
Sabadell, Barcelona, Spain

Sebastian Aparicio
Department of Business
Universitat Autònoma de Barcelona
Cerdanyola del Vallès, Barcelona, Spain

Centre for Entrepreneurship and Social Innovation Research (CREIS)
Universitat Autònoma de Barcelona
Sabadell, Barcelona, Spain

ISBN 978-3-031-34385-8 ISBN 978-3-031-34386-5 (eBook)
https://doi.org/10.1007/978-3-031-34386-5

This Palgrave Macmillan imprint is published by the registered company Springer Nature Switzerland AG.
The registered company address is: Gewerbestrasse 11, 6330 Cham, Switzerland

Preface

A classical contest between Adam Smith and Karl Marx has brought different perspectives regarding the role of entrepreneurs and business owners in the economic development process. Great contributions had been made to the literature on economic development, spanning from linear theories of development that include substantial investments in capital factor, savings, and technological change as the main drivers of economic growth, to theories of physical capital accumulation, human capital, labor capital mobilization across economic sectors, economic dependency from less developed to more developed countries, as well as balanced and unbalanced growth approaches. Although these theoretical developments might have different perspectives, it is suggested that the drivers of economic development remain disparate. This is also a matter of reality as many countries' growth and development move in different directions. These main differences stem from low technology and weak institutional structure, as well as little innovation and entrepreneurial activity in regions and countries.

Explorations concerning different development paths and growth divergence are not new. For example, the idea of creative destruction has

The original version of the book has been revised. A correction to this book can be found at https://doi.org/10.1007/978-3-031-34386-5_14.

emerged to explain upward fluctuations in favor of both developed and developing economies. This is an idea that has been further developed in terms of both innovation and entrepreneurship as key sources of economic development, echoing the public policy sphere that moves from theory to practice. As an example, successful policies have been observed in countries such as Germany, South Korea, Ireland, and Singapore, among others. In these cases, politicians were able to go beyond populism and work for all the actors who are part of the economic system. Key political strategies consisted of encouraging people to start a new venture and supporting them to achieve growth through the investment of productive projects.

Drawing on past successful events, the literature studying the effects of entrepreneurship and innovation on fundamental indicators that spur development has been growing. Despite the extant evidence, scholars and policymakers are still clamoring for studies dealing with the exploration of those factors that enable a positive association between entrepreneurship, innovation, and economic development. For instance, in developing countries, institutional reforms have been considered precursors of lagged economies, which are usually characterized by high levels of necessity-driven entrepreneurship.

Placing emphasis on these economies helps us disentangle the formation, and hence the role, of entrepreneurship and innovation in these countries. For example, the (formal and informal) institutional structure of Latin American countries has influenced a divergent process of economic development. Corruption has affected not only entrepreneurship but also other institutional aspects that alter economic decisions. In this sense, it has been important to identify the harmful effect of taxes on economic development. Extant evidence has suggested that this relationship varies depending on the socioeconomic structure of the countries. Yet, the association between these institutional characteristics and entrepreneurship and innovation seems to be less explored in developing countries such as Latin America.

Given the severity of institutional problems in less developed countries, governments have been interested in capturing dimensions of development beyond economic terms. Policy initiatives to diagnose poverty, inequality, living standards, and so on in these countries have unveiled the problem of turning theory into practice. For example, there is still a discrepancy in how to measure economic development since it depends on many factors. Given this difficulty, approaches such as sociotechnical subsystems have emerged to bring different insights into the economic development discussion. Yet, there is still a long way to go in linking institutions to economic development through innovation and entrepreneurship.

In this regard, this book offers literature and theoretical analyses, as well as empirical evidence across regions and countries (with special emphasis on Latin America), aimed at exploring the complexity involved in the economic development process, which considers institutions (i.e., fundamental), as well as entrepreneurship and innovation (i.e., proximate) as key elements that explain the existence of developed and lagged economies. To this end, institutional economics, a sociotechnical subsystems approach, and growth theories are used to frame our analysis. Similarly, the utilization of systemic and simultaneous structures is considered in this book to comprehend the effect of entrepreneurship and innovation on economic development.

The obtained findings suggest that innovative entrepreneurship is definitely a key piece within the complex engine of economic development. Corporate taxes are squeezing and asphyxiating new ventures and small- and medium-sized enterprises, preventing them from exploring other international markets, enhancing performance, and contributing to economic growth. Regulating this institutional characteristic is not enough. The sociotechnical subsystem approach shows that different elements should be synchronized to explain not only economic growth but also poverty alleviation, inequality, human development, and sustainability.

Thanks to these results, this book provides different perspectives on theories, methodological approaches, and cases that might attract attention from a wide-ranging audience, spanning from academics and policymakers to students interested in economics, management, and business. Cross-country comparisons are helpful for understanding the economic development phenomenon as, presumably, a common global purpose. Yet, the emphasis on Latin America evidences the misalignment between institutions, entrepreneurship, innovation, and economic development.

The elaboration of this book counted on many friends and colleagues, who have contributed through comments in conferences, seminars, meetings, and so on. We are grateful to all of those who have read and attended sessions where we had the opportunity to present our preliminary findings. Also, many thanks to the anonymous reviewers and editors who, through their comments, have enhanced this book. A special appreciation goes to Diego Martinez-Moya, who has contributed to a number of chapters and supported the development of others.

Diego Gomez acknowledges Fundación ECSIM for their constant assistance and financial support during the development of this book. Sebastian Aparicio and David Urbano acknowledge the financial support from the project ECO2017-87885-P (Spanish Ministry of Economy & Competitiveness). In particular, Sebastian Aparicio, as a Serra Húnter Fellow, acknowledges the Serra Húnter Program and the Catalan government for their constant support. Additionally, Sebastian acknowledges the COLCIENCIAS Ph.D. program (617/2013), as well as Sapiencia-Enlaza Mundos (Municipio de Medellín), for their financial support during his Ph.D. studies. Finally, David acknowledges the financial support from the 2017-SGR-1056 project (Economy & Knowledge Department, Catalan Government) and ICREA under the ICREA Academia program.

Last but not least, we are very grateful to Liz Barlow and Esther Rani from Palgrave Macmillan and Springer Nature for their constant support and encouragement. We appreciate their enthusiastic help, as well as their wisdom, care, and effort, in guiding and motivating us to move this passionate project forward.

Medellín, Colombia; Barcelona, Spain

Diego Gomez
Sebastian Aparicio
David Urbano

Contents

List of Contributors

Sebastian Aparicio Department of Business and Centre for Entrepreneurship and Social Innovation Research (CREIS), Universitat Autònoma de Barcelona, Cerdanyola del Vallés, Barcelona, Spain

Diego Gomez Fundación ECSIM, Medellin, Colombia

Diego Martinez-Moya Fundación ECSIM, Medellin, Colombia

David Urbano Department of Business and Centre for Entrepreneurship and Social Innovation Research (CREIS), Universitat Autònoma de Barcelona, Cerdanyola del Vallés, Barcelona, Spain

List of Figures

List of Tables

1

General Introduction

Diego Gomez, Sebastian Aparicio, and David Urbano

1.1 Main Motivation

Every economy, in its most simplified form, can be viewed from the supply side or the demand side. Customers and suppliers constantly interact with each other, generating a huge quantity of transactions that motivate new forms of human interaction. Observing, understanding, controlling, and, above all, motivating such exchanges is difficult due to the high complexity involved in markets and across their members. Baumol (1990) suggests that people respond to (institutional) incentives, which are utilized to make productive, unproductive, and destructive decisions. Taking this idea into consideration, do these incentives explain the

D. Gomez
Fundación ECSIM, Medellin, Colombia

S. Aparicio (✉) • D. Urbano
Department of Business, Universitat Autònoma de Barcelona,
Cerdanyola del Vallés, Barcelona, Spain

Centre for Entrepreneurship and Social Innovation Research (CREIS),
Universitat Autònoma de Barcelona, Sabadell, Barcelona, Spain
e-mail: Sebastian.Aparicio@uab.cat

D. Gomez et al. (eds.), *Driving Complexity in Economic Development*,
https://doi.org/10.1007/978-3-031-34386-5_1

growth and development process? If incentives are key elements, why do differences across regions and countries still exist? Although the secret of economic development may appear to be well known, the way in which all elements form a system where actions and reactions emerge to explain growth and development is still a mystery (Helpman, 2004).

The development quest is certainly not new. Classic works such as Adam Smith (1775), David Ricardo (1817), and others had these questions in mind. However, all their efforts were limited to explaining economic growth, leaving space for exploring the chaos involved in the development process. Smith, for example, began his work *The Wealth of Nations* with the study of the division of labor. From there, he built a complete perspective with very coherent ideas that led to the explanation of why one nation is richer than another. Similarly, David Ricardo analyzed countries' production based on factor endowments (e.g., land, capital, and labor), their respective advantages over other nations, and their relations with foreign markets, which determine the social and economic differences across countries.

Both classical views set up the main pillars upon which traditional economic thought rests and builds its evolution. Although topics such as unemployment, interest rates, quality of life, and other issues related to economic development are noted in the classical perspective, Smith's and Ricardo's purpose was focused on explaining countries' production.

Economic thought gained maturity under classical ideas, which were evolving to the neoclassical perspective. Through this approach, scholars and policymakers paid attention to the configuration of markets via optimization processes, whose assumption implies that all actors behave in a rational way. Drawing on this idea, Schumpeter (1911) appeared to have a similar objective, as his goal was to understand the fluctuations of the economic cycle. From this viewpoint, suppliers (i.e., firms) are not taken for granted. Accordingly, the way in which economies grow and develop is due to the existence of entrepreneurs and their innovations. In this way, people involved in entrepreneurship and innovation take a greater role in the performance of regions and countries by generating a series of economic and social benefits. Schumpeter (1911) suggests that the entrepreneur, who is motivated by profits and market penetration, performs innovative activities (via research and development—R&D), demands more qualified personnel, requires better institutions, generates a reallocation of factors, and encourages changes in demand patterns.

Motivated by these ideas, Nelson and Winter (1982) proposed an evolutionary vision of economic change. That is, the economy is viewed in a more dynamic and changing way over time, but supported by the idea of a better economic development based on business opportunities, as well as the adequate performance of new and established companies. All this generates greater competition in the economy for products and services with high added value. Moreover, this obligates the economy to constantly increase the training of the working population, who, in addition to entrepreneurs, are key actors that search for productive innovations. Therefore, from the supply side, it is the new ventures that serve as the engine for achieving better economies in all dimensions.

The Schumpeterian perspective is helpful in understanding those gears (i.e., entrepreneurs and firms) that directly move an existing economic engine forward. Yet, the way these elements are configurated is partly explained through this research stream. While Nelson and Winter (1982) also showed curiosity about the interaction between the external and internal environments, as well as the way both interact with each other, there was not a clear framework that helped in further comprehending how the external environment occurs and configures exchanges and interactions among economic agents. North (1990, 2005), from a historical perspective, introduced the notion of institutions, which constitute the set of rules and incentives within which people make decisions. Metaphorically speaking, institutional economics frames all gears that intervene within a huge engine such as a national economy.

The evolution of all these ideas suggests that economic development depends on direct (e.g., entrepreneurs, firms, or innovation) and fundamental factors (institutions), which differ across regions and countries (North & Thomas, 1973). Hence, by using a systemic perspective, this book seeks to explore the elements that constitute an institutional environment that is conducive for entrepreneurship and innovation as a catalyst of economic development. The book offers a series of chapters that explain using theory and extant literature the association between innovative entrepreneurial firms and the development path of countries, which is conditioned by institutions such as regulation, taxes, culture, and so on. Empirically speaking, the book provides evidence from across the globe, but due to important differences between developed and developing economies, a special emphasis is given to Latin American countries.

1.2 Research Contribution

The use of evidence observed through different lenses helps this book contribute to the entrepreneurship and economic development literature in different ways. First, by conducting a detailed study of the previous literature, it is possible to identify the true role of entrepreneurship and innovation in the economic development process. This entails an exhaustive review of the direct relationship between entrepreneurship and economic growth, as well as a detailed analysis of existing development theories. By doing so, this book emphasizes entrepreneurship and innovation as central elements into the economic thought.

Second, embracing complexity enables us to strengthen a systemic view through the identification of socio-technical subsystems, which becomes a versatile approach to better measure and comprehend economic development. By employing this approach, it is possible to embrace different elements (e.g., income, labor, and government size) that constitute interrelated equations boosted by institutions, entrepreneurship, and innovation.

Third, by reaching beyond economic factors by incorporating gross domestic product (GDP), the human development index (HDI), and the Gini index, we provide a more compelling perspective regarding the importance of entrepreneurship and innovation for different dimensions of development. In this regard, we contribute to the literature about entrepreneurship and economic development, in which traditional views have been adopted to estimate production functions. Using socio-technical subsystems helps us embrace the existing interdependence among economic development variables that include growth, poverty, and inequality.

Fourth, while we observe case studies of successful nations promoting entrepreneurship and innovation to achieve economic development, it may be possible to diagnose existing shortcomings in developing countries such as those in Latin America and discuss blueprints to improve current development, which allows us, fifth, to examine the role of the institutional structure in facilitating economic development in emerging economies.

Sixth, we emphasize the true effect of the taxation system on innovation and entrepreneurship as a helpful way of understanding the unstable institutional structure. Through these contributions, we hope to make clear policy recommendations for developing countries to boost innovation and entrepreneurship, while highlighting the consequences of weak institutional structures and the harmful dependence upon factors such as taxes. Academia may find our contributions useful for the discussion of case studies, theoretical debates, and literature support, which emphasize the importance of entrepreneurship and innovation for economic development.

Finally, we find that although entrepreneurship, institutions, and innovation are fundamental to the economic development of countries, there are forces that have not yet been identified because of the difficulty of bringing them down to a macroeconomic level. These include the profitability of investment projects (internal rate of return), operating costs, country risk, access to financing, and some other variables that directly affect the main actors of the story, households, and firms, which make investment decisions and carry out entrepreneurial processes that are the driving force of the economy.

1.3 Theoretical Aspects

Development theories do not always reach a consensus regarding the definition of economic development. Some of them are more attached to economic growth, and others are more related to social issues, such as inequality, well-being, and quality of life. For example, for Sen (1988), economic development represents the capacity and freedom that nations have to not only create wealth, but also promote and maintain prosperity and well-being in economic, political, environmental, and cultural terms. Another traditional concept suggests that economic development is the process of productive transformation that allows a reallocation of the existing resources in an economy, all via industrialization (Meier, 2001; Syrquin, 1988). The classical view focused on the importance of investment and capital accumulation (Solow, 1956; Swan, 1956). However, when designing policies, classical theories fell short, since these disregarded some elements that are fundamental for the development of a country (e.g., geography and institutions).

After a stagnation in economic development theories, new proposals emerged to try to answer the million-dollar question (why are some economies more developed than others?), by including a series of elements perhaps assumed in traditional theories. Thus, aspects such as institutions, in addition to technological and pecuniary externalities, as well as the quality of life, labor formality, education, and endogenous innovation have arisen. From here, development is assumed to be a matter of social engineering, which is presented as a process similar to that of an organization, which results from the coherent and articulated effort of the entire society (Hausmann & Rodrik, 2003).

This new idea consists of conceiving development as a system of continuous flows of social decisions, where individuals, companies, and governments interact at the same time. Hence, individuals are considered the core of society; firms are the engine driving the dynamics of development; and governments facilitate the interaction between individuals and companies (Aparicio et al., 2016). Accordingly, rethinking development implies the recognition of new ventures as entities capable of generating employment, innovation, and competitiveness, articulating the whole society to achieve better levels of well-being (Audretsch, 2007).

Therefore, it is worth asking, what are the effects of new venture creation on economic development? The vast literature is conclusive regarding the impact on job creation (Urbano et al., 2019; van Praag & Versloot, 2007). However, this becomes a vaguely achieved objective since formal jobs, with trained and skilled personnel, are what economies need (Acs et al., 2013). The persistent creation of formal jobs may generate high income, which motivates individuals to pursue a goal such as entrepreneurship.

Achieving formality requires appropriate institutions. North (1990, 2005) defines them as the rules that regulate economic and non-economic transactions. Accordingly, societies need a set of incentives that can be created through rules, norms, and regulations (i.e., formal institutions), as well as culture, social codes, and habits (i.e., informal institutions). If institutions incentivize entrepreneurs to contribute to the economy and society, formal jobs are created (Baumol, 1990). An appropriate system of incentives entails, for instance, eliminating an unnecessary number of procedures required to open a new business; a clear contracting method and enforcement of contracts; an efficient taxation system that guarantees the proper functioning of new and established small- and medium-sized enterprises (SMEs); and the legitimacy of property rights (North, 2005; Williamson & Winter, 1991). Consequently, to comprehend the process of economic change fueled by new firms, the alignment of institutions across all levels and sectors is essential (Williamson, 2000).

Institutions can also encourage entrepreneurship (directly) and economic development (indirectly) by facilitating funding, through either the private or the public sector (Baumol, 1990). Investment support and hence decisions are encouraged if entrepreneurs identify productive projects that effectively lead to higher firm growth (Acs et al., 2013). As a result, new products or production processes appear, which can cause spillover effects, incentivizing greater competition for both these new products and their required inputs (Acs et al., 2013).

The effect of permanent innovation helps countries to specialize to a greater extent in different products, achieving comparative advantages in goods with higher added value. In this way, it is possible to think of better levels of competitiveness that make it easier for them to face the difficult competition that arises in the globalized world. Drawing on this idea, Hausmann and Rodrik (2003) comment on the importance of learning in innovative processes, which have two basic pillars: discipline and promotion. With these elements, new business opportunities can be identified and then materialized.

Hence, economic development depends on an adequate process, where institutions, entrepreneurship, and innovation interact simultaneously with national performance. With these basic elements, as well as the variables around them, it would be possible to have an economy, not only with a higher level of production but also with a better quality of life and well-being.

1.4 Structure of the Book

Motivated by the theoretical basis and gaps explained in this introductory chapter, a collection of literature, theoretical, and empirical analyses is brought together in this book. The departure point is the exploration of existing literature that links entrepreneurship to economic growth (Chap. 2). In this chapter, a systematic literature review over the 1993–2021 period is conducted. Nuances in entrepreneurship measures such as self-employment, business owners, and total early-stage entrepreneurial activity are identified, and a meta-regression analysis complements what the literature confirms regarding the positive relationship between entrepreneurial activity and economic growth. However, previous works have also revealed that entrepreneurship does not always benefit the economy. In this regard, it is important to define and explore economic development as a potential outcome of activities such as entrepreneurship and innovation (Chap. 3).

Given the vast literature on the economic development of nations, in this chapter, we chronologically review the most influential theories regarding economic development. First, this chapter reviews the classical theories, taking as its fundamental focus those involving endogenous and exogenous economic growth. Second, it reviews Schumpeterian development theories, which introduce a key part of the "heart" of this book: innovation. Finally, this chapter contributes to the discussion between accumulationists and assimilationists, as well as introduces the concept of "social capacity" within the new theories relating to system dynamics.

As divergent patterns exist, Chap. 4 reviews the growth path of some successful countries in terms of economic development, exploring the reasons why some countries have been more successful because of innovation and entrepreneurship. We analyze a battery of indicators for countries such as Korea, Singapore, Japan, Germany, and Ireland. In addition, a business perspective is considered, as some multinationals have been part of the innovation and entrepreneurship that have led to the success of these countries.

As these concepts are present in the economic development process, it is important to formally understand how different elements interact with each other to explain long-term outcomes. In this regard, Chap. 5 utilizes the notion of circular flow to mathematically represent an economy where entrepreneurs interplay with households and financial systems. Such a representation provides the basis for conducting simulations that are helpful in understanding how certain interventions (e.g., higher taxes) affect the decisions involved in undertaking entrepreneurial and innovative projects that, ultimately, affect the economy as a whole.

After highlighting the importance of innovation and entrepreneurship for the economic development of developed and developing countries in the previous chapters, Chap. 6 focuses on describing the devastating effects of taxation on innovation and entrepreneurship, and thus on economic development. First, this chapter demonstrates the strong dependence of taxation on the performance of government institutions. It then translates dependence into the negative effects of tax burdens on development in developing and developed countries.

Given that a large portion of the taxes collected in a country comes from the tax burden on businesses, Chap. 7 analyzes, from a systemic perspective, the importance of the profitability of investment projects at the country level for the economic development of countries. First, the effect of country risk/cost variables on profitability such as the internal rate of return is observed. Second, a return-on-equity variable is identified for comparison with the previous results. This chapter also studies the effects of both variables on the economic development of developing and developed countries through a three-stage estimation methodology.

Chapter 8 focuses on the Latin American case. In this regard, a number of SMEs are observed as actors constantly involved in adaptation processes to survive the negative effects of unstable institutions. In this chapter in particular, different barriers at the country, city, and firm levels are identified to examine whether companies are embedded in a harmful environment that stops them from exploring international markets. A dynamic capabilities approach is adopted to analyze those factors assisting SMEs with the adaptation process.

After unveiling the effect of country and organizational barriers on development in the previous chapter, Chap. 9 seeks to focus on studying the relationship between entrepreneurship and income generation, specifically in a developing country such as Colombia. This provides a broad picture of what is happening in developing countries, especially when individuals have differing motivations to enter productive or unproductive activities. These differences explain the existing variation across regions in Colombia.

As cross-country and regional differences exist due to corporate taxes, and profits (from companies to countries) have a strong influence on the effects on economic development, a door remains open to analyze what happens at the corporate level in developing and developed countries. Therefore, Chap. 10 sets out to study the effect of firm size across developed and developing countries. Here, the analysis of SMEs becomes essential for exploring the configuration of firms across countries, which complements the types of entrepreneurs and their macroeconomic effects observed in Chap. 9.

The evidence offered in previous chapters shows that institutions, entrepreneurship, firm growth, and innovation explain economic outcomes. Yet, other social effects have still not been considered. Chapter 11 conducts a principal components analysis regarding entrepreneurship, inequality, and poverty in developing and developed countries. First, the chapter unveils the fundamental factors underlying both inequality and poverty, which are created from the principal component analysis. This analysis allows the grouping of related variables into specific factors, which are helpful for suggesting indicators based on the fundamental factors that are better suited to explaining poverty and inequality in developed and developing countries.

Given the application of factor analysis and the identified lacuna in the theories of economic development, Chap. 12 proposes complex methodologies based on socio-technical subsystems to study and understand the complexity of a broad phenomenon such as development. On the one hand, this chapter addresses socio-technical subsystems as a fundamental theory for the study of economic development in developing and developed countries. On the other, it defines innovation and entrepreneurship as the key subsystem in the search for such cross-country development. Based on this approach, subsystems such as per capita GDP, the HDI, and the Gini coefficient are key factors that represent economic development.

Finally, Chap. 13 brings together all the ideas and conclusions derived from all the previous chapters. It highlights the main learning aspects relating to developed economies to discuss potential public strategies conducive to the economic development of developing countries.

References

Acs, Z. J., Audretsch, D. B., & Lehmann, E. E. (2013). The knowledge spillover theory of entrepreneurship. *Small Business Economics, 41*(4), 757–774.

Aparicio, S., Urbano, D., & Gómez, D. (2016). The role of innovative entrepreneurship within Colombian business cycle scenarios: A system dynamics approach. *Futures, 81*, 130–147.

Audretsch, D. B. (2007). Entrepreneurship capital and economic growth. *Oxford Review of Economic Policy, 23*(1), 63–78.

Baumol, W. J. (1990). Entrepreneurship: Productive, unproductive, and destructive. *Journal of Political Economy, 98*(5), 893–921.

Hausmann, R., & Rodrik, D. (2003). Economic development as self-discovery. *Journal of Development Economics, 72*(2), 603–633.

Helpman, E. (2004). *The mystery of economic growth*. MIT Press.

Meier, G. (2001). The old generation of development economics and the new. In G. Meier & J. Stiglitz (Eds.), *Frontiers of development economics. The future in perspective*. World Bank.

Nelson, R., & Winter, S. (1982). *An evolutionary theory of economic change*. Harvard University Press.

North, D. C. (1990). *Institutions, institutional change and economic performance*. Cambridge University Press.

North, D. C. (2005). *Understanding the process of economic change*. Princeton University Press.

North, D. C., & Thomas, R. P. (1973). *The rise of the western world: a new economic history*. Cambridge University Press.

Ricardo, D. (1817). *On the principles of political economy*. J. Murray.

Schumpeter, J. A. (1911). *The theory of economic development: an inquiry into profits, capital, credit, interest, and the business cycle*. New Jersey: Transaction Books.

Sen, A. (1988). The concept of development. In H. Chenery & T. N. Srinivasan (Eds.), *Handbook of development economics* (Vol. I). North Holland.

Smith, A. (1775). *The Wealth of Nations: An inquiry into the nature and causes of the Wealth of Nations*. Harriman House.
Solow, R. M. (1956). A contribution to the theory of economic growth. *The Quarterly Journal of Economics, 70*(1), 65–94.
Swan, T. W. (1956). Economic growth and capital accumulation. *Economic Record, 32*(2), 334–361.
Syrquin, M. (1988). Patterns of structural change. In H. Chenery & T. N. Srinivasan (Eds.), *Handbook of development economics* (Vol. 1). North Holland.
Urbano, D., Aparicio, S., & Audretsch, D. (2019). Twenty-five years of research on institutions, entrepreneurship, and economic growth: What has been learned? *Small Business Economics, 53*(1), 21–49.
van Praag, C. M., & Versloot, P. H. (2007). What is the value of entrepreneurship? A review of recent research. *Small Business Economics, 29*(4), 351–382.
Williamson, O., & Winter, S. (1991). *The nature of the firm: Origins, evolution and development*. Oxford University Press.
Williamson, O. E. (2000). The new institutional economics: taking stock, looking ahead. *Journal of Economic Literature, 38*(3), 595–613.

2

Entrepreneurial Activity and Economic Growth: A Literature Review

Sebastian Aparicio, David Urbano, and Diego Gomez

2.1 Introduction

Without a doubt, entrepreneurship is directly linked to economic growth (Acs et al., 2012; Audretsch et al., 2013; Audretsch & Keilbach, 2008; Urbano et al., 2019), yet certain nuances exist in regard to the types and quality of entrepreneurial activity, which might explain the different roles entrepreneurship plays in the development process of various countries. Previous authors have provided evidence of the importance of entrepreneurship for growth, distinguishing among self-employment, business ownership, and entrepreneurship capital, among others (Audretsch &

S. Aparicio (✉) • D. Urbano
Department of Business, Universitat Autònoma de Barcelona, Cerdanyola del Vallés, Barcelona, Spain

Centre for Entrepreneurship and Social Innovation Research (CREIS), Universitat Autònoma de Barcelona, Sabadell, Barcelona, Spain
e-mail: Sebastian.Aparicio@uab.cat

D. Gomez
Fundación ECSIM, Medellin, Colombia

D. Gomez et al. (eds.), *Driving Complexity in Economic Development*,
https://doi.org/10.1007/978-3-031-34386-5_2

Keilbach, 2004a, 2004b, 2004c; Blanchflower, 2000; Carree et al., 2002, 2007). Hence, several researchers have been motivated by the economic benefits of entrepreneurship, which has been studied in the economics discipline since the 1940s and is nowadays one of the key issues explored in the subdiscipline of entrepreneurship (Carlsson et al., 2013; Tsvetkova, 2012). Although quite extensive literature exists regarding the effects of entrepreneurial activity on economic growth, there remains a need to understand the evolution of this relationship through a systematic literature review (Van Praag & Versloot, 2007). Audretsch et al. (2008) raised questions about what lens is used to perceive the relationship between entrepreneurship and economic growth, what additional variables can be used for international comparisons, and what other effects could result from this relationship.

Thus, our objective in this chapter is to analyze the content and evolution of research focused on the relationship between entrepreneurial activity and economic growth, highlighting the theoretical approaches that have been advanced and the empirical strategies that have been used. The methodology consists of categorizing and selecting the articles according to a systematic literature review. Hence, using the Web of Science database, we defined two criteria to identify the most relevant articles dealing with this relationship. First, the paper must have focused on the studies that have been the most often cited, considering the keywords that link entrepreneurship with economic growth. Second, in order to describe the results that apply to entrepreneurship and economic growth and that are based on state-of-the-art research methods, only literature between 1993 and 2021 was selected.

This chapter focuses on the results we found by applying keywords and identifying journals, years, authors, hypotheses proposed, theoretical frameworks, and methods used to relate entrepreneurship to economic growth. The search was conducted according to the following keywords in the title, abstract, and text of the articles: "entrepreneurship capital," "entrepreneurial activity," "ownership firms," "self-employment," "business ownership," "economic growth," and "economic development." We found that entrepreneurship and economic growth yielded 2438 results, followed by entrepreneurship and economic development, with 3189 results. We then used variations of "entrepreneurship," such as "entrepreneurship capital and economic growth" (247 results) or "entrepreneurship capital and economic development" (197 results), "entrepreneurial activity and economic growth" (259) or with "economic development" (380), "ownership firms" (326 with "economic growth" and 301 with "economic development"), "self-employment and economic growth" or with "economic development" (142 and 169, respectively), and "business ownership and economic growth" or with "economic development" (196 and 278, respectively). To filter these results we first dropped articles that were repeatedly selected using different key word combinations, and then we considered only articles that focused on the causality from entrepreneurial activities to economic growth. Thus, the number of articles selected to explain this relationship was 90; these were classified according to three types of literature to which most of the articles related: (1) empirical issues (67), followed by (2) theory (17), and (3) the introduction of special issues (6).

Furthermore, we assessed the effect of entrepreneurship on economic growth by using meta-regression analysis (MRA) as a tool. According to Hunter and Schmidt (2004) and Stanley (2008), an MRA can be performed only on the basis of a sample of studies that all measured a certain type of relationship. Only 15 articles provided the information required to conduct this type of methodology, which consists of collecting the average relationship of economic growth and entrepreneurship as well as the sample size. In some cases, we assumed that the same value is based on a similar data set used in different articles found in the literature review. To avoid differences in units, we used a natural logarithm to express all measures in percentages (Harbord & Higgins, 2008). In addition, most authors report several regressions arising from testing procedures and/or from comparative analyses of different specifications (e.g., different sectors or different types of countries). However, the selection criterion was in each case to take the authors' preferred or base specification(s) for the MRA database, although in some cases the reader is left to identify these. Even base specifications usually permitted more than one regression per study because the author(s) often applied their preferred specification(s) to different samples, different entrepreneurship indices, different periods, and different endogeneity assumptions. These were recorded as independent regressions because our purpose was to investigate the implications of these heterogeneities for the reported effects. The MRA allowed an understanding of the positive effect of entrepreneurship on economic growth.

After this introduction, this chapter is structured as follows. In the next section, we present the different frameworks used to link entrepreneurship with economic growth. We then report the results in terms of key words used, number of papers per author and per journal, common hypotheses proposed, theoretical frameworks used, and techniques for assessing the relationship. Next, we discuss and analyze the results presented in the previous sections, complementing them through MRA. Finally, we present the conclusions and highlight the challenges of researching the link between entrepreneurship and economic growth from the perspective of institutional economic theory.

2.2 Conceptual Framework: Linking Entrepreneurship to Economic Growth

One of the basic questions in economics is "What drives economic growth?" Although neoclassical theory has identified that investment in physical capital and labor are the main drivers (Solow, 1956; Swan, 1956), *endogenous growth theory* (Romer, 1986, 1990) has emphasized the importance of knowledge accumulation and hence the creation of knowledge capital. Thus, a new class of growth model recognizes some aspects of social factors that are also important in the generation of economic growth. According to this literature, entrepreneurship could be an important factor in economic growth (Minniti & Lévesque, 2010), and therefore it should be encouraged where investments in social capital are greater (Amin, 2000; Simmie, 2003; Smith, 2003).

Minniti and Lévesque (2010) used this idea to incorporate entrepreneurship behavior in the *Solow–Swan growth model*. A theoretical structure has been developed to demonstrate how entrepreneurship influences the national steady state. Aparicio, Urbano, and Audretsch (2016), Audretsch and Keilbach (2004a, 2004b, 2004c, 2005, 2008), Bjørnskov and Foss (2013), Bosma et al. (2018), Iyigun and Owen (1999), and Urbano et al. (2020) have assessed econometrically the effect of entrepreneurship on economic growth. They included entrepreneurship as a new input in the Solow–Swan model to find its relative importance in the growth process. Other authors, such as Carree et al. (2002, 2007), have studied how disequilibrium in the entrepreneurship rate could affect growth in a sample of countries at different development stages. All of these studies have used different frameworks to relate entrepreneurship to economic growth. Thus, it is possible to identify three theoretical streams to understand this relationship: (1) neoclassical economic growth theory, (2) Schumpeterian theory, and (3) endogenous growth theory.

First, Solow (1956) and Swan (1956) based their model of economic growth on the neoclassical production function whose key factors are capital and labor. Ever since then, research has relied on the model of the production function as a basis for explaining the determinants of economic growth. Romer's (1986, 1990) and Lucas's (1988) critique of the Solow approach was not of the basic model of the neoclassical production function. Instead, they introduced variables, such as human capital and externalities, into this analysis to differentiate the types of labor. They found that more skilled labor generates positive externalities as well as more economic growth. Iyigun and Owen (1999) and Blanchflower (2000) have used the neoclassical production function, taking into account human capital as well as entrepreneurship (self-employment) as the special characteristics of individuals. Hence, entrepreneurship is assessed in the economic growth model to identify its impact and complementarity.

Second, according to Schumpeter (1934), entrepreneurs are agents capable of generating shocks in the economic cycle through the innovation process. Schumpeter developed a theory of economic development that is based on the process of creative destruction generated by entrepreneurial activity. Additional advances in this line have combined the Schumpeterian framework with endogenous growth models (Aghion & Howitt, 1992). Drawing on this, some authors have focused on the relationship between entrepreneurship and economic growth, taking into account the stages of economic development, finding that business ownership and gross domestic product (GDP) per capita have a *U*-shaped form (Carree et al., 2002, 2007; Van Stel & Carree, 2004). On the basis of this theory, other authors have proposed that entrepreneurship is a conduit of knowledge that affects economic growth (Agarwal et al., 2007; Audretsch, 2007; Audretsch & Keilbach, 2008; Noseleit, 2013).

Third, according to Baumol (1993), the relationship between entrepreneurship and economic growth can be studied from the perspective of endogenous growth theory (Romer, 1990), in which entrepreneurship, instead of labor, could be the key to progress. Apart from entrepreneurial activity, this theory includes complementary variables such as innovation, human capital, and geography, among others. Some authors have used this theory, indicating that it provides an adequate framework for understanding the relationship between entrepreneurship and economic growth (see, among others, Acs et al., 2012; Acs & Szerb, 2007; Berkowitz & DeJong, 2005; Braunerhjelm & Henrekson, 2013; Carree & Thurik, 2007).

These frameworks have been adopted because they offer the possibility of studying the direct link between entrepreneurship and economic growth. However, they do not offer explanations of the environment in which entrepreneurship influences economic growth (Wennekers & Thurik, 1999). Prior research suggests that institutions and cultural factors frame the decisions of the millions of entrepreneurs in small firms and of entrepreneurial managers working within large companies (Bjørnskov & Foss, 2016; Huggins et al., 2018; Urbano et al., 2019). Likewise, Aparicio et al. (2021a), Audretsch (2007), Audretsch et al. (2008), Audretsch and Keilbach (2004a, 2004b, 2004c, 2005, 2007), and Urbano and Aparicio (2016) have been explicit about the limitations of studying the effect of entrepreneurship on economic growth regardless of institutional and environmental factors. Thus, they have suggested the importance to future research of institutions in understanding the framework in which entrepreneurship and economic growth interact. This idea was supported by Baumol and Strom (2007) and Galor and Michalopoulos (2012), who suggested that institutions that shape entrepreneurial behavior have a vital influence on the growth and innovation that characterize each economy. Institutional economics proposes that economic growth is achieved through the adequacy of the institutions that affect human behavior (North, 1990, 2005). Indeed, institutions define a stable structure for human interaction through both formal (laws, regulations, government policies, etc.) and informal (beliefs, values, and social norms, among others) rules. These rules represent both formal and informal institutions. Using this theory, scholars have extensively studied entrepreneurial activity, including where environmental factors condition new business creation (Aidis et al., 2008; Thornton et al., 2011; Veciana & Urbano, 2008; Welter & Smallbone, 2011). Nevertheless, the literature on entrepreneurial activity and economic growth that takes into account environmental factors is limited; the issue of the proper identification of institutions that encourage entrepreneurship and positively affect economic growth still persists.

2.3 Findings of the Literature Review

Among the 90 selected articles, we identified several hypotheses, frameworks, and methodologies. We focused on the different identification strategies the authors used to conduct their studies. Thus, we found different approaches represented in hypotheses, supported by different theoretical frameworks, and that were empirically tested using different techniques. To understand the literature review, it is important to identify the starting point of each author(s), taking into account the story behind this relationship. For instance, Iyigun and Owen (1999) presented an endogenous growth model by which individuals choose to increase either their human capital or their experience through entrepreneurial activity. They found that both decisions positively affect economic growth. Also, Wennekers and Thurik (1999) presented a literature review about the positive effects of entrepreneurship, not only as a direct driver of growth but also as a conduit for knowledge and innovation. Similarly, Blanchflower (2000) and Carmona et al. (2016) used self-employment as a proxy for entrepreneurship to analyze its determinants and its effect on economic growth across countries. They found a negative and positive relationship, respectively, between entrepreneurship and economic growth. Following that, Carree et al. (2002) and Prieger et al. (2016) established the hypothesis that the relationship between these two variables has a *U*-shaped form, which was helpful in understanding the optimal level of entrepreneurship. Countries with low income levels have high self-employment rates; medium-income countries have low self-employment rates; more developed economies have self-employment rates that are higher than those of medium-income economies but lower than those of developing economies. In summary, there are hypotheses about the effects of entrepreneurship and economic growth, as well as about the *U*-shaped curve that shows the different relationships with economic development, depending on the stage in which each country is.

In theoretical articles, some authors have analyzed the *entrepreneurship–economic growth hypothesis* (Gries & Naudé, 2009; Minniti & Lévesque, 2010; Sternberg & Wennekers, 2005; Van Praag & Versloot, 2007; Wennekers & Thurik, 1999). In fact, our literature review suggests that entrepreneurship can be approached from different points of view. Thus, each article tests the hypothesis, depending on data availability. Self-employment data, for example, were used by Blanchflower (2000), Iyigun and Owen (1999), and Van Stel et al. (2005), whereas data about business owners were used by Carree and Thurik (2007), locus and content of knowledge by Carlsson et al. (2009), and number of entrepreneurs by Braunerhjelm et al. (2009). Other authors, such as Acs et al. (2018), Aparicio et al. (2021a), Bosma et al. (2018), Castaño et al. (2016), Hessels and Van Stel (2009), Nissan et al. (2011), Urbano et al. (2020); Valliere and Peterson (2009), Wennekers et al. (2005), and Wong et al. (2005) used the entrepreneurial activity captured in the Total Early-Stage Entrepreneurial Activity index, which was developed by Global Entrepreneurship Monitor (GEM). A different approach was taken by Audretsch (2007) and Urbano and Aparicio (2016), who used entrepreneurship capital as an independent variable in the neoclassical economic growth model and regional economic growth as a dependent variable.

Regarding the regional level, another hypothesis was identified, which consists of how entrepreneurship affects regional economic growth. Indeed, Audretsch and Fritsch (2002), Audretsch and Keilbach (2004a, 2004b, 2004c, 2005), Brixy (2014), Belitski and Desai (2016), Capello and Lenzi (2016), Content et al. (2020), Fritsch and Wyrwich (2017), Gonzalez-Pernía and Peña-Legazkue (2015), Huggins et al. (2018), Müller (2016), and Noseleit (2013) used regional data to assess whether there is a positive impact of entrepreneurship on regional economic growth. Berkowitz and DeJong (2005), Mueller (2007), and Stephens and Partridge (2011) tested this hypothesis in other regions and found similar results. This could indicate that the effects of entrepreneurship are robust, both at the national and regional levels.

From a theoretical point of view, geography plays a role in this relationship and helps facilitate an understanding not only of economic growth but also of economic development. This is the other type of hypothesis we found in the literature review. First, some studies, such as those by Acs and Szerb (2007), Carree et al. (2002, 2007), Liñán and

Fernandez-Serrano (2014), and Van Stel and Carree (2004), related entrepreneurship to economic development (GDP per capita) depending on the stage of development. Thus, a new hypothesis is proposed, which is that there is a relationship between entrepreneurship and economic growth in a *U*-shaped form. Second, studies such as those by Acs, Desai, and Hessels (2008), Amorós et al. (2012), Biondi (2008), Brouwer (2003), and Naudé (2009) found positive effects of entrepreneurship on economic development. Biondi (2008) and Brouwer (2003) commented on the relationship in a theoretical sense, and Acs, Desai, and Hessels (2008), Amorós et al. (2012), and Naudé (2009) tested the hypothesis using different types of data.

Although previous research has shown that entrepreneurship plays a direct role in the achievement of economic growth, it has also considered the idea of considering entrepreneurship as a conduit of knowledge spillover that positively affects economic growth (Acs, Desai, & Klapper, 2008; Acs et al., 2012; Agarwal et al., 2007, Audretsch, 2007; Audretsch & Keilbach, 2004a, 2004b, 2004c, 2008; Noseleit, 2013). It is worth emphasizing that Audretsch (2018) opened the possibility to further explore the capacity entrepreneurs have to absorb and create knowledge, which brings benefits to society and the economy through innovative projects and ideas.

To achieve such effects, Audretsch and Keilbach (2004a, 2004b, 2004c), Bjørnskov and Foss (2016), and Urbano et al. (2019) suggested that entrepreneurship requires an adequate context for generating more impact on economic growth and multiplying knowledge spillover. Thus, it is important to take into account institutions in the analysis. Therefore, a new hypothesis was proposed by Baumol and Strom (2007), Bjørnskov and Foss (2013), Braunerhjelm and Henrekson (2013), Cumming et al. (2014), King and Levine (1993), and Van de Ven (1993), suggesting that institutions explain the relationship between entrepreneurship and economic development. Baumol and Strom (2007) discussed the importance of institutions in understanding the relationship between entrepreneurship and economic development, and Alwakid et al. (2021), Aparicio et al. (2021a, 2021b), Aparicio, Urbano, and Audretsch (2016), Bjørnskov and Foss (2013), Bosma et al. (2018), Braunerhjelm and Henrekson (2013), and Urbano et al. (2020) tested the effect of institutions on economic development.

We found other hypotheses in the literature review, such as that social diversity is conducive to entrepreneurship (Audretsch & Keilbach, 2007), that entrepreneurship requires an infrastructure to affect economic growth (Van de Ven, 1993), that the stage of innovation of entrepreneurship may affect growth (Etzkowitz & Klofsten, 2005), that the link between entrepreneurship and development can be explained by clusters (Rocha, 2004), and that entrepreneurship also brings benefits in terms of sustainable development (Alwakid et al., 2021; Aparicio et al., 2020) and inclusive growth (Aparicio et al., 2021a).

The hypotheses proposed in the articles already mentioned have used different theoretical frameworks to support each research question. The first approach used the neoclassical economic growth theory that consists of identifying the factors that affect economic growth in the short and long term. Authors such as Audretsch and Keilbach (2004a, 2004b, 2004c, 2005, 2007, 2008), Bjørnskov and Foss (2013), Du and O'Connor (2018), Erken et al. (2018), Iyigun and Owen (1999), and Urbano and Aparicio (2016) have assessed the effect of entrepreneurship on economic growth through econometric techniques in a Solow–Swan specification. It is important to note that this theory does not take into account entrepreneurship explicitly because it is assumed in production decisions.

The theory that takes into account entrepreneurs and their behavior is the Schumpeterian theory because it includes the idea that entrepreneurship encourages the innovation process that affects development. Some authors, such as Agarwal et al. (2007), Aparicio, Urbano, and Gómez (2016), Audretsch and Fritsch (2002), Biondi (2008), Bjørnskov and Foss (2013), Brouwer (2003), Carree et al. (2002, 2007), Ferreira et al. (2017), King and Levine (1993), Nissan et al. (2011), Rocha (2004), Sternberg and Wennekers (2005), Van de Ven (1993), Van Stel and Carree (2004), Van Stel et al. (2005), Wennekers and Thurik (1999), and Wong et al. (2005) have used this theory to support each hypothesis that relates entrepreneurship not only to economic growth but also to economic development. This theory allows the possibility of discussing the role of entrepreneurship in the growth and development process, and it includes, with theoretical support, entrepreneurship variables in the growth models.

By taking into account new variables in the economic growth model supported by theoretical frameworks it is possible discuss an evolution of neoclassical growth theory, as mentioned by Baumol (1993). In Baumol's words, entrepreneurship can be an important driver of growth both in the short and long term. When we included this idea together with the previous approach, the number of published articles increased considerably, because, since then, many authors have tested their hypotheses with the structured theory of growth. Thus, authors such as Acs et al. (2012), Acs and Szerb (2007), Aparicio et al. (2018), Audretsch and Keilbach (2008), Berkowitz and DeJong (2005), Braunerhjelm et al. (2009), Braunerhjelm and Henrekson (2013), Carlsson et al. (2009), Carree and Thurik (2007), Fritsch (2007), Gries and Naudé (2009), Hessels and van Stel (2009), Mueller (2007), Noseleit (2013), Stephens and Partridge (2011), Valliere and Peterson (2009), and Van Praag and Versloot (2007) have argued that the link between entrepreneurship and economic growth is supported in endogenous growth theory. However, Audretsch and Keilbach (2004a, 2004b, 2004c, 2008), who used both neoclassical growth theory and endogenous growth theory, highlighted not only the importance of relating entrepreneurship to economic growth but also the relevance of taking into account the context in which this relationship occurs.

Authors who have argued for the importance of institutions when considering the context that enhances new firms and positively affects economic growth have used institutional economics theory. Baumol and Strom (2007), Bjørnskov and Foss (2016), Brouwer (2003), Naudé (2009), and Urbano et al. (2019) have discussed the importance of this theory. According to their discussion, the next step in understanding the link between entrepreneurship and economic growth is through institutions. In this sense, Acs et al. (2018), Aparicio et al. (2021b), Bjørnskov and Foss (2013), Bosma et al. (2018), and Nissan et al. (2011) have introduced institutions, specifically, formal institutions in the production function. Others, such as Aparicio et al. (2021b), Aparicio, Urbano, and Audretsch (2016), Aparicio, Urbano, and Gómez (2016), and Urbano et al. (2020), have assessed the effect of institutions (both formal and informal) on entrepreneurship, which in turn impacts economic growth. These recent articles show some tendency to consider that the institutional theory is apparently quite an important framework for understanding the relationship between entrepreneurship and economic growth.

In most articles that used neoclassical economic growth theory, Schumpeterian theory, or endogenous growth theory, the a priori expectation was that the methodology most often used would be time series because the Solow–Swan model requires short- and long-term analysis. However, the literature review indicates that other methods have been used to analyze the relationship between entrepreneurship and economic growth. According to Wooldridge (2010), depending on the data, cross-section, time series, or panel data used, which have different techniques of estimation, other literature reviews and qualitative approaches have also been used. For example, Bjørnskov and Foss (2016) and Urbano et al. (2019) have thoroughly explored the current state of the art of the articles that considered the existing sequence starting from institutions through entrepreneurship and ending with economic growth. Dean et al. (2019) and Huggins et al. (2018) have deeply analyzed the potential associations between entrepreneurial activity and economic growth across regions and countries. Qualitative lenses were used to grasp details (e.g., gender inclusion and regional barriers) that escape to traditional data sets.

2.4 Analysis and Discussion: Where Is This Relationship Now, and Where Should It Advance in the Future?

Most articles found a positive effect of entrepreneurship on economic growth, even using different theoretical frameworks and techniques. At the national level, Acs et al. (2018), Aparicio et al. (2021a, 2021b), Aparicio, Urbano, and Audretsch (2016), Aparicio, Urbano, and Gómez (2016), Audretsch (2007), Audretsch and Keilbach (2008), Bosma et al. (2018), Braunerhjelm et al. (2009), Carlsson et al. (2009), Carree and Thurik (2007), Gries and Naudé (2009), Hessels and van Stel (2009), Iyigun and Owen (1999), Minniti and Lévesque (2010), Nissan et al. (2011), Noseleit (2013), Sternberg and Wennekers (2005), Urbano and Aparicio (2016), Urbano et al. (2020), Valliere and Peterson (2009), Van Praag and Versloot (2007), Wennekers et al. (2005), Wennekers and Thurik (1999), and Wong et al. (2005) all found evidence of the positive effect of entrepreneurship on economic growth. Only one article found a negative effect of self-employment on economic growth (Blanchflower, 2000). This general outcome represents an important result, considering that many of these articles have used different measures of entrepreneurship (entrepreneurship capital, self-employment, and the Total Early-Stage Entrepreneurial Activity index, among others).

At the regional level, Aparicio et al. (2018), Audretsch and Keilbach (2004a, 2004b, 2004c, 2005, 2007), Berkowitz and DeJong (2005), Content et al. (2020), Fritsch and Wyrwich (2017), Mueller (2007), Müller (2016), and Stephens and Partridge (2011) found a positive effect of entrepreneurship on growth. Audretsch and Keilbach (2004a, 2004b, 2004c) introduced the concept of entrepreneurship capital and tested it using data from German regions; Stephens and Partridge (2011) used small businesses and self-employment data to study the effect of entrepreneurship on lagging regions and found a positive impact, even in regions with low technological progress. Moreover, the impact of entrepreneurship in advanced regions was higher. Finally, Berkowitz and DeJong (2005) and Mueller (2007) used new firm creation data to study their impact on regional growth in Russian and German regions, respectively, and the impact of entrepreneurship on growth was positive as well.

Although most studies discussed above found a positive relationship between entrepreneurship and economic growth, we conducted an additional exercise based on meta-analysis techniques to assess this positive impact on growth. According to Hunter and Schmidt (2004), meta-analysis is a useful technique to take advantage of all information found in each article selected in a literature review. Among others, the methods offered by meta-analysis allow one to compare systematic similarities or differences across the findings of several articles. Put specifically, it is conducted as a meta-regression in order to assess the direction and magnitude of entrepreneurship to economic growth (Harbord & Higgins, 2008; Sharp, 1998). According to Hunter and Schmidt, using meta-regression makes it possible to conduct an estimation corrected by the sample size used in each article. They suggested that at least 20 articles could report enough information to validate the relationship stated in the research question.

To compare previous results with other studies, we carried out a search of articles that related entrepreneurship to economic growth; however, no articles that study this relationship using MRA were found. Similar assessments, such as one article that related entrepreneurship and regional development (Akgün et al., 2011); one article that dealt with education and entrepreneurship (Van der Sluis et al., 2008); and three articles that used MRA to regress economic growth in function of income inequality (De Dominicis et al., 2008), institutions (Efendic et al., 2011), and social capital (Westlund & Adam, 2010) were found. One important conclusion of the last study is the role of entrepreneurship as a societal setting in which to explain economic growth, which should be addressed in future studies. Although these articles are not related to the purpose of this chapter, they highlight the importance of MRA to complement and extend the analysis.

Given the amount of the empirical articles selected in this literature review (67), information such as mean, standard deviation, sample size, R^2 adjusted, coefficient (only regarding entrepreneurship measures), and level of analysis (national or regional) was extracted. On the basis of this sample, we used information from 21 regressions based on 15 articles to conduct an MRA. Table 2.1 presents the results of three different models: (1) only regarding the constant, (2) the assessment of entrepreneurship on economic growth, and (3) a similar regression but corrected by sample size. The results presented in Table 2.1 suggest a positive and higher impact of entrepreneurship on economic growth. Model 2 reveals lower $\hat{\tau}^2$ and higher R^2 adjusted values than Model 3, which means that this relationship presents systematic similarities within the group of articles used to conduct this exercise.

Table 2.1 Results of meta-regression analysis. Economic growth as dependent variable

	Model 1	Model 2	Model 3
Entrepreneurship		2.269***	2.300*
		(0.769)	(0.803)
Sample size			0.004
			(0.017)
Constant	7.936*	−1.461	−2.263
	(4.019)	(4.667)	(6.144)
T	338.2	243.8	256.8
R^2-adjusted		0.279	0.24
Observations	21	21	21

Note: * $p < 0.10$; *** $p < 0.01$

On the basis of Model 2, Fig. 2.1 illustrates the fitted model with only entrepreneurship as the independent variable. The circles represent the estimates from each article, sized according to the precision of each estimate. Notice that each article found a coefficient between 0 and 2, similar to the results of meta-regression. Even though the model assumes linearity, the meta-regression suggests a positive relationship between entrepreneurship and economic growth. However, the difficulties in carrying out this exercise suggest that more empirical studies regarding this relationship are needed. Hence, the importance of entrepreneurship to achieving economic growth remains not only at the policy-implication level but also at the theoretical and empirical levels, which could explore the interaction and complementary effects of other variables, as Carlsson et al. (2013) suggested.

Regarding previous results, in which most articles found a positive relationship, it is important to also consider this relationship in the development stage, as Carree et al. (2002, 2007), Fritsch (2007), Van Stel and Carree (2004), and Van Stel et al. (2005) found. According to these authors, there is a possibility of obtaining a negative effect of entrepreneurship, but they also found a positive effect of this variable. The finding was that the countries with low income levels tend to have a higher rate

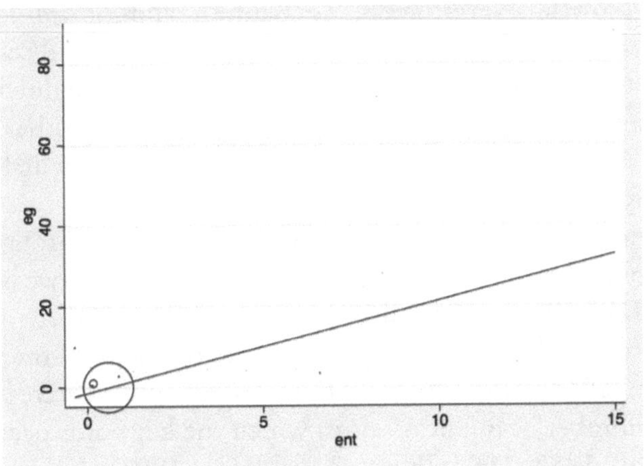

Fig. 2.1 Graph of fitted economic growth model. Note: eg, economic growth; ent, entrepreneurship

of entrepreneurial activity, whereas the countries with high income levels tend to have a lower rate of entrepreneurship; thus, depending on the stage of development, entrepreneurship has a different impact, which means that the relationship between entrepreneurship and economic growth has a *U*-shaped form.

In regard to stage of development, other authors who wanted to test the effect of entrepreneurship on economic development used the new economic growth theory. Authors such as Acs, Desai, and Hessels (2008), Acs, Desai, and Klapper (2008), Acs and Szerb (2007), Amorós et al. (2012), Biondi (2008), Brouwer (2003), Naudé (2009), and Rocha (2004) looked inside the development characteristics of each country and took into account productivity, competitiveness, and spillovers, among other factors; they concluded that entrepreneurship is useful as a conduit for knowledge and innovation. Moreover, other authors found that entrepreneurship affects export orientation (Aparicio et al., 2021b; Hessels & Van Stel, 2009).

Finally, Aparicio, Urbano, and Audretsch (2016), Bjørnskov and Foss (2013), Bosma et al. (2018), and Nissan et al. (2011) found that institutions affect economic growth; specifically, a formal institution approach, such as procedures or the time to create a new business, indicating that regulation can influence the context in which entrepreneurship affects economic growth. Nevertheless, as Baumol and Strom (2007) and Audretsch and Keilbach (2004a, 2004b, 2004c) have discussed, it is important to understand how entrepreneurship is configured by taking into account culture, beliefs, and social values, among other factors, to obtain the best understanding of the role of entrepreneurship in economic growth.

To certain extent, Fig. 2.2 illustrates these concerns through different clusters about additional keywords also used in the papers we have already analyzed. The technique is called *networks of co-occurrences of keywords*, defined by the authors or extracted from the title and abstract (Van Eck & Waltman, 2014). Accordingly, the number of clusters is created according to the number of publications in which the keywords occur together (Callon et al., 1983, 1986; Peters & Van Raan, 1993). As Fig. 2.2 shows,

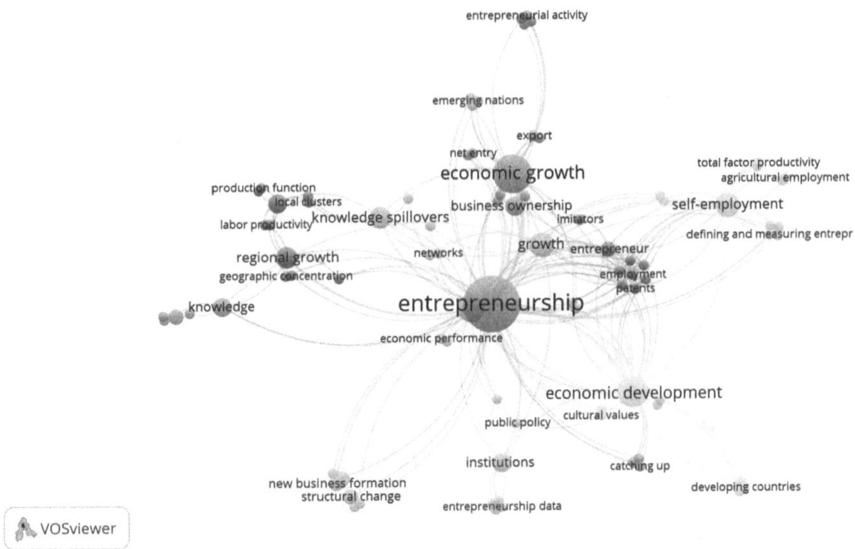

Fig. 2.2 Co-occurrence network of additional keywords used in selected papers. Note: The co-occurrence network was created through VOSviewer software. See Van Eck and Waltman (2010) for further details

the central cluster (in green) is generated by the co-occurrence of entrepreneurship and economic growth, which is related to the remaining clusters.

Despite the clusters observed in Fig. 2.2, some research questions about understanding the role of entrepreneurship in the field of economic growth persist. Hence, including the role of context and culture in the analysis of institutional economics can be useful. Thus, it is necessary to incorporate institutional variables to test which of them encourage entrepreneurial activity, which in turn may affect economic growth.

2.5 Conclusions

The relationship between entrepreneurship and economic growth was first mentioned by Schumpeter (1934). The boon of entrepreneurship research has led to the exploration of this relationship, not only at a theoretical level but also at an empirical one. Since 1999, seminal papers based on studies that used quantitative methodologies have found a positive effect of entrepreneurship on economic growth (Iyigun & Owen, 1999); however, Blanchflower (2000) found that the effect of self-employment on economic growth is negative. Carree et al. (2002) found, in effect, that a negative relationship between these two variables exists, but they also found a positive relationship and concluded that there is a *U*-shaped relationship between entrepreneurship and income level.

In regard to the different results, we analyzed the content and evolution of research that has focused on the relationship between entrepreneurship and economic. We conducted a rigorous search of articles published in journals within the Web of Science through an exploratory analysis focused on this relationship. We found that more articles were published on the hypothesis about the positive effect of entrepreneurship on economic growth, and it was determined by special issues written by Acs and Szerb (2007) and published by *Small Business Economics* journal. Since then, authors have used different measures of entrepreneurship and economic growth, concluding that there is a positive effect of entrepreneurship on economic growth. Also, the authors identified in the literature review showed that entrepreneurship is a conduit of knowledge and innovation and that it positively affects export orientation.

In addition, a meta-regression analysis validated the positive relationship between entrepreneurship and economic growth and suggested that this relationship needs be explored further, not only in terms of policy implications but also in regard to theoretical and empirical issues. As Carlsson et al. (2013) suggested, the effects of entrepreneurship could consider antecedent or complementary effects joined with other variables to unveil the significant impact of entrepreneurship on growth. Following this idea, authors such as Aparicio, Urbano, and Audretsch (2016), Bjørnskov and Foss (2013), Nissan et al. (2011), and Urbano et al. (2019)

found that institutions also affect economic growth. Nevertheless, as Audretsch et al. (2008), Audretsch and Keilbach (2004a), and Baumol and Strom (2007) discussed, it is important to understand how institutions affect entrepreneurship, and therefore it is possible to identify how entrepreneurship and economic growth interact, given each context (culture, beliefs, social values, etc.).

Some research questions persist in seeking an understanding of the role of entrepreneurship in the field of economic growth. Here, institutional economics can be useful for including context and culture in the analysis. It is thus necessary to incorporate institutional variables to test which of them encourages entrepreneurial activity, which in turn affects economic growth. Moreover, according to this account, it is possible to obtain separate effects for opportunity and necessity entrepreneurship. Finally, the convergence analysis can add elements to the discussion of the policy implications of growth in each country.

References

Acs, Z. J., Audretsch, D. B., Braunerhjelm, P., & Carlsson, B. (2012). Growth and entrepreneurship. *Small Business Economics, 39*, 289–300.

Acs, Z. J., Desai, S., & Hessels, J. (2008). Entrepreneurship, economic development and institutions. *Small Business Economics, 31*, 219–234.

Acs, Z. J., Desai, S., & Klapper, L. F. (2008). What does "entrepreneurship" data really show? *Small Business Economics, 31*, 265–281.

Acs, Z. J., Estrin, S., Mickiewicz, T., & Szerb, L. (2018). Entrepreneurship, institutional economics, and economic growth: an ecosystem perspective. *Small Business Economics, 51*(2), 501–514.

Acs, Z. J., & Szerb, L. (2007). Entrepreneurship, economic growth and public policy. *Small Business Economics, 28*, 109–122.

Agarwal, R., Audretsch, D., & Sarkar, M. B. (2007). The process of creative construction: knowledge spillovers, entrepreneurship, and economic growth. *Strategic Entrepreneurship Journal, 1*, 263–286.

Aghion, P., & Howitt, P. (1992). A model of growth through creative destruction. *Econometrica, 60*, 323–351.

Aidis, R., Estrin, S., & Mickiewicz, T. (2008). Institutions and entrepreneurship development in Russia: A comparative perspective. *Journal of Business Venturing, 23*, 656–672.

Akgün, A. Y. A., Baycan-Levent, T. N., Nijkamp, P., & Poot, J. (2011). Roles of local and newcomer entrepreneurs in rural development: A comparative meta-analytic study. *Regional Studies, 45*, 1207–1223.

Alwakid, W., Aparicio, S., & Urbano, D. (2021). The influence of green entrepreneurship on sustainable development in Saudi Arabia: The role of formal institutions. *International Journal of Environmental Research and Public Health, 18*(10), 5433.

Amin, A. (2000). Industrial districts. In E. Sheppard & T. Barnes (Eds.), *Companion to economic geography*. Blackwell.

Amorós, J. E., Fernández, C., & Tapia, J. (2012). Quantifying the relationship between entrepreneurship and competitiveness development stages in Latin America. *International Entrepreneurship and Management Journal, 8*, 249–270.

Aparicio, S., Audretsch, D., & Urbano, D. (2021a). Does entrepreneurship matter for inclusive growth? The role of social progress orientation. *Entrepreneurship Research Journal, 11*(4), 20190308.

Aparicio, S., Audretsch, D., & Urbano, D. (2021b). Why is export-oriented entrepreneurship more prevalent in some countries than others? Contextual antecedents and economic consequences. *Journal of World Business, 56*(3), 101177.

Aparicio, S., Turro, A., & Noguera, M. (2020). Entrepreneurship and intrapreneurship in social, sustainable, and economic development: Opportunities and challenges for future research. *Sustainability, 12*(21), 8958.

Aparicio, S., Urbano, D., & Audretsch, D. (2016). Institutional factors, opportunity entrepreneurship and economic growth: Panel data evidence. *Technological Forecasting and Social Change, 102*, 45–61.

Aparicio, S., Urbano, D., & Gómez, D. (2016). The role of innovative entrepreneurship within Colombian business cycle scenarios: A system dynamics approach. *Futures, 81*, 130–147.

Aparicio, S., Urbano, D., & Gómez, D. (2018). Entrepreneurship and regional economic growth in Antioquia: An empirical analysis. *Economics and Business Letters, 7*(2), 84–91.

Audretsch, D. B. (2007). Entrepreneurship capital and economic growth. *Oxford Review of Economic Policy, 23*, 63–78.

Audretsch, D. B. (2018). Entrepreneurship, economic growth, and geography. *Oxford Review of Economic Policy, 34*(4), 637–651.

Audretsch, D. B., Bönte, W., & Keilbach, M. (2008). Entrepreneurship capital and its impact on knowledge diffusion and economic performance. *Journal of Business Venturing, 23*, 687–698.

Audretsch, D. B., & Fritsch, M. (2002). Growth regimes over time and space. *Regional Studies, 36*, 113–124.

Audretsch, D. B., & Keilbach, M. (2004a). Does entrepreneurship capital matter? *Entrepreneurship Theory and Practice, 28*, 419–429.

Audretsch, D. B., & Keilbach, M. (2004b). Entrepreneurship capital and economic performance. *Regional Studies, 38*, 949–959.

Audretsch, D. B., & Keilbach, M. (2004c). Entrepreneurship and regional growth: an evolutionary interpretation. *Journal of Evolutionary Economics, 14*, 605–616.

Audretsch, D. B., & Keilbach, M. (2005). Entrepreneurship capital and regional growth. *The Annals of Regional Science, 39*, 457–469.

Audretsch, D. B., & Keilbach, M. (2007). The localization of entrepreneurship capital: Evidence from Germany. *Papers in Regional Science, 86*, 351–365.

Audretsch, D. B., & Keilbach, M. (2008). Resolving the knowledge paradox: Knowledge-spillover entrepreneurship and economic growth. *Research Policy, 37*, 1697–1705.

Audretsch, D. B., Link, A. N., & Peña-Legazkue, I. (2013). Academic entrepreneurship and regional economic development: Introduction to the special issue. *Economic Development Quarterly, 27*, 3–5.

Baumol, W. J. (1993). *Entrepreneurship, management and the structure of payoffs*. MIT-Press.

Baumol, W. J., & Strom, R. J. (2007). Entrepreneurship and economic growth. *Strategic Entrepreneurship Journal, 1*(3-4), 233–237.

Belitski, M., & Desai, S. (2016). Creativity, entrepreneurship and economic development: city-level evidence on creativity spillover of entrepreneurship. *The Journal of Technology Transfer, 41*(6), 1354–1376.

Berkowitz, D., & DeJong, D. N. (2005). Entrepreneurship and Post-socialist Growth. *Oxford Bulletin of Economics and Statistics, 67*, 25–46.

Biondi, Y. (2008). Schumpeter's economic theory and the dynamic accounting view of the firm: neglected pages from the Theory of Economic Development. *Economy and Society, 37*, 525–547.

Bjørnskov, C., & Foss, N. (2013). How strategic entrepreneurship and the institutional context drive economic growth. *Strategic Entrepreneurship Journal, 7*, 50–69.

Bjørnskov, C., & Foss, N. J. (2016). Institutions, entrepreneurship, and economic growth: what do we know and what do we still need to know? *Academy of Management Perspectives, 30*(3), 292–315.

Blanchflower, D. G. (2000). *Self-employment in OECD countries. Labour economics, 7*, 471–505.

Bosma, N., Sanders, M., & Stam, E. (2018). Institutions, entrepreneurship, and economic growth in Europe. *Small Business Economics, 51*(2), 483–499.

Braunerhjelm, P., Acs, Z. J., Audretsch, D. B., & Carlsson, B. (2009). The missing link: knowledge diffusion and entrepreneurship in endogenous growth. *Small Business Economics, 34*, 105–125.

Braunerhjelm, P., & Henrekson, M. (2013). Entrepreneurship, institutions, and economic dynamism: lessons from a comparison of the United States and Sweden. *Industrial and Corporate Change, 22*, 107–130.

Brixy, U. (2014). The significance of entry and exit for regional productivity growth. *Regional Studies, 48*, 1051–1070.

Brouwer, M. T. (2003). Weber, Schumpeter and Knight on entrepreneurship and economic development. In J. T. Metcalfe & U. Cantner (Eds.), *Change, transformation and development* (pp. 145–167). Springer.

Callon, M., Courtial, J. P., Turner, W. A., & Bauin, S. (1983). From translations to problematic networks: An introduction to co-word analysis. *Social Science Information, 22*(2), 191–235.

Callon, M., Rip, A., & Law, J. (Eds.). (1986). *Mapping the dynamics of science and technology: Sociology of science in the real world.* Cham, Switzerland: Springer.

Capello, R., & Lenzi, C. (2016). Innovation modes and entrepreneurial behavioral characteristics in regional growth. *Small Business Economics, 47*(4), 875–893.

Carlsson, B., Acs, Z. J., Audretsch, D. B., & Braunerhjelm, P. (2009). Knowledge creation, entrepreneurship, and economic growth: a historical review. *Industrial and Corporate Change, 18*, 1193–1229.

Carlsson, B., Braunerhjelm, P., McKelvey, M., Olofsson, C., Persson, L., & Ylinenpää, H. (2013). The evolving domain of entrepreneurship research. *Small Business Economics, 41*, 913–930.

Carmona, M., Congregado, E., Golpe, A. A., & Iglesias, J. (2016). Self-employment and business cycles: searching for asymmetries in a panel of 23 OECD countries. *Journal of Business Economics and Management, 17*(6), 1155–1171.

Carree, M. A., & Thurik, A. R. (2007). The lag structure of the impact of business ownership on economic performance in OECD countries. *Small Business Economics, 30*, 101–110.

Carree, M., Van Stel, A., Thurik, R., & Wennekers, S. (2002). Economic development and business ownership: an analysis using data of 23 OECD countries in the period 1976–1996. *Small Business Economics, 19*, 271–290.

Carree, M., Van Stel, A., Thurik, R., & Wennekers, S. (2007). The relationship between economic development and business ownership revisited. *Entrepreneurship and Regional Development, 19*, 281–291.

Castaño, M. S., Méndez, M. T., & Galindo, M. Á. (2016). The effect of public policies on entrepreneurial activity and economic growth. *Journal of Business Research, 69*(11), 5280–5285.

Content, J., Bosma, N., Jordaan, J., & Sanders, M. (2020). Entrepreneurial ecosystems, entrepreneurial activity and economic growth: new evidence from European regions. *Regional Studies, 54*(8), 1007–1019.

Cumming, D., Johan, S., & Zhang, M. (2014). The economic impact of entrepreneurship: Comparing international datasets. *Corporate Governance: An International Review, 22*, 162–178.

Dean, H., Larsen, G., Ford, J., & Akram, M. (2019). Female entrepreneurship and the metanarrative of economic growth: A critical review of underlying assumptions. *International Journal of Management Reviews, 21*(1), 24–49.

De Dominicis, L., Florax, R. J. G. M., & De Groot, H. L. F. (2008). A meta-analysis on the relationship between income inequality and economic growth. *Scottish Journal of Political Economy, 55*, 654–682.

Du, K., & O'Connor, A. (2018). Entrepreneurship and advancing national level economic efficiency. *Small Business Economics, 50*(1), 91–111.

Efendic, A., Pugh, G., & Adnett, N. (2011). Institutions and economic performance: A meta-regression analysis. *European Journal of Political Economy, 27*, 586–599.

Erken, H., Donselaar, P., & Thurik, R. (2018). Total factor productivity and the role of entrepreneurship. *The Journal of Technology Transfer, 43*(6), 1493–1521.

Etzkowitz, H., & Klofsten, M. (2005). The innovating region: toward a theory of knowledge-based regional development. *R&D Management, 35*, 243–255.

Ferreira, J. J., Fayolle, A., Fernandes, C., & Raposo, M. (2017). Effects of Schumpeterian and Kirznerian entrepreneurship on economic growth: Panel data evidence. *Entrepreneurship & Regional Development, 29*(1-2), 27–50.

Fritsch, M. (2007). How does new business formation affect regional development? Introduction to the special issue. *Small Business Economics, 30*, 1–14.

Fritsch, M., & Wyrwich, M. (2017). The effect of entrepreneurship on economic development—an empirical analysis using regional entrepreneurship culture. *Journal of Economic Geography, 17*(1), 157–189.

Galor, O., & Michalopoulos, S. (2012). Evolution and the growth process: Natural selection of entrepreneurial traits. *Journal of Economic Theory, 147*, 759–780.

Gonzalez-Pernía, J. L., & Peña-Legazkue, I. (2015). Export-oriented entrepreneurship and regional economic growth. *Small Business Economics, 45*(3), 505–522. https://doi.org/10.1007/s11187-015-9657-x

Gries, T., & Naudé, W. (2009). Entrepreneurship and structural economic transformation. *Small Business Economics, 34*, 13–29.

Harbord, R. M., & Higgins, J. P. (2008). Meta-regression in Stata. *Stata Journal, 8*, 493–519.

Hessels, J., & Van Stel, A. (2009). Entrepreneurship, export orientation, and economic growth. *Small Business Economics, 37*, 255–268.

Huggins, R., Waite, D., & Munday, M. (2018). New directions in regional innovation policy: a network model for generating entrepreneurship and economic development. *Regional Studies, 52*(9), 1294–1304.

Hunter, J. E., & Schmidt, F. L. (Eds.). (2004). *Methods of meta-analysis: Correcting error and bias in research findings*. Sage.

Iyigun, M. F., & Owen, A. L. (1999). Entrepreneurs, professionals, and growth. *Journal of Economic Growth, 4*, 213–232.

King, R. G., & Levine, R. (1993). Finance, entrepreneurship and growth. *Journal of Monetary Economics, 32*, 513–542.

Liñán, F., & Fernandez-Serrano, J. (2014). National culture, entrepreneurship and economic development: different patterns across the European Union. *Small Business Economics, 42*, 685–701.

Lucas, R. E., Jr. (1988). On the mechanics of economic development. *Journal of Monetary Economics, 22*, 3–42.

Minniti, M., & Lévesque, M. (2010). Entrepreneurial types and economic growth. *Journal of Business Venturing, 25*, 305–314.

Mueller, P. (2007). Exploiting entrepreneurial opportunities: The impact of entrepreneurship on growth. *Small Business Economics, 28*, 355–362.

Müller, S. (2016). A progress review of entrepreneurship and regional development: What are the remaining gaps? *European Planning Studies, 24*(6), 1133–1158.

Naudé, W. (2009). Entrepreneurship, developing countries, and development economics: new approaches and insights. *Small Business Economics, 34*, 1–12.

Nissan, E., Galindo Martín, M. A., & Méndez Picazo, M. T. (2011). Relationship between organizations, institutions, entrepreneurship and economic growth process. *International Entrepreneurship and Management Journal, 7*, 311–324.

North, D. C. (1990). *Institutions, institutional change and economic performance*. Cambridge University Press.

North, D. C. (2005). *Understanding the process of economic change*. Princeton University Press.

Noseleit, F. (2013). Entrepreneurship, structural change, and economic growth. *Journal of Evolutionary Economics, 23*, 735–766.

Peters, H. P., & Van Raan, A. F. (1993). Co-word-based science maps of chemical engineering. Part I: Representations by direct multidimensional scaling. *Research Policy, 22*(1), 23–45.

Prieger, J. E., Bampoky, C., Blanco, L. R., & Liu, A. (2016). Economic growth and the optimal level of entrepreneurship. *World Development, 82*, 95–109.

Rocha, H. O. (2004). Entrepreneurship and development: The role of clusters. *Small Business Economics, 23*, 363–400.

Romer, P. (1990). Endogenous technological change. *Journal of Political Economy, 98*, 71–102.

Romer, P. M. (1986). Increasing returns and long-run growth. *The Journal of Political Economy, 94*, 1002–1037.

Schumpeter, J. (1934). *The theory of economic development: An inquiry into profits, capital, credit, interest, and the business cycle*. Transaction.

Sharp, S. (1998). Meta-analysis regression. Stata Technical. *Bulletin, 7*, 16–22.

Simmie, J. (2003). Innovation and urban regions as national and international nodes for the transfer and sharing of knowledge. *Regional Studies, 37*, 607.

Smith, H. (2003). Knowledge organizations and local economic development: The case of Oxford and Grenoble. *Regional Studies, 37*, 33.

Solow, R. M. (1956). A contribution to the theory of economic growth. *The Quarterly Journal of Economics, 70*, 65–94.

Stanley, T. D. (2008). Meta-regression methods for detecting and estimating empirical effects in the presence of publication selection. *Oxford Bulleting of Economics and Statistics, 70*, 103–127.

Stephens, H. M., & Partridge, M. D. (2011). Do entrepreneurs enhance economic growth in lagging regions? *Growth and Change, 42*, 431–465.

Sternberg, R., & Wennekers, S. (2005). Determinants and effects of new business creation using global entrepreneurship monitor data. *Small Business Economics, 24*, 193–203.

Swan, T. W. (1956). Economic growth and capital accumulation. *Economic Record, 32*, 334–361.

Thornton, P. H., Ribeiro-Soriano, D., & Urbano, D. (2011). Socio-cultural and entrepreneurial activity: An overview. *International Small Business Journal, 29*, 105–118.

Tsvetkova, A. (2012). Book review: Entrepreneurship, growth, and economic development. *Economic Development Quarterly, 26*, 279–280.

Urbano, D., & Aparicio, S. (2016). Entrepreneurship capital types and economic growth: International evidence. *Technological Forecasting and Social Change, 102*, 34–44.

Urbano, D., Aparicio, S., & Audretsch, D. (2019). Twenty-five years of research on institutions, entrepreneurship, and economic growth: What has been learned? *Small Business Economics, 53*(1), 21–49.

Urbano, D., Audretsch, D., Aparicio, S., & Noguera, M. (2020). Does entrepreneurial activity matter for economic growth in developing countries? The role of the institutional environment. *International Entrepreneurship and Management Journal, 16*(3), 1065–1099.

Valliere, D., & Peterson, R. (2009). Entrepreneurship and economic growth: Evidence from emerging and developed countries. *Entrepreneurship and Regional Development, 21*, 459–480.

Van Eck, N. J., & Waltman, L. (2014). CitNetExplorer: A new software tool for analyzing and visualizing citation networks. *Journal of Informetrics, 8*(4), 802–823.

Van der Sluis, J., Van Praag, M., & Vijverberg, W. (2008). Education and entrepreneurship selection and performance: A review of the empirical literature. *Journal of Economic Surveys, 22*, 795–841.

Van de Ven, H. (1993). The development of an infrastructure for entrepreneurship. *Journal of Business Venturing, 8*, 211–230.

Van Praag, C. M., & Versloot, P. H. (2007). What is the value of entrepreneurship? A review of recent research. *Small Business Economics, 29*, 351–382.

Van Stel, A., & Carree, M. (2004). Business ownership and sectoral growth: An empirical analysis of 21 OECD countries. *International Small Business Journal, 22*, 389–419.

Van Stel, A., Carree, M., & Thurik, R. (2005). The effect of entrepreneurial activity on national economic growth. *Small Business Economics, 24*, 311–321.

Veciana, J. M., & Urbano, D. (2008). The institutional approach to entrepreneurship research: Introduction. *International Entrepreneurship and Management Journal, 4*, 365–379.

Welter, F., & Smallbone, D. (2011). Institutional perspectives on entrepreneurial behaviour in challenging environments. *Journal of Small Business Management, 49*, 107–125.

Wennekers, S., & Thurik, R. (1999). Linking entrepreneurship and economic growth. *Small Business Economics, 13*, 27–56.

Wennekers, S., Van Stel, A., Thurik, R., & Reynolds, P. (2005). Nascent entrepreneurship and the level of economic development. *Small Business Economics, 24*, 293–309.

Westlund, H., & Adam, F. (2010). Social capital and economic performance: A meta-analysis of 65 studies. *European Planning Studies, 18*, 893–919.

Wong, P. K., Ho, Y. P., & Autio, E. (2005). Entrepreneurship, innovation and economic growth: Evidence from GEM data. *Small Business Economics, 24*, 335–350.

Wooldridge, J. (2010). *Introduction to econometrics. A modern approach* (4th ed.). Thomson.

3

A Review of Economic Development Thinking and the Role of Innovative Entrepreneurship: Past, Present, and Future

Diego Gomez, Sebastian Aparicio, and David Urbano

3.1 Introduction

In the classic book *The Mystery of Economic Growth*, Helpman (2004) expresses his opinion on what has happened in the last 50 years of economists' work on the economic growth phenomenon, but above all, on his life devoted to research on endogenous growth and development. However, the book title is disturbing since in recent decades the author has been one of the most important and active in the so-called new growth theory current (Clark, 2007).

D. Gomez
Fundación ECSIM, Medellin, Colombia

S. Aparicio (✉) • D. Urbano
Department of Business, Universitat Autònoma de Barcelona, Cerdanyola del Vallés, Barcelona, Spain

Centre for Entrepreneurship and Social Innovation Research (CREIS), Universitat Autònoma de Barcelona, Sabadell, Barcelona, Spain
e-mail: Sebastian.Aparicio@uab.cat

D. Gomez et al. (eds.), *Driving Complexity in Economic Development*,
https://doi.org/10.1007/978-3-031-34386-5_3

It is even challenging for research work on the dynamics of social transformation that the issue in question comes under the category of mystery. The situation for an important group of researchers who had opted to follow the path of the new growth theory is that they have reached a plain where the path vanished without having been able to put together a consistent proposal to trigger economic growth processes (Galor, 2005; Leick & Lang, 2018). One of the purposes of this chapter is to try to advance in the knowledge of the dynamics of transformation, hoping that its understanding may help us unveil the supposed mystery of growth.

In the past 70 years, a large group of countries (e.g., Singapore, Ireland, Israel, Korea, Hong Kong, and Taiwan) has managed to overcome levels of underdevelopment and join the group of high-income economies. These countries have maintained their dynamism and high levels of economic growth. Other economies such as China, Botswana, Malaysia, Indonesia, and India maintain high growth rates and are rapidly closing the gap.

It is interesting that none of the experiences of these countries either supports or categorically contradicts the central arguments that economic growth theorists have argued, only that the elements suggested from the endogenous development (human capital and technology) or the neoclassical model (physical and human capital accumulation) seem to have been the determinants. The evidence, as Helpman (2004) suggests, seems rather to say that the key issue remains unraveled. What contents are there in the countries' transformations that allow us to unravel the dynamics of transformation? This is important and will therefore be one of the axes of the discussion.

Helpman (2004, p. 10) notes that "for centuries economists have been concerned with the growth of nations, and have studied this subject continuously since Adam Smith. This effort has produced a better understanding of the sources of economic growth. But the subject has proved elusive and many mysteries remain." In the last 70 years, there have been two phases of discussion on economic growth. The first phase began with the work of Solow (1956) in which he proposed that growth is explained by technological change linked to capital accumulation. The second came later when the concept of capital was broadened by introducing the accumulation of human capital to explain technological change. Mankiw et al. (1990) developed key research in this regard. Their work arose as a re-evaluation of the neoclassical growth model after the initial contributions of Lucas (1988) and Romer (1986, 1992), which appeared in the second half of the 1980s, giving origin to the second phase of the discussion, endogenous growth.

The neoclassical perspective on development economics and the recent contributions from the "new growth theory" constitute the mainstream. Landau (1991) reviews the subject in "How competitiveness can be achieved: fostering economic growth and productivity." The author notes that in recent years there has been an increase in curiosity about the economic study of the innovation process, as a result of new evidence presented in various studies, which shows that the competitiveness of companies, economic growth, and therefore a country's quality of life are closely related to its capacity to successfully introduce technological innovations. Paradoxically, in Solow's model, given the size of the residual, it was concluded that technical progress was the main determinant of economic growth, and yet the models made little mention of the mechanisms by which technological change occurs. These cannot be adequately analyzed using the framework of the early theories of economic growth (Solow, 1957), which, according to the author, employ oversimplified assumptions about the role of technological change as a determinant of growth. Neoclassical models assume that technology is exogenous, that is, although technical progress is considered one of the fundamental variables in determining growth, neither its origin nor its dependence on both decisions and the interaction between various agents is specified. In the context of neoclassical models, the only explanation for this phenomenon is that production grew due to exogenous technological changes, which the model does not explain. Therefore, the part of the growth that could not be attributed to the increase in the use of production factors was called "technical progress" (or "Solow residual").

In the research of Mankiw et al. (1990), we find the idea in which the Solow residual is a measure of ignorance, but after a decade of work by the new growth theory, its researchers would also have to accept that the inability to explain the residual statistically would now be matched by the multiple attempts to explain with regressions the productivity of capital, labor, and total factor productivity. According to this, the title of Helpman's book depicts this recognition. This intense regression exercise began in the late 1980s with Romer's (1990) contributions. From there, the role of technology in economic growth and its effects on the competitiveness of companies began to be considered. The proposed models are known as "endogenous growth" models. In these new models, technology was an endogenous variable, so that it ceased to be the "manna from heaven"—a term used by Freeman—of the Solow residual, and became the result of the decisions of companies that use the scientific knowledge available, invested in R&D activities to develop innovations that could be exchanged in the market.

The emergence of this second phase of work on economic growth, as Helpman (2004) points out, was marked by a strong academic controversy over the ability of the neoclassical model to explain growth and the real evidence that endogenous models were indeed succeeding in doing so. Meanwhile, emerging countries continued growing, not thanks to a theory, but to real dynamics these countries had built. However, the vast majority of developing nations was still experiencing low growth rates and structural problems of poverty and exclusion. The group of developed countries was widening the income gap at a historically unprecedented rate, showing that there was not a process of convergence either, as suggested in theory, but quite the opposite. Thus, Helpman's (2004) work was fundamental in opening a new phase of discussion. Grossman and Helpman (1991) elaborated a model of technological change to conclude that part of the differences in growth is due to "different experiences in technological progress" (Grossman & Helpman, 1991, p. 28). The debate with the defenders of the neoclassical model of capital accumulation is not yet closed, although Helpman insists that "it has indeed been the factors that have increased productivity that have managed to better explain economic growth and not capital accumulation: the growth of per capita income is due to more capital, more human capital and more productivity" (Helpman, 2004, p. 31). But he then concludes: "The puzzle remains" (Helpman, 2004, p. 17).

Given the vast literature on the economic development of nations, in this chapter, we take a trip back in time to review chronologically the most influential theories of economic development. First, this chapter reviews the classical theories of economic development, taking the theories of endogenous and exogenous economic growth as its fundamental focus. Second, it reviews development theories, which introduce a key part of the "heart" of this book: entrepreneurship and innovation. In addition, this chapter takes part in the discussion between accumulationists and assimilationists. Finally, dynamic systems, as part of the solution to the impossibility of using classical theories to unravel the mystery of the growth of nations, are introduced.

3.2 Behind the Supposed Mystery of Development

William Easterly, a contemporary of Helpman, expresses the same concerns about the mystery of economic development, bringing insights into the discussion on endogenous growth. In his book *The Elusive Quest for Growth* (Easterly, 2002), he notes: "Fifty years ago, after World War II, we economists began our bold quest: the discovery of how the poor countries of the tropics could become rich like the rich countries of Europe and North America." He further states: "The precious object offered by us (multilateral entities) ranged from foreign aid for investment in machinery, to strengthening education, to controlling population growth, to loans conditioned on reforms to give relief on debts that had been given conditioned on reforms. None of this has delivered what was promised" (Easterly, 2002, p. XI). The current acknowledged uncertainties and limitations surrounding growth are even present in the conventions of experts on the subject. In 2004, at the Barcelona World Fair, there was a meeting of economists working on development and economic growth. For those who follow the discussion on proposals to overcome poverty problems, the document "The Barcelona Declaration" that originated from the meeting leaves a feeling of certain impotence, of recognition of little consensus, that each country faces a specific problem and that it must, based on a specific analysis of its situation based on the work of Hausmann, Rodrik, and Velasco (2005): "Diagnosis of Growth," propose its development strategy: "Each country will find its development path."

The same authors of the base study, Hausmann and Rodrik, continued their research on growth processes, especially in the cases of countries that had rapid growth phases. In one of the papers that followed the Barcelona meeting, "Growth Accelerations," they point out that these are not associated with the factors that have traditionally been pointed out and that they seem to have an idiosyncratic character (Hausmann et al., 2004). In another research, "Economic development as self-discovery"

(Hausmann & Rodrik, 2002), they open a new search path in which they propose to determine the specialization patterns of countries, that is, what they know how to do, as a determining factor of the state of development, which in turn needs to begin to be understood as a learning process. This discussion, which we have been following in the previous paragraphs, is the one that has been taking place within the economic "mainstream." But other currents within the study of economics, not exempt from these debates either, have been progressively converging around the construction of social capabilities from innovation as the central axis of development processes. The point at which the discussion takes place suggests a path of exploration around the nature of these dynamics and the policies that should lead us to the development.

According to this, the World Bank, in its publication "World Development Report 2002," states: "How do we explain the persistence of poverty amid plenty? If we know the sources of abundance, why don't poor countries simply adopt the policies that contribute to it. … We must create incentives for people to invest in more efficient technology, have better skills, and organize more efficient markets. These incentives are embodied in institutions" (Banerji et al. 2002). The truth is that the sources of abundance seem neither so well-known nor so clear, and the matter is not so easy to solve with only more efficient markets and technologies. Why do so many countries with low rates of development and high rates of poverty not enter into processes of social transformation and growth, while a few others have done so in the last 40 years? (Banerji et al. 2002).

That is why it is so interesting to find Douglass North, the Nobel Prize laureate who in 2002 noted the above concerns, continuing and deepening the search in the book *Understanding the Process of Economic Change*, which he published in 2005, 4 years after the previous statement. In his reflection on what we have not yet understood about development, he points out that a complete theory of economic change will have to integrate theories of demography, knowledge accumulation, and institutional change. "We are still far from having good theories for any of the three, much less for them together, but we are working on it" (North, 2005, p. 1). North's proposal in this book is that the key to economic development is "the deliberate effort of human beings to control their environment" (North, 2005, p. 1). Intentionality is what explains development. This element is fundamental in the construction of an approach to development as a learning process. Intentionality is expressed in decisions, in projects, in new undertakings, which, when they are successful and generate transformations, bring about what we call "learning." In the preface he explains:

> The economic paradigm—neoclassical theory—was not created to explain the process of economic change. We live in a world of uncertainty and continuous change that is constantly unraveling new and novel ideas. Standard theories are of little help in this context. Seeking to understand economic, social, and political change (and not one of them without the others) requires a rethinking of the way we think. Can we develop a dynamic theory comparable in elegance to general equilibrium theory? The answer is possibly no. (North, 2005)

If the social transformation generated by innovation and learning is understood as a complex set of chaotic emergencies, it is possible to enter into the space of uncertainty and continuous change suggested by North. But if, in addition, these dynamics are subject to non-deterministic simulations but rather to the exploration of multiple future scenarios, new formalization options could be proposed to initiate the exploration of a proposal for a dynamic model of the economy in the terms suggested by North. But in the meantime, the previous proposals of the "mainstream" would be insufficient in their genesis. Xavier Sala-i-Martin, one of the most important authors of the "new growth theory," agrees with this when he takes stock of the progress made. The neoclassical assumption of diminishing returns of each of the factors had as an almost devastating consequence the fact that long-term growth due to the accumulation of capital was unsustainable. This is why neoclassical researchers were forced to introduce exogenous technological growth, the ultimate engine of growth (Sala-i-Martin, 2000, 2002, p. 5). Pritchett refers to these doubts when he entitles an article "The Continuing Question" and quotes Sala-i Martin when he analyzes why "four million regressions" have not yet resolved the questions (Pritchett, 2006).

These statements by Sala-i-Martin and Pritchett, added to North's statement on general equilibrium models, establish a radical position on their limitations. They would be, then, incapable of modeling development processes. It should be noted that this judgment comes from two of today's most important and renowned development economists. Further on, Sala-i-Martin notes: "Put differently, if we want to model technological progress endogenously, we have to abandon the world of perfect competition and Paretian optimality, which are the foundations of neoclassical theory, and allow for imperfect competition" (Pritchett, 2006, p. 13)—that is, to abandon the assumptions that give mathematical consistency to the neoclassical model, which implies proposing a new mathematical foundation. This would imply abandoning the general equilibrium paradigm to unveil "the mystery of development."

Different contributions from other currents suggest transformations in socioeconomic capabilities as key elements to explain and unleash development processes. The Comisión Económica para América Latina y el Caribe (CEPAL) proposed a development process of productive restructuring with equity. Chapter 7 of the book *Globalization and Development* (CEPAL, 2002) proposes the strengthening of national innovation systems and technological development. It expresses concern about the existence of the assumption that macroeconomic stability and the opening of markets, proposed from the neoclassical perspective, would be sufficient conditions for technological flows and innovation to take place in the region, which has not occurred. This coincides with the criticisms of Helpman, Easterly, North, Hausmann, and Rodrik. The CEPAL document proposes strategies on how to achieve the technological transformation required to achieve systemic competitiveness. It explains that in the case of Latin America there was a stage of industrialization led by the state, and the National Innovation System responded to this policy.

In this regard, CEPAL states:

> [S]tructural reforms caused the reorientation of the regional productive apparatus towards nontradable goods and services, on the one hand, and static comparative advantages, on the other, but failed to create dynamic comparative advantages based on learning and knowledge, which would increase the value added of exports and improve the insertion of the region's companies in world markets. (CEPAL, 2002, p. 220)

In addition, they point out that four patterns of post neoclassical reform behavior were presented that explain the transformation of the new scheme for the acquisition of technological and innovative capabilities in productive systems and companies: first, a simultaneous process of innovation and inhibition of national capacities; second, marginalization and destruction of national productive chains; third, unequal specialization in the production of knowledge; finally, transfer of some preexisting R&D activities abroad. Thus, CEPAL's proposals were: to strengthen national innovation systems with active policies and financing; accelerate the use of information and communications technologies; and establish intellectual property policies. These proposals, formulated from a general ad hoc discussion, have not led to a consensus on the policies and measures needed. Although they have been applied, there is some skepticism about their effectiveness. But they coincide with the new proposal that Hausmann and Rodrik are beginning to formulate.

Jorge Katz, a CEPAL researcher for several decades, in *Structural Reform, Productivity and Technological Change in Latin America*, notes: "The approach (of the book) is in line with the Schumpeterian metaphor of the process of creative destruction. Latin America is undergoing fundamental changes in modes of production and organization as well as regulatory regimes. Countries have become importers of capital goods and intermediate manufacturing goods while increasing their exports of low value-added products" (Katz, 2001, p. 24). "There is an urgent need for innovation policies that help develop domestic capabilities to accelerate the process of reaching the international productivity frontier" (Katz, 2001, p. 26). This is what some have also called the "neo-structuralist approach" of CEPAL, which points to innovation as a central process, triggering development processes. As we have pointed out, this coincides with the proposals now being made by Hausmann and Rodrik. The critical issue is to carry out an explanatory process that allows the construction of social consensus and the design of development policies for the region.

However, the explanation of the accelerated growth processes of the newly developing countries in Asia is neither clear nor complete. Sanjaya Lall, one of the experts on the processes of accelerated development in Southeast Asia, in his paper "Creating Comparative Advantage: The Role of Industrial Policy" (Lall, 1996), says:

> It has repeatedly been argued that sustained economic growth generally depends on productivity. Productivity growth, in turn, at the aggregate level is composed of two factors. First, it reflects the shift in the direction of the production structure towards activities with higher levels of productivity. And second, it signals productivity growth in particular activities. (Lall, 1996, p. 117)

In other words, process and product innovation would explain the Asian processes.

The same author, in one of his papers on Southeast Asian development, says in contrast to the neoclassical simplification to explain development processes:

> In the 1980s it was widely discussed that the East Asian export development model proved the validity of neoclassical prescriptions. It was generally accepted that outward orientation was synonymous with liberal trade and industrial policies, it was assumed that the success of these countries proved the benefits of market-driven resource allocation. This line of argument has been completely demolished by the evidence. The latest in a line of publications suggests, on the one hand, that there is no single 'East Asian model' and, on the other, that in many of these countries there were numerous selective and functional interventions. These are the conclusions of the Banerji et al. (2002) on the East Asian miracle. (Lall, 1996, p. 138)

The discussion on development processes has also been active in the last decade with other authors in the institutionalist school. This is the reason for the title of the book recently published by the OECD *Development is Back*. This is the publication with which the OECD celebrates its 40 years of existence. It emphasizes the central proposal of this trend: The quality of institutions and government are conducive to development in a globalized world (OECD, 2002). The reflection in this paper revolves fundamentally around the role of the firms: "The role of the firm as the locus of productivity growth in society, and the importance of healthy inter-firm price competition in driving that growth, mean that, more than ever, the firm is at the heart of development" (OECD, 2002, p. 123). Firms and their role as innovative agents and managers of learning, as pointed out by North (2005), are delineated as a key to the development process.

Cohen's paper "Growth in Theory and Practice" is part of this compilation. This author points out that the difference in income between developed and developing countries has multiplied in the last 200 years (Cohen, 2002, pp. 48 and 49), and there does not seem to be clear evidence to support the hypothesis of convergence in development paths. The author argues that this is because new technologies were not assimilated in low-income countries and a phase of strong divergence was unleashed (Cohen, 2002, p. 50). But he points out in a challenging way: "For poor countries, new technologies and globalization are both a refreshing challenge and a source of convergence with rich countries" (Cohen, 2002, p. 58). He also indicates that the task requires active policies of technological change, human capital formation, and the development of institutional networks. "The sample is the counterexamples of underdevelopment, Japan yesterday, Singapore today, there are many messages of hope" (Cohen, 2002 p. 59). The essential point is that the development processes of countries that have undergone rapid growth processes converge to the income levels of developed countries as the processes of innovation and learning bring them closer to the same patterns of specialization. In a different research, Cohen (2007) refers to the effects of human capital and education. In this paper, the discussion seeks to explore how learning, changing patterns of specialization, and productive transformation are common to the approaches proposed. It also explores why there is still no explicit consensus on development proposals or agreements on policies. What they agree on as common elements are technology and productivity and their contributions to development. In the evolution of development theories, reflection on the role of technology, innovation, and the construction of human and social capital are at a point of discussion where the currents are beginning to converge.

Acemoglu, in his 2009 book *Introduction to Modern Economic Growth*, states:

> Returning to the first question, there are innumerable fundamental causes of economic growth that various economists, historians, and social scientists have proposed over the ages. Listing and cataloging them is neither informative nor useful. Instead, I classify the main candidate root causes of economic growth into four categories of hypotheses. Although this classification does not do justice to some of the nuances of the literature, it is

> satisfactory for our purpose of highlighting the main factors affecting cross-country income differences and economic growth. The first is the luck hypothesis. The second is the geography hypothesis. Third, is the culture hypothesis. Finally, the institutions hypothesis. (Acemoglu, 2009, p. 110)

For Acemoglu, business and innovation do not seem to be relevant issues.

Economic growth, and development more broadly, seems to be more of a systemic problem, yet to be defined more comprehensively, than a mystery or an elusive quest as suggested by Helpman (2004), Easterly (2002), and Acemoglu (2009) in their books and more recent articles. Approaching the problem from a systemic and dynamic perspective would introduce important elements into the discussion. One of them is the multicausality of the dynamics of change, another is the reinforcement of virtuous or degrading dynamics, another understanding the historical and adaptive behaviors of social systems, and perhaps most importantly, fully integrating these elements.

The fact that it is a systemic dynamic implies continuing the search for a process of self-discovery, which is built from one's idiosyncrasies, as suggested by Hausmann and Rodrik in their works on growth accelerations and development like a self-discovery (Hausmann et al., 2004; Hausmann & Rodrik, 2002). This assumes that there are dynamics of learning and transformation but that the processes are specific and contextualized within the possibilities and realities of each country. It implies an important approach to the work of chaos theory and systemic conception of society and its forms of organization (Jantsch, 1980).

But more broadly, what does development as a systemic problem consist of? What would allow us to affirm that it is indeed behavior that evidences systemic characteristics? The discussion of development in high-income countries seems to look for some kind of switches or levers from which to activate a change. After identifying a significant one, they discuss at length whether or not it is the most important one, without econometric exercises being able to go beyond establishing a basic association between the specific variable and growth. As Sterman (2006) points out in "Learning from evidence in a complex world," the complexity of the system hides multiple key behaviors and the system's dynamics approach allows us to improve our ability to discover those key elements that explain the fundamental aspects of policy design.

They have ended up with a very wide range of "switches," but each one alone has failed to provide a satisfactory explanation, to the point that, after the intricate econometric paths, the researchers of the "new growth theory" have reached a plateau without being able to solve the problem of explaining economic growth. Some, like Helpman and Easterly, make their bewilderment evident. Thus, the state of underdevelopment and the social dynamics that would lead to overcoming it are observed in underdeveloped countries in a more comprehensive manner as a systemic problem of incapacities, disarticulations, and exclusions, in which the switches, levers, and the dynamics themselves are multiple and interdependent and must be articulated integrally. Development should then be understood as a process of learning, and of building the capacity to generate well-being. This is the exploration that will be undertaken.

3.3 Developmental States as Systemic Balance Sheets

The first phase of the discussion of growth (as Easterly called it) began with the publication by Solow of his growth model in 1956 and 1957, based on his proposal to understand growth as the result of the accumulation of factors, in which technology was exogenous to the model and was incorporated through investments. This generated the need to make a continuous effort to construct information that would allow growth accounting exercises to be carried out to study how the accumulation of physical and human capital can explain economic growth.

From this approach, several of the "shared beliefs" about economic growth emerge, as Hausmann (2006a) titles a paper in which he presents the current state of the development discussion. The beliefs shared by the "mainstream" are as follows[1]:

[1] Taken from Hausmann's (2006) article "Economic Growth: Shared Beliefs, Shared Disappointments."

- Openness to global markets generates sales opportunities for products and thus expansion of the economy.
- Openness to investment and financial markets allows new projects to be financed.
- Sound public finances and stable currency allow opportunities to be exploited without risk.
- Property rights and contract enforcement allow for the generation of new activities.

All four beliefs are associated with the accumulation of physical capital, which is the fundamental proposal of the neoclassical model. The first is associated with the creation of incentives proposed by Easterly. The fourth is associated with the work of Coase and North on the need for institutions for innovation and the reduction of transaction costs. But clearly, the context in which it is expressed is aimed at facilitating capital accumulation. In other words, despite the advances of the so-called second phase of work on economic growth, which emphasized the construction of human capital and technology, their contributions are not a fundamental part of these "shared beliefs."

But neither have these so-called shared beliefs been shown to be sufficient to generate growth processes. "One of the readings from these experiences (the fast-growing countries) is that achieving growth is difficult. It is not enough to bring inflation from three digits to one, open the economy to the market and investment, privatize state enterprises and reform the financial system. There is much more to do" (Hausmann, 2006a, 2006b, p. 5).

The "second phase" sought to endogenize technological change because the evidence pointed to the insufficiency of capital accumulation as a determining factor. Helpman points out that more than half of the variation in per capita income of countries is explained by differences in total factor productivity (TFP) (Helpman, 2004, p. 34). Therefore, a priority issue is the explanation of this variation.

Romer (1986) concludes that models such as those proposed by Solow, with a constant exogenous increase in technological change, are inadequate to explain long-run growth trends (Helpman, 2004; Romer, 1986). With this paper, Romer introduced the externalities that generate increasing returns to scale through the accumulation of knowledge, and the search for the endogeneity of technological change began. The next work was developed by Lucas (1988) in which he introduced human capital with increasing effects on productivity (Lucas, 1988).

After these initial works, a broad phase of research was generated in which productivity growth is associated with a wide range of factors. In the first of these, by Romer (1990), the author associates investment in research and development with growth. Subsequent work by Grossman and Helpman (1991), and Aghion and Howitt (1992) continued along this path by introducing the effects of product quality improvements and "creative destruction" into the model. Subsequent papers by these authors further developed this line of research.

After the publication of Solow's work generated the need to establish and standardize a growth accounting that would allow the quantification of TFP, the information bases were built that decades later allowed the exploration of the "second phase" with empirical evaluations and correlations of multiple factors (Hulten, 2000).

Charles Hulten wrote a paper for the NBER (National Bureau of Economic Research) entitled "Total Factor Productivity: A Short Biography." He points out how, based on econometrics, it was possible to begin to separate TFP in terms of increasing returns to scale, factor cost, and innovation (Hulten, 2000, p. 24). This allowed the generation of dozens of papers, some validating mathematical approximations of the AK type and others correlating growth with multiple factors (Hulten, 2000, p. 32). However, before Hulten's work, Robert Barro had also carried out for the NBER a first "balance" between the contributions of the endogenous and neoclassical models in the paper "Notes on Growth Accounting." The author concludes that the contribution is important but that both approaches are complementary, but not conclusive (Barro, 1998b, pp. 24–25). In the same year Barro himself published an extensive paper on determinants with empirical data on a broad base of countries over 30 years. His main conclusions were that development depended fundamentally on respect for laws, controlled government consumption, and lower inflation (Barro, 1998a). This work was one of the foundations of what is called "shared beliefs."

Back to Hulten, he points out that the "new growth theory" challenged traditional conceptions by introducing noncompetitive markets, increasing returns to scale, and innovation as an endogenous part of the economic system. This forced the statistical basis to be refined to meet the needs of empirical testing (Hulten, 2000, p. 32) and is the foundation of a multiplicity of econometric exercises to explain growth from various perspectives, which have not been exempt from criticism about the validity, consistency, and completeness of their conclusions. Hulten and Isackson (2007) takes up the classic discussion on which is the fundamental explanation of growth, productivity, or capital accumulation. He again concludes that it is productivity, which again depends on a multiplicity of factors.

From another perspective, the document "Growth Econometrics" by Durlauf et al. (2004) gives a historical account of this process of theoretical exercises with econometric validations throughout the "second phase" of the study of growth (Durlauf et al., 2004). The process has consisted of the search for the determinants of development based on cross-country growth regressions that explain the differences in growth between countries (Durlauf et al., 2004, pp. 27 and 73). The authors did a compilation of the many exercises proposed in the economic growth literature to date. They consolidated 145 exercises and classified them into "43 different growth theories" with the requirement that the determinant in question was significant in at least one study (Durlauf et al., 2004, pp. 74–75). The irony of the exercise is that it seems to serve more to demonstrate to us the futility than the usefulness of these regressions. If we have 43 possible nonexclusive reasons, it is as much as saying that economic growth, and in broader terms, development, has everything to do with everything. Therefore, the problem is stated as follows: "So, if one has a set of K potential growth theories, all of which are logically compatible with each other (and all derived subtheories), then there are $2k–1$ potential theoretical specifications, each of which corresponds to a particular combination of theories" (Durlauf et al., 2004, p. 76).

It is evident that the so-called second phase of growth only had as a consensus the purpose of endogenizing technological change and finding the determinants of growth. But from that starting point, a search was opened that opened up many paths: geographical conditions, demographics, capitalism, education, investment, foreign trade, ethnic homogeneity, finance, foreign investment, governance, industrial structure, inequality, infrastructure, religion, social capital and so on. "This plethora of potential regressors illustrates very well one of the fundamental problems with empirical growth research, expressed in the absence of any consensus on which determinants should go into the growth model" (Durlauf et al., 2004, p. 75).

The authors established in the exercises that there is a correlation between a variable and growth, but not whether it is a cause, condition, or result of the process. The authors point out: "An obvious and frequent criticism of growth regressions is that they are weak in establishing directions of causality. At some level, there is a standard problem in that two variables may be correlated but together depend on a third" (Durlauf et al., 2004, p. 116). Dani Rodrik is also emphatic in assessing the possible conclusions of these exercises. He states that they allow us to ensure that there are multiple externalities, evidence that the "residual" shows an improvement in technological efficiency and the state of technology and a better allocation of resources in the economy. But there is no causal decomposition: "We cannot interpret the decompositions of 'sources of growth' in a causal way" (Rodrik, 2006).

A key aspect to consider at this level of the discussion on economic growth is the appearance of a compilation and balance of what has been achieved, at a time when it seems that the contributions of the new growth theory have stopped. The balances are both at the conceptual level, such as those discussed by Barro, Easterly, North, and Helpman, and at the empirical level, with the consolidation of statistical exercises such as those of Barro, Hulten, Durlauf et al., Bosworth and Collins, which we will discuss below.

However, as an ex post evaluation of what was an important effort of more than 15 years, now its protagonists themselves are approaching it with a retrospective and self-evaluative vision. A good contribution in this sense is that of Xavier Sala-i-Martin. In 2002, he held a conference in Chile entitled "15 Years of New Growth Economics: What We Have Learned." He points out in his lecture that the empirical literature on cross-country regressions is extensive and from it one can conclude:

1. There are no simple determinants of development.
2. The level of initial income is the most important and robust variable.
3. The size of the state does not seem to be very important, what is important is the quality of government.

4. The relationship between the main measures of human capital and growth is weak.
5. Institutions affect the efficiency of the economy (Sala-i-Martin, 2002, p. 17).

With these conclusions, he not only ratifies the “shared beliefs” but also expresses and acknowledges that the correlation exercises seem to have reached an impasse. In the book *Economic Growth* that he published with Robert Barro in 2004, the vade mecum of growth theory, they express these same conclusions and further state: “growth increases with favorable movements in the terms of trade,” and the relationship with investment is positive but depends on it being accompanied by the above factors (Barro & Sala-i-Martin, 2004, p. 541).

As Sala-i-Martin expressed at the aforementioned conference, the discussion process unleashed by Paul Romer’s article on increasing returns and long-run growth brought about a resurgence of research on economic growth. The literature multiplied and the work of economists was definitively changed. But the consensus achieved was only on a few basic lines. Hausmann (2006a, 2006b) points out: “That vein is exhausted.”

Another approach that rescues the effort of this collective operation of chaotic generation of knowledge on economic growth and development is that behind it lies a more important consideration, and that is that development could be approached as a systemic state. Each “state” implies a systemic balance among multiple indicators. For example, one cannot claim to have a good infrastructure endowment for an economic apparatus that does not require it. This implies that progressively overcoming different levels of development must be understood as a process of learning, capacity building, and therefore of social transformation.

An exercise that serves to explore this line of approach to development as a systemic state is carried out by Barry Bosworth and Susan Collins (2003) of the Brookings Institution. As noted above, it is also another “stocktaking” of what has been advanced in this phase of the new growth theory, but it has some features that are important and very useful for this exercise of systemic characterization. It constructs a database for a group of 84 countries for a period between 1960 and 2000. The authors make a comparative exercise between the multiple theoretical approaches and determinants allowing one to evaluate which determinants are more relevant, as well as to evaluate how much and how they contribute to explaining TFP and the productivities of physical and human capital. They begin their paper by noting: "The past decade has seen an explosion of empirical research on economic growth and its determinants, but many of the central issues remain unresolved" (Bosworth & Collins, 2003, p. 113). They state that there is no consensus on the relative contributions of capital accumulation and improvements in TFP, or on the role of education or economic policy. The point is that the two traditional empirical research tools, growth accounting to compare countries and time-series regressions to assess correlation in given countries, are also both being challenged (Bosworth & Collins, 2003, p. 113). Therefore, Bosworth and Collins seek to show that, properly implemented, both tools are relevant.

The result is very useful for this discussion. A set of relevant determinants is obtained with which a statistical exercise can be assembled that allows us to establish whether systemic states of development exist and whether countries that have grown at an accelerated rate have moved from lower to higher states. The authors explain that "as part of our effort to compile a standard set of growth accounts for 40 years, we have also selected a set of the main determinants of growth from the empirical literature and expanded those data where necessary to cover 84 countries" (Bosworth & Collins, 2003, p. 152). A large panel of data, 84 countries, and extended in time, was constructed—sufficient to perform an in-depth statistical exercise to allow us to evaluate a systemic approach.

Even so, this leaves us with one key question: Are entrepreneurship and innovation key to understanding the dynamics of development?

In the previous pages, it was discussed how development is the result of a dynamic of systemic transformation. Approaching it in this way requires progress on three fronts within this chapter: first, in the methodology for approaching the processes of social transformation and with it the discussion of economic growth; second, in the understanding of development as a learning process generated by innovation, with what this implies in policy design; third, in mathematical modeling and simulation of the dynamics of transformation.

Firstly, in the methodological aspect, the systemic approach to development is an important contribution to the discussion of development as a dynamic of social transformation that takes place in a complex sociotechnical system. The fact that, as presented in the previous chapter, the levels of development are associated with multiple variables and processes makes it necessary to explore the fact that it is a systemic problem within the dynamics of complexity. As proposed by Sterman (2006), Radzicki (2003), and Sterman and Radzicki (1994), in other research, partial approaches do not allow us to understand either the dynamics of transformation or the reasons for the multiple collateral effects that occur in this type of system.

Secondly, we will seek to further explore how innovation can trigger a learning dynamic that generates social transformation processes, the empirical evidence that supports this assertion, and the effect on the type of policies that should be applied to activate the dynamics of social transformation.

Thirdly, from the perspective of systems engineering and its construction of simulation techniques and applications, one of the most interesting aspects of this work is aimed at exploring the possibility of advancing sufficiently in the modeling of social transformation dynamics that derive in higher levels of development. The first element to be explored is the type of causal relationships and dynamic processes that are generated in a relationship structure that is energized by learning and innovation processes. Then, we will seek to investigate the type of mathematical modeling that represents the behavior of the system. Finally, a simulation methodology will be proposed that will allow both the type of dynamics and the complex characteristics of the system to be captured.

Thus, the hypothesis proposed is that the approximation to socioeconomic development as a systemic and complex dynamic allows us: first, to understand that the development process is a transformation generated from the learning that is generated in innovation; and second, to dynamically simulate the processes of social transformation from the dynamics of innovation.

The role of entrepreneurship and innovation is the central axis of this chapter. The discussion process between the neoclassical growth models and the new growth theory, with its endogenous models, which took place between 1986 and 2004, generated an important contribution, in the sense that it opened up empirical and conceptual research in multiple fields and perspectives. But the dozens of econometric research and the multiple theories that accompanied them eventually lead to the conclusion that development is a systemic state in which the society involves an internal balance between its different subsystems.

This has two implications in dynamic terms. First, the system has its inertia that resists change, which together with the natural characteristics of resilience allows it to assimilate changes and accommodate itself without fundamentally changing its structure (Bar-yam, 2004; Stiglitz, 1999). Second, not all subsystems can be generators of transformation dynamics. Ecogeography is more of a conditioning factor than a possible lever for a development process (Sachs et al., 1999; Warner, 2002). In turn, no change can occur if it does not include the other subsystems in the transformation dynamics.

A necessary task is the empirical evaluation of the development processes that have taken place in the world in these 50 years, regardless of whether or not they applied elements that were in the theoretical discussion that was held around endogenous and exogenous models. The most important thing in the last 50 years of economic growth theory according to Hoff and Stiglitz (2001) is that "we know that development is possible, but not inevitable." In addition, Stiglitz himself, after a review of five decades and as a director of the World Bank, is the one who proposes a systemic approach to development, a new paradigm that takes into consideration the interdependence between the institutional, human capital, social capital, and productive capacities (Stiglitz, 1998).

The issue with this systemic approach is that it also implies that there are interdependencies that generate inertias that retard or disable development. The challenge is to explore what could be the key dynamics capable of triggering the transformation processes that are development itself (Stiglitz, 1999). The intention here is to discuss how innovation can be one of these key dynamics.

Innovation has a relative character (OECD, 1993, 1997). For a country or a society, what is new is that which it does not have or does not do. For this chapter, on the one hand, innovation will be understood as the introduction, in a country's economic activity, of new products and services that were not previously generated in that society. This approach has its origin in the work of Schumpeter in the 1930s and is the same as that applied by Lall, Hausmann, and Rodrik in their work (Hausmann, Rodrik, & Velasco, 2005; Lall, 2000). On the other hand, productivity in its broadest sense is understood as the capacity of individuals in a society to generate value.

At this stage of the discussion, within the different approaches to the problem of development, we will investigate how learning and innovation have determined the development processes of fast-growing countries. In the exploration carried out in this chapter, the reading we propose makes a somewhat different interpretation from the directions of the actions. Innovation, understood as the incorporation of new activities, involves building new capabilities, and this was possibly what marked development. If so, it would be a leap from endogenous development to induced development mediated by collective decision-making and systemic emergences. The answer must come from the empirical evidence of these processes. This inquiry can give more certain indications of the dynamics of learning and innovation in countries with accelerated growth, and of how societies are constantly transforming themselves and changing their patterns of organization and welfare.

The first general approach to the economic system was developed by Adam Smith in the second half of the eighteenth century with his books *The Theory of Moral Sentiments* and *Inquiry into the Nature and Causes of the Wealth of Nations.* He elaborated an approach to the problem from the ethics of free enterprise, the production capacity of societies, and the division of labor as a production scheme that would allow the expansion of these capacities.

Structural changes in the modes of production were the construction of economists, social thinkers, and also of nascent engineers. In 1805, Eli Whitney showed how rifle parts could be mass-produced independently and then assembled, something that had previously been impossible to do in the handcrafted production process of piece-by-piece adjustment until the final rifle was obtained. The development of the standardization of assembly parts, the division of labor for mass production, the source of the motive power of steam engines, the freedom to innovate and to make business, and the consolidation of institutions that regulated incentives and intellectual property formed the basis for the transformations, the generation of wealth, and the social conflicts that would follow (Landes, 2003; North, 2005; Olson, 1982).

A few decades later, Malthus, in A *Summary View of the Theory of Population* (final edition of 1827, in which the different versions since 1803 are compiled), introduced the problem of the limitation of natural resources to the discussion. The society of the time had a consumption basket centered on the agricultural exploitation of the land. Technological change in land exploitation techniques was almost nonexistent, while the population had a high exponential growth rate—a theory recently indirectly supported by Jones (2020), which indicates that economic growth would be ended by population reduction. In this context, Malthus's reflections had an enormous impact on English society. Then, in 1898, Veblen introduced into the debate the role of technology and institutions and their effects on social capabilities. In his article "Why Economics Is Not an Evolutionary Science," he describes how established social structures oppose the changes brought about by technology. The problem of the dynamics of change and how social transformations occur is then raised. Strictly speaking, this discussion by Veblen was the first to introduce innovation and technological change as determinants of economic development (Veblen, 1898).

However, it was Joseph Schumpeter in the 1930s and 1940s who definitively marked the discussion on the impact of technology on society and the role of the entrepreneur and innovation. Schumpeter's work marked path research on innovation and its effects on social transformation of which this work is part, introducing those models of systems with nonlinear dynamics that he said he needed, capable of capturing the effects he proposed and which he pointed out could not be captured by general equilibrium models. These only represented a stationary state that technology and entrepreneurs were constantly breaking (Schumpeter, 1939, 1983).

Other approaches from cultural history currents have made an important contribution to the discussion on the role of innovation in social transformations. Mancur Olson, in *The Rise and Decline of Nations* from 1982, criticizes conventional approaches, indicating that they did not explain the incentives to save or innovate, or how societies moved from one state to another of greater development. He pointed out that we only really knew how to accumulate capital, but very little about how we accumulated knowledge, which is the major source of economic growth and social transformation (Olson, 1982, pp. 3–5). Olson assigns a central role to technology and innovation in development. In his work, he explains how market structures and some of their characteristics facilitate or inhibit innovation processes. An example is usually trade unions or oligopolistic structures where innovation can generate processes of change that vary the income conditions of workers or companies, with rents derived from artificially maintaining suboptimal structures (Olson, 1982, pp. 62 and 86). Similarly, he argues that regulatory barriers that prevent the reallocation of resources in the economy may reduce the rate of growth (Olson, 1982, p. 65). He notes that technology has played a central role in US leadership (Olson, 1982, p. 90), making a strong criticism of general equilibrium models, which he argues are not capable of representing and explaining the multiple disequilibria produced by growth processes, much less the processes of social transformation, technological change, or capital accumulation (Olson, 1982, pp. 187, 188, 194, 196).

Within this current historic-institutionalist analysis, the book by David Landes, *The Wealth and Poverty of Nations*, discusses the reasons for the existence of winners and losers in the development process throughout history. He explains how the division of labor studied by A. Smith and technological changes generated the preponderance of the West in the Europe of the Middle Ages (Landes, 2003, p. 45). The role he assigns to innovation in social transformation is paramount. He presents and explains how a group of inventions led to the emergence of modern society. The water wheel was a source of motive power that allowed the beginning of multiple industrial processes. Eyeglasses extended the working life of skilled labor and craftsmen. The mechanical clock introduced time management and the concept of productivity into the culture and strengthened the concept of linear time in Western culture. The printing press improved the processes of dissemination, conservation, and consolidation of knowledge. Gunpowder provided military power and served to cement a new structure of power and government (Landes, 2003, pp. 45–59). With regard to the clock, he notes: "The invention of the mechanical clock anticipated in its effects the economic analysis of Adam Smith: it increased the wealth of nations derived directly from the productivity of their labor force" (Landes, 2003, p. 50). In addition, he notes that one of the key reasons for this expansion based on innovation was the freedom of the market and enterprise that allowed innovation to be profitable and generate new wealth (Landes, 2003, p. 59). In Chapter 18, "The Wealth of Knowledge," an approach to the growth and transformation of societies based on knowledge is made (Landes, 2003, p. 276). In fact, in Europe during the Industrial Revolution, the emigration of qualified personnel in different specialties was prohibited in various periods and by various states (Landes, 2003, p. 276). According to Landes, knowledge and its diffusion became the source that allowed innovation and the emergence of multiple industries, such as metalworking in England and chemistry in Germany (Landes, 2003, pp. 285–286).

In this discussion on the role of innovation and the dynamics of entrepreneurship and learning intimately linked to it, the work of Nelson and Pack (1998) for the World Bank, "The Asian Miracle and the Modern Growth Theory," is relevant. There, the authors discuss the basic assumptions of the new growth theory and make a leap from endogenous development to induced development strategies. In the paper, they state:

> The Asian miracle is explained by entrepreneurship, innovation, and learning. These are the significant factors in the rapid growth of the Asian tigers. Theories about the Asian miracle can be divided into two groups: First, 'accumulationist' theories emphasize the role of capital investments and their effects on the production function of these countries. If countries make investments and get the resources, the development will follow. Second, 'assimilationist' theories emphasize entrepreneurship, innovation, and learning. They see investment in physical and human capital as essential but insufficient without a process of assimilation. (Nelson & Pack, 1998, pp. 1 and 3)

Nelson and Pack (1998) explain in detail the differences between the accumulationist and assimilationist approaches to these issues and explain the processes of development by innovation. They explain it as follows:

- Business decision-making. Accumulationists do not pay attention to firms. They focus on macroeconomic incentives and constraints. For assimilationists it is firms that learn and are the key to rapid growth.

- The nature of technology. Accumulationists assume that technology is available and can be adopted by firms. Assimilationists argue that only a small part of it is available in catalogs and much of it is tacit learning from the application of knowledge and continued practice.
- The potential economic capabilities of a well-educated workforce. Accumulationists try to explain labor productivity gains as resulting from alternative technologies. Assimilationists emphasize the ability to learn, undertake, and innovate.
- The role of exports in a fast-growing country. Accumulationists assume that the increase in exports is to be expected from the increase in human and physical capital stocks. Assimilationists observe that this is the result of active policies of governments, firms, innovative capacity, and the learning of firms, which allows them to compete in world markets. External markets strengthen learning in two ways: competitive demands and technical assistance from foreign customers. (Nelson & Pack, 1998, pp. 4–5)

This last assertion is precisely where it is important to generate the linkage with the last part of the discussion: Can exports provide us with empirical evidence of how innovation has transformed societies and support Nelson and Pack's assertion that development processes are associated with learning, entrepreneurship, and innovation? It would seem so.

The answer to this question has made some important contributions in the last 5 years. In the neo-Schumpeterian line of research, Lall (2000) carried out several works that record information that provides an answer to this question. In "The Technological Structure and Performance of Developing Country Manufactured Exports, 1985–1998," he works on statistics for the period. He found that export structure has implications for growth and development and that the growth of exports of higher-technology products explains faster growth. He found that Asian countries dominated the study period with 70% of exports. He notes: "[I]nternational trade theory does not explain the emergence of countries' export growth trajectories" (Lall, 2000, p. 29), but instead points out that countries with a "good learning system" can innovate and change their pattern of specialization (Lall, 2000, pp. 30, 31).

The same author with other researchers in a 2005 paper, "The Sophistication of Exports: A New Measure of Product Characteristics," carried out an exercise to qualify the sophistication of products. In the document, they construct a sophistication indicator based on which they make a comparative analysis of countries and again find empirical evidence that shows, as in the previous work, a relationship between the level of sophistication of exports and levels of development (Lall, 2000; Lall et al., 2005, p. 28).

Another line of work that has coinciding findings comes from the World Bank. Daniel Lederman works along these lines. In 2002, together with Maloney, he published the document "Trade Structure and Growth," in which the following trade variables are analyzed: export concentration, intra-industry exports, and abundance of natural resources (Lederman & Maloney, 2002). The study begins to hint that concentration and natural resource orientation have negative effects on growth. In 2005, Lederman published the paper "Innovation and Development Around the World, 1960–2000" together with Saenz. The paper concludes: "Econometric results suggest that innovation may have a strong positive effect on long-term development" (Lederman & Saenz, 2006, p. 1). Econometric analyses on R&D investment variables, number of patents, and technical and research personnel also indicate a high potential for the endogeneity of innovation (Lederman & Saenz, 2006).

Other works that are very relevant in the verification of the effect of innovation on development and growth are those carried out by Bayley Klinger of the CID/KSG Harvard. In "Diversification, Innovation, and Imitation Inside the Global Technological Frontier," through the use of export statistics and controlling with data that evidence market failures, they find that export diversification grows in the initial levels of development and then concentrates on the higher levels of development. In the same direction, the patenting process grows (Klinger & Lederman, 2006a). The authors point out that they do not find much empirical work on the relationship between the emergence of new products (innovation) and economic development, which is where they direct their research and which is exactly along the lines of this discussion. This is what they explore in depth in the following work: "Innovations and export portfolios." In the methodology they use, they take up the characterization of innovation events that they identified in the previous work and control against the size and export concentration of the countries. They conclude: "There is a clear negative relationship between the concentration of innovation portfolios and performance: countries that are more successful in the search process have a broader success in the range of industries than poor performers" (Klinger & Lederman, 2006b). An important contribution of the methodology suggests that the emergence occurs chaotically. Therefore, they conclude that a broad-spectrum policy that allows for the emergence of these "success stories" is preferable to a selection of winning sectors.

A set of works that end up configuring a robust set of empirical evidence that innovation has an endogenous causal relationship with development processes are the works of Ricardo Hausmann, Hausmann with Rodrik, and Hausmann with Bailey Klinger himself. The first of these is "Economic Development as Self-Discovery," published by Hausmann and Rodrik (2002). The work is based on a two-sector general equilibrium model, one modern and the other traditional, similar in its conception to those used by the neo-Schumpeterian tradition, although the latter simply does not assume the restrictions necessary for general equilibrium to occur. The model is used to explain the learning processes in economies and how these take place around self-discovery of new activities, that is, around innovations (Hausmann & Rodrik, 2002, p. 35). In another research by the same authors with Andrés Velasco on constraints to growth, called "Growth Diagnostics," the model of analysis leads them to a similar conclusion: A structural constraint is when there is "very low adoption of technology or self-discovery" (Hausmann, Rodrik, & Velasco, 2005, p. 19). On innovation and self-discovery, they say: "To get a sense of how these can be the engines of growth, suppose that either through chance or deliberate action, a new product appears on the scene" (Hausmann, Rodrik, & Velasco, 2005, p. 26). In Schumpeter's terms, the steady state—equilibrium—is broken, if it existed at all, or in Bar-Yam's terms, the complex system changes its structure.

In December 2005, Hausmann, Rodrick, and Hwang published the paper "What You Export Matters." This paper is a key contribution to the discussion on the relationship between innovation and the transformation of specialization patterns. The paper takes a broad export database of 5000 products for a period between 1992 and 2003. They use it to construct two indicators: The first refers to the type of country exporting a given product, and the second to the set of goods exported by a country. The conclusions are important: There is a clear relationship between exports and the level of per capita income, and countries that have learned to produce products that are typical of richer countries grow faster. In other words, what was proposed in the previous chapter and this one is verified: There is a systemic relationship between the capacity to generate welfare and the level of development measured by income, and innovation can generate a dynamic of transformation. The respective relationships are shown in Figs. 3.1 and 3.2.

In a more recent paper, Hausmann and Klinger (2006) presented the paper "Structural Transformation and Patterns of Comparative Advantage in the Product Space." In this work, they perform a statistical work of

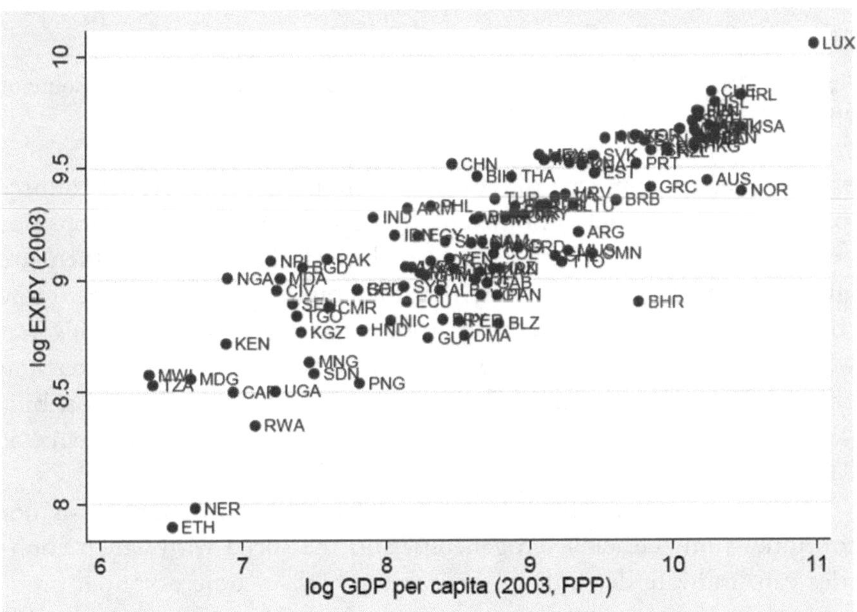

Fig. 3.1 Relationship between per capita income and EXPI export portfolio. Source: "What You Export Matters" (Hausmann et al., 2005)

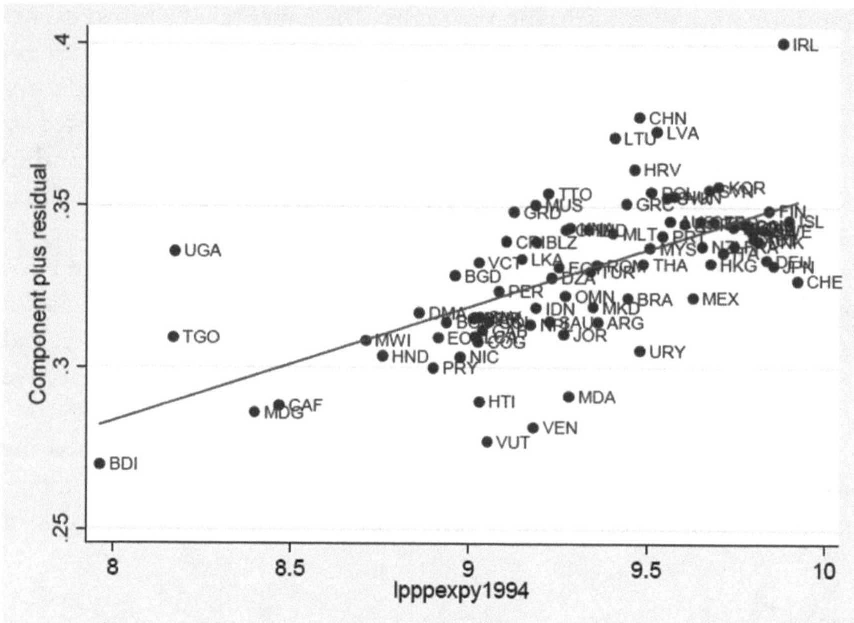

Fig. 3.2 Partial relationship between EXPI export portfolio and subsequent growth. Source: "What You Export Matters" (Hausmann et al., 2005)

probabilities for a universe of more than a thousand products per country for the period 1962–2000. Based on this, a network of interrelationships between products is constructed in which the linkages between them are given in terms of the probability that they can be produced in the same country. A framework for reading product typologies is built on this network, using the one proposed by Leamer. This network allows a reading of countries' context given by the products they export and the possibilities they have of learning how to develop new products (Hausmann & Klinger, 2006).

The exercise reveals that the variety of products in countries is not continuous but rather heterogeneous, and the speed with which countries can innovate depends on how many high-income potential products, with a good probability of being realized, they have close to their current production pattern. This is what the authors call "open forest"

(Hausmann & Klinger, 2006, p. 20). Again, this exercise provides empirical evidence between innovation and economic growth.

If we focus on recent research by some Latin American authors, we have as references the works of Ricardo Hausmann and Eduardo Lora. On the one hand, Hausmann (2016) states that "know-how is the hardest component of technical progress to be mobilized, and as such can become the binding constraint of the development process," highlighting the importance of this factor in a key determinant of development such as innovation. Balland et al. [Hausmann] (2022) understand that in addition to innovation, economic development has to be approached from a new paradigm of economic complexity in which technological change and other indicators carry out a systemic interaction. On the other hand, Castellani and Lora (2014) propose that not only innovation but also entrepreneurship is a key transmission channel to achieve social mobility in Latin America.

The set of results and conceptual approaches that have been presented support the important way in which innovation, learning, and entrepreneurship have a direct relationship with the dynamics of transformation that are expressed in economic and social development. These three factors are fundamental for the development of countries (especially entrepreneurship), and some notable authors on economic development have even mentioned their importance.

Jones (2021a) states that growth has substantially exceeded its long-run rate because of rising educational attainment, declining misallocation, and rising (global) research intensity, implying that frontier growth could slow markedly in the future. Thus, the author points out that to avoid stagnation, the actions of an economic agent, firms, are necessary, since they are the ones that introduce technology into the market. In another key research, Jones (2021b) demonstrates that combinatorial growth in the number of draws from standard thin-tailed distributions leads to exponential economic growth; these exponential growth rates are strongly influenced by innovative capabilities, some of which are generated by the firms themselves.

Bloom et al. (2013) highlight the importance of firms as generators of innovation in favorable environments such as trade liberalization and low wages, while Oman et al. (2002) states that the firm is at the heart of development, since the role of the firm as the locus of productivity growth in society, and the importance of healthy inter-firm price competition, drive economic growth. From a more structural perspective, Pritchett et al. (2017) state that for there to be sustained economic growth, there must be a structural transformation, in which firms must be the main axis—firms that desire a more open business environment, make more complex products and services, and are represented in the political settlement. Additionally, in recent high-impact literature, there has been a wave of articles related to how firms are synonymous with entrepreneurship, which is strongly related to economic development through innovation and entrepreneurial dynamics mechanisms (Aparicio et al., 2016; Audretsch & Keilbach, 2008). For example, Rico and Cabrer-Borrás (2019) analyze whether the divergences in the economic growth of the Spanish regions are a result of sectoral differences, company size, or the technological level of the new firms that emerge in the market, and find that both the creation of new firms and entrepreneurial activity have a positive effect on productive efficiency and can explain the differences in the economic growth of the regions. Including spatial analysis, Adler et al. (2019) support the hypothesis that tech-startup entrepreneurship is organized across two distinct but related spatial scales, which act on entrepreneurial activity through different mechanisms, suggesting that local diversity and local specialization can simultaneously potentiate innovation.

According to the different currents, but especially from the neo-Schumpeterian current, the effects of social transformations can be approached from the observation of the impact on societies, and the degree of innovation they have in their portfolio of economic activities through firms. Normative approaches can be built around this to propose models derived from these discussions on the dynamics of the system. This can be useful if innovation is reviewed from its effects on the transformation of societies, and from there, a theoretical approach is proposed and a development policy proposal is made. From the theoretical point of view, this research is aimed at exploring how to structure (model) socio-economic dynamics to simulate how innovations generate transformations in which the firms play a fundamental role.

3.4 Dynamics of Entrepreneurship, Learning, and Innovation

As previously discussed, development does not seem to be such an elusive mystery. It is rather a systemic state in which the multiple social, human, cultural, productive, and institutional aspects of society maintain a balance, interdependence, and mutual correlation. But societies are constantly changing, transforming themselves, and are capable of overcoming inferior states of development and acquiring new capacities.

One of the patterns of change has as a dynamic of transformation the learning of new activities for the generation of well-being, or what we call here "innovation processes," the construction of new capabilities for making new and more complex products. As noted in the previous section, these innovation dynamics have the potential to transform society. However, how can these dynamics be understood in more detail and how can they be developed more dynamically?

One of the purposes of this chapter is to explore how entrepreneurship and innovation can trigger a learning dynamic that generates processes of social transformation and to review the empirical evidence to support this assertion. The basic hypothesis is that innovation unleashes a dynamic of societal transformation. The work of Hausmann and Rodrik in 2005 on export portfolios, of Lall on exports and their level of sophistication in 2000 and 2005, of Klinger and Lederman on innovation in 2006, and those that have been working on the relationships between export patterns, innovation indicators, and levels of development, clearly indicate that the introduction of new activities in societies generates a virtuous dynamic of transformation that progressively converts it into one of higher income and level of development (Gómez, 2002a, 2002b, 2002c; Hausmann et al., 2005; Hausmann & Klinger, 2006; Klinger & Lederman, 2006a, 2006b; Lederman & Maloney, 2002; Lederman & Saenz, 2006).

This approach suggests that each innovation is the result of a deliberate action that is configured as a project. In terms of knowledge construction, each project is also a learning process. It is also proposed that innovations take the form of two types of improvements: new products and new processes. Each of them surpasses what previously existed in society or introduces something that did not exist before. This classification of innovations is in line with Bell and Pavitt (1993), which has been widely discussed and cited within innovation theory. In the approach proposed here, a new good is generated in the case of radical innovation, or a new process in the case of incremental innovation, both of which in turn generate an expansion in production capacity in the case of processes, or an expansion in the portfolio of goods offered by society, that is, an expansion in the demands that society can meet. Ultimately, this is what is called "social capacity": what a community can produce and deliver both to its community and others (see Fig. 3.3).

In Fig. 3.3, we use a schematic representation of the relationships between variables. The arrows indicate the direction of causality, and the sign indicates whether the effect is positive or negative. This same scheme will be used throughout the discussion.

As noted, Bell and Pavitt (1993) is one of the most cited articles on the relationship between development, technological change, and innovation (technological accumulation and industrial growth). This article discusses growth processes and is one of the important contributions that support the relationship between innovation and economic growth. It proposes that technical change and technological learning are key factors in explaining the differences between developed countries in their performance, growth, and trade. The authors emphasize trying to understand the processes of technological accumulation in the industrialized world (Bell & Pavitt, 1993, p. 157), differentiating between two types of

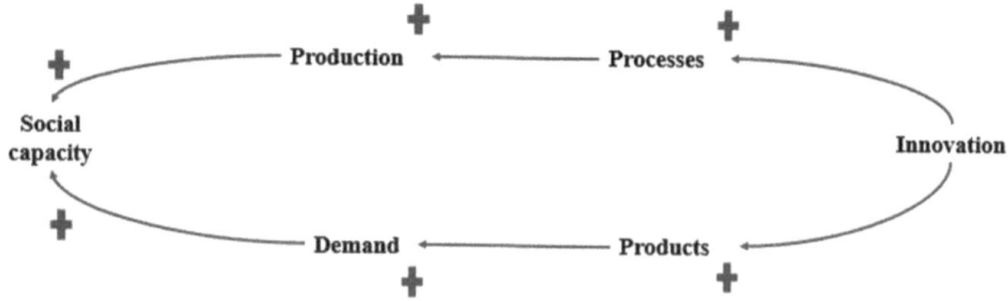

Fig. 3.3 Innovation and expansion of social capacity. Source: Own elaboration

resources, skills, and physical goods. The authors propose that technology accumulation takes place in the former, and analyze the processes of technology diffusion and how they allow developing countries to advance without incurring the costs of innovation (Bell & Pavitt, 1993, p. 158).

Technological innovation is concentrated in developed countries, while diffusion is a process specific to developing economies. They argue that these dynamics are what generate the continuous imbalances in the economies, due to the dynamics of competition, imitation, innovation, learning, and competitiveness (Bell & Pavitt, 1993, p. 158). Market structures generate pressures and barriers in the diffusion processes. These structures are typical of the level of development of the technology. They note that development trajectories are associated with countries' learning processes. For this reason, the authors conclude that learning activities—their nature, determinants, and dynamic effects on the economy—may become the focus of analysis and policy attention in the future (Bell & Pavitt, 1993, p. 164).

This, as Bell and Pavitt point out, is precisely the core of the discussion in this chapter. This dynamic of expansion of social capabilities through innovation represents a progressive, adaptive, and permanent process through which societies learn and transform themselves. It is the type of dynamics described by Bijker in his work on societies and their artifacts and what he describes as the "sociology of science" (Bijker, 1999; Bijker et al., 1987; Bijker & Pinch, 1984).

Observing another posture, Nicholas Stern (2002) held the conference "Dynamic Development: Innovation and Inclusion." In it, he states that innovation is at the heart of the strategy for the transformation of societies:

> I will present a strategy for development based on what we have learned from development experiences. The strategy is based on two pillars: creating an investment climate for the dynamics of growth to happen and empowering people to participate in the growth process. Innovation and inclusion are at the heart of this strategy and the actions of the plan. This is the reason for the title of this conference: "Development Dynamics: Innovation and inclusion." (Stern, 2002, pp. 4 and 5)

Innovations generate a process of social assimilation, which in turn generates an increase in social capabilities. This gives rise to a virtuous process of social transformation and increased knowledge. Each innovation in turn builds knowledge. This dynamic was discussed by Olson and Landes in their studies on economic transformation and the history of civilizations. Veblen had analyzed this dynamic since the nineteenth century and had also explained that innovations have a direct effect on society by changing its consumption and even behavioral patterns. Taken together, this configures what Carlota Pérez describes as a technical-economic paradigm (Landes, 2003; Olson, 1982; Perez, 2004; Veblen, 1898).

Therefore, innovation transforms society, but in turn, new social capabilities generate and feed new dynamics. Each learning process generates new knowledge, which in turn is the basis for the construction of new learning processes. This is what Hausmann and Klinger find and empirically validate in what they call "open forest"—those new products that are placed within the possibilities of society each time it manages to introduce a new product that expands demand. Also, as Bijker explains, each new artifact in society is built around a new arrangement of suppliers, services, facilities, and knowledge of use. In other words, each new social capability brings with it a new transformation of that society. Both transformations and knowledge feed back into the innovation process, maintaining a dynamic of new learning (see Fig. 3.4).

The point is that some societies manage to maintain permanent learning processes, as in the case of American society over the last 200 years.

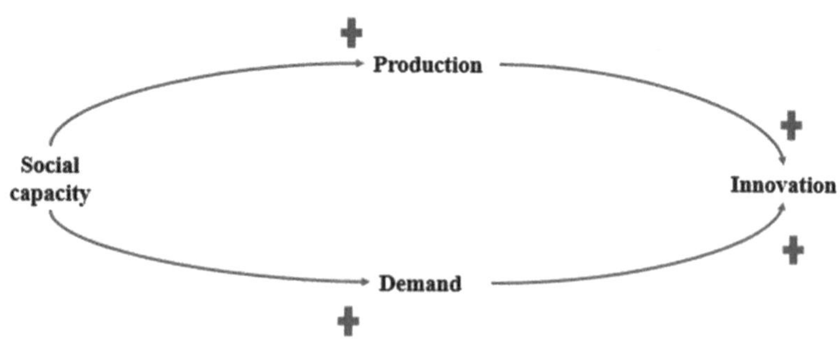

Fig. 3.4 Social capacity, knowledge, social transformation. Source: Own elaboration

Others manage to establish them after having remained static for long periods and without having built precedents that could explain them, such as Singapore and Korea, and others even seem to involute, such as Argentina (Landes, 2003). North (2005), in the book *Understanding the Process of Economic Change*, approaches this concept when he states that "the driving force in the development of mankind has been the stock of knowledge, which has revolutionized production technologies" (North, 2005, p. 43). Then, in his discussion of democracy, he returns to the concepts of learning and discovery processes (North, 2005, p. 56), as the basis for the construction of societies.

This process has to do with an element that North calls "intentionality." This social construct establishes a referent that it seeks to achieve and that determines its collective action (North, 2005). In our analysis, we will call this referent the "innovation referent" and it depends fundamentally on the level of knowledge in society. As Einstein suggested, societies define their actions within their levels of thinking. A society that increases its level of knowledge has the opportunity to set more ambitious goals than one that is less capable (see Fig. 3.5).

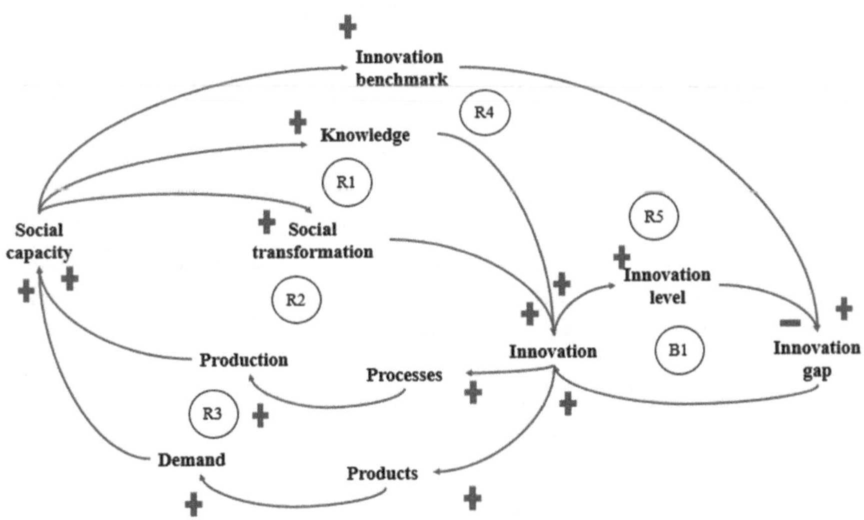

Fig. 3.5 The innovation benchmark and social capability. Source: Own elaboration

In this model, the basic social capabilities are associated with knowledge and the capacity to generate initial goods. The economy will grow according to the innovation benchmark that this society sets as a target.

There are many social examples of the construction of referents. One of them is the American decision to put a man on the moon after they felt that the Soviets had surpassed them technologically. Other examples more relevant to this analysis are the goals set by Lee Kuan Yew and Park Chung Hi for Singapore and Korea, respectively. In each case, they set the level that their society should aim for and aligned their efforts in that direction.

The whole dynamic of the process is quite suggestive. Progressively (see Fig. 3.5), new processes and products expand social capabilities for generating well-being. In turn, knowledge and structures expand and evolve, generating new possibilities for innovation. Society is self-directed and self-organized (in terms of complex thinking and systems theory) (Bar-yam, 2004), building a referent that marks its transformation intentionality (North, 2005).

Trajectories are an important aspect of this dynamic process of development. Although, as Cohen notes, there is no evidence of the general convergence suggested by neoclassical trajectories, there could be a specific pattern of learning, innovation, and growth for a society that follows the "logistic curve" behavior presented in Fig. 3.6. Cohen (2002) explains that countries break their dynamic of slow growth and enter a virtuous and exponential dynamic of growth until they approach the levels of the leading countries in terms of income and technology, initiating the third phase of lower growth but also of convergence as the pattern of specialization is reached and the gap with the most innovative countries is reduced.

The behavior over time of such a dynamic is shown in Fig. 3.6. Initially, the possibilities for innovation are enormous, but real capacities are limited, and the process of capacity expansion is slow. Then it accelerates and maintains a significant pace. In the last phase, as the benchmark is reached, the possibilities for innovation are fewer and each project will require greater effort. This is the phase in which, for example, Korea's insertion in the world home appliance markets begins to stabilize its

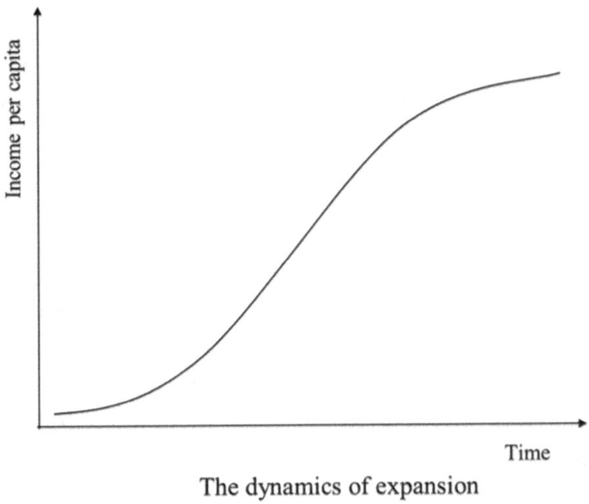

Fig. 3.6 The dynamics of expansion. Source: Developed by the author

participation and the entire market structure of the sector accommodates and assimilates the new players. This process has occurred in micro dimensions, with the introduction of new products, or at the scale of economies, as in the case of Korea, and continues to occur permanently in the processes of insertion into new markets.

Within the processes of technology diffusion, market expansion, the introduction of innovative products, which have been studied within the fields of systems dynamics research, the result of an expansion of economies that show a behavior of successive "s" is familiar, intuitive, and discussed. The common reaction is: "how, and economists didn't know this?" Within the economic schools closer to innovation and development issues the topic is well known. Innovation has been approached in system dynamics fundamentally from the perspective of its diffusion processes, which are assimilated to the processes of epidemic propagation (Sterman, 2000; Sterman & Ford, 1998). Other research in recent years has studied the dynamics of innovation over time in sectors with high rates of technological change (Milling, 2002) and the dynamics of innovation in companies. Maier, in 1998, published "New Product Diffusion Models in Innovation Management: A System Dynamics Perspective," in which he returns to logistic curves and evaluates the effects of delays and managerial decisions on the configuration of the curve.

Another discussion that is introduced in system dynamics is that of competitive behavior among several agents that compete for the markets of new products. A dynamic of demand expansion reinforcement is proposed by the effort to capture the potential market. Within the evolutionary and neo-Schumpeterian tradition of research on innovation processes, Harvey and McMeekin critique simple diffusion models in "Between Demand and Consumption: A Framework for Research" (Harvey et al., 2001). On the one hand, for the economic discussion in the neo-Schumpeterian current, it is important to have a mathematical formalization of these dynamics. Schumpeter advocated the use of mathematical tools to formalize his theoretical intuitions on the effects of innovation, entrepreneurship, and process improvements. For the theoretical current, this represents a severe break with neoclassical theory, due to these behaviors assuming not the existence of a state of equilibrium but a dynamic of transformation to higher states of social capacity. Ironically, paraphrasing Neil Armstrong, a small step for systems dynamics is an enormous step for neoclassical economics, and one that it may not need to take because its central problem of discussion is not economic growth but macro stability in the short term. On the other hand, in development economics, the discussion has been very broad. The neoclassical theory of economic development faces the dilemma of overcoming general equilibrium models to advance in the understanding of the dynamics of economic development.

As already noted, after the appearance of Romer's work (1986), a new phase of interest began in the late 1980s in work on economic growth and specifically in the economic study of the innovation process, largely as a result of the results of various studies showing that the competitiveness of companies, economic growth, and therefore the quality of life of a country are closely related to its capacity to successfully introduce technological innovations or "technical progress" (or "Solow residue"). It was Solow who did the first work within the neoclassical tradition, pointing out the importance of technological change, paradoxically explained by the size of the residual in econometric regressions. He concluded that technical progress was the main determinant of economic growth, yet the models were silent on the mechanisms by which technological change occurs. They cannot be adequately analyzed using the framework of early economic growth theories (Solow, 1956), which employ oversimplifying assumptions about the role of technological change as a determinant of growth (Solow, 1956, 1994).

Although Solow's discussion is clear in indicating the effect of technology, there was no proposal to explain the dynamics of technology generation and its social transformations. In fact, in these models, technology was considered to be exogenous, that is, although technical progress was considered to be one of the fundamental variables in determining growth, neither its origin, nor its dependence on decisions, nor the interaction between various agents was specified.

The contributions of the early 1990s began to consider the role of technology in economic growth, and its effects on the competitiveness of companies are known as "endogenous growth by innovation" models. In these new models, technology was an endogenous variable, so that it ceased to be an ad hoc appearance and became the result of the decisions of companies that, using available scientific knowledge, invested in R&D activities to develop marketable innovations in the market (Romer (1990) and Grossman and Helpman (2004) are examples of these models).

The type of model proposed in the new growth theory seeks to endogenize technology while maintaining the condition of complying with general equilibrium restrictions. The most recent approaches to the effects of innovation and productivity approach the problem with mathematical formulations based on a production function such as the following one presented by Sala-i-Martin on innovation:

$$Y_t = A \times K_t^{\alpha} \times L_t^{1-\alpha} \tag{3.1}$$

where Y_t is the output, A is the company efficiency parameter, L is labor, K is the compound of aggregate intermediate and capital goods, and α is the capital elasticity. Then, if we clear for K, we have:

$$K_t = \left(\sum_{j=1}^{N_t} X_{jt}^{\alpha} \right)^{\frac{1}{\alpha}} \tag{3.2}$$

Then, replacing Eq. (3.2) in Eq. (3.1):

$$Y_t = A \times L_t^{1-\alpha} \times \left(\sum_{j=1}^{N_t} X_{jt}^{\alpha} \right)$$

This function has to comply with the basic criterion of constant or decreasing returns to scale that allows the construction of a general equilibrium system so that the function does not expand and end up without a solution (Sala-i-Martin, 2000, 2002). The models are of the type of formulations presented in Fig. 3.7, also called "AK models."

The most recent works by Rodrick and Hausmann point out that the behavior of growth processes according to the neoclassical and endogenous growth approaches are as presented in Fig. 3.8 (Hausmann et al.,

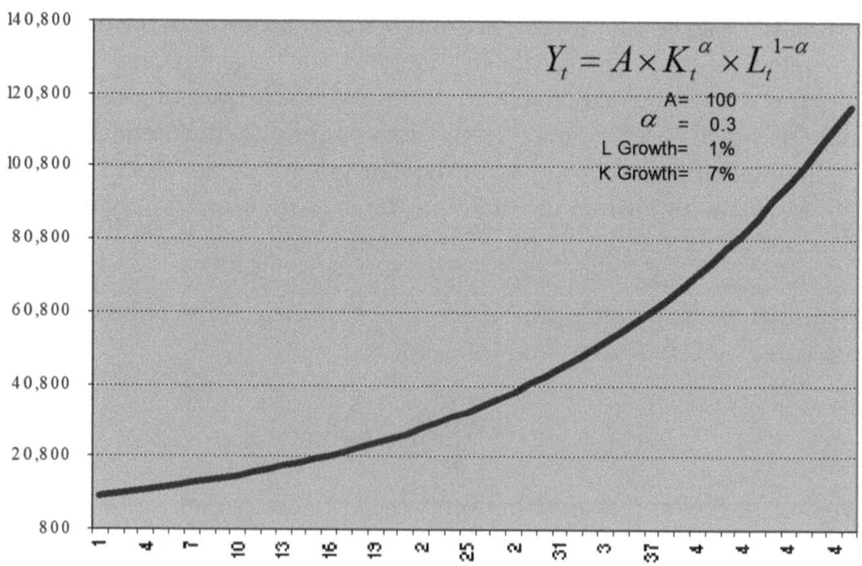

Fig. 3.7 AK models. Source: Author's simulation

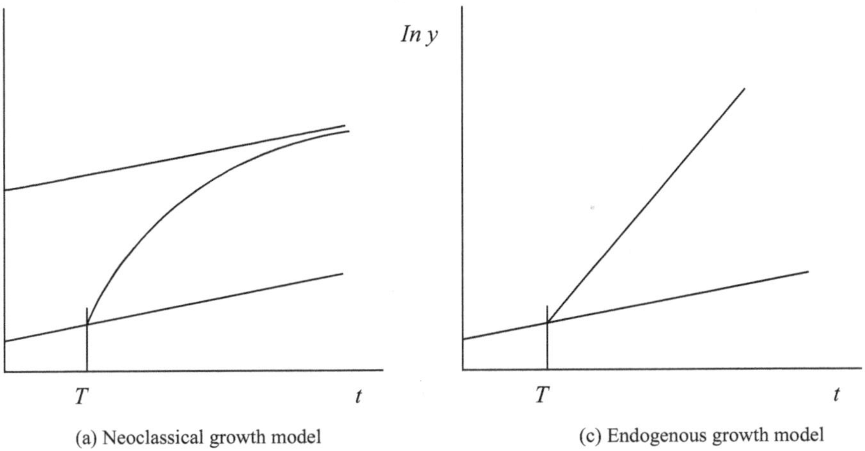

Fig. 3.8 Evolution of per capita output in the neoclassical and endogenous models. Source: Hausmann, Rodrik, & Velasco (2005)

2004). Classical theory suggests a convergence process following a curve with a decreasing slope. Endogenous growth assumes a constant slope that is consistent with general equilibrium assumptions. The truth is that the final behavior of the AK models without diminishing returns, but rather increasing ones, at a constant rate, ends up generating an expansive trajectory as shown in Fig. 3.8.

Sala-i-Martin himself has explained the insufficiency of the neoclassical approach to describe the empirical evidence that the growth process can be induced by innovation dynamics, which in turn are fed by knowledge construction processes, which could be approximated from mathematical constructions that allow the cybernetic and feedback processes that occur in these dynamics to be captured (Sala-i-Martin, 2000, 2002).

With a more critical view, Metcalfe makes a harsh critique of general equilibrium and its ability to understand the processes of innovation and development, stating that:

> Hicksian temporary equilibrium is defined as the state in which markets empty and supply and demand equalize. The point is that if an equilibrium is a solution to some problem, we need to know which problem we are

> dealing with. In Nelson and Winter's perspective, if the problem is economic development and the role of innovation in the development of the economy is an "evolutionary" problem, then the equilibrium has an internal problem of consistency in providing the required solution. (Metcalfe, 2001, p. 14)
>
> The main issue is that equilibrium and evolution are incompatible. How is it that the market is orderly and never in equilibrium? The key is that the different elements of the system change at different rates, and these characteristics define the system. (Metcalfe, 2001, p. 17)

The point is that the empirical evidence suggests that the behaviors seem to be more of the type presented in Fig. 3.6. The per capita income trajectories of Korea, Singapore, and Ireland are good examples of these behaviors. They show deliberate processes of innovation and learning that generate dynamics in the progressive phases of growth.

To advance in this discussion, the behaviors evidenced in countries with recent development processes will be discussed in depth and will be reviewed around a modeling proposal with system dynamics that allow these economic processes to be represented and discussed more comprehensively, representing the dynamics of learning and innovation inherent to these processes.

The dynamics shown in Figs. 3.5 and 3.6 have a possible mathematical formalization. Per capita income, or in broader terms the total product of an economy or a society, is showing its capacity to generate welfare. That social capacity is called "C." To understand it, it will be represented in this way: It is all the products and services that are made or rendered in a given period. It is as if everything that society does were placed in a Walmart or on a counter. In other words, C is a portfolio of goods and services. Every period, on that counter, all the products and services in the possible quantities are demanded by the society and the "warehouse" is emptied. These sales or outflows will be called "FS." In turn, in every period, the company generates new production and replenishes this Walmart. This production flow will be called "FP." The change of social capabilities C over time will be described by the changes in the input and output flows, that is, the production of the period, FP, and the demand, FS; that is, if we compare what has just been sold with what has just been supplied, we will be able to observe the new things we have learned to do.

In other words, the change in social capabilities is evidenced by the new products introduced in the portfolio.

This change is represented by the following equation:

$$\frac{dC}{dt} = \text{FP} - \text{FS} = C \times K_i \tag{3.3}$$

where K_i is the effective innovation rate. The change in production flow that is associated with the social capacity to generate goods depends on the capacity for product and process innovation presented in Fig. 3.3. It will depend on the social resources applied to innovation and on the possibility that this innovation is effective, that is, that society has not reached the innovation threshold. As society reaches the maximum level of possibilities within the innovation level, the effect of the resources applied to innovation is reduced. Expressed formally, we have the following structure:

$$K_i = K_e - \frac{C}{C_d} \tag{3.4}$$

where K_e is the basic innovation, C is the social capacity, C_d is the innovation benchmark, while the expression $\frac{C}{C_d}$ is the reduction of innovation effectiveness.

Therefore, what society delivers is linked to the capacity to innovate products and is limited by the achievable level of development. As explained, the level of innovation is marked by a benchmark that aspires to reach: the higher it is, the higher the level that society achieves. In turn, societies know that they cannot aspire to move from the plow to the satellite launching business, but they can aspire to semi-industrial organic products that are in their "open forest," in Hausmann and Klinger's terms, or at an attainable level of sophistication, in Lall's terms (Hausmann & Klinger, 2006; Lall et al., 2005).

The capacity to innovate will be determined by the ratio between the current and expected social capacity. As the social capacity grows and approaches the innovation "frontier," the number of innovations is gradually reduced until the proposed benchmark is reached. The complete differential equation that represents this dynamic, without yet endogenizing knowledge, is Eq. (3.5):

$$\frac{dC}{dt} = K_e \times C - C \times \left(\frac{C}{C_d} \right) \tag{3.5}$$

After solving the differential equation (3.4), we arrive at the following expression for social capacity (Eq. 3.6):

$$C(t) = \frac{-K_e \times C_0 \times e^{K} e^{t}}{\left(\frac{C_0}{C_d} - K_e \right) - \frac{C_0}{C_d} \times e^{K} e^{t}} \tag{3.6}$$

where C_0 is the initial value of c.

In the steady state, Eq. (3.7):

$$\begin{gathered} \frac{dC}{dt} = 0 \\ K_e \times C = C \times \left(\frac{C}{C_d} \right) \\ C = K_e \times C_d \end{gathered} \tag{3.7}$$

which will be the social capacity that can be effectively achieved in this learning process. If this equation is simulated, Fig. 3.9 is obtained:

The simulated equation is Eq. (3.7), with a benchmark of an EXPI of \$10,000 and a final innovation and assimilation capacity K_e of 0.85.

The model obtained is a classical dynamic within system dynamics. It consists of stock with two input and output flows, which is nothing more than a differential equation. This is represented in the form shown in Fig. 3.10. You will recall that "SOCIAL CAPACITY" is represented in this model as the set of products that society makes. The metaphor is that

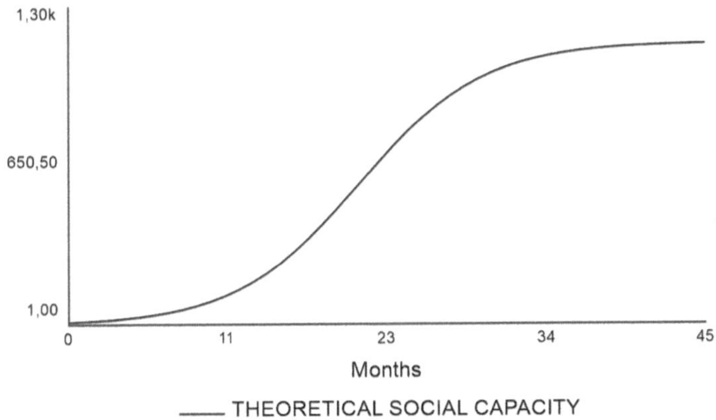

Fig. 3.9 Social capability simulation. Source: Developed by the authors

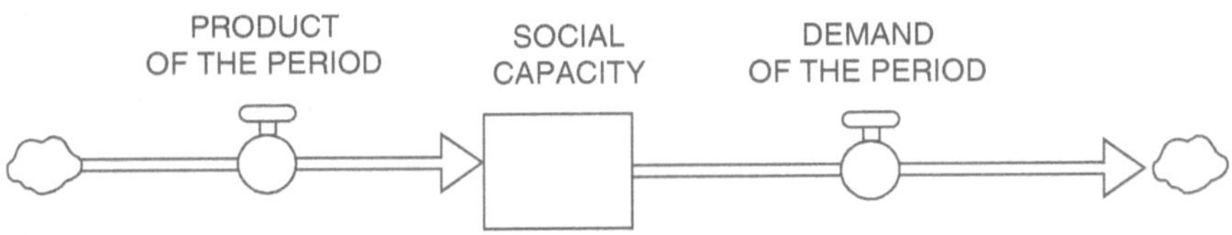

Fig. 3.10 System flow structure. Source: Developed by the authors

of a large warehouse where all the goods and services that society knows how to make and is capable of generating in a given period are available.

The diagram of the complete system with the simulation of the theoretical formula is shown in Fig. 3.11. It is important to highlight the character of the "social capacity" stock. It is emptied in each period and replenished simultaneously. This means that the demand served expresses the social capacity to generate welfare.

The simulated theoretical formula is the following equation, and it is organized in such a way that on the first line is the numerator and on the next two lines are the two terms of the denominator.

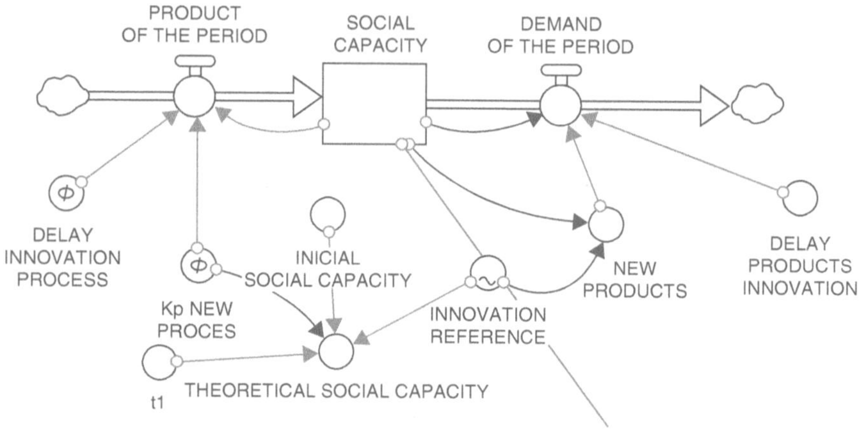

Fig. 3.11 Complete system structure. Source: Developed by the authors

$$\text{THEORETICAL SOCIAL CAPACITY} = \left(\begin{array}{l}-\text{Kp\_NEW\_PROCESSES}^{*}\text{INITIAL\_SOCIAL\_CAPACITY}^{*}\text{EXP} \\ (\text{Kp\_NEW\_PROCESSES}^{*}\text{t1})\end{array}\right) / \left(\begin{array}{l}\left(\begin{array}{l}(\text{INITIAL\_SOCIAL\_CAPACITY / INNOVATION\_REFERENCE\_A}) \\ -\text{Kp\_NEW\_PROCESSES}\end{array}\right) \\ -\text{INITIAL\_SOCIAL\_CAPACITY}^{*}\text{EXP}(\text{Kp\_NEW\_PROCESSES}^{*}\text{t1}) \\ /\text{REFERENCE\_INNOVATION\_REFERENCE\_A} \\ \end{array}\right)$$

Kp of the model is Ke and t1 is a mechanism to introduce time in the theoretical equation. In the simulation, Fig. 3.12 compares the curve obtained by the structure of the model and the one obtained by the simple mathematical calculation of the formula. One and the other are perfectly superimposed. To differentiate them in the model structure, a small delay was introduced that allows the simulation of the equation to be out of phase with the theoretical one. This distinction and precision are important to differentiate the curves. In Fig. 3.12 the delay is enlarged.

The system is highly sensitive to lags associated with assimilation factors. In Fig. 3.12, the model does not incorporate any lag period necessary for process or product innovation. Its only natural lag is the feedback from product innovation to process innovation via the stock of social

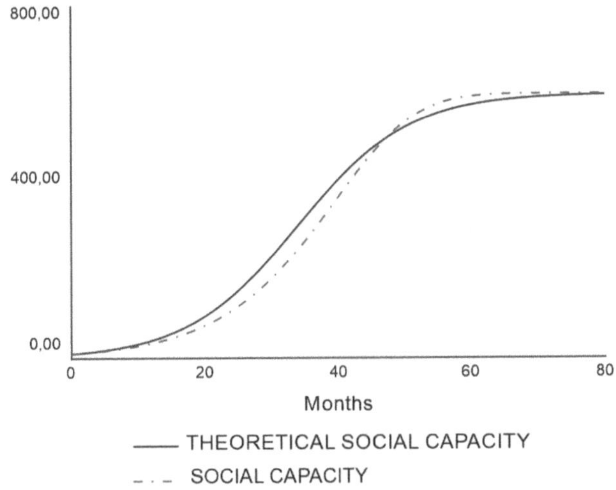

Fig. 3.12 The system without delays. Source: Developed by the authors

capability. In Fig. 3.13, some periods required for the process and product innovation were introduced, which generates delayed responses in the system. The actual behavior, once delays are introduced, is substantially different from the behavior considered without delays and feedback.

The system starts to adopt behaviors that are even more similar to real socioeconomic processes but its mathematical complexity increases and it is now only possible to solve it with computational numerical methods. In the basic model that exemplifies the behaviors, the consistency between the mathematical formula and the simulation structure is verified. When a model of successive learning phases that introduces three different learning phases is built, a behavioral profile like this one is obtained (see Fig. 3.14).

Without intending to emulate the graph, there is a structural consistency of the system represented by the learning evolution of Singapore in particular and with the behaviors presented in Fig. 3.15. As shown in Fig. 3.5, the successive "s" corresponds to decisions to move to more ambitious innovation benchmarks.

The problem refers to the type of behavior shown by the development processes of fast-growing countries and their inconsistency with the trajectories proposed in the models currently used to study growth dynamics. Figure 3.15 shows the processes of accelerated growth in a group of

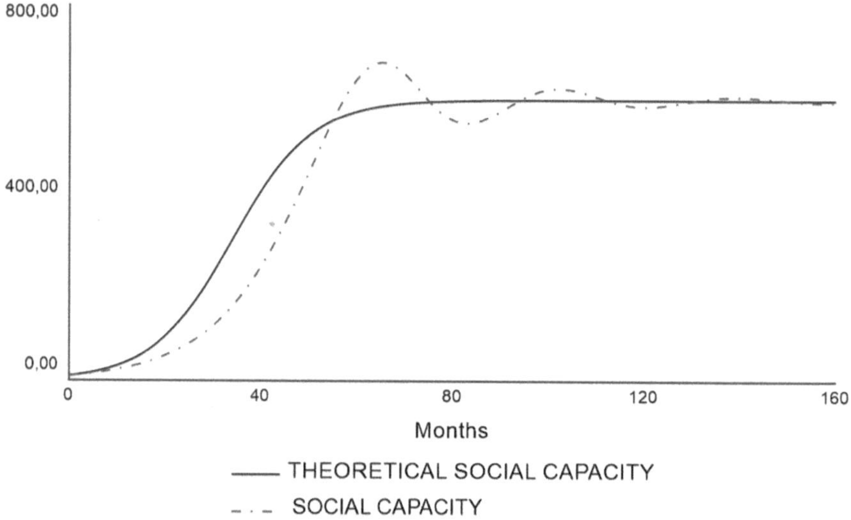

Fig. 3.13 The system with delays in processes and new products. Source: Developed by the authors

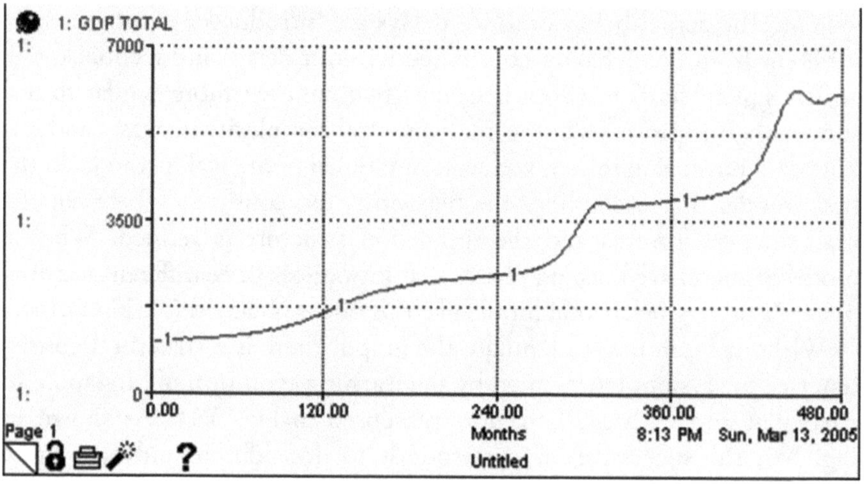

Fig. 3.14 The development process with three innovation leaps. Source: Developed by the authors

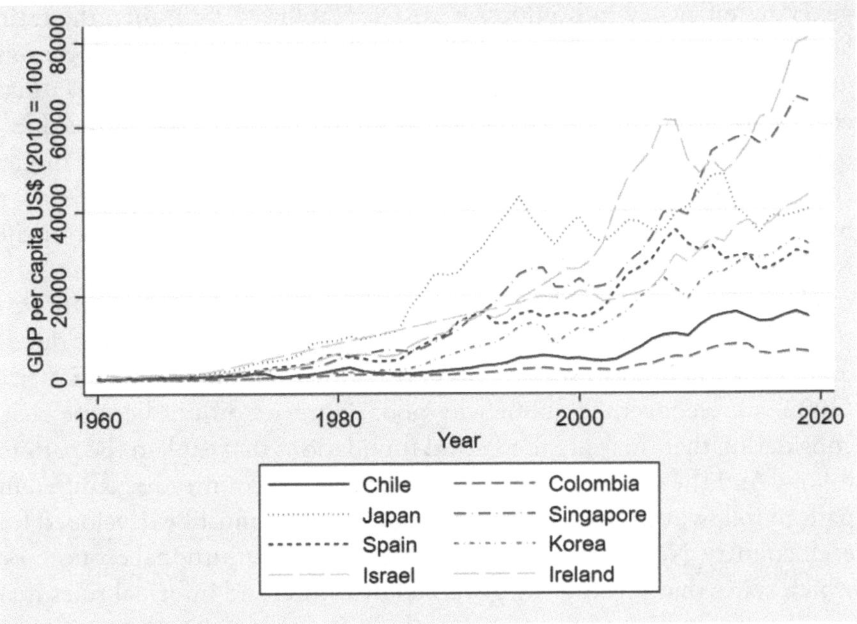

Fig. 3.15 Evolution of per capita output. Source: Authors' calculations, based on data from World Bank, WDI

countries whose development trajectories are represented as per capita GDP growth.

The behavior of per capita output shown in the curves suggests that the productivity and innovation that have accompanied the growth of these countries generate successive phases of "s." From the neoclassical or new growth theory approaches, there is no theoretical or mathematical approach to adequately discuss these processes.

3.5 Conclusions

In this chapter, we have taken a journey through the predominant theories of economic growth of the past and present centuries. It starts with the first phase of growth explained by exogenous growth theories, where growth is explained mainly by a "manna" falling from the sky that generates efficiency in productive capacity (Solow, 1957); then the train leaves the station of "ignorance" and disembarks at the endogenous growth theories, which explain through the work of Solow (1957) that economies grow due to technological progress called "Solow Residue"; however, this process is generated intrinsically in the economic model (Lucas, 1988), to which a few years later researchers would develop a mathematical framework capable of serving as the basis for most of the relevant research on economic growth in the world.

However, at the beginning of this century, Helpman (2004) criticized the state of economic growth theories, concluding that economic development remains an unsolved "mystery." Other authors such as Easterly (2002) were concerned about why poor countries do not become rich, considering that there are theoretical foundations that explain the path to follow. And the conclusion was reached that each country has a different path to follow; therefore, a theory of development must be developed for each country. North (1990) founded the basis of institutional economics, which states that societies are governed by formal and informal rules that establish the behavior of economic agents. The economy could not follow a correct path without considering institutions, which was the first step toward concluding that economic growth involves many actors.

Authors such as Hausmann et al. (2004) and North (2005) began to argue that the growth of a nation depends to a large extent on the capacity to learn and innovate, taking the technological change used in endogenous growth theories one step further to generate a process of social transformation. An example of rapid growth was seen in some Asian countries such as South Korea and Singapore, and the explanation for this phenomenon divided researchers into two groups: accumulationists and assimilationists. The accumulationist theories emphasize the role of capital investments and their effects on the production function of these countries. If countries make investments and get the resources, development will follow. "Assimilationist" theories emphasize entrepreneurship, innovation, and learning. They see investment in physical and human capital as essential but insufficient without a process of assimilation (Nelson & Pack, 1998, pp. 1 and 3).

This is how the importance of the role of entrepreneurship and innovation for economic growth emerges, a relationship that has been widely studied in the literature (Bosma et al., 2018; Maradana et al., 2017; Wennekers & Thurik, 1999). Therefore, development is not such an elusive mystery; it is rather a systemic state in which the multiple social, human, cultural, productive, and institutional aspects of society maintain a balance, interdependence, and mutual correlation. However, societies are constantly changing, transforming themselves, and are capable of overcoming inferior states of development and acquiring new capacities.

One of the patterns of change has as a dynamic of transformation the learning of new activities for the generation of well-being, what we call here "innovation processes," the construction of new capabilities for making new and more complex products. Thus, one of the purposes of this chapter was to explore how entrepreneurship and innovation can trigger a learning dynamic that generates processes of social transformation and to review the empirical evidence to support this assertion. The basic hypothesis was that innovation unleashes a dynamic of societal transformation and the works of Hausmann et al. (2005), Hausmann and Klinger (2006), Klinger and Lederman (2006a), and Lederman and Saenz (2006) indicate that the introduction of new activities in societies generates a virtuous dynamic of transformation that progressively converts it into one of a higher income and level of development.

But another purpose of this chapter was to try to propose a model capable of capturing all these learning processes. The model obtained was a classical dynamic within system dynamics. It consists of stock with two input and output flows, which is nothing more than a differential equation. This is represented in the form shown in Fig. 3.10. Remember that "SOCIAL CAPACITY" is represented in this model as the set of products that society makes. The metaphor is that of a large warehouse where all the goods and services that society knows how to make and is capable of generating in a given period are available. The model results in an "s" behavior that replicates the learning phases of countries such as Singapore and South Korea. Thus, it is concluded that it is necessary to carry out dynamic models that are more complex and closer to reality to understand the phenomenon of economic growth and put them into practice in countries with low economic performance.

References

Acemoglu, D. (2009). *Introduction to modern economic growth*. Princeton, NJ.: Princeton University Press.

Adler, P., Florida, R., King, K., & Mellander, C. (2019). The city and high-tech startups: The spatial organization of Schumpeterian entrepreneurship. *Cities, 87*, 121–130. https://doi.org/10.1016/j.cities.2018.12.013

Aghion, P., & Howitt, P. (1992). A model of growth through creative destruction. *Econometrica, 60*, 323–351. Blackwell.

Aparicio, S., Urbano, D., & Audretsch, D. (2016). Institutional factors, opportunity entrepreneurship and economic growth: Panel data evidence. *Technological Forecasting and Social Change, 102*, 45–61.

Audretsch, D. B., & Keilbach, M. (2008). Resolving the knowledge paradox: Knowledge-spillover entrepreneurship and economic growth. *Research Policy, 37*(10), 1697–1705.

Balland, P. A., Broekel, T., Diodato, D., Giuliani, E., Hausmann, R., O'Clery, N., & Rigby, D. (2022). The new paradigm of economic complexity. *Research Policy, 51*(3), 104450.

Banerji, A., Cull, R. J., Demirguc-Kunt, A., Djankov, S., Dyck, A., Islam, R., Kraay, A., Mcliesh, C., & Pittman, R. (2002). Building institutions for markets - overview (English). World Development Report Washington, D.C.: World Bank Group. Url: http://documents.worldbank.org/curated/en/228361468140407049/World-development-report-2002-building-institutions-for-markets-overview

Barro, R. (1998a). *Determinants of economic growth. A cross country empirical study*. MIT Press.

Barro, R. (1998b). *Notes on growth accounting* (NBER, 6654).

Barro, R., & Sala-i-Martin, X. (2004). *Economic growth* (2nd ed.). MIT Press.

Bar-yam, Y. (2004). *Making thinks work*. NECSI/Knowledge Press.

Bell, M., & Pavitt, K. (1993). Technological accumulation and industrial growth. *Industrial and Corporate Change, 2*(2), 157–211.

Bijker, W. (1999). *Of bicycles, bakelites and bulbs. Toward a theory of sociotechnical change*. MIT Press.

Bijker, W., Huges, T., & Pinch, T. (1987). *The social construction of technological systems*. MIT Press.

Bijker, W., & Pinch, T. (1984). The social construction de facts and artefacts: or how the new sociology of the science and the new sociology of the technology might benefit each other. *Social Studies of Science, 14*(3), 399–441.

Bloom, N., Romer, P. M., Terry, S. J., & Van Reenen, J. (2013). A trapped-factors model of innovation. *American Economic Review, 103*, 208–213. https://doi.org/10.1257/aer.103.3.208

Bosma, N., Content, J., Sanders, M., & Stam, E. (2018). Institutions, entrepreneurship, and economic growth in Europe. *Small Business Economics, 51*(2), 483–499. https://doi.org/10.1007/s11187-018-0012-x

Bosworth, B., & Collins, S. (2003). *The empirics of growth: An update*. Brookings Institution.

Castellani, F., & Lora, E. (2014). Is entrepreneurship a channel of social mobility in Latin America? *Latin American Journal of Economics, 51*(2), 179–194. https://doi.org/10.7764/LAJE.51.2.179

CEPAL. (2002). *Globalización y Desarrollo*. Disco Compacto B. Santiago de Chile.

Clark, G. (2007). *A farewell to alms: A brief economic history of the world (STU-student edition)*. Princeton University Press. http://www.jstor.org/stable/j.ctt7srwt

Cohen, D. (2002). Growth in theory and in practice. In J. B. de Macedo, C. Foy, & C. P. Oman (Eds.), *The development is back* (p. 47). OECD.

Cohen, D. (2007). Growth and human capital: good data, good results. *Journal of Economic Growth, 12*(1), 51–76.

Durlauf, S. Johnson, P., & Temple, J. (2004). *Growth econometrics* (Vassar College Economics Working, 61).

Easterly, W. (2002). *The elusive quest for growth*. MIT Press.

Galor, O. (2005). Chapter 4: From stagnation to growth: Unified growth theory. In P. Aghion & S. Durlauf (Eds.), *Handbook of economic growth*. Elsevier. https://doi.org/10.1016/S1574-0684(05)01004-X

Gómez, D. (2002a). Colombia 9000.3: Construcción de lo posible; un marco prospectivo para el desarrollo del país., Cámara de Comercio de Medellín.

Gómez, D. (2002b). *La productividad y la innovación en los procesos de desarrollo*. Centro de Ciencia y Tecnología de Antioquia.

Gómez, D. (2002c). *Los procesos de desarrollo en el mundo*. Cámara de Comercio de Medellín.

Grossman, G. M., & Helpman, E. (1991). Quality ladders in the theory of growth. *The Review of Economic Studies, 58*(1), 43–61.

Grossman, G., & Helpman, E. (2004, July). Managerial incentives and international organization of production. *Journal of International Economics, 3*(2).

Harvey, M., McMeekin, A., & Randles, S. (2001). *Between demand & consumption: A framework for research* (Discussion paper No. 40).

Hausmann, R. (2006). Economic Growth: Shared Beliefs, Shared Disappointments? CID Working Paper No. 125.

Hausmann, R. (2006a). Economic growth: Shared beliefs, shared disappointments?. Harvard University, CID, 125. Harvard, Kennedy School of Government, CID.

Hausmann, R. (2006b). *Doomed to choose: Industrial policy as Predicament*. Harvard, Kennedy School of Government, CID.

Hausmann, R. (2016). Economic development and the accumulation of know-how. *Welsh Economic Review, 24*, 13. https://doi.org/10.18573/j.2016.10049

Hausmann, R., Hwang, J., & Rodrik, D. (2005). What you exports matters. RWP05-063. Harvard, Kennedy School of Government, CID.

Hausmann, R., Rodrik, D., & Velasco, A. (2005). Growth diagnostics. CID Working Paper, url: http://www.tinyurl.com/y3y5zksu.

Hausmann, R., & Klinger, B. (2006). Structural transformation and patterns of comparative advantage in the product space. RWP06-041. Harvard, Kennedy School of Government, CID.

Hausmann, R., Pritchett, L., & Rodrik D. (2004). *Growth accelerations* (National Bureau of Economic Research. Vol. Working Paper 10566).

Hausmann, R., & Rodrik, D. (2002). *Economic development as self-discovery* (NBER Working Paper Series, vol. Working Paper 8952). http://www.nber.org/papers/w8952.

Helpman, E. (2004). *The mystery of economic growth*. MIT Press.

Hoff, K., & Stiglitz, J. (2001). Modern economic theory and development. In G. M. Meier & J. E. Stiglitz (Eds.), *Frontiers of development economics* (pp. 399–457). Oxford University Press.

Hulten, C. (2000). *Total productivity factor: A short biography*. 7471. NBER.

Hulten, C., & Isaksson, A. (2007). *Why development levels differs: The sources of differential economic growth in a panel of high and low income countries*. NBER Working Paper No. 13649. https://doi.org/10.3386/w13469

Jantsch, E. (1980). *The self organizing universe*. Pergamon Press.

Jones, C. I. (2020). *The end of economic growth? Unintended consequences of a declining population* (No. w26651). National Bureau of Economic Research.

Jones, C. I. (2021a). *The past and future of economic growth: A semi-endogenous perspective* (No. w29126). National Bureau of Economic Research.

Jones, C. I. (2021b). *Recipes and economic growth: A combinatorial march down an exponential tail* (No. w28340). National Bureau of Economic Research.

Katz, J. (2001). *Structural reform, productivity and technological change in Latin America*. CEPAL.

Klinger, B., & Lederman, D. (2006a). *Diversification, innovation, and imitation inside the global technological frontier*. World Bank.

Klinger, B., & Lederman, D. (2006b). *Innovations and export portfolios*. World Bank.

Lall, S. (1996). En: Desarrollo endógeno, J. Acosta (Comp.).

Lall, S. (2000). The technological structure and performance of developing country manufactured exports, 1985-1998 44.

Lall, S., Weis, J., & Zhang J. (2005). *The "sophistication" of exports: A new measure of product characteristics* (QEH Working Paper, 123).

Landau, R. (1991). How competitiveness can be achieved: fostering economic growth and productivity. In R. Landau (Ed.), *Technology and economics*. National Academy Press.

Landes, D. (2003). *The wealth and poverty of nations*. New York Press.

Lederman, D., & Maloney, W. (2002). Trade structure and growth.

Lederman, D., & Saenz, L. (2006). Innovation and development around the world, 1960-2000. 3774.

Leick, B., & Lang, T. (2018). Re-thinking non-core regions: planning strategies and practices beyond growth. *European Planning Studies*. https://doi.org/10.1080/09654313.2017.1363398. Routledge.

Lucas, R. J. (1988). On the mechanics of economic growth. *Journal of Monetary Economics, 22*, 3–42.

Maier, F. H. (1998). New product diffusion models in innovation management a system dynamics perspective. *Systems Dynamic Review, 14*(4), 285–308. Wiley.

Malthus, T. (1803). *An essay on principle of population*. Oxford University Press. Versión reimpresa 1998.

Mankiw, G., Romer, D., & Weil, D. (1990). A contribution to the empirics of economic growth, 3541.

Maradana, R. P., Pradhan, R. P., Dash, S., Gaurav, K., Jayakumar, M., & Chatterjee, D. (2017). Does innovation promote economic growth? Evidence from European countries. *Journal of Innovation and Entrepreneurship, 6*(1). https://doi.org/10.1186/s13731-016-0061-9

Metcalfe, G. (2001). *Institutions and progress* (CRIC Discussion Paper No. 45).

Milling, P. M. (2002). Understanding and managing innovation processes. *Systems Dynamic Review, 18*(1), 73–86.

Nelson, R., & Pack, H. (1998). *The Asian miracle and the modern growth theory. 1881*. The World Bank; Development Research Group.

North, D. C. (1990). *Institutions, institutional changes and economic performance*. Cambridge University Press.

North, D. C. (2005). *Understanding the process of economic change*. Princeton University Press.
OECD. (1993). Manual de Frascati, medición de las actividades científicas y tecnológicas propuesta de norma práctica para encuestas de investigación y desarrollo experimental.
OECD. (1997). Manual de OSLO. Segunda versión.
OECD. (2002). Development is back. OECD 40 years.
Olson, M. (1982). *The rise and decline of nations* (1st ed.). Yale University Press.
Oman, C., Braga de Macedo, J., & Colm, F. (2002). *Development is back*. OECD.
Perez, C. (2004). El cambio tecnológico y las oportunidades de desarrollo como blanco móvil. *Revista de la CEPAL, 2001*(75), Diciembre 2001.
Pritchett, L. (2006). The quest continues. *Finance and Development, 43*(1).
Pritchett, L., Sen, K., & Werker, E. (2017). *Deals and development: The political dynamics of growth episodes*. Oxford University Press.
Radzicki, M. (2003). Institutional economics, post Keynesian economics, and system dynamics: Three strands of heterodox economics braid. In J. T. Harvey & R. F. Garnet (Eds.), *The future of heterodox economics* (96th ed.). Michigan University Press.
Rico, P., & Cabrer-Borrás, B. (2019). Entrepreneurship, firms creation and regional performance. *European Journal of Management and Business Economics, 28*(2), 158–173. https://doi.org/10.1108/EJMBE-07-2018-0077
Rodrik, D. (2006). *Desarrollo Económico. PED 106 Notas de Clase*. KSG/Harvard.
Romer, P. (1986). Increasing returns and log-run growth. *Journal of Political Economic, 94*, 1002–1037.
Romer, P. (1990). Endogenous technological change. *Journal of Political Economic, 98*, 71–102.
Romer, P. (1992). Economic growth. In *The fortune encyclopedia of economics*.
Sachs, J., Gallup, J. L., & Mellinger, A. (1999). *Geography and economic development 1*. Harvard, Kennedy School of Government, CID.
Sala-i-Martin, X. (2000). *Apuntes de Crecimiento Económico*. Antoni Bosch Editor.
Sala-i-Martin, X. (2002). *15 years of new growth economics: What have we learnt*. Banco Central de Chile, 172.
Schumpeter, J. A. (1939). *Business cycles*. McGraw Hill.
Schumpeter, J. A. (1983). *Capitalismo, socialismo y democracia*. ORBIS.
Solow, R. (1956). A contribution to the theory of economic growth. *The Quarterly Journal of Economics, 70*(1), 65–94. MIT Press.
Solow, R. M. (1957). Technical change and the aggregate production function. *The Review of Economics and Statistics, 39*(3), 312–320.

Solow, R. (1994). Perspectives on growth theory. *The Journal of Economic Perspectives, 8*(1).
Sterman, J. (2000). *Business dynamics: Systems thinking and modeling for a complex world.* Irwin McGraw-Hill.
Sterman, J. (2006). Learning from evidence in a complex world. *American Journal of Public Health, 96*(3), 505–515.
Sterman, J., & Ford, D. (1998). Dynamic modeling of product development processes. *Systems Dynamic Review, 14*(1).
Sterman, J., & Radzicki, M. (1994). Evolutionary economics and system dynamics. In R. W. England (Ed.), *Evolutionary concepts in contemporary economics.* Michigan Press.
Stern, N. (2002). *Dynamic development: Innovation and inclusion 19.* FMI.
Stiglitz, J. (1998). Towards a new paradigm for development: Strategies, policies, and processes.
Stiglitz, J. (1999). Participation and development: Perspectives from comprehensive development paradigm.
Veblen, T. (1898). Why economics is not an evolutionary science? *Cambridge Journal of Economics, 22*, 403–414.
Warner, A. (2002). Institutions, geography, regions, countries and the mobility bias 91.
Wennekers, S., & Thurik, R. (1999). Linking Entrepreneurship and Economic Growth. *Small Business Economics, 13*(1), 27–56. https://doi.org/10.1023/A:1008063200484

4

Why Do Some Nations Succeed While Others Fail? The Role of Culture and Regulations in Entrepreneurship and Innovation

Diego Gomez, Sebastian Aparicio, and David Urbano

4.1 Introduction

The title of this chapter finds its inspiration in Acemoglu and Robinson's (2012) book *Why Nations Fail: The Origins of Power, Prosperity, and Poverty*. In this book, interesting hypotheses are put forward regarding why some nations fail while others succeed; however, perhaps the most important conclusion is that "inclusive institutions," such as representative legislatures, good public schools, open markets, and strong patent systems, which are capable of providing incentives in the economic

D. Gomez
Fundación ECSIM, Medellin, Colombia

S. Aparicio (✉) • D. Urbano
Department of Business, Universitat Autònoma de Barcelona, Cerdanyola del Vallés, Barcelona, Spain

Centre for Entrepreneurship and Social Innovation Research (CREIS), Universitat Autònoma de Barcelona, Sabadell, Barcelona, Spain
e-mail: Sebastian.Aparicio@uab.cat

D. Gomez et al. (eds.), *Driving Complexity in Economic Development*,
https://doi.org/10.1007/978-3-031-34386-5_4

growth process, are needed. Although this statement is accurate in the context of institutional economics (North, 2010; Williamson, 2000), in this chapter, we seek to approach the core of the problem to understand why some countries have had successful processes of economic growth and have been able to include a large part of the population in this accelerated process (Dinda, 2014). Thus, the purpose is to study countries' learning and transformation dynamics and to consider whether the empirical and historical evidence shows social learning processes with innovation and entrepreneurship (not with capital flows) explaining the "diffusion" behavior of learning stages.

To achieve this objective, we will first develop a theoretical framework to identify the cornerstone of economic growth, focusing mainly on the explanation of capitalism as the economic model of large nations (Bakshi & Chen, 1996). Accordingly, we will use the literature on exogenous and endogenous growth theories to our advantage to explain some hypotheses. Although the theories of exogenous growth that led to those of endogenous growth were fundamental in laying the foundations of all economic theories based on general equilibrium, perhaps they were taken lightly and interpreted from a superficial point of view; capital and technological change, following the work of Solow (1957), gained strength as the main engines of growth, the former attracting more media recognition since the word capitalism derives from it. However, is this capital more important than technological change? Do they need each other, and to what extent? In our theoretical framework, we will try to answer these questions through literary analysis and a stylized factual exercise.

Then, we will proceed to create an empirical strategy that will allow us to recognize some key indicators of inclusive development, such as education, entrepreneurship, and economic complexity (most of them taken from the World Development Indicators [WDI]), and to carry out a comparison of stylized facts from different countries and regions. This comparison will finally allow us to reveal why some countries have successful growth processes and how some poor countries could adopt such a growth path.

4.2 Theoretical Framework

The Theoretical, Technical, and Practical Aspects of Capital

According to Glyn (2007), after a turbulent century of unprecedented social and technological change, capitalism appeared as the main ideology and model for economic growth in most developed countries. It is therefore worthwhile inquiring further into capitalism. Some authors have taken it upon themselves to understand this phenomenon in depth (Thrift, 2005), analyze its development historically (Rueschemeyer et al., 1992), and review the culture that it has unleashed (Sennett, 2006). However, it is worth asking the question "what is capitalism?" Capitalism is defined as an economic and social system based on private ownership of the means of production, in which capital plays the role of a wealth generator. Thus, capital is the main axis of the entire productive apparatus that drives growth. Based on this concept, we allow ourselves to establish that capitalism by definition does not exist.

The finding is not recent, dating back to 1957, and its author did not give it much importance. He was interested in how it could contribute to the growth of economies by identifying the determinants. Robert Solow was awarded the Nobel Prize in 1988 for his work on economic growth. In 1956, he formulated the mathematical structure of the model, and in 1957, he carried out an empirical exercise to establish the behavior of the model's parameters (Solow, 1957). Using data from the US economy between 1909 and 1949, Solow determined that only 12.5% of economic growth is explained by the increase in capital and the remaining 87.5% of economic growth is explained by technological change, the so-called Solow Residual.

We reconstructed the exercise with data from the last decades for the United States and other countries (Spain, Japan, the United Kingdom, and Australia); this reconstruction will be discussed later. The conclusion is the same: what explains growth is the technological change in values ranging from 70 to 95% for these countries. Therefore, it is not capital that explains the transformation of economies; hence, capitalism does not exist. What exists is an open system in which societies undertake, learn, and innovate. What exists is the society of the Schumpeterian entrepreneur.

Jean Louis Blanc used the term "capitalist" in 1850 to describe business owners in a pejorative way (Marks, 2012). The term had been used before, among others by David Ricardo in 1817 and Pierre-Joseph Proudhon in 1840. Carl Marx used it not only in a pejorative but also in a condemnatory way, making him guilty of a terrible crime, appropriating surplus value. The myth of the exploitative businessman was created, which was useful for sowing hatred but limited the understanding of the role of the businessman in generating development and building the social fabric.

Open societies were left with the insult of being capitalist and assimilated it with a certain stoicism. Nevertheless, for the statist scheme of the closed society, the curse of error and the tragic fate that has destroyed societies for decades remained. By wanting to eradicate the "capitalist" entrepreneur, what was undertaken was to deprive society of its adaptive capacity to learn, articulate innovations with capabilities, and generate interaction networks through which we all contribute to the common welfare.

Ironically and elegantly, Solow's equation allows us to explain why and how communist countries have fallen behind and even stopped over time. Cuba and Venezuela are on a dramatic journey to stagnation and degradation. Entrepreneurs are the natural heroes of these innovative societies (Al-Dajani & Marlow, 2013; Aparicio et al., 2022). In precariously stagnant societies, entrepreneurs are more tied to inherited capital and concentrated on conventional activities. In these societies, the myth of the "capitalist" falls on fertile ground and becomes an ideological instrument that ends up disabling society. This is the case in Latin America, which is mired in basic specialization patterns. The ideas of the Comisión Económico para América Latina y el Caribe (CEPAL) and the leftist policies are aimed at controlling the "capitalist" entrepreneur and have made the dynamics of innovation in the region impossible in three ways: high taxes prevent the creation of new companies or the growth and reinvention of existing ones, high operating costs impose a heavy burden of subsidies and tariffs, and high financing costs result from the country risk generated by inflation rates and decisions not to pay debts. Therefore, we believe that there are myths that stagnate entire societies. Returning to the technical section of the discussion, we will look at the detailed work carried out by Solow, consider the conclusions that the author reached, and reconstruct this process for some countries, analyzing their behavior to compare the results.

In Robert Solow's 1957 article "Technical Change and the Aggregate Production Function," the author sought a new elementary way of separating changes in per capita output due to technical change (which some authors call "resource-saving" technical change [Hulten & Nakamura, 2017]) from those due to changes in per capita capital availability. For this work, Solow emphasized the collection of information and made it clear that the variable used for the GDP excludes information from the agricultural sector to avoid generating relative importance biases between sectors (homogeneity). Two of the most important assumptions on which the author based his proposal are first that markets behave under a scheme of perfect competition and second that the factor payments are equal to their marginal productivities (in addition to these assumptions, the author stressed the importance of the function being homogeneous of degree 1). These assumptions are crucial because they allowed Solow to develop the procedures necessary to reach the steady-state levels in his equations more smoothly and coherently (at the mathematical level). Since Solow's objective required the disaggregation of the influences of factors on the GDP, there was a price to pay, which was to obtain a new time series for the share of labor or property in the total income.

Having made the assumptions clear, Solow used a production function of the following form (neutral case):

$$Q = A(t) \times f(k,l) \tag{4.1}$$

where $A(t)$ measures the cumulative effect of technological changes over time. Through this equation, the author developed the whole mathematical framework, making use of the assumptions, to arrive at the following equation:

$$\frac{\dot{q}}{\dot{q}} = \frac{\dot{A}}{\dot{A}} + w_k \frac{\dot{k}}{\dot{k}} \tag{4.2}$$

where $\frac{q}{\dot{q}}$ is the output per worker, $\frac{\dot{k}}{\dot{k}}$ is the capital per worker, and w_k is the capital share. With these three time series, it would only be necessary to clear for $\frac{\dot{A}}{\dot{A}}$.

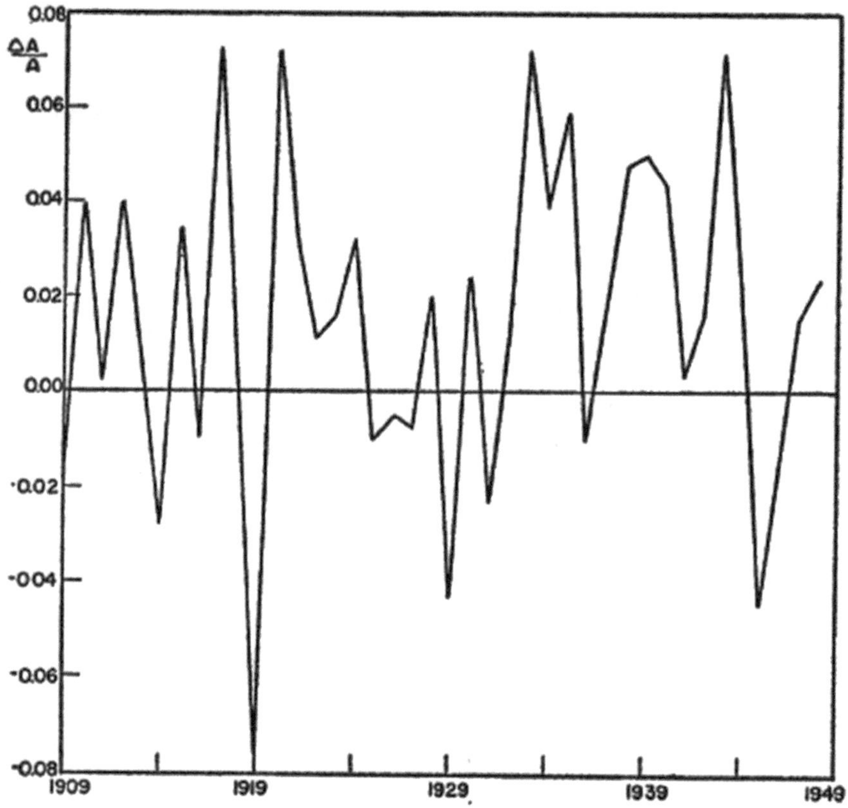

Fig. 4.1 US technological change, 1909–1949, by Robert Solow. Source: Extracted from Solow (1957)

Having developed the technical part, Solow provided an application for the United States from 1909 to 1949, reaching very interesting conclusions. First, he stressed that A(t) during this period was neutral on average (see Fig. 4.1). Second, the upward shift of the production function occurred, apart from fluctuations, at a rate of 1% per year in the first half of the period and 2% per year in the second half (see Fig. 4.2). Third, the gross output per labor hour doubled over the period (from $0.623 to $1.275), with 87.5% of the increase attributable to technical change and the remaining 12.5% to increased use of capital (Solow, 1957).

These results are important because they provide relevant information on theoretical and policy implications regarding the significance of

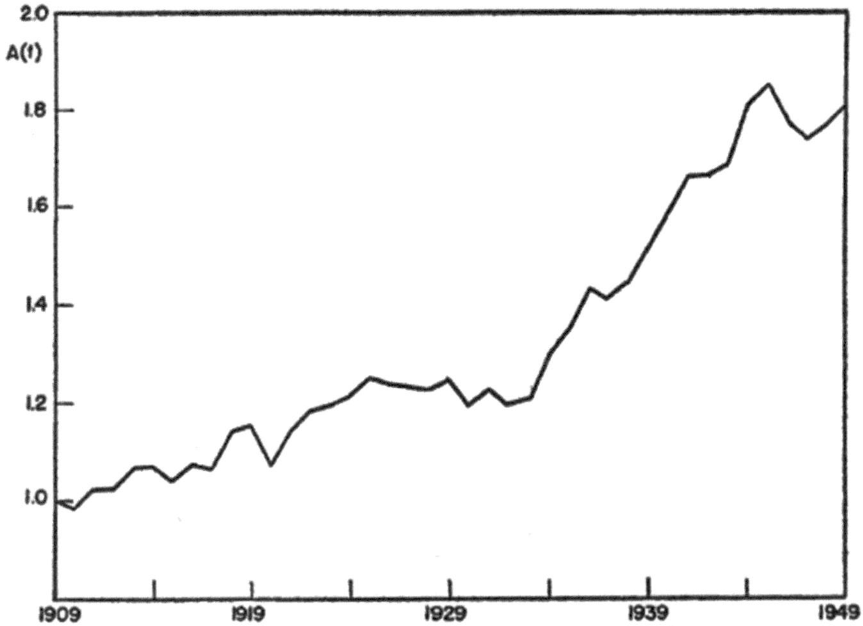

Fig. 4.2 The cumulative effect of technological change in the US, 1909–1949, by Robert Solow. Source: Extracted from Solow (1957)

technological change for the economic growth of nations. After all, although capital is important for the proper development of an economy, at the end of the day, what is fundamental is technological change or innovation.

To observe the behavior of the cumulative effect of technological change over time, we replicate the Solow model from 1960 to 2015 (for the US economy). To calculate capital and output per capita, we use the International Monetary Fund (IMF) database; for hours worked and employment, we use the OECD database; and, finally, we use a capital factor of 0.3 for all economies, intending to simplify the exercise and not calibrate this coefficient for each country. It should be noted that, in this exercise, unlike the one carried out by Solow, the agricultural sector of the US economy is not set aside. With this information, we are able to obtain the time series of technological change and its cumulative effects (Fig. 4.3). Reviewing what happens with these time series, we can observe in Fig. 4.3 that, like the period analyzed by Solow, technological change

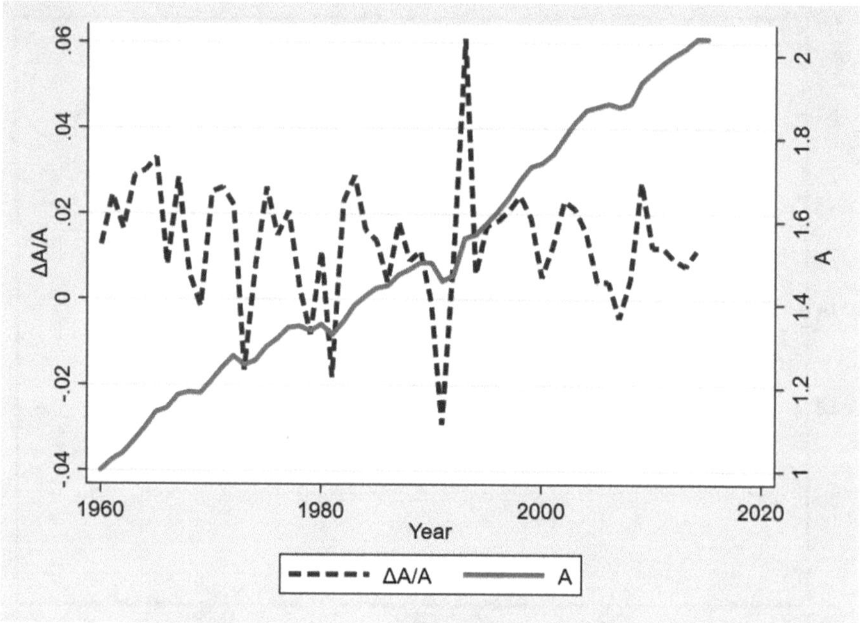

Fig. 4.3 Technological change and its cumulative effect on US economy, 1960–2015. Source: Developed by the authors with OECD and IMF data

is neutral (blue line), taking into account a large fluctuation between 1990 and 1995. Something revealing about this time series is that, although there was a drop in 2008 (the mortgage crisis), it was not as dramatic as that in the 1990s. This may indicate that technological change is affected less strongly by shocks related to the mortgage sector and more by the productivity behavior of firms. This is a key finding because it supports the theory and literature indicating that productivity, innovation, and entrepreneurship through firm creation are the axis of economic growth. Now, if we look at the red line in Fig. 4.3, corresponding to the cumulative effect of technological change, we can see that it has a positive slope with few strong oscillations.

Table 4.1 summarizes the effects and disaggregation of GDP growth for the US over the period studied. This table indicates two key results. First, the GDP growth corresponding to capital is 22%. Second, the percentage of GDP growth corresponding to technological change is 78%. This shows that, as in the Solow model, most of the growth in the GDP

Table 4.1 Summary of effects of technological change behavior, 1960–2015 (US economy)

Concept	Value
GDP growth 1960–2015 $mill	28.31
GDP corrected by unit of technological change $ mill.	21.13
GDP growth with corrected GDP $mill	6.33
% of GDP growth due to capital	0.22
% of GDP growth due to technological change	0.78

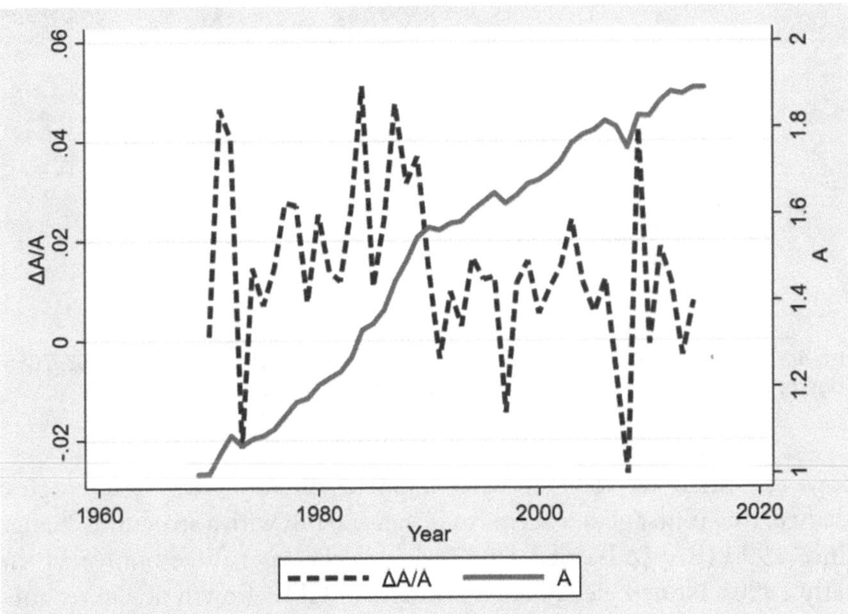

Fig. 4.4 Technological change and its cumulative effect on Japan, 1970–2015. Source: Developed by the authors with OECD and IMF data

is due to technological change, while a small part is due to capital. This makes it clear that technological change is fundamental for the growth and development of nations, highlighting the need for public policies focused on encouraging technological change and innovation.

Performing the same exercise for Japan's economy from 1970 to 2015 (Fig. 4.4), we can observe similar behavior to the United States cumulative effect of technological change, being increasing and positive;

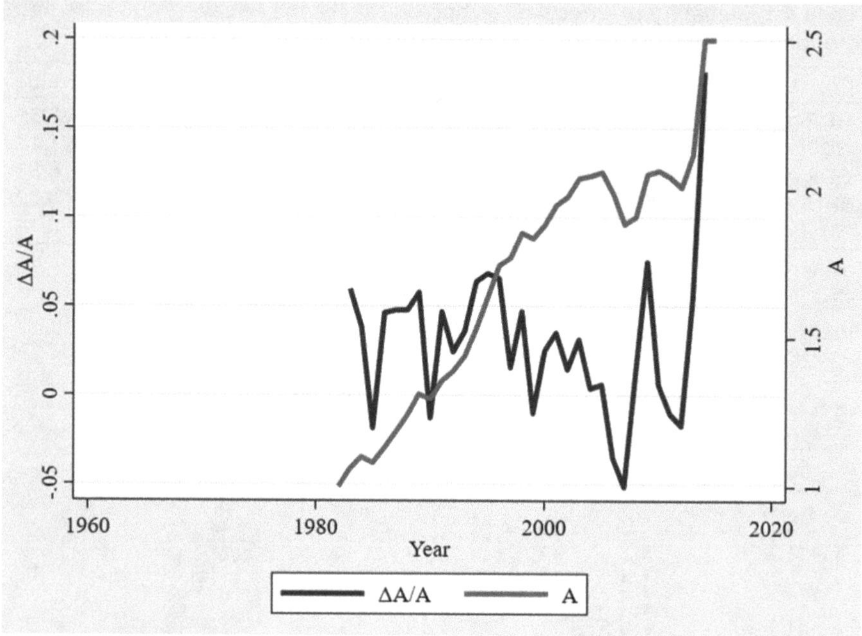

Fig. 4.5 Technological change and its cumulative effect on Ireland, 1983–2015. Source: Developed by the authors with OECD and IMF data

however, when we look at what happens directly with technological change, this at first glance seems to be neutral but with a structural change since 1990 (Bec & Bastien, 2007) due to the asset price bubble in the early 1990s. Nonetheless, the percentages of GDP growth due to technological change and capital are 71% and 29%, respectively, which are similar values to those of the US economy.

If we consider the case of the Irish economy (Fig. 4.5), we can observe that the cumulative effect of technological change increases until 2007. This is because the Irish economy bases its GDP growth on technological change and less on capital, given that the GDP growth corresponding to technological change is 88%, while the remaining 12% corresponds to capital. By 2008, Ireland was affected by the global financial crisis; however, by 2010, it was showing accelerated improvements, and the cumulative effect of technological change began to increase.

This exercise is important for two specific reasons. First, it reveals that technological change is crucial for the growth of nations, as pointed out in growth accounting models (Hulten, 2010). Second, economies that depend on innovation and technological change do not suffer dramatic declines in their GDP. This leads to policy recommendations aimed at encouraging the creation of new enterprises, innovation and productivity within them, and facilities for entrepreneurs. As a conclusion, and based on this exercise, we can establish that, given that the economic growth of developed countries depends to a large extent on their technological change and not on the flow of capital, capitalism does not exist as we know it.

4.3 Empirical Strategy

Empirical Evidence of Learning Dynamics: Data and Results

The purpose is to study countries' learning and transformation dynamics and to determine whether the empirical and historical evidence shows social learning processes with innovation and entrepreneurship (not with capital flows) explaining the "diffusion" behavior of learning stages that have "s" behavior. Thus, an important part of the discussion will focus on the work that Richard Nelson and Howard Pack carried out for the World Bank: the Asian miracle and the modern growth theory. The authors stated that the Asian miracle can be explained by entrepreneurship, innovation, and learning. These are the significant factors in the rapid growth of the Asian tigers (Nelson & Pack, 1998, p. 1).

Productivity and innovation are not factors that successful economies (Japan, Korea, Singapore, and Ireland) have driven since they closed their gap with the developed world; they are factors that were present throughout the process. From the early stages of their industrialization, that is, from those moments when industrialization was oriented toward labor-intensive activities, the governments of Japan, Korea, Ireland, and Singapore were aware of the importance of productivity improvements and directed policies to promote the determinants of productivity and innovation, as shown in Figs. 4.6 and 4.9.

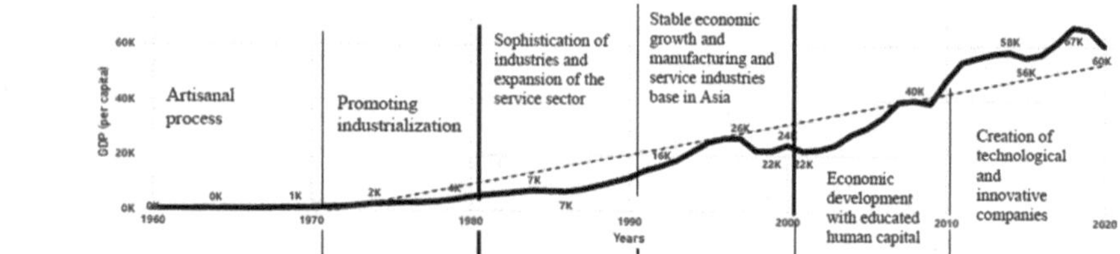

Industries that drive economies into the future	Secondary industries (handicrafts, etc.)	· Light industries (textiles, etc.) · Labor intensive industries	· Labor-intensive processes in high-tech industries · Financial industries	· Electronic Industries · Information technology industries	· Technologic services Industries	· Electronics and services industry (creation of technology companies)
Incremental capital-output ratio (ICOR). ICOR= Investment rate/Incremental rate of GDP		4.3 (1970-1979)	4.8 (1980-1989, ex. 1985,1986)	4.5 (1990-1997)	11.2 (2000-2010)	5.7 (2000-2010)
Economic and industrial policies	· Creation of the Singapore Economic Development Board · National economic strategies	· Promoting export-oriented industries · introduction of foreign capital	· Promoting technologic-oriented industries · Manufacturing sector target of 25% share in GDP	Transforming into the financial and commercial center of Asia	Sustainable economic development policies	Education and innovation as development policies

Fig. 4.6 Singapore's economic transformation process. Source: Own elaboration with data from WDI and excerpts from Singapore Productivity Center

To achieve high levels of economic development, these governments invested more in education and sought improvements in its quality, and they promoted entrepreneurship and technological modernization of the economy. For example, in Japan, Korea, Ireland, and Singapore, in the first phase of development, the abundant factor in the economy was labor, so labor-intensive industries had priority in accessing new technological knowledge. However, part of the new technology was oriented toward the development of new sectors, in which the technological gap could be exploited (Figs. 4.6 and 4.9).

Broadly, a series of papers reviewed the behavior of a group of countries from this perspective of innovation (Gómez, 2002d). Gómez (2002a, 2002b) conducted a descriptive analysis of the development processes of different countries—Germany, Singapore, Japan, Ireland, Spain, the United States, Russia, Korea, Taiwan, Hong Kong, Hungary, Bulgaria, Vietnam, Chile, Mexico, Brazil, and Colombia—to identify the role of productivity and innovation in the economic development of each of them and their influence on economic and social results. The author found that countries that had accelerated growth processes during some period in their history had achieved significant improvements in terms of innovation—technical progress, including technological advances and the introduction of new products. There were continuous improvements in their productivity, diversification of their exports, and high rates of economic growth (as will be shown below). These high growth rates, reflected in high levels of per capita income, meant the transformation of consumption. Systemically, this whole process led to important social transformations. In addition, it was observed that the assimilation of innovation is a fundamental determinant of long-term productivity growth. Its effects depend not only on its incidence in productive branches that are intensive in the use of new technologies but also, to a large extent, on the capacity of the business fabric to incorporate advances in knowledge, absorb technical progress, and adapt their production processes, human resource management, and corporate strategies.

Japan and the so-called Asian tigers have had successful development processes, with very significant results in terms of growth, export diversification, and social benefits. First, Japan's highest economic growth occurred from World War II until the early 1990s, when the economy expanded about 55 times (Fig. 4.7). Second, Singapore experienced high

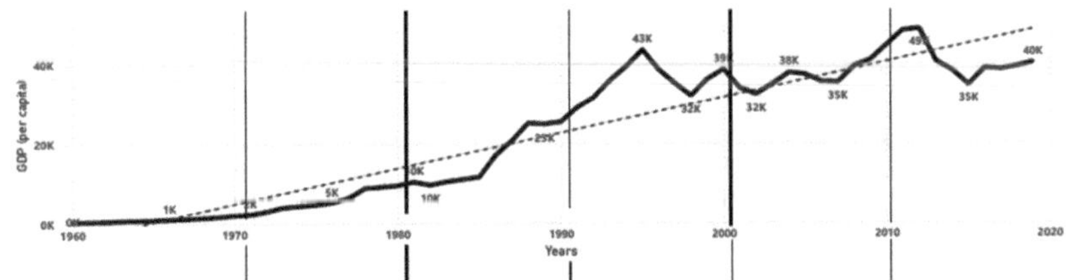

Value-added component (Industries and goods)	· Heavy industries · Aluminum · Chemicals · Carbon · Rubber · Shipbuilding	· Heavy electrical engineering · Precision engineering · Bearings · Machine tools · Consumer products · Accessories	· Highly specialized industries · Advanced Electronics · Specialty aeronautics · Biotechnology · Information technology · Information Technology · Medium electronics · New materials	Lost decade due to price bubble · Falling asset prices · Insolvent companies and banks · Purchase of gold and government bonds	· Strengthening the financial sector · Creation of leading companies in state-of-the-art technology · Development of aerospace materials · Advanced electronics · Mechatronics	· Automotive Sector Electronification · High-impact bioengineering and biotechnology · Pharmaceuticals · Petrochemicals · Aerospace products

Fig. 4.7 Japan's economic transformation process. Source: Own elaboration with data from WDI and excerpts from Japan Productivity Center (METI)

growth rates a little later, in 1960, and they lasted until 1995 and averaged 8.25% growth annually (Fig. 4.6); in the same period, the GDP per capita growth was faster in Singapore (6.25%) than in any other country in Asia except South Korea. Both Singapore and Japan are economies that are currently at the stage of innovation at the technological frontier, so their exports are mostly composed of technology- and human capital-intensive goods. However, Japan is currently lagging behind Singapore, the United States, Korea, and several European countries in terms of information technology (Fig. 4.8).

Like Japan and Singapore, the remarkable performance of the Irish economy has earned it the label "miracle," and it has been compared to those countries as the "Celtic tiger." Although Ireland undertook an industrialization process later than the European average and Japan and Singapore, within a decade, it evolved from a natural resource-intensive economy (with agriculture playing a leading role) to a technology- and knowledge-intensive economy with a strong export orientation. Between 1987 and 2000, the Irish economy grew at an average annual rate of 7%, and between 1995 and 2001, it grew at a rate of more than 10% and reached rates of up to 11.5% (Fig. 4.9).

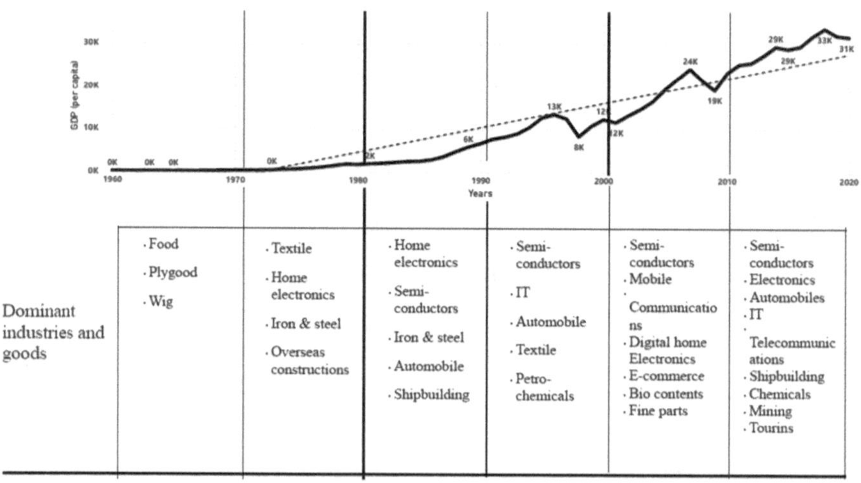

Fig. 4.8 Korea's economic transformation process. Source: Own elaboration with data from WDI and excerpts from Chaired Research Fellow Institute for International Economic Policy

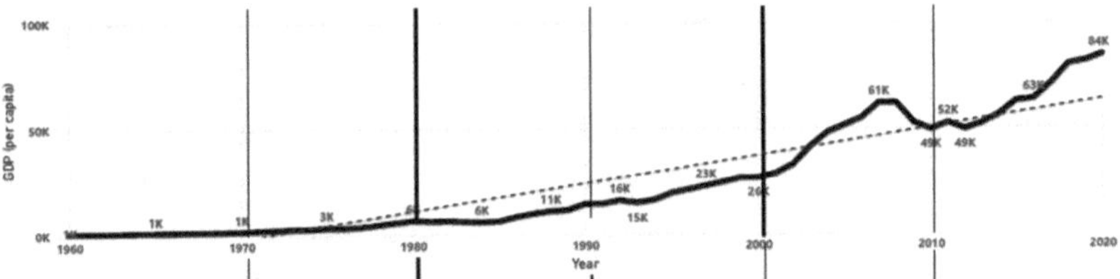

Industries that spur economic performance	· Agriculture · Fishing	· Banking sector · Textiles · Mining · Agriculture	· Textiles · Mining · Agriculture · Fishing	· Agriculture and mining tachnification · Large exporter of raw materials (with high productivity)	· Services and high-tech industries · Financial Service Industry · Export And Trade Industry	· Services and high-tech industries · Pharmaceutical And Medical Technology Industries · Software And ICT Industries
Economic and industrial policies	· Foreing direct investment (FDI)	· Joined to the European Economic Community	· Political inestability · High tax rates	· Low tax rates · High FDI	"Celtic tiger" focusing on economic growth	Economic development policies

Fig. 4.9 Ireland's economic transformation process. Source: Own elaboration with data from WDI

Countries such as the United States, Japan, and (West) Germany, which managed to grow economically and maintain this growth at high rates for relatively long periods, started from a certain level of human and social capital before reaching or maintaining high rates of economic growth. In other words, the high rates of social development in these countries were not obtained solely as a consequence of their extraordinary economic growth; however, it should be recognized that they were greatly increased and potentiated by the economic dynamism achieved. Thus, in these countries, virtuous circles were formed in which the growth of human and social capital facilitated the growth of income, which, in turn, fed back into the circuit, further increasing human and social capital. The formation of these reinforcing feedback loops is the phenomenon that comes closest to what we call development.

So far, we have remarked that these countries (Singapore, Japan, Korea, and Ireland) have undergone a process of economic transformation in key sectors, transforming their artisanal production into technified production processes with high-impact technologies. Therefore, we could deduce that the economic complexity of the countries is the key to the development process. Since the seminal work of Hidalgo and Hausmann

(2009), the academic community has been interested in analyzing the countries' economic complexity, which translates into the number of products (and their complexity of production) that a country successfully exports. The importance of this indicator seems to be bearing research fruits as the literature on the subject is beginning to grow.

van Dam and Frenken (2020) proposed a combinatorial model of economic development, making it clear that an economy develops by acquiring new capabilities allowing for the production of an ever-greater variety of products with increasing complexity. Considering the case of Great Britain's economy, Bishop and Mateos-Garcia (2019) sought to gain a better understanding of the mechanism connecting economic complexity with economic performance, creating a measure of emergent technological activity in a location based on a combination of novel data sources including text from UK business websites and CrunchBase (technology company directory). The results highlight the potential value of the novel, unstructured data sources for the analysis of the links between economic complexity and regional economic development. Two important pieces of research involving developing economies are those by Caous and Huarng (2020) and Erkan and Ceylan (2021). First, Caous and Huarng (2020) used hierarchical linear modeling as a statistical tool to analyze 87 developing countries from 1990 to 2017, finding that human development (the Human Development Index) increased with greater economic complexity (the Economic Complexity Index). Second, Erkan and Ceylan (2021) analyzed annual data from 1996 to 2017 for 22 countries called transitional economies using the panel causality method, concluding that transitional economies need to increase their level of economic complexity to obtain a larger share of the global added value and increase their competitiveness. Other research on economic complexity and analyses of its role alongside institutions has been relevant (Hartmann et al., 2017). Taking this literature into account, we consider it necessary to study the stylized facts of economic complexity for countries such as Singapore, Japan, Korea, and Ireland and to investigate the importance of such complexity for the process of economic growth.

Figure 4.10 shows us the Economic Complexity Index contrasted with the GDP per capita for a sample of 58 countries in the years 2000, 2010, and 2019. When we separate the observations into two quantiles (we will

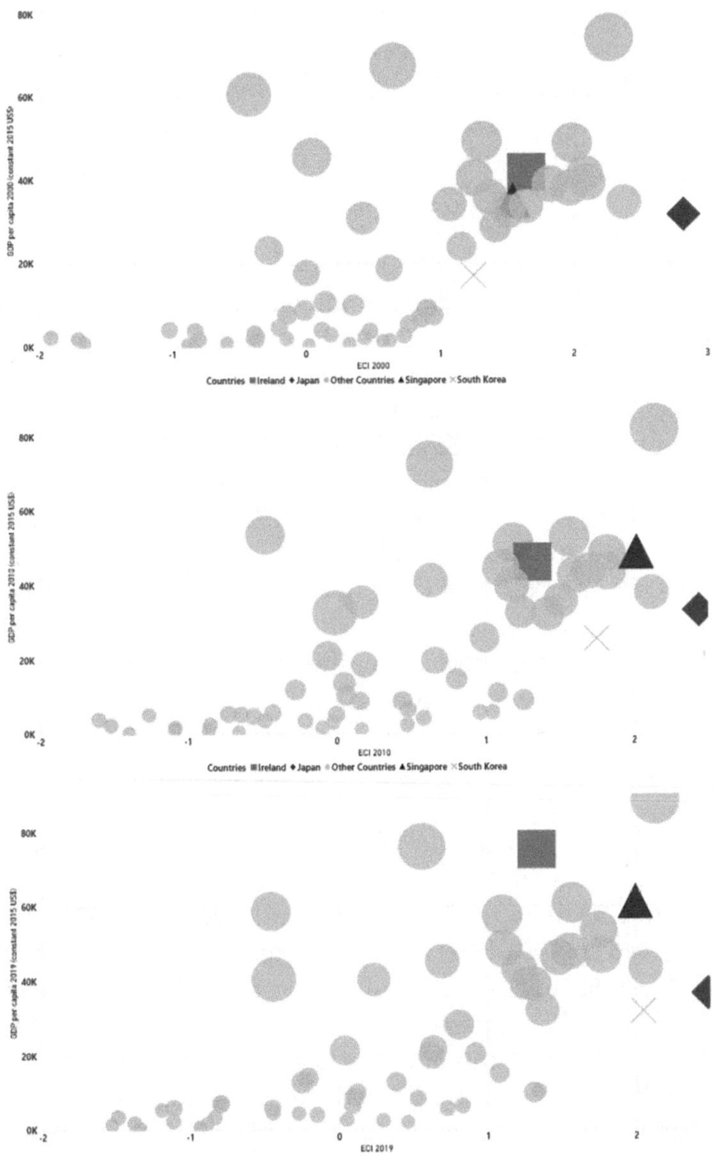

Fig. 4.10 Economic complexity index versus GDP per capita (2000–2010–2019). Source: Own elaboration with WDI and ATLAS of economic complexity data

call them developing and developed countries, distinguished by the size of the circles), we find that the mean of the ECI for developing countries is -0.37 in 2000, -0.45 in 2010, and -0.49 in 2019. In other words, the economic complexity index for developing countries is deteriorating. Now, if we consider what happens with developed countries, we have an index of 1.37 in 2000, 1.29 in 2010, and the same in 2019. This indicates that, although the index for developed countries decreases, it remains positive and high while developing countries endure a "trap" of low specialization, technification, and complexity of the products that they export.

Focusing on the countries that we are analyzing throughout the chapter, for the three scenarios (2000, 2010, and 2019), Singapore, Japan, Korea, and Ireland's ECI is around the average.

Figure 4.11 shows that Japan is the only one of the four countries to have suffered stagnation in the ECI; however, its GDP per capita rose from $31,430 in 2000 to $36,362 in 2019. Analyzing the case of Korea, it has been the most stable of the four countries, although, through slow and progressive growth, its ECI rose from 1.24 to 2.04 between 2000 and 2019, while its GDP per capita increased by 86.4%, from $16,992 to $31,682, in the same period. The technological development that Korea has achieved throughout this century is well known, and this process of both innovation and entrepreneurship has borne fruit.

Figure 4.10 shows that both Singapore and Ireland are success stories in the process of specialization and economic growth. Singapore's ECI increased from 1.54 in 2000 to 1.99 in 2019, while Ireland's decreased from 1.64 to 1.33. If we focus on the performance of the GDP per capita, Ireland showed growth of 80%, while Singapore attained growth of 75%. This considerable growth is due not only to the stability and increases in the ECI (this can be supported by a simple regression for the 58 countries, in which the ECI turns out to be positive and significant [$p < 0.001$] for the GDP per capita [a 1 unit increase in the ECI results in increases of $11,629 in 2000, $13,324 by 2010, and $14,517 by 2019]) but also to the transformation process that both countries have undergone in terms of their development policies and the promotion of highly technological industries.

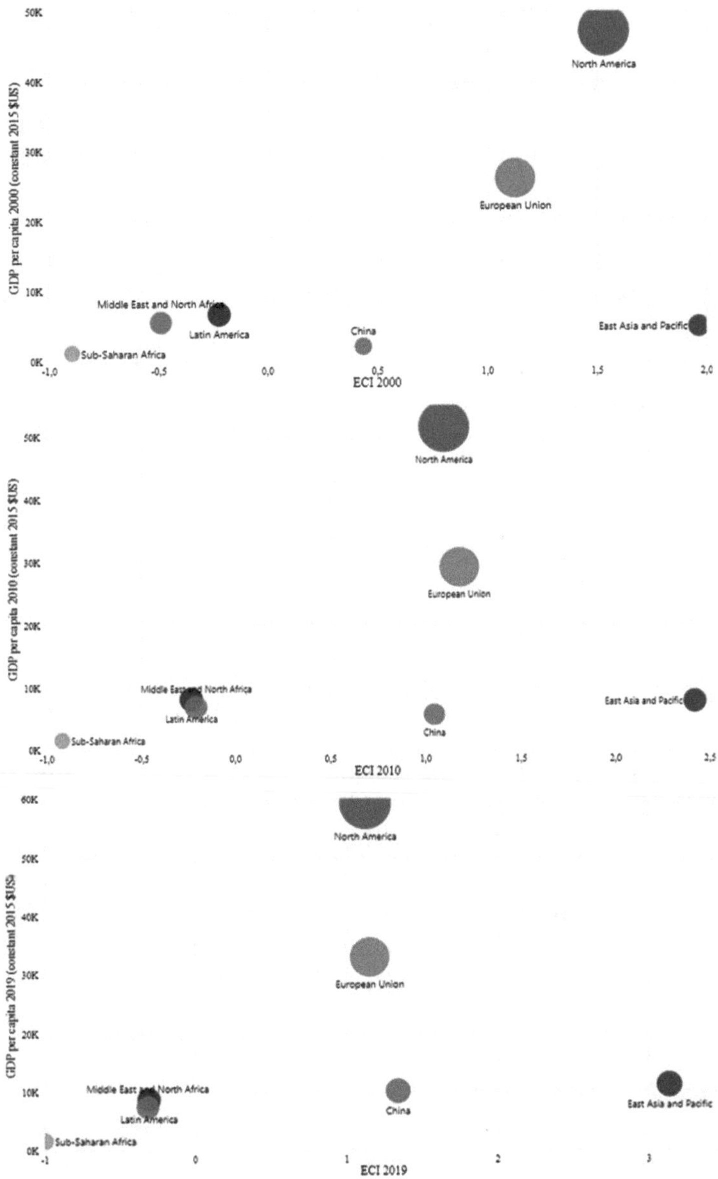

Fig. 4.11 ECI versus GDP per capita for country groups (2000–2010–2019). Source: Own elaboration with WDI and ATLAS of economic complexity data

Figure 4.11 presents the same relationship as Fig. 4.10 but for groups of countries, such as North America, Latin America (some Caribbean countries), China, the European Union, Sub-Saharan Africa, the Middle East and North Africa, and East Asia and the Pacific. This graph shows that North America and the European Union, both of which are groups with good ECI indices, contain the countries with the highest economic development (GDP per capita), while the groups with a low ECI comprise the least developed countries (Latin America [and some Caribbean countries], the Middle East and North Africa, and Sub-Saharan Africa). However, the China and East Asia groups present different behavior since, despite having a good ECI, in 2000, their development is not as expected. However, it is worth noting that the ECI is a powerful dimensionality reduction technique used to predict and explain future economic growth, income inequality, and greenhouse gas emissions; it is therefore expected that both groups will have a higher level of development in later years. This is the case as China presented growth in its GDP per capita of 362% and East Asia and Pacific growth of 123% in 19 years, which can be seen in the graph through the growth of the circles representing the size of these economies. Meanwhile, the groups of countries with low development seem to expect stagnation in their growth as their ECI is decreasing.

We have already seen through the previous figures that productive specialization (ECI), development policies, and the promotion of new technified industries are strongly related to the growth of countries that have achieved success in terms of economic development. However, behind this process of technification and productive specialization are hidden key factors in the achievement of such success, namely skilled human capital, innovation, and entrepreneurship. We will review some of the literature that has supported this assumption and the stylized facts for the analyzed countries (Singapore, Korea, Japan, and Ireland).

The studies carried out by Barro on the determinants of growth showed that human capital is an important factor for a country's growth; thus, the author placed special emphasis on education, a variable contained in human capital, for which the author, through his model of economic growth, demonstrated its significance (Barro, 1998a, 1998b; Barro & Sala-i-Martin, 2004). Later, Lucas (1988) highlighted human capital accumulation as an alternative source of sustained growth. He distinguished between two main resources of human capital accumulation: education and learning by doing. According to Lucas, the role of human capital in growth is significant since it allows an economy to achieve long-term growth on its way to innovation through the learning or training of its labor force. In addition, according to Nelson and Phelps (1966), economic growth and the rate of innovation should increase with the level of educational attainment, particularly with enrollment in secondary and higher education, which better reflects the number of potential researchers in an economy. For these authors, human capital is the main resource for innovation since it enables the introduction of new sectors through knowledge and technology spillovers—originating in trade—and learning, in turn allowing the development of new technologies.

Other pieces of research have highlighted the fundamental role of knowledge, its creation, and its assimilation. On the one hand, Dowrick (2003) stated that, if the knowledge spillovers are substantial and if knowledge exhibits dynamic feedback effects, then small changes in the resources devoted to knowledge production can lead to substantial changes in economic development, thus highlighting the positive correlation between knowledge and development through its different diffusion mechanisms. On the other hand, Aghion and Howitt (1992) emphasized the important role that innovation plays in an economy; according to these authors, the fundamental innovative activity is achieved through research and development and the secondary activity through learning by doing, hence highlighting knowledge and its creation and assimilation as an essential factor for the development and importance of policies that provide the opportunity for local entrepreneurs to learn from experience. Research, as the authors stated, opens new windows of opportunity or new product lines, and the development of learning activities makes it possible to take advantage of those windows and achieve incremental improvements in the product lines. In this way, the positive effects of research, education, and learning on development processes have been recognized (Hulten & Ramey, 2019), highlighting that these effects are fundamental to the ability to take advantage of the benefits of learning and technology spillovers.

Regarding the essential value of education for long-term outcomes, Lee and Lee (2016) conducted a seminal work in which they presented new data sets on long-run enrollment ratios, educational attainment, and human capital stock measures for numerous countries. The authors found that, over the past two centuries, there has been remarkable growth in the average educational attainment and human capital stock as well as a narrowing of the gap in the average educational attainment between nations. This research was vital as it led to the most reliable database on the educational level of countries: "the Barro–Lee educational attainment dataset" developed in 2018. The following is an analysis of stylized facts regarding education (using the Barro–Lee dataset) and the GDP per capita for a group of 53 developed and developing countries.

Figure 4.12 shows us the economic average years of schooling with the GDP per capita for a sample of 53 countries in the years 2000, 2010, and 2017. Splitting the sample again into two quantiles (we will call them developing and developed countries, also represented by the size of the circles), we find that the average years of schooling for developing countries are 7.48 in 2000, 8.31 in 2010, and 8.97 in 2017. This means that, for developing countries, the average years of schooling have been increasing over the years, but the average remains low. Meanwhile, for developing countries, the average years of schooling were 10.45 in 2000, 11.79 in 2010, and 12.05 by 2017. Through a simple regression, we can see that an increase of 1 year of schooling causes an increase of US$ 6213 in the GDP per capita, which is a significant effect. Therefore, education is paramount for adequate economic development, but it seems that developing countries have not yet realized this.

Considering the particular case of the countries that we have analyzed so far, in Fig. 4.12, we find that all four countries, Japan, Singapore, South Korea, and Ireland, have increased their average years of schooling, and they have all been able to increase their GDP per capita. Korea's average years of schooling rose from 10.6 in 2000 to 12.1 in 2017, and its GDP per capita increased by 44% over the same period; Singapore recorded 8.9 average years of schooling in 2000 and 11.5 in 2017, and it increased its GDP per capita by 70% over the same period; Japan's average years of schooling increased from 10.7 in 2000 to 12.8 in 2017, and its GDP per capita increased by 14.2% over the same period; and the

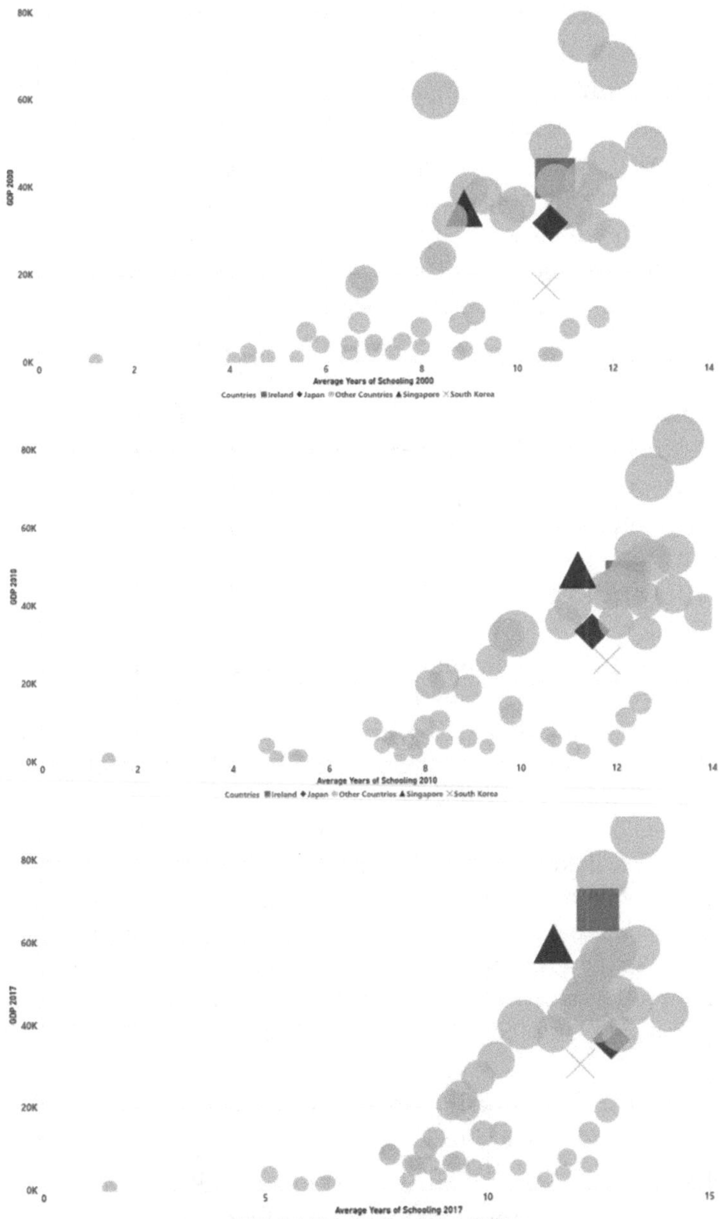

Fig. 4.12 Average years of schooling versus GDP per capita (2000–2010–2017). Source: Own elaboration with WDI and Our World in data (Oxford University)

average years of schooling in Ireland rose from 10.8 in 2000 to 12.5 in 2017, with its GDP per capita increasing by 62% over the same period. These countries are clear examples of the long-term relationship of education with economic development represented by the GDP per capita. However, what happens in some countries in which the high average years of schooling are not reflected in the level of development? If we look at Fig. 4.13, in which we analyze the relationship between the GDP per capita and the average years of schooling for the same groups of countries as in Fig. 4.11, we can see that the regions of Latin America and the Caribbean and the Middle East and North Africa have more average years of education than China; however, by 2017, the former ended up with a lower GDP per capita than the latter, even though they have a higher figure in 2000. This suggests that there are well-educated countries that are not able to develop their potential and that there is still a missing link in our understanding of these countries' success other than specialization and education.

According to CEPAL (2002):

> Firms respond to signals from their environment to acquire and adapt technology and improve it over time, to build technological capabilities and competitive advantages. Such decisions are influenced by the incentive structure, factor, and resource markets (skills, capital, technology, suppliers) and the institutions (education and training, technological, financial, etc.) with which the firm interacts. For this reason, innovation is an interactive process, linking agents that act following market incentives, such as companies, with other institutions that act under strategies and rules that do not respond to market mechanisms. The set of agents, institutions, and rules that support the processes of technology incorporation has been called the innovation system, which determines the pace of generation, adaptation, and diffusion of technological knowledge in all activities.

Following the World Bank, organizational diversity has enabled companies to respond quickly to competitive pressures, to develop market innovations, and to adapt their internal practices to stimulate innovative activity. National innovation systems are an approach based on institutions and social systems to explain how innovation dynamics are

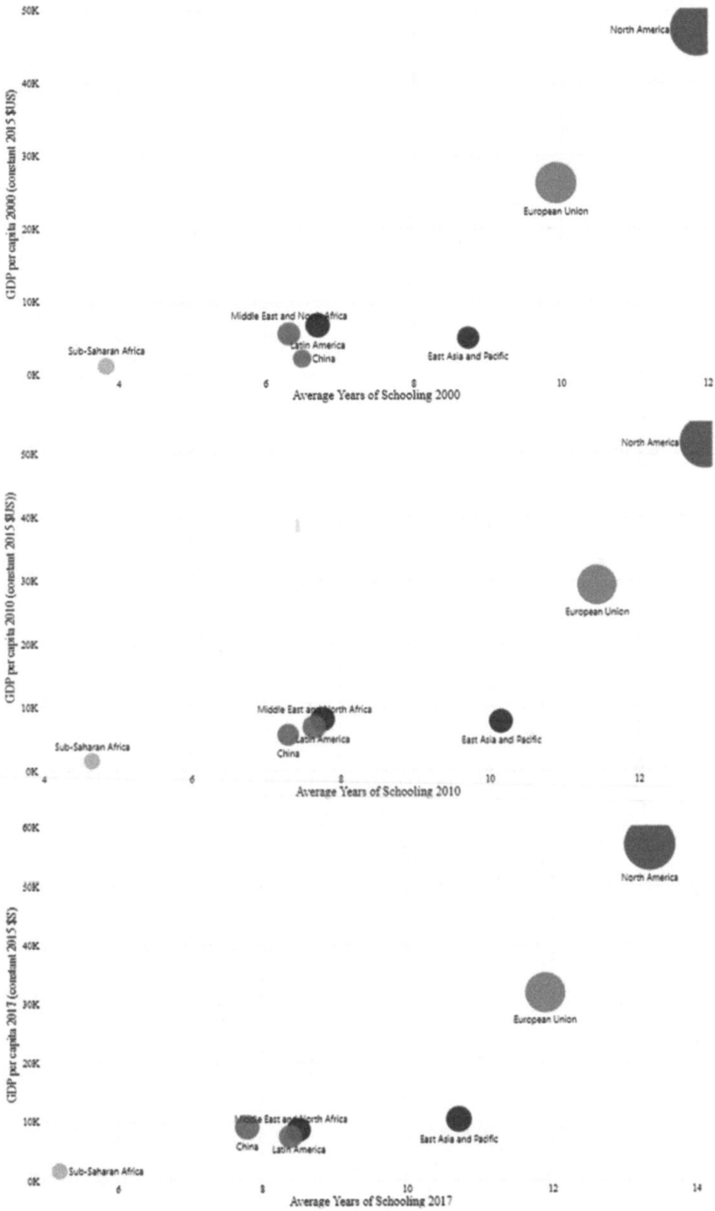

Fig. 4.13 Average years of schooling versus GDP per capita for country groups (2000–2010–2017). Source: Own elaboration with WDI and Our World in data (Oxford University)

articulated and generated. These systems have been the key to the economic growth of countries such as Ireland, Japan, Singapore, and Korea because, through them, a link has been achieved between industry, universities, laboratories, and research institutes to create a solid infrastructure in science and technology.

There are other contributions concerning how the processes of innovation and entrepreneurship mark the dynamics of societies' transformation (Aglietta, 2002; Mole, 1987). On the one hand, Mole (1987) understood innovation as a social process and its effects on society; furthermore, regarding the process of the social construction of technology, he proposed that technology is socially constructed and technological artifacts are influenced by social relations in their creation. The author argued that the innovation process is multidirectional as there are always multiple alternative solutions to technological problems. Therefore, he asserted that the design of alternative products is based on the inclusion of different social groups and ranks, which limits and establishes the technology. On the other hand, Aglietta (2002) approached innovation from the concepts of transformation and reproduction.

Other relevant pieces of research in this regard are those by Metcalfe (2001) and Drucker (2002). Drucker, in "Innovation and the Innovative Entrepreneur," stated that "[i]nnovation and entrepreneurship are treated as a career and a discipline." Innovation and the innovative entrepreneur were presented as products of decision, as a task that must be organized, and as systematic work. The author introduced the concept of "Society as an innovative enterprise: they are societies that are not planned but focused on opportunity." He explained that what we need is an innovative entrepreneurial society in which innovation and innovative entrepreneurship are common, fluid, continuous things and that innovation and innovative entrepreneurship must become a vital, integral activity in our organizations, our economy, and our society (Drucker, 2002, p. 293). Meanwhile, following the institutionalist approach to the firm, Metcalfe (2001) assigned a determinant role to the firm, establishing that the firm is the machine in the innovation process. This means that the private enterprise system has an unlimited capacity for self-induced, highly decentralized, and uncoordinated adaptation, which allows it to invent and innovate within the constraints imposed by the market (Metcalfe, 2001, p. 5).

The importance of entrepreneurship does not only date back to the beginning of this century as significant recent research has highlighted the role of entrepreneurship in the economic and social development of nations. Rico and Cabrer-Borrás (2019) investigated whether the divergences in the economic growth of the Spanish regions are a result of sectoral differences, company size, or the technological level of the new firms that are emerging in the market. The authors found that entrepreneurship, understood as both the creation of new firms and entrepreneurial activity, has a positive effect on productive efficiency and can explain the differences in regions' economic growth. Crudu (2019) analyzed the role of innovative entrepreneurship in European Union member countries' economic development, finding that innovative entrepreneurs are more present in countries with higher development levels and higher incomes, being motivated by the improvement opportunity that they see in becoming entrepreneurs; however, the creation of new firms does not substantially contribute to accelerated economic development. This indicates that the road to studying the role of entrepreneurship is a long one. In a policy study, Qian and Haynes (2014) evaluated the efficacy of the US Small Business Innovation Research (SBIR) program from the perspective of promoting high-technology entrepreneurship, showing that this program may also serve as an effective entrepreneurship policy.

Therefore, given the importance that entrepreneurship seems to have for economic growth and development, we will now review the stylized facts of entrepreneurship and GDP per capita. In Fig. 4.14, we analyze the behavior of entrepreneurship versus GDP per capita for 49 countries, entrepreneurship being measured as the new business density figure of the World Bank.

Contrary to the previous figures, in which the relationship between the variables seems to have an exponential behavior, this relationship seems to be logarithmic because, as countries experience greater entrepreneurship, they reach higher GDP levels; however, a ceiling is apparent at which the GDP does not grow anymore. This may be because external factors that influence entrepreneurship must be considered for it to be sustainable (Lee, 2019). Moving on to the data, and separating the

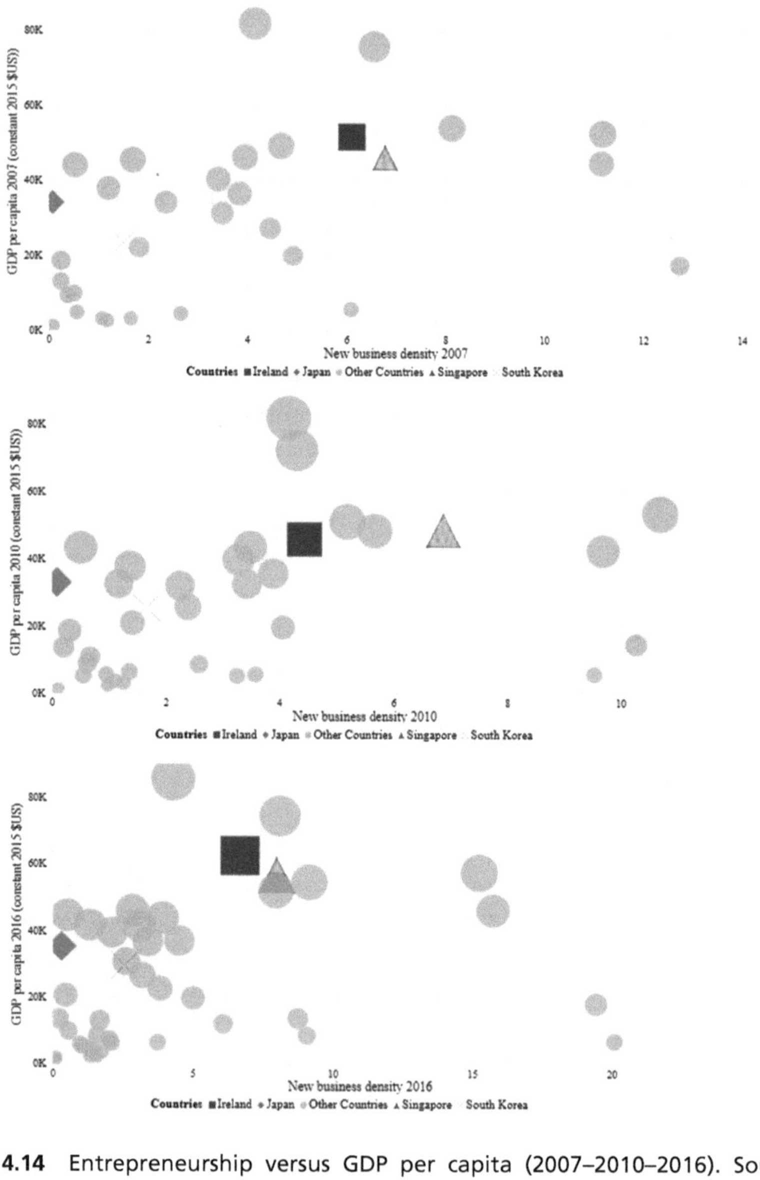

Fig. 4.14 Entrepreneurship versus GDP per capita (2007–2010–2016). Source: Own elaboration with WDI data

countries into developed and developing countries, we find that, for the developed countries, the mean of new business density was 5.34 in 2007, 4.36 in 2010, and 5.60 in 2016; meanwhile, for the developing countries, the mean was 2.48 in 2007, 2.43 in 2010, and 4.08 in 2016. This shows that countries seem to consider the need to promote entrepreneurship because, accompanied by appropriate policies, it can become a factor that generates economic development.

Regarding the cases of Korea, Singapore, Japan, and Ireland, we can see in Fig. 4.14 that the stagnation of the Japanese economy is perhaps due to the lack of progress in entrepreneurship in recent years, while, for the other countries, it seems to be their salvation. As countries such as Ireland and Singapore increased their entrepreneurship, they boosted their economies. Meanwhile, Korea seems to be undergoing a process of slow growth.

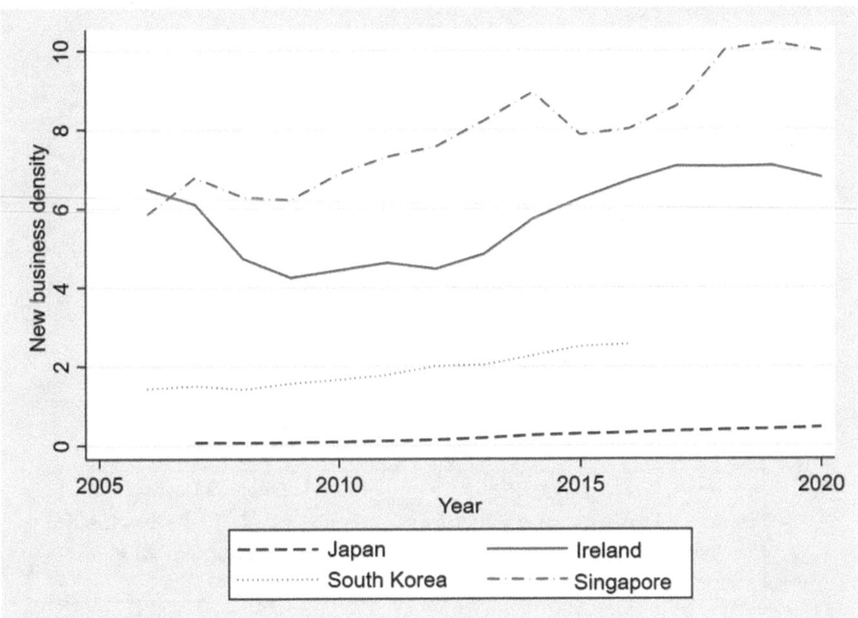

Fig. 4.15 Entrepreneurship trend over time (Singapore, Japan, Korea, and Ireland). Source: Own elaboration with WDI data

Entrepreneurship over the years can be seen in Fig. 4.15, which shows that Ireland and Singapore have driven the growth of their business. However, as of 2017, a decrease in this indicator can be observed, which raises the possibility that entrepreneurs in these countries perhaps need a more favorable environment (institutional context) in which to carry out their ventures. This leads us to conclude that entrepreneurship is the key to the countries' development because, in 2016, an increase in the new business density of 1 unit generated a significant increase of US$ 1117 in the GDP per capita. This may be due to the dynamics generated by the creation of companies, that is, employment and social mobility, among others.

If we perform the same analysis for the groups of countries that we have been observing, three interesting conclusions can be drawn from Figures 4.14, 4.15 and 4.16. First, countries with low levels of entrepreneurship have low levels of economic development (such as GDP per

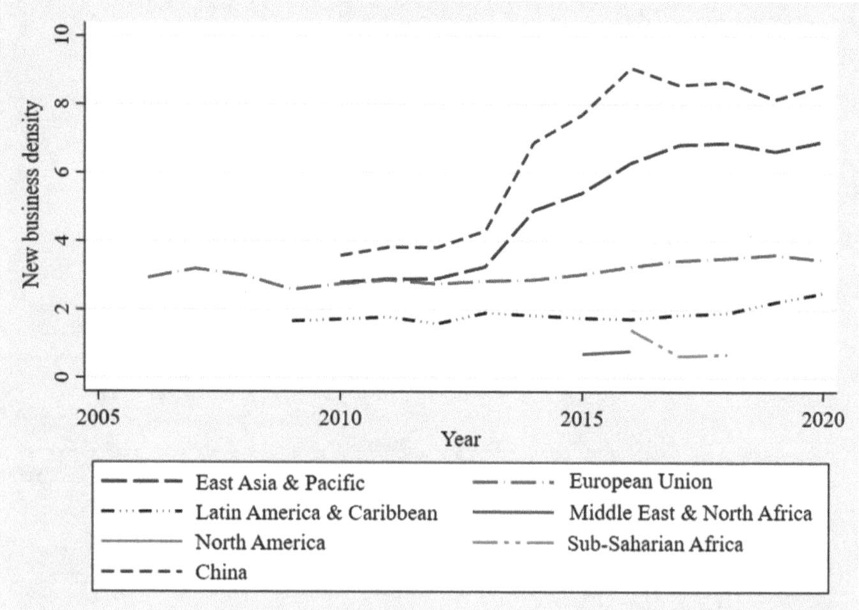

Fig. 4.16 Entrepreneurship trend over time (country groups). Source: Own elaboration with WDI data

capita) since Latin American and African countries have low levels of entrepreneurship while their economies are the most underdeveloped, making the possibility of growth with low levels of education and productive specialization more difficult. Second, the stability of the European economy may be due to the behavior of entrepreneurship in this region as Fig. 4.16 shows that the behavior of this variable over time for this region is somewhat stable. Finally, Fig. 4.16 also presents the accelerated growth of entrepreneurship in China and the East Asia and Pacific region, where economies have increased their development over the years (see Fig. 4.13).

4.4 Conclusions

Although the claim that capitalism or capital does not exist as we know it is a little bold, it has strong foundations based on empirical evidence. Countries such as the United States, Japan, and Ireland have a share of technological change in GDP growth of more than 70%, demonstrating that, although capital is important in the development of countries' productive apparatus, what is most important in such growth is technological change because, if new learning capabilities, new entrepreneurial projects, or a wide range of new specialized products are not created, a nation is destined for stagnation and will not enjoy a successful process of inclusive economic growth and development.

The different variables evaluated with the GDP per capita indicate that countries such as Korea, Singapore, Japan, and Ireland reformed and built new social capabilities, which sustained the gradual process of specialization in high-value-added products through education, entrepreneurial dynamics, and innovation, although it is clear that each process had its emphasis and particularities. As indicated in the literature, human and social capital are the basis for absorbing, implementing, and appropriating new technologies through spillovers of R&D processes. The high significance of and positive correlation between the GDP per capita and the labor force with secondary and tertiary education show the importance of the contribution of knowledge to a country's development. According to the World Bank, tertiary education has a direct influence on national productivity, which establishes better living standards and determines a country's ability to compete in the global economy.

In this way, knowledge has been a basis for the growth of countries such as Korea, Singapore, and Ireland. Betting on the education and training of their labor force to obtain goods and services with high technological content has paid off in higher productivity and higher incomes for their population. A country with adequate infrastructure, skilled labor, and high investment in research and development makes an economy attractive for investment, and these factors have contributed to the successful growth of some countries. The specialization and entrepreneurship indicators show that a country lagging in international trade must direct its policies to changes in its production and export structure to new specialization patterns to achieve sustained growth toward becoming a knowledge-based economy.

Hausmann et al. (2008) developed key growth diagnostics; however, although this diagnosis stresses the importance of human capital, it does not emphasize the importance and fundamental role of entrepreneurship in countries' growth process. This is undoubtedly the contribution of our diagnosis as we give its place to entrepreneurship, innovation, human capital, and education, which, together with institutions and policymakers, have contributed to the success of countries such as Japan, Ireland, Singapore, and Korea in the growth process. Therefore, in this book, factors such as institutions, innovation, and entrepreneurship will be the cornerstone of the explanation of economic development.

References

Acemoglu, D., & Robinson, J. A. (2012). Why nations fail: The origins of power, prosperity, and poverty. Currency.

Aghion, P., & Howitt, P. (1992). A Model of Growth Through Creative Destruction. *Econometrica, 60*(2), 323–351. https://doi.org/10.2307/2951599

Aglietta, M. (2002). *Regulación y crisis del capitalismo*. Siglo XXI Editores.

Al-Dajani, H., & Marlow, S. (2013). Empowerment and entrepreneurship: A theoretical framework. *International Journal of Entrepreneurial Behaviour & Research, 19*(5), 503–524.

Aparicio, S., Audretsch, D., Noguera, M., & Urbano, D. (2022). Can female entrepreneurs boost social mobility in developing countries? An institutional analysis. *Technological Forecasting and Social Change, 175*, 121401.

Bakshi, G. S., & Chen, Z. (1996). The spirit of capitalism and stock-market prices. *American Economic Review, 86*(1), 133–157.

Barro, R. (1998a). *Determinants of economic growth. A cross-country empirical study*. MIT Press.

Barro, R. (1998b). *Notes on growth accounting* (NBER, 6654).

Barro, R., & Sala-i-Martin, X. (2004). *Economic growth* (2nd ed.). MIT Press.

Bec, F., & Bastien, A. (2007). The transmission of aggregate supply and aggregate demand shocks in Japan: Has there been a structural change? *Studies in Nonlinear Dynamics and Econometrics, 11*(4). https://doi.org/10.2202/1558-3708.1342

Bishop, A., & Mateos-Garcia, J. (2019). Exploring the link between economic complexity and emergent economic activities. *National Institute Economic Review, 249*(1), R47–R58. https://doi.org/10.1177/002795011924900114

Caous, E. L., & Huarng, F. (2020). Economic complexity and the mediating effects of income inequality: Reaching sustainable development in developing countries. *Sustainability (Switzerland), 12*(5). https://doi.org/10.3390/su12052089

CEPAL. (2002). Globalización y Desarrollo. Disco Compacto B. Santiago de Chile. Chile.

Crudu, R. (2019). The role of innovative entrepreneurship in the economic development of EU member countries. *Journal of Entrepreneurship, Management and Innovation, 15*(1), 35–60. https://doi.org/10.7341/20191512

Dinda, S. (2014). Inclusive growth through creation of human and social capital. *International Journal of Social Economics, 41*(10), 878–895. https://doi.org/10.1108/IJSE-07-2013-0157

Dowrick, S. (2003). Ideas and education: Level or growth effects? NBER Working Paper No. 9709, doi: 10.3386/w9709

Drucker, P. (2002). *La innovación y el empresario innovador*. Editorial Norma.

Erkan, B., & Ceylan, F. (2021). Determinants of economic complexity in transitional economies. *Transition Studies Review, 28*(2), 57–80. https://doi.org/10.14665/1614-4007-28-2-004

Glyn, A. (2007). *Capitalism unleashed: Finance, globalization, and welfare* (pp. 1–272). Oxford University Press. https://doi.org/10.1093/acprof:oso/9780199226795.001.0001

Gómez, D. (2002a). Colombia 9000.3: Construcción de lo posible; un marco prospectivo para el desarrollo del país., Cámara de Comercio de Medellín.

Gómez, D. (2002b). *La productividad y la innovación en los procesos de desarrollo*. Centro de Ciencia y Tecnología de Antioquia.

Gómez, D. (2002c). *Los procesos de desarrollo en el mundo*. Cámara de Comercio de Medellín.

Gómez, D. (2002d). *Dinámica del desarrollo social* (pp. 1–14). System Dynamics Society.

Hartmann, D., Guevara, M. R., Jara-Figueroa, C., Aristarán, M., & Hidalgo, C. A. (2017). Linking economic complexity, institutions, and income inequality. *World Development, 93*, 75–93. https://doi.org/10.1016/j.worlddev.2016.12.020

Hausmann, R., Klinger, B., & Wagner, R. (2008). *Doing growth diagnostics in practice: a 'mindbook'* (Center for International Development, 177).

Hidalgo, C. A., & Hausmann, R. (2009). The building blocks of economic complexity. *Proceedings of the National Academy of Sciences of the United States of America, 106*(26), 10570–10575. https://doi.org/10.1073/pnas.0900943106

Hulten, C., & Nakamura, L. (2017). *Accounting for growth in the age of the internet: The importance of output-saving technical change* (No. w23315). National Bureau of Economic Research.

Hulten, C. R. (2010). Growth accounting. In B. H. Hall & N. Rosenber (Eds.), *Handbook of the economics of innovation* (Vol. 2, pp. 987–1031). North-Holland.

Hulten, C. R., & Ramey, V. A. (2019). The importance of education and skill development for economic growth in the information era. In *Education, skills, and technical change* (pp. 115–146). University of Chicago Press. https://doi.org/10.7208/chicago/9780226567945.003.0003

Lee, H. J. (2019). What factors are necessary for sustaining entrepreneurship? *Sustainability (Switzerland), 11*(11). https://doi.org/10.3390/su11113022

Lee, J. W., & Lee, H. (2016). Human capital in the long run. *Journal of Development Economics, 122*, 147–169. https://doi.org/10.1016/j.jdeveco.2016.05.006

Lucas, R. J. (1988). On the mechanics of economic growth. *Journal of Monetary Economics, 22*, 3–42. Elsevier.

Marks, S. G. (2012). The word "capitalism": The Soviet Union's gift to America. *Soc, 49*, 155–163. https://doi.org/10.1007/s12115-011-9520-x

Metcalfe, G. (2001). *Institutions and progress* (CRIC Discussion Paper No. 45).

Mole, V. (1987). *Enterprising Innovation: An alternative approach*. Frances Pinter.
Nelson, R., & Pack, H. (1998). *The Asian miracle and the modern growth theory. 1881*. The World Bank; Development Research Group.
Nelson, R., & Phelps, E. (1966). Investment in humans, technological diffusion, and economic growth. *American Economic Review, 56*(2), 69–75.
North, D. C. (2010). *Understanding the process of economic change. Understanding the process of economic change*. Princeton University Press. https://doi.org/10.2307/20034365
Qian, H., & Haynes, K. E. (2014). Beyond innovation: The small business innovation research program as entrepreneurship policy. *Journal of Technology Transfer, 39*(4), 524–543. https://doi.org/10.1007/s10961-013-9323-x
Rico, P., & Cabrer-Borrás, B. (2019). Entrepreneurship, firms creation and regional performance. *European Journal of Management and Business Economics, 28*(2), 158–173. https://doi.org/10.1108/EJMBE-07-2018-0077
Rueschemeyer, D., Stephens, E. H., & Stephens, J. D. (1992). *Capitalist development and democracy*. University of Chicago Press. https://doi.org/10.1590/0101-35172004-1610
Sennett, R. (2006). *The culture of the new capitalism* (pp. 1–214). Yale University Press. https://doi.org/10.5860/choice.43-4789
Solow, R. M. (1957). Technical change and the aggregate production function. *The Review of Economics and Statistics, 39*(3), 312. https://doi.org/10.2307/1926047
Thrift, N. (2005). *Knowing capitalism* (pp. 1–65). SAGE. https://doi.org/10.4135/9781446211458
van Dam, A., & Frenken, K. (2020). Variety, complexity and economic development. *Research Policy*. https://doi.org/10.1016/j.respol.2020.103949
Williamson, O. E. (2000). The new institutional economics: Taking stock, looking ahead. *Journal of Economic Literature, 38*(3), 595–613. https://doi.org/10.1257/jel.38.3.595

5

Diagnosing the Dynamics of Economic Growth

Diego Gomez, Sebastian Aparicio, and David Urbano

5.1 Introduction

Hausmann et al. (2005) published the base document of what would become a series of papers on economic growth diagnostics in different countries (Brazil, El Salvador, and the Dominican Republic). The basic assumption was that economic growth occurred if investments were profitable. The authors used a theoretical and methodological framework in which a static model compatible with the general equilibrium state was developed. Although that research agenda represents a starting point in the logic of economic growth, it is possible to advance in a consistent way in how the

---

D. Gomez
Fundación ECSIM, Medellin, Colombia

S. Aparicio (✉) • D. Urbano
Department of Business, Universitat Autònoma de Barcelona,
Cerdanyola del Vallés, Barcelona, Spain

Centre for Entrepreneurship and Social Innovation Research (CREIS),
Universitat Autònoma de Barcelona, Sabadell, Barcelona, Spain
e-mail: Sebastian.Aparicio@uab.cat

D. Gomez et al. (eds.), *Driving Complexity in Economic Development*,
https://doi.org/10.1007/978-3-031-34386-5_5

theoretical and practical process is represented, ensuring that the stylized facts match the theoretical and methodological sections. That is why, in this chapter, we propose a methodology that mathematically models the dynamics of growth arising from the creation and transformation of companies and viable investments, with a review of the drivers of this growth.

The basic hypothesis in this chapter is that economic growth is derived from an investment dynamic that implies the development of viable projects. This requires conditions of demand and price, as well as a structure of costs, expenses, and taxes, that together allow an Internal Rate of Return (IRR) to be obtained that enables the project to be carried out by investors (Hajdasinski, 2004; Patrick & French, 2016). The model utilized for the analysis of growth conditions is a dynamic flow model that allows us to approximate the dynamics of investment and its effects on the economy over time. From this model we frame the fundamental determinants of investment as the basis of economic growth, making it clear that households and firms are the key agents in the system. From Hausmann et al. (2005) idea, a new set of investment determinants is proposed.

This chapter ends with a suggested diagram that shows the importance of the decision-making of companies and people (households) on the viability of projects and on the creation of companies capable of generating transformation processes. For this, it is key to mention that the hidden innovation behind transformation processes is essential to making a business decision and generating new ventures. This idea is developed throughout the book, which explains that economic development means not only a calculation of the percentage growth in what we produce, but also employment generation, poverty reduction, increased income, institutional support, education, reduction of taxes, and improvement of living conditions.

5.2 Theoretical Framework

The puzzle of economic development is still missing certain pieces, and authors have pointed out how complex it is for many countries to reach this state (Ahmad et al., 2021; Sautet, 2013). Hausmann et al. (2005) propose a mathematical approach, motivated by three considerations. First, "while development is a broad concept entailing the raising of human capabilities in general, we believe increasing economic growth rates is the central challenge that developing nations face." Thus, these authors consider that higher living standards are the most direct route to achieving improvements in social and human indicators. Second, "trying to come up with an identical growth strategy for all countries is unlikely to prove productive. Growth strategies are likely to differ according to domestic opportunities and constraints." Third, "it is seldom helpful to provide governments with a long list of reforms, many of which may not be targeted at the most binding constraints on economic growth." Despite the authors' endeavors, they conclude that working toward a general methodology of economic development through growth is almost unfeasible. Why is this the case? Is it a structural problem in how we see the economic world?

Perhaps the answers to these questions begin with resolving how we understand the economy. In economics during the twentieth century and, more specifically, after the contributions of Leon Walras (Walras, 1868, 1896) and Vilfredo Pareto (1892–1893, 1898), the synthesis carried out by Samuelson (1947, 1966), the Arrow and Debreu (1954) model, and, more recently, the developments of Mas-Colell (1985), the dominant metaphor has been the demonstration of an existing general equilibrium, understood as the state that occurs after (all minus one) markets equalize their demands and offer at a price that allows this equilibrium. During the same years in which Walras and Marshall were making their fundamental contributions, two other approaches were being discussed and proposed. The first suggested an understanding of the economy as circular flows of goods and money (Patinkin, 1973a, 1973b). The second approach is called cumulative circular causality (CCC) (Berger, 2009). This states that processes in economics are determined by the previous states of both the same variable and other related variables. However, the metaphor that ultimately prevailed was that of general equilibrium because it could be used for value determination and for explaining the operation of markets. General equilibrium is represented mathematically with timeless equations that represent the economy as a closed market event with labor, goods, and money, subject to the optimization of marginal costs.

Drawing on the idea that any economy can be represented through a set of equations, this chapter presents a mathematical and theoretical basis upon which different relationships are developed and subsequently analyzed under the circular flow scheme. Employing circular flows,

Knight (1921) supported his theories of costs and prices being related to the role of the entrepreneur and households in economic activity. The circular flow model, or the *Wheel of Fortune*, as Knight called it, implies a behavior that has not been explored or represented mathematically: a continuous flow of goods and money that can and should be represented by a system of differential equations that capture the cybernetics (autoregressive nature) of the system. This behavior also reflects and explains the CCC approach and, in fact, integrates into the same model the cumulative effects of money, export capacities, and investment, among other things. All of these have been the subject of partial studies by Myrdal (1939, 1957), Kaldor (1940), and Lucas (1975), among others.

This approach implies that the equations must be expressed with time dependencies on previous periods which therefore determine current and future events. This type of model does not require markets to be closed, as it assumes a continuous process of consumption, production, and investment decisions, and, on the contrary, the non-existence of closed markets is an initial condition that determines agents' decisions for future periods. In other words, general equilibrium is not a requirement, it is not necessary and possibly it does not occur. This approach also allows us to address two fundamental issues in economics: economic cycles and the transformations that generate growth and development. This is what we will seek to explain with the system of equations that will be constructed below.

5.3 Mathematical Approach

We start with the construction of the flow-by-flow model. Hulten (2006) introduces a system of equations that represent the circular model of the economy proposed by Samuelson (1947, 1966) and taken up by Mankiw et al. (1992). This system is represented in Fig. 5.1.

According to Fig. 5.1, what households and firms trade in the factor market is labor (denoted by L), and what is traded in the goods and services market is quantities (represented by Q). For Hulten, both these markets are closed in quantities and prices at a given instant. Hence Hulten (2006) defines equalities between rent and expenditures and

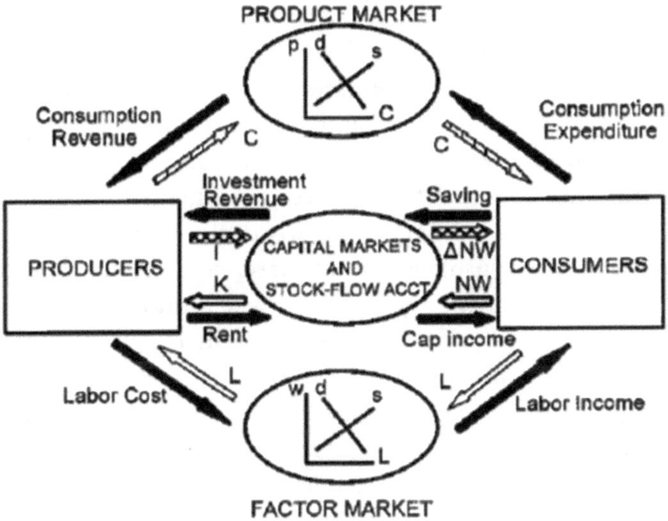

Fig. 5.1 Circular model of the economy. (Source: Hulten (2006)

revenues and costs (wages, rents, and profits). Theoretically speaking, the prices associated with labor (P_L) and quantities (P_Q) are defined.

Thus, the equality between income and expenditure is $P_L * L = P_Q * Q$, and the equality between revenues and costs is $P_Q * Q = P_L * L$. From these identities, we establish market equilibria that guarantee that, at any given time, the laws of supply and demand are satisfied. From the basic scheme, Hulten begins by introducing dynamics to the model (in physical terms, the dimension of time), considering the moment of equilibrium in the same identity, and including a time factor, that is, $P_L(t) * L(t) = P_Q(t) * Q(t)$ and $P_Q(t) * Q(t) = P_L(t) * L(t)$.

From the last equality, Hulten establishes the distinction between nominal and real national accounts. As far as constant prices are concerned, he introduces a productivity factor (A) to observe efficiency-based changes in real output. In other words, this allows him to deflate the expansions by presenting output in constant terms, thus making it possible to observe the real change produced in the economy. At the same time, this productivity factor generates changes in the decisions of individuals, introducing variations in consumption and work patterns.

Hulten suggests that this productivity is obtained from the savings (S) generated by households, given that over time deferred consumption allows the accumulation of resources destined for investment in the acquisition of new technologies and human capital. Thus, individuals have to make an intertemporal decision between saving and borrowing. The total time value of wealth generated over time, taking into consideration savings or debt acquired, is composed of expenditure and income, respectively, plus the return or price of debt service, which is denoted by (r).

For Hulten, these savings generated in the economy should, in principle, support two things. On the one hand, there are the debts acquired with the rest of the world (abroad), which must be balanced by the balance of trade created by trading with other countries; and on the other hand, savings must be able to sustain the investment that generates changes in the economy. In addition, for Hulten, it is necessary to handle the concept of the inventories that appear in the national accounts. The first concept is that savings are a non-consumption that is temporarily represented in the inventories of goods destined for investment in subsequent period(s); and the second one is that not everything that is produced in a period is necessarily consumed, but, on the contrary, part of that production is expected to be consumed in the future.

However, the matter may be even more interesting. By deepening this scheme in its temporal effects and accumulated causality, it is possible to build a model of the economy in which the multiple effects, decisions, and processes that occur in the dimension of time are collected and structured. That is to say, the circular model and the accumulated causality it implies can be mathematically modeled, in advance on the initial scheme elaborated by Hulten (2006). Moreover, what is modeled is an economy in which time plays a determining role both in production and investment processes and in consumption decisions. It is therefore a matter of understanding the economy as a system similar to a thermodynamic system.

Thus, the construction of the model will start by considering the two main agents in the economy: firms and households. In the case of firms, these are represented by four basic components: production, capital stock, cash, and inventories; while on the household side, four other components are represented: consumption, labor supply (understood as the economically active population), labor, and cash.

5.3.1 Production and Demand: The Goods and Services Cycle

The generation and consumption cycle is constructed first. The cycle starts with the production function, then uses the demand function for consumer goods and consumption goods, and ends with the participation in work by families.

5.3.2 Production

The first of the components to be constructed is a basic production function. We understand this as the social capacity (SC) to generate goods and services. This function assumes the use of the installed capacity of the system, which is associated with the capital stock. This use depends on the level of the labor force. The effectiveness of utilization is associated with a productivity factor as shown in Eq. (5.1). This factor ρ_t establishes what society is able to do on average per worker.

$$SC(t) = L(t)\rho_t \tag{5.1}$$

Here $L(t)$ represents the number of people working at time t and ρ_t represents how many units of goods or services each unit of labor produces, that is, ρ_t is a productivity factor whose behavior is strongly influenced by variables such as investment and innovation. In the first phase of the model, it is assumed to be static, and in later versions, it is endogenized; using this factor, the processes of learning, innovation, and entrepreneurship, which explain the processes of accelerated development, are analyzed. The production aspect is crucial, given that, as will be seen in the development of the mathematical approach, companies are in charge of generating value through innovation.

5.3.3 Consumption

On the consumption side, it is assumed that the money people spend during time t is a proportion ς_t of the money they earned as remuneration for their work, or as income for their goods, in period $t - 1$.

$$C(t) = \frac{\left(L(t-1)P_L(t-1) + R(t-1)\right)\varsigma_t}{P_C(t)} \tag{5.2}$$

In this equation, $P_L(t - 1)$ represents the price of each unit of labor in period $t - 1$, $P_C(t)$ means the price of each unit of consumption in period t, and $R(t - 1)$ represents the income received at time $(t - 1)$. This income is considered, at this stage of the model, as a percentage rh of the economy's product. This is expressed in Eq. (5.3).

$$R(t) = P_C(t-1) * SC(t-1) * rh \tag{5.3}$$

5.3.4 Labor, EAP, and Unemployment

The dynamics of these components consist of the description of the growth of the labor supply by families, represented as the economically active population (EAP), and the dynamics of the demand for labor by companies, denoted as L. The goods of an economy are demanded by households, by the same companies for investment, by government, and for exports. To meet this demand, employers must hire enough personnel to produce the quantities that these four agents need, subject to the level of productivity of the average employee in the economy. From the above, it is assumed that the number of employees in an economy is the ratio between the demand and the level of productivity of the employees, as described in Eq. (5.4).

$$L(t)=\frac{D(t-1)-\frac{dINV}{dt}(t-1)}{\rho_t} \tag{5.4}$$

The EAP is the population that is able and willing to work, and it is assumed that this population has a growth rate δ_1, given by demographic factors that are assumed to be an exogenous constant.

$$\frac{dEAP}{dt}=\delta_1 EAP(t) \tag{5.5}$$

The labor force peaks at the available EAP. The equation is as follows:

$$L(t)=\begin{cases} \mathcal{L}(t) & if \quad EAP(t)>L(t) \\ PEA & if \quad EAP(t)\le L(t) \end{cases} \tag{5.6}$$

The model built up to this point is shown in Fig. 5.2. This is what is called the real economy, where goods, services, and labor flow. It is important to note that the decisions of how much labor force to employ depend on the demand and change in inventories from the previous period and the change in the productivity of the economy (Fig. 5.2).

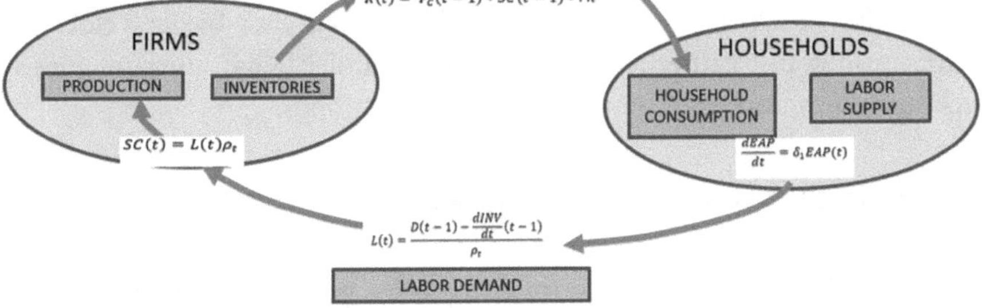

Fig. 5.2 Flow economy model. (Source: Own elaboration)

5.3.5 Revenues and Payments

The household dynamic is summarized as four parts: consumption, EAP, labor, and cash. In turn, the dynamics of firms are represented by: production, capital stock, cash, and inventories. This section discusses the cash flows, which represent the payment of salaries and rent by companies, and the purchases of goods and services by households. This is done by representing the cash balances of each of the agents.

5.3.6 Household Cash Balance

The dynamics of household cash flow are described by Eq. (5.7).

$$\frac{dHC}{dt} = \left(P_L(t)L(t) + R(t-1)\right) - \left(L(t)\rho_t P_C(t)\right)\varsigma_t \qquad (5.7)$$

where HC means household cash, and its rate of change, as expressed in the equation, is defined as the difference between income and expenses. The income is made up of the remuneration for work at time t and the income generated for one period before, while the expenditures for this case represent only the consumption of goods and services which, in Eq. (5.7), are a proportion of the production of the previous period. This proportion is determined by a factor of propensity to consume, which is denoted by ς_t. The model proposes that all the money that households do not spend is saved by being deposited in the financial system, which allows this money later to become an investment, which in turn increases the capital stock. For this reason, the household cash balance does not store money but rather simply serves to establish what amount goes to consumption and what amount goes to investment.

5.3.7 Cash Balance of Companies

The behavior of the cash flow of companies is reciprocal to that of the cash flow of households, meaning that, in the case of companies, the income is the consumption of households, and the outgoings are the salaries and rents the companies must pay. This is shown in Eq. (5.8).

$$\frac{dCC}{dt} = \left(P_L(t-1)L(t-1) + R(t-2)\right)\varsigma_t - \left(P_L(t)L(t) + R(t-1)\right) + \frac{dHC}{dt}(t-1) \tag{5.8}$$

This model assumes that the surplus amount of money once wages have been paid is also paid to households as income from their investments, meaning that the cash balance of companies, like that of households, does not show storage of money but serves as an intermediate step to establish what amount is salary and what amount is income.

The following figure presents the integrated flow dynamics. The monetary flows are directly linked to the flows of goods and labor through the prices of goods and the price of labor (Fig. 5.3).

5.3.8 Inventories and Investment

Inventories are a crucial element in this circular model approach. The existence of inventories evidences the existence of a dynamic in which accumulations and deaccumulations are a central part of a complex systems with delays. More specifically, the presence of inventories accounts

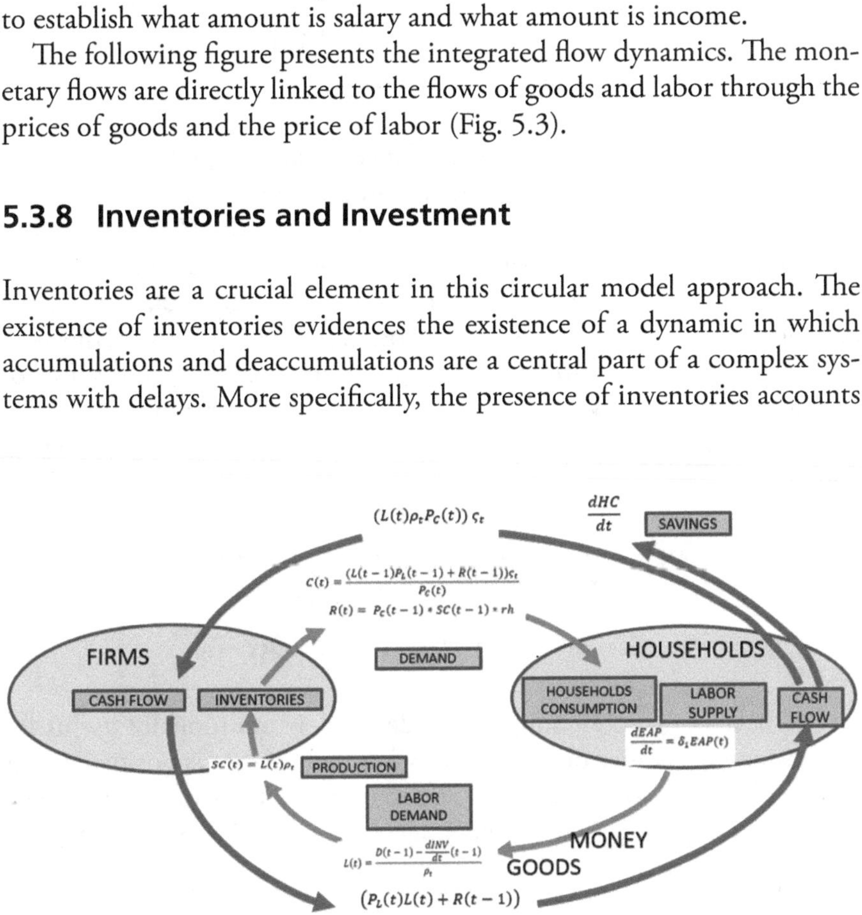

Fig. 5.3 Flow economy model with flows of families and payments of goods and services. (Source: Own elaboration)

for the behavior of markets that adjust in an autoregressive manner and in which periods are needed to adjust the capacities, products, and investments required. Below are the equations that are used to represent the dynamics of inventory accumulation.

The behavior that this equation seeks to demonstrate is the gap between the quantities produced and the quantities demanded in a period; we will call this SD(t).

$$SD(t) = SC(t-1) - \frac{L(t-1)P_L(t-1) + R(t-1))\varsigma_t}{P_C(t)} - EN(t) - GC(t) - ID(t) \tag{5.9}$$

The variable SD expresses the imbalance between supply and demand, and is constructed to monitor whether production is sufficient to supply people's needs, *EN* is the quantity of exported goods, *ID* is investment demand, and *GC* the government consumption. As can be seen, it is constructed simply as the difference between the social capacity of the economy and the consumption intentions of the population. In this way, inventories change according to this balance and according to the level of people's savings, which are destined to buy investment goods. Thus, the effective variation of the inventories is obtained with the following equation:

$$\frac{dINV}{dt} = SC(t) - \frac{L(t-1)P_L(t-1) + R(t-2))\varsigma_t}{P_C(t)} - EN(t-1) - GC(t-1) - ID(t-1) \tag{5.10}$$

The balance between supply and demand is traditionally useful for establishing consumer prices, that is, when the balance is positive, prices tend to decrease and when it is negative, prices tend to increase. This sensitivity is represented by the parameter γ of Eq. (5.10), which describes the previous situation.

$$\frac{dP_c}{dt} = -\gamma_t SD(t) \tag{5.11}$$

Thus, the demand for a good is represented by:

$$D(t) = HD(t) + EN(t) + GC(t) + ID(t) \tag{5.12}$$

where *HD* represents household demand and is, in turn, represented by Eq. (5.13) below, ID is investment demand, represented in Eq. (5.14) below, and EN is the quantity of exported goods.

$$HD(t) = \frac{L(t-1)P_L(t-1) + R(t-2))\varsigma_t}{P_C(t)} \tag{5.13}$$

$$ID(t) = \frac{I_n}{P_C(t)} \tag{5.14}$$

Based on the previous analysis and equations, we can conclude that household demand is equal to its consumption (Eq. (5.13) = Eq. (5.2)), and that government consumption is part of the mathematical framework but will not be taken into account in the explanation of the flow since its role is that of a resource manager.

The concept of capital stock is understood as the assets of a society that are necessary for the generation of the goods and services it requires (Boratyński & Osiewalski, 2021). The dynamics of the capital stock of companies are determined by investment goods, which represent an increase in the installed capacity of companies and are acquired with the financing obtained from the system's reserves, which consist fundamentally of household savings. This means that the goods produced have two final destinations: some are bought by households for consumption, and others are purchased by companies to increase their productive capacity. The foregoing suggests that changes in the capital stock are a result of decisions of the agents to expand the productive capacity and are financed by household savings in previous periods. This is illustrated in Eq. (5.15).

$$\frac{dSK}{dt} = \frac{dHC}{dt}(t-a) \tag{5.15}$$

where a is the time it takes for the capital increase to become effective from the moment people invest their savings. This occurs under the assumption that everything that people save is constituted as investment and that the economy produces goods independently of demand. The system behaves in a more complex way: the economy invests to produce what is expected to be demanded. This implies that the investment and the demand for the labor force are determined according to the expectations of the growth of the demand.

The dynamics of investment, therefore, are determined by the level of utilization of the capacity of companies; that is, entrepreneurs invest when the demand for their goods exceeds a certain percentage of their production capacity, and in this way the investment is determined as a percentage of the capital stock *SK*, as expressed in Eq. (5.16).

$$In(t)=\begin{cases} \dfrac{\left(COR(t)-\dfrac{Cap(t)-SC(t)}{SC(t)}\right)*OI(t)*SK(t)}{LI(t)} \\ \text{if } COR(t)-\dfrac{Cap(t)-SC(t)}{SC(t)}>0 \\ 0 \\ \text{if } \quad COR(t)-\dfrac{Cap(t)-SC(t)}{SC(t)}<0 \end{cases} \tag{5.16}$$

where *COR* is the idle capacity required, that is, the level of idleness that companies maintain to be prepared for sudden increases in demand. *Cap* is the total production capacity of companies; *SC*, the social capacity, is what is produced; and *OI* is the level of overinvestment. It is assumed that, once the demand exceeds the established percentage of the capacity of production, entrepreneurs invest *OI* times the idle capacity they have left to prepare for permanent increases in demand. The investment to be made does not enter the system immediately: it has an executive capacity, and there is a delay in its entry into operation. Therefore, the equation is divided by the investment lag factor *LI*, so that the investment is made during *LI* periods until the total is reached.

For Eq. (5.15) to be calculated, it is necessary to determine the total capacity *Cap*, which is a function of the productivity of capital. In other words, to calculate the total production capacity, it is necessary to know the production capacity of each unit of monetary capital. We denote that value as *LUK* and it is represented in Eq. (5.17):

$$LUK(t) = \frac{\gamma SK(t-1)}{L(t-1)\rho_t} \tag{5.17}$$

where γ represents the level of capital utilization. Thus constructed, *LUK* represents the amount of capital needed to produce a consumer good, from which the total capacity is found as the ratio between the total capital stock and the *LUK*, as shown by Eq. (5.18).

$$Cap = \frac{SK(t)}{LUK(t)} \tag{5.18}$$

The economic flow model with the inclusion of inventories and investment is shown in Fig. 5.4.

This model is put into practice through Ithink, a system dynamics software that allows the generation of the system of equations that has been built and is represented in Fig. 5.4. With this it is possible to obtain a graphical representation of the behavior of some key variables of the model, such as investment, the investment decision, the production capacity of firms, household income, and household cash flow, among others. Figure 5.5 shows us dynamically the behavior of key variables such as the income and investments of households and firms, in addition to representing the scheme of the model. Runs 1, 2, and 3 are different

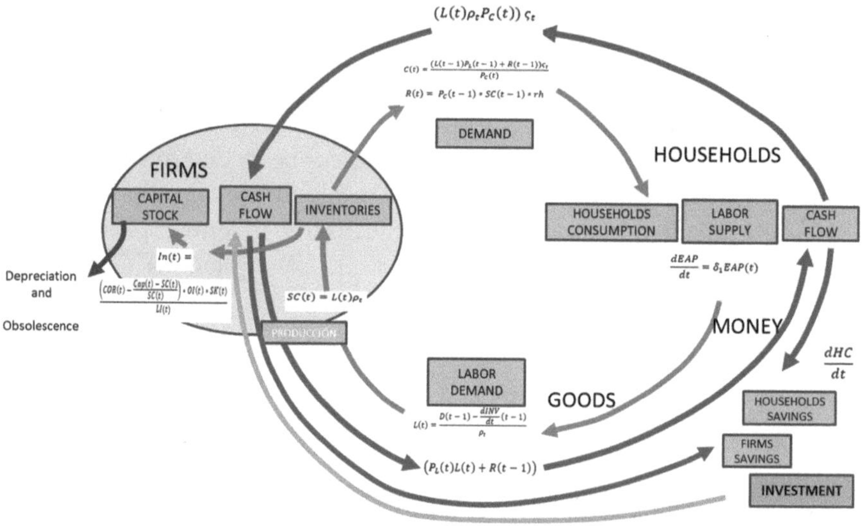

Fig. 5.4 Flow economy model with flows of families and payments of goods and services, inventories, and investment. (Source: Own elaboration)

because of different investment levels. Run 4 shows the effect of a change in the execution times of the investment. Over time, it can be seen that the investment produces cycles. With higher levels of investment, higher incomes are obtained for households and firms, since higher investment translates into better future production and higher income.

The same model when run through Simulink/Matlab allows us to generate a system of equations with mathematical software, with which we obtain the results of the system that are presented in Fig. 5.6.

In addition, these simulations make it possible to identify the fundamental role played by firms in the expansion of the economy, since it is firms that, through investment, generate new capacities and dynamics in the system, generating employment and income for families.

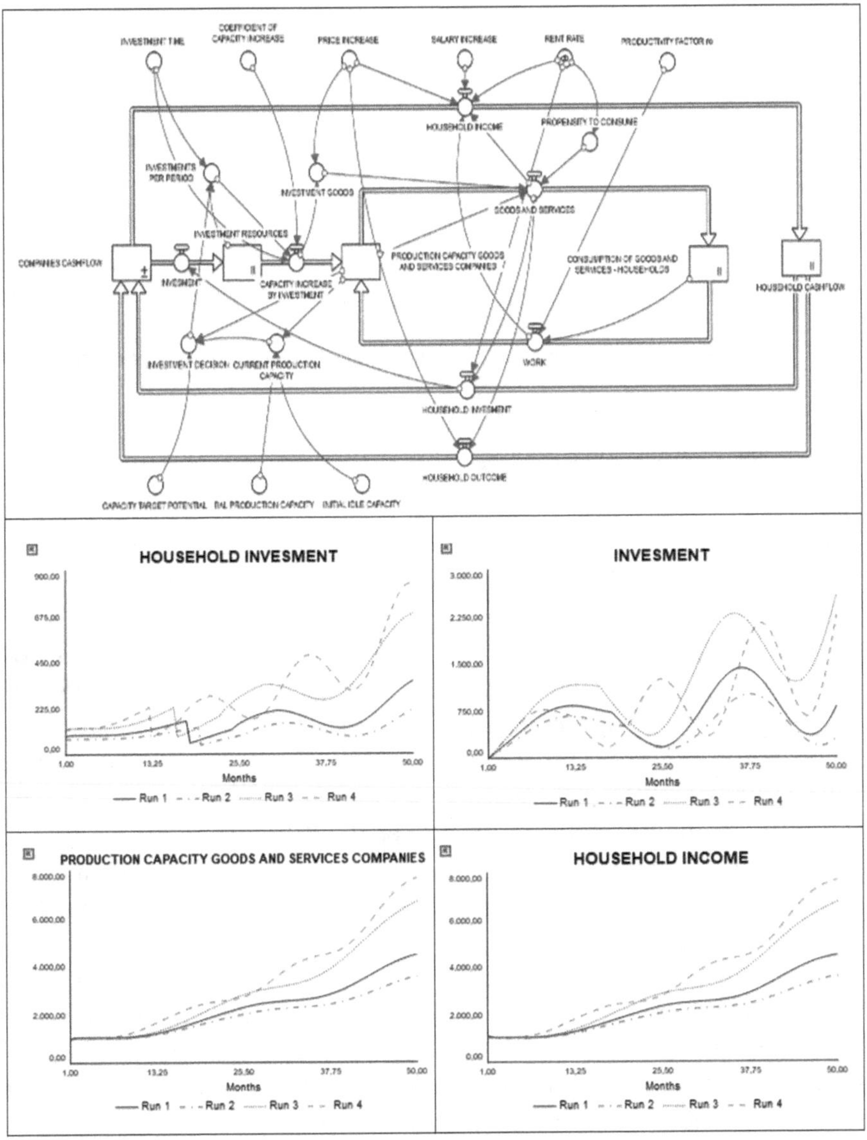

Fig. 5.5 Dynamic simulations. (Source: Own elaboration)

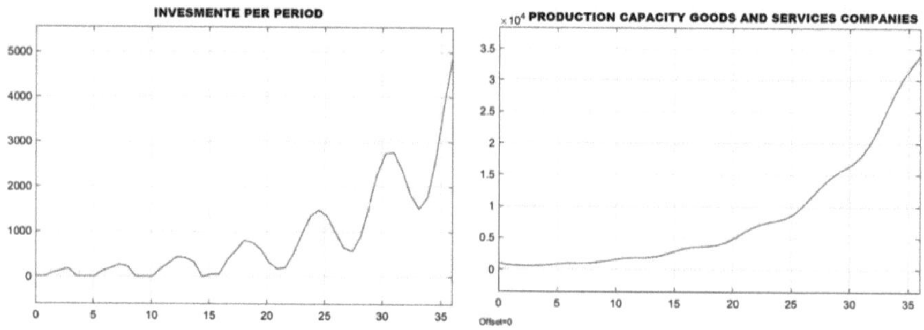

Fig. 5.6 Dynamic simulations whit Simulink/Matlab. (Source: Own elaboration)

5.4 The Role of Firms

The main result of the development of the mathematical approach is to raise the importance of companies and their relationship with other market agents in an economic model through a flow structure. The literature has been concerned with studying certain drivers of economic development, such as savings (Cavallo et al., 2018; Din et al., 2021), GDP (Sajith & Malathi, 2020; Stjepanović et al., 2017), education (Hamdan et al., 2020; Kruss et al., 2015), and the financial system (Beck et al., 2000; King & Levine, 1993). However, it has looked away from firms and their role in the economic process (Aparicio et al., 2016).

As we may appreciate from the initial part of the mathematical approach, companies and households are the backbone of the economic structure: companies produce goods that households consume and also jobs in which people in households are employed. Households obtain wage remunerations that are destined for consumption but also for savings, and these savings are then spent on either investment or more consumption. In parallel, firms earn profits from the sale of goods and services through inputs and inventory, and these profits are invested in future periods. In short, companies are major generators of social welfare. That is why, in addition to a mathematical approach that gives importance to firms in the development process, we want to propose a flow diagram of how this development is produced through firms.

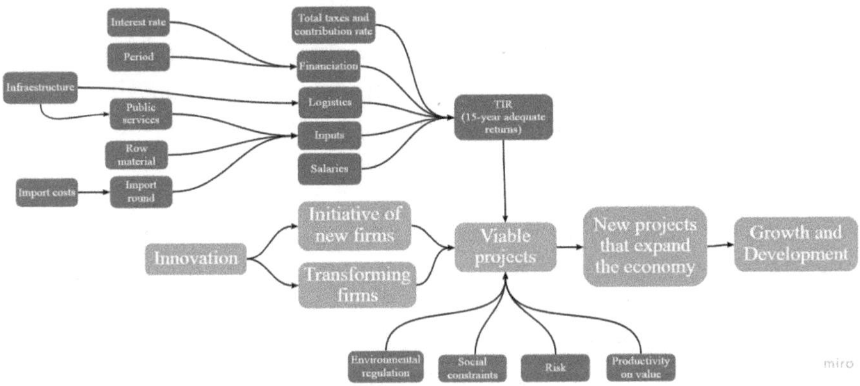

Fig. 5.7 Importance of firms in the transformational dynamic

Figure 5.7 shows the process through which firms play a fundamental role in value creation in society, and thus lead to economic development. First, in society, there are economic variables that are in constant interaction with firms and households, but for the creation of a new firm (entrepreneurship) there must be a viable project with a possible future profitability. Such viable projects depend directly on variables such as environmental regulations, social constraints, innovation, risk, and productivity, in addition to an innovative initiative. However, how should these viable projects be evaluated? This is done through the internal rate of return (IRR).

The internal rate of return is the profitability offered by an investment (project). In our specific case, we consider that it depends on variables such as wages, inputs, financing, logistics, and taxes. IRR and its effect on economic development will be further analyzed in a later chapter, but it should be noted that IRR is one of the cornerstones of our research, along with other institutional variables that allow IRR to have positive effects. Thus, we will review, in a bottom-up manner, the key variables that make up the proposed diagram and that converge to give economic growth and development. First, we analyze some characteristics and effects of IRR; second, we observe the environment in which projects are assessed to determine their viability; and finally, we consider the processes of initiatives, innovation, and investment for the development of ventures.

IRR is defined as an interest rate that equates the present worth of a cash flow stream to zero. When it has a unique value, it provides valuable information about the return on investment and is often viewed as a measure of efficiency (Hartman & Schafrick, 2004). However, this definition falls away when there are multiple internal rates of return, a situation that may arise when a project is defined by a mixture of positive and negative cash flows. Still, Hartman and Schafrick (2004) show that this rate always produces decisions consistent with present worth under the assumption that at least one real internal rate of return exists. Patrick and French (2016) support the idea that IRR is a wonderfully simple benchmark but one that should be used in conjunction with other analysis to appraise projects, so that the researcher can determine its correctness in the context of other benchmarks. It is precisely this conclusion that makes us think that IRR should be used not only as a driver of development but also as part of the transmission mechanism of other initial effects.

In the literature, IRR has a multidisciplinary use, and some of its uses and characteristics are shown in research related to public-private partnerships (PPPs), productivity and wages, financing projects through other methodologies, developments of the measure, and new interpretations. De Albornoz et al. (2018) provide a clear proposition to determine the potential number of real positive IRRs that a cash flow may have, which depends on the number of sign variations and the value of the net present value (NPV) calculated with a discount rate equal to 0 for PPPs. Lopes and Teixeira (2013) investigate the extent to which the productivity gains associated with workplace training are shared by both the firms concerned and their workers. The authors propose that productivity increases due to improved worker learning practices improve the IRR, concluding that training investments are good or they would not even be considered by firms. However, more accurate knowledge of the gains captured by firms (and workers) is critical for policymakers in their decision-making processes. The estimates found in the paper show that firm training is a genuinely worthwhile investment for all participants. Other research has been concerned with developing different features and improvements for IRR. Dhavale and Sarkis (2018) consider an investment decision involving a sustainable, energy-efficient, greenhouse gas-reducing asset, and incorporate the value of carbon emission allowances for the investing company, utilizing a Bayesian model for IRR that uses the Gibbs sampler. The authors show that IRR is influenced by the volatility and uncertainty of carbon credit cash flows, so that ignoring those uncertainty characteristics and simply using the expected values of cash flows can result in a significantly inaccurate investment rate of return. From another perspective, Milanesi (2016) introduces the average internal rate of return (AIRR) into the mathematical fuzzy frame, as an alternative method for estimating returns in ambiguous situations. However, the results of this new measure are not sufficiently intuitive. In general, the IRR can depend on many factors inherent to the production process of a company in any sector, from inputs, adequate infrastructure, and budget, to all kinds of internal and external factors such as country risk or the behavior of the regional economy.

This is strongly related to our second key concept, since viable projects are determined not only by IRR but also by environmental factors. The first and perhaps the most important environmental factor is the initiative for a new firm, or what is also known in the literature as the entrepreneurial decision. The literature on entrepreneurial decisions is extensive and has followed different approaches (Shepherd et al., 2015). Long et al. (2021) examine the effects of entrepreneurial decision-making logic on new venture sustainability, using 259 entrepreneurs as a sample, and develop a logistic regression analysis as a research method. The authors show that goal orientation plays a negative role in promoting new venture sustainability, while avoiding contingencies has a positive influence on it. Partnerships are conducive to new venture sustainability, while means orientation and leveraging contingencies have a negative effect. From a similar perspective, Maine et al. (2015) investigate effectuation and causation as two opposing decision-making modes leading to opportunity creation and recognition. (A causation approach implies that the entrepreneur focuses on a predefined goal and then aims to find the means to reach this goal; while the effectuation approach implies that the entrepreneur focuses on the means at hand, which they aim to transform into one or more goals that were not necessarily predefined.) These authors utilize the embedded case study method to investigate 30 decisions made by three scientist-entrepreneurs creating commercial platforms for biotechnology inventions. The results show the iterative nature of opportunity generation and decision-making modes, as entrepreneurs respond to their evolving environment and to regulatory and funding constraints, such that entrepreneurs can shift from effectuation to causation, remain in one particular mode, or adopt a combination of the two modes. This study provides evidence of the role played by the environment, since regulations and budgetary barriers are crucial in entrepreneurial decisions.

Two other important pieces of research reveal the factors that influence the entrepreneurial decision. First, Yi et al. (2020) examine the influences of entrepreneurial passion on entrepreneurial decision-making and entrepreneurial expectation among 427 Chinese college students. They find that students with high entrepreneurial passion scores also have high entrepreneurial decision-making scores. Students' entrepreneurial expectation and ability mediate, respectively, the relationship between entrepreneurial passion and entrepreneurial decision-making, and the relationship between entrepreneurial passion and entrepreneurial decision-making through entrepreneurial expectation. Second, Wang et al. (2020) adopt a collective perspective in the study of entrepreneurial decision-making processes and empirically analyze how social relationships between family members can shape their collective entrepreneurial decision-making behavior. The authors find a significant relationship between the cognitive dimension of family social capital and the entrepreneur's decision-making. Additionally, there has been research on the perception of risk. Ma et al. (2021) discuss how entrepreneurs and non-entrepreneurs may make different decisions when they face the same opportunities, and show that entrepreneurs and non-entrepreneurs assess an opportunity differently because of how they take into account the inherent risk of that opportunity. Other research focuses more on the implications for firms (Davidsson et al., 2021; Lam, 2017; Shahriar et al., 2021). Therefore, it is evident that the entrepreneurial decision through innovation not only affects the viability of the project but is also influenced by environmental, budget, risk, and social aspects.

Finally, our last cornerstone is entrepreneurship (new projects that expand the economy), since this is determined by the viability of projects, which is influenced by internal (innovation) and external (i.e., risk, environment) factors and IRR, and can also have positive effects on economic dynamics. The literature on the determinants and effects of entrepreneurship is extensive and of high theoretical and practical quality (Chepurenko, 2015; Mehmood et al., 2019; Simpeh, 2011). An important part of this literature supports the idea that entrepreneurship, together with other measures such as innovation, drives the dynamics of the transformation of societies through firms. Schaltegger et al. (2016) develop a theoretical framework to analyze co-evolutionary business model development for sustainable niche pioneers and conventional mass market players, aiming for the sustainable transformation of markets. In this research, the authors seek to identify the basic evolutionary processes of business model variation, selection, and retention, as well as evolutionary pathways, to support a structured analysis of the dynamics between business model innovation and market sustainability transformation, that is, the way in which, through entrepreneurship, the market can be transformed for the convenience of firms and society. Using a different approach, Chrisanty et al. (2021) study the consequences of transformational entrepreneurship, in terms of increased organizational readiness for change, minimized counterproductive work behavior, and enhanced employee performance. These authors also aim to understand the extent to which organizational readiness for change and counterproductive work behavior affect employee performance. Using structural equation modeling, the authors find that transformational entrepreneurship positively and significantly affects organizational readiness for change and employee performance, and negatively and significantly affects counterproductive work behavior. In addition, their results demonstrate a significantly positive effect of organizational readiness for change on employee performance and a significantly negative effect of counterproductive work behavior on employee performance. This research seeks to promote, first, a dynamic of transformation within firms, through better methodological and innovative processes, and then a social transformation through the sale of better products that generate productive employment dynamics.

Thus, our diagram proposes firms as its main axis, since it is through firms that viable projects are evaluated through the IRR and the environment, and firms are also responsible for implementing the innovation that generates a dynamic transformation of social inclusion.

5.5 Conclusions

In this chapter, we have established a mathematical basis capable of expressing economic growth through investment projects; households and firms form a fundamental part of the model. It could be said that they are the cornerstones of the system or the circular flow model. Using the literature and developing the mathematical foundation, we have come to several conclusions.

First, if one reviews the literature, it is easy to conclude that the stagnation of economic development theories is due to the lack of use of unconventional methodologies. The literature has focused on studying the economic development of endogenous growth models and indicators, and although these provide a glimpse of the characteristics of development, they still do not allow us to identify with certainty the whole transmission mechanism that is hidden in the puzzle called economic development. This is why in this chapter we are encouraging the building of a mathematical basis through a different methodology, using a flow model that allows us to identify the main agents of the whole economic apparatus.

Second, using the two economic agents of households and firms, we build a model of circular reinvestment flows in which both agents have their respective roles. On the one hand, firms are composed of production, capital stock, cash, and inventories. On the other hand, households are composed of consumption, labor supply, and cash. However, going into the logic of the model, what gives the dynamic capacity is investment, since households receive wages for their work and firms receive profits from the sale of their products, then they decide whether to invest the profits, consume them, or save them for future consumption or investment. In this way, the model feeds back.

Third, given that the model indicates that the growth of the economy is the result of an investment dynamic that implies the development of viable projects, price and demand conditions are required, as well as a structure for costs, expenses, and taxes that allow investors to make decisions. This is how we can understand the importance of firms in the economy, given that through investment decisions they allow for adequate economic development or stagnation. How do firms make investment decisions? This leads us to the following fourth conclusion. There are three key concepts involved in business decision-making: IRR, viable projects, and entrepreneurship. As a first step, companies analyze their returns, which depend on different variables such as inputs, wages, infrastructure, financing, and logistics (i.e., their entire cost and expense structure). Then, together with the IRR, they analyze the entrepreneurial decision of new firms or projects, regulations, social constraints, risk, productivity, and innovation, and this makes companies or individuals decide whether or not a project is viable. Finally, viable projects give rise to entrepreneurship, which is nurtured by new ideas and transformation processes, leading to a dynamic of social transformation called economic development.

References

Ahmad, M., Jabeen, G., Irfan, M., Işık, C., & Rehman, A. (2021). Do inward foreign direct investment and economic development improve local environmental quality: Aggregation bias puzzle. *Environmental Science and Pollution Research, 28*(26), 34676–34696. https://doi.org/10.1007/s11356-021-12734-y

Aparicio, S., Urbano, D., & Gómez, D. (2016). The role of innovative entrepreneurship within Colombian business cycle scenarios: A system dynamics approach. *Futures, 81*, 130–147.

Arrow, K. J., & Debreu, G. (1954). Existence of an equilibrium for a competitive economy. *Econometrica, 22*(3), 265–290.

Beck, T., Levine, R., & Loayza, N. (2000). Finance and the sources of growth. *Journal of Financial Economics, 58*(1–2), 261–300. https://doi.org/10.1016/s0304-405x(00)00072-6

Berger, S. (2009). *The foundations of non-equilibrium economics: The principle of circular and cumulative causation* (pp. 1–224). Taylor and Francis. https://doi.org/10.4324/9780203873731

Boratyński, J., & Osiewalski, J. (2021). Bayesian estimation of capital stock and depreciation in the production function framework. *Central European Journal of Economic Modelling and Econometrics, 4*, 455–486. https://doi.org/10.24425/cejeme.2021.139837

Cavallo, E., Eichengreen, B., & Panizza, U. (2018). Can countries rely on foreign saving for investment and economic development? *Review of World Economics, 154*(2), 277–306. https://doi.org/10.1007/s10290-017-0301-5

Chepurenko, A. (2015). Entrepreneurship theory: New challenges and future prospects. *Foresight Russia, 9*(2), 44–57. https://doi.org/10.17323/1995-459X.2015.2.44.57

Chrisanty, F. N., Gunawan, M. S., Wijayanti, R. W., & Soetjipto, B. W. (2021). The role of transformational entrepreneurship, readiness to change and counterproductive work behavior in enhancing employee performance. *Organizacija, 54*(1), 63–81. https://doi.org/10.2478/orga-2021-0005

Davidsson, P., Grégoire, D. A., & Lex, M. (2021). Venture Idea Assessment (VIA): Development of a needed concept, measure, and research agenda. *Journal of Business Venturing, 36*(5). https://doi.org/10.1016/j.jbusvent.2021.106130

De Albornoz, V. A. C., Galera, A. L., & Millán, J. M. (2018). Is it correct to use the internal rate of return to evaluate the sustainability of investment decisions in public private partnership projects? *Sustainability (Switzerland), 10*(12). https://doi.org/10.3390/su10124371

Dhavale, D. G., & Sarkis, J. (2018). Stochastic internal rate of return on investments in sustainable assets generating carbon credits. *Computers and Operations Research, 89*, 324–336. https://doi.org/10.1016/j.cor.2017.02.014

Din, S. U., Khan, M. Y., Khan, M. J., & Nilofar, M. (2021). Nexus between sustainable development, adjusted net saving, economic growth, and financial development in South Asian emerging economies. *Journal of the Knowledge Economy*. https://doi.org/10.1007/s13132-021-00818-6

Hajdasinski, M. M. (2004). Technical note—The internal rate of return (IRR) as a financial indicator. *Engineering Economist, 49*(2), 185–197. https://doi.org/10.1080/00137910490453437

Hamdan, A., Sarea, A., Khamis, R., & Anasweh, M. (2020). A causality analysis of the link between higher education and economic development: Empirical evidence. *Heliyon, 6*(6). https://doi.org/10.1016/j.heliyon.2020.e04046

Hartman, J. C., & Schafrick, I. C. (2004). The relevant internal rate of return. *Engineering Economist, 49*(2), 139–158. https://doi.org/10.1080/00137910490453419

Hausmann, R., Rodrik, D., & Velasco, A. (2005). *Growth diagnostics*. https://growthlab.cid.harvard.edu/publications/growth-diagnostics-0

Hulten, C. (2006). A new architecture for the US national accounts. In *The architecture of capital accounting: Basic design principles*. University of Chicago Press.

Kaldor, N. (1940). A model of the trade cycle. *The Economic Journal, 50*, 78–92.
King, R. G., & Levine, R. (1993). Finance and growth: Schumpeter might be right. *Quarterly Journal of Economics, 108*(3), 717–737. https://doi.org/10.2307/2118406
Knight, F. H. (1921). *Risk, uncertainty and profit*. Книга.
Kruss, G., McGrath, S., Petersen, I., & Gastrow, M. (2015). Higher education and economic development: The importance of building technological capabilities. *International Journal of Educational Development, 43*, 22–31. https://doi.org/10.1016/j.ijedudev.2015.04.011
Lam, J. (2017). *Implementing enterprise risk management*. John Wiley & Sons, Inc.. https://doi.org/10.1002/9781118922415
Long, D., Wang, H., & Wang, P. (2021). Built to sustain: The effect of entrepreneurial decision-making logic on new venture sustainability. *Sustainability (Switzerland), 13*(4), 1–20. https://doi.org/10.3390/su13042170
Lopes, A. S., & Teixeira, P. (2013). Productivity, wages, and the returns to firm-provided training: Fair shared capitalism? *International Journal of Manpower, 34*(7), 776–793. https://doi.org/10.1108/IJM-02-2012-0033
Lucas, R. E. (1975). An equilibrium model of the business cycle. *Journal of political economy, 83*(6), 1113–1144.
Ma, D., Fiet, J. O., & Dubofsky, D. A. (2021). Entrepreneurial decision-making under risk. *Entrepreneurship Research Journal*. https://doi.org/10.1515/erj-2020-0051
Maine, E., Soh, P. H., & Dos Santos, N. (2015). The role of entrepreneurial decision-making in opportunity creation and recognition. *Technovation, 39–40*(1), 53–72. https://doi.org/10.1016/j.technovation.2014.02.007
Mankiw, N. E., Romer, D., & Weil, D. N. (1992). A contribution to the empirics of economic growth. *Q J Econ, 107*(2), 407–437.
Mas-Colell, A. (1985). *The theory of general economic equilibrium: A differentiable approach (No. 9)*. Cambridge University Press.
Mehmood, T., Alzoubi, H. M., Alshurideh, M., Al-Gasaymeh, A., & Ahmed, G. (2019). Schumpeterian entrepreneurship theory: Evolution and relevance. *Academy of Entrepreneurship Journal, 25*(4), 1–10.
Milanesi, G. S. (2016). The fuzzy average internal rate of return: Development and applications. *Journal of Economics, Finance and Administrative Science, 21*(40), 39–47. https://doi.org/10.1016/j.jefas.2015.12.001
Myrdal, G. (1939). *Monetary equilibrium*. Augustus M. Kelley.
Myrdal, G. (1957). *Economic theory and underdeveloped regions*. Gerald Duckworth.

Pareto, V. (1892–1893). Considerazioni sui principi fondamentali dell'economia politica pura. *Giornale degli Economisti* [21] 4 (May 1892), 389–420; 4 (June 1892), 485–512; 5 (August 1892), 119–57; 6 (January 1893), 1–37; 7 (October 1893), 279–321.

Pareto, V. (1898). *Comment se pose Ie probleme de l'economie pure*. Memoire presente en decembre 1898, a la Societe Stella. Lausanne, 1898 (privately published), 12 pp. Reprinted in Vilfredo Pareto, Oeuvres Completes, Vol. 4: Marxisme et economie pure. Librairie Droz, 1966.

Patinkin, D. (1973a). In search of the "wheel of wealth": On the origins of Frank Knight's circular-flow diagram. *The American Economic Review, 63*(5), 1037–1046. http://www.jstor.org/stable/1813935

Patinkin, D. (1973b). Frank Knight as teacher. *The American Economic Review, 63*(5), 787–810. http://www.jstor.org/stable/1813905

Patrick, M., & French, N. (2016). The internal rate of return (IRR): Projections, benchmarks and pitfalls. *Journal of Property Investment and Finance*. Emerald Group Publishing Ltd. https://doi.org/10.1108/JPIF-07-2016-0059

Sajith, G. G., & Malathi, K. (2020). Applicability of human development index for measuring economic well-being: A study on GDP and HDI indicators from Indian context. *The Indian Economic Journal, 68*(4), 554–571. https://doi.org/10.1177/0019466221998620

Samuelson, P. A. (1947). *Foundations of economic analysis*. Harvard University Press.

Samuelson, P. A. (1966). *The collected scientific papers of Paul A. Samuelson*. 2 vols. Ed. J. E. Stiglitz. MIT Press.

Sautet, F. (2013). Local and systemic entrepreneurship: Solving the puzzle of entrepreneurship and economic development. *Entrepreneurship: Theory and Practice, 37*(2), 387–402. https://doi.org/10.1111/j.1540-6520.2011.00469.x

Schaltegger, S., Lüdeke-Freund, F., & Hansen, E. G. (2016). Business models for sustainability: A co-evolutionary analysis of sustainable entrepreneurship, innovation, and transformation. *Organization and Environment, 29*(3), 264–289. https://doi.org/10.1177/1086026616633272

Shahriar, M. S., Hasan, K. B. M. R., Hossain, T., Beg, T. H., Islam, K. M. A., & Zayed, N. M. (2021). Financial decision making and forecasting techniques on project evaluation: A planning, development and entrepreneurial perspective. *Academy of Entrepreneurship Journal, 27*(4), 1–7.

Shepherd, D. A., Williams, T. A., & Patzelt, H. (2015). Thinking about entrepreneurial decision making: Review and research agenda. *Journal of Management, 41*(1), 11–46. https://doi.org/10.1177/0149206314541153

Simpeh, K. N. (2011). Entrepreneurship theories and empirical research: A summary review of the literature. *European Journal of Business and Management, 3*(6), 1–9.

Stjepanović, S., Tomić, D., & Škare, M. (2017). A new approach to measuring green GDP: A cross-country analysis. *Entrepreneurship and Sustainability Issues, 4*(4), 574–590. https://doi.org/10.9770/jesi.2017.4.4(13)

Walras, L. (1868). Méthode de conciliation ou de synthèse. In *Oeuvres économiques complètes / Auguste et Léon Walras. Tome 9—Études d'économie sociale—théorie de la répartition de la richesse sociale* (pp. 151–173). Economica.

Walras, L. (1896). Théorie de la propriété. In *Oeuvres économiques complètes/ Auguste et Léon Walras. Tome 9—Études d'économie sociale—théorie de la répartition de la richesse sociale* (pp. 177–212). Economica.

Wang, C., Flamini, G., Wang, K., Pei, R., & Chen, C. (2020). Entrepreneurial decision-making and family social capital. *Management Decision, 59*(5), 938–952. https://doi.org/10.1108/MD-10-2019-1414

Yi, R., Lyu, B., Wang, H., & Huang, W. (2020). Entrepreneurial passion, entrepreneurial expectation and entrepreneurial decision-making among college students. *Journal of Psychology in Africa, 30*(4), 323–329. https://doi.org/10.1080/14330237.2020.1796094

6

Taxes and Economic Growth: The Role of the Central Government

Diego Gomez, Sebastian Aparicio, David Urbano, and Diego Martinez-Moya

6.1 Introduction

The literature on the various effects of taxes on economic growth is extensive (Easterly & Rebelo, 1993; Stokey & Rebelo, 1995), not only in the short term (Baiardi et al., 2019) but also in the long term (Alinaghi & Reed, 2021). However, most of these studies focus on the direct effects of tax structure on economic growth such as GDP and do not pay attention to the effects of tax structure on the determinants of economic growth, such as Gross National Income (GNI), New Business Density (NBD), and Gross Fixed Capital Formation (Diacon & Maha, 2015; Fritsch &

D. Gomez • D. Martinez-Moya
Fundación ECSIM, Medellin, Colombia

S. Aparicio (✉) • D. Urbano
Department of Business, Universitat Autònoma de Barcelona, Cerdanyola del Vallés, Barcelona, Spain

Centre for Entrepreneurship and Social Innovation Research (CREIS), Universitat Autònoma de Barcelona, Sabadell, Barcelona, Spain
e-mail: Sebastian.Aparicio@uab.cat

D. Gomez et al. (eds.), *Driving Complexity in Economic Development*,
https://doi.org/10.1007/978-3-031-34386-5_6

Mueller, 2008; Meyer & Meyer, 2019; Tyler, 1981). The studies also leave aside the tautological role of the performance of government institutions in determining the taxes that end up affecting economic growth. It is precisely these gaps in the literature that we are trying to fill through the development of this research.

To achieve this, we use Steinmo (1989) and North's (1990) theoretical frameworks, which established the existence of "rules of the game," creating incentives that drive the economic behavior and intentions of individuals, but also of the government (North & Weingast, 1989), and also that institutional structures are the context in which political actors must necessarily define their policy preferences and determine their strategic objectives (Steinmo, 1989). Having established this theoretical framework, we proceed to propose a couple of hypotheses that support the fundamental role played by the performance of government institutions through their total debt on the determination of taxes, and how these taxes disincentivize some determinants of economic growth such as GNI, NBD, and Gross Fixed Capital Formation. To test these hypotheses, we use the World Development Indicators to create an unbalanced panel data with a maximum of 4749 observations from 2000 to 2018 and also use a multi-level equation model (i.e., simultaneous equations) to develop a three-stage estimation (3SLS) (Wooldridge, 2002) that considers both the direct effect of taxes on economic growth determinants and the direct and indirect effects that government performance and entrepreneurship have on national economic growth.

Results show that when government performance, such as total central government debt (as a percentage of GDP) and claims on central government (annual growth as a percentage of broad money), increases by 1%, taxes (namely income profits and capital gains) increase by 0.32% and 0.46%, respectively, supporting what Bassetto and Kocherlakota (2004) state. These authors find that when taxes on income, profits, and gain increase by 1%, economic growth determinants such as GNI growth, NBD, and Gross Fixed Capital Formation decrease by 0.41%, 1.01%, and 0.15%, respectively. These findings reinforce the knowledge in current literature (for instance Alves, 2019; Belitski et al., 2016; Iwamoto & Shibata, 2008). This leads to literature and policy implications that allow us to propose some recommendations for policymakers on where to redirect efforts to obtain benefits in economic growth and business creation.

This chapter is structured as follows: The next section presents the theoretical framework, where we establish institutional economics and institutional structures as the main axis of the research. Afterward, we explain the methodology, involving the source of the data and the empirical strategy. Then, results are presented. Finally, we conclude, and generate a discussion on theoretical and policy implications.

6.2 Conceptual Framework

6.2.1 Theoretical Foundations

According to Steinmo (1989), institutional structures are the context in which political actors must necessarily define their policy preferences and determine their strategic objectives, thus providing a central link between individual choice behavior and macro policy outcomes, including tax policies. This is in line with North's (1990) institutional economics framework that established the existence of "rules of the game," creating incentives that drive not only the economic behavior and intentions of individuals but also governments (North & Weingast, 1989). North (1990, 2005) defines different types of rules, which are grouped into two main categories. First, formal institutions exist that encompass regulations, laws, policies, and so on. All of them are contained in written official documents that aim to achieve particular social, economic, and political objectives. Second, and complementarily, there are unwritten norms that represent the cultural sphere of any society: These consist of habits, social perceptions, and preconceptions that support or exert pressure on human behavior.

Stimulated by this internal and external influence on economic behavior and individual decision-making, economic growth research has adopted the institutional economics framework in order to understand how tax policies can modify economic outcomes (Aparicio et al., 2016; Belitski et al., 2016; Lee & Gordon, 2005; Neog & Gaur, 2020) and affect the decision-making of individuals about fiscal policies (Androniceanu et al., 2019; Gokalp et al., 2017). Therefore, the institutional framework for the study of this phenomenon is of crucial importance.

6.2.2 Hypothesis Development

In the development of the hypotheses, we focus on two fundamental aspects of the research: first, how taxes depend on institutions—mainly public policies and government institutions, and their economic performance. Second, we will establish the importance of taxes on economic growth.

In economic history, the importance of fiscal policies for the proper development of society through revenue collection has been proven (Auerbach & Gorodnichenko, 2012; Barro, 1974; Easterly & Rebelo, 1993), even now, during the COVID-19 pandemic (Faria-e-Castro, 2021). Taxes play perhaps the most important role in fiscal policies (Barro, 1974; Lucas & Stokey, 1983) and have direct effects on the main economic variables. These effects are on variables such as education (Oyarzo & Paredes, 2021), health (Blakely et al., 2020; Room et al., 2005), entrepreneurship (Darnihamedani et al., 2018; Djankov et al., 2010), labor (Eissa & Liebman, 1996; Johnston, 2021), productivity (Romero-Jordán et al., 2020), and, of course, on economic growth (Neog & Gaur, 2020; Stokey & Rebelo, 1995), which is a core element throughout this research. This is where we find a gap in the literature, given that although much research focuses on showing the effects of taxes on the economy, there is still not much academic investigation of what determines these taxes.

For example, some research has focused its efforts on identifying the importance of institutions and public policies in the determination of taxes (Arbel et al., 2019; Ricciuti et al., 2019). In the realm of public policies, Arbel et al. (2019) reveal a new implication of the Yule–Simpson paradox with public policy repercussions, and find that statistical test outcomes support Laffer's controversial claim that for the few upper-bracket taxpayers, an efficient collection is associated with tax reduction, rather than a tax increase. On the other side, Ricciuti et al. (2019) estimate the long-term impact of political institutions distinguishing between the accountability and transparency of fiscal institutions (impartiality) and their effectiveness in extracting revenues. These authors find that stronger constraints on the executive foster the impartiality of tax systems, impacting total tax revenues and income revenues. Von Schiller (2016) explores the relationship between socio-political institutions and tax composition in developing countries and argues that strong business organizations and stable political party systems reduce the uncertainty of fiscal contracts for economic elites that can accept a larger share of the tax burden. Consequently, governments more intensively collect taxes using progressive taxation. However, political institutions do not seem to be the only ones to play an important role in determining taxation. Bruno (2019) analyzes the relationship between tax enforcement, compliance, and morale within countries characterized by the rapid introduction of market institutions and the slow evolution of political regimes, such as transition economies. The author finds that the lower the quality of political institutions and the weaker the tax morale, the less tax compliance can be achieved. Therefore, having political institutions of good quality is not a sufficient condition conducive to tax enforcement or compliance, as confirmed by results like those of Cox et al. (2018). Research on the effects of government institutions on taxation is even more furtive. Alt and Lowry (1994) conclude that (i) aggregate state budget totals are driven by different factors under Democrats and Republicans, the net result being that Democrats target spending (and taxes) to higher shares of state-level personal income; (ii) divided government is less able to react to revenue shocks that lead to budget deficits, particularly where different parties control each chamber of the legislature; and (iii) unified party governments with restricted ability to carry deficits into the next fiscal year (outside the South) have sharper reactions to negative revenue shocks than those without restrictions. Thus, we can observe that the relationship between government institutions and taxation is not yet sufficiently explored, as the research carried out focuses more on tax compliance and evasion.

Bassetto and Kocherlakota (2004) offer perhaps the key research for understanding the relationship between government performance and taxation. These authors consider a government that can only raise funds by levying distortionary taxes. They allow the government to collect taxes in a given period that are based on incomes earned in previous periods. The results show that once they do so, given any debt path, the government can adjust its tax policy to attain that debt path without affecting equilibrium allocations or prices. The above allows us to establish the following hypothesis:

Hypothesis 1: Government performance such as total central government debt (as GDP%) and claims on central government (annual growth as % of broad money) have a positive effect on taxes (income profits and capital gains).

The literature on the various effects of taxes on economic growth is extensive (Easterly & Rebelo, 1993; Stokey & Rebelo, 1995); hence, it is important to give an overview of these effects and review the proxies used to approach these variables. Lee and Gordon (2005) explore how tax policies affect a country's growth rate, using cross-country data between 1970 and 1997. These authors find that statutory corporate tax rates are significantly negatively correlated with cross-sectional differences in average economic growth rates, controlling for various other determinants of economic growth and other standard tax variables. In fixed-effect regressions, they again find that increases in corporate tax rates lead to lower future growth rates within countries. The coefficient estimates suggest that a cut in the corporate tax rate by 10 percentage points will raise the annual growth rate by one to two percentage points. Along the same lines, Arnold et al. (2011) present empirical results that support theoretical beliefs that economic growth (per capita GDP) can be increased by gradually moving the tax base toward consumption and immovable property (especially residential property). Authors discuss the point that in some cases, such as the reduction of corporate taxes and the top rate of personal income tax, it is unlikely that these growth-enhancing changes will help the recovery from the current crisis. At the same time, there are tax changes that appear to be bad for growth, such as reductions in sales taxes (particularly if they take the form of exemptions and reductions) and property taxes that would do little to speed recovery. They conclude that any necessary increases in revenue after recovery would be least harmful to growth if they were based on increasing recurrent taxes on immovable property and consumption taxes. The above reveals that the tax structure of a country is crucial for economic growth.

Sabir (2019) examines the impact of fiscal policy and institutional quality on the inclusive growth process of selected developing Asian countries. The author uses the system generalized method of moments to address the problem of endogeneity and omitted variable bias. Furthermore, this author finds that both fiscal policy and institutions have positive effects on inclusive growth (negative for the effect of tax revenue). These empirical results confirm that fiscal policy can work more efficiently in the presence of good quality institutions in the developing Asian countries and demonstrate that there is a need to transform the tax structure of the countries with a huge emphasis on the progressive tax system; this is likely to benefit the lower segment of the population. Sabir concludes that there is a need to develop institutions as they serve as a road map for the development of a country. Using an endogenous growth model, Denaux (2007) provides a theoretical and empirical investigation of the simultaneous effects of taxes and government spending on long-run economic growth. The author uses a two-sector model—one sector produces physical output and the other produces human capital—observing that the property tax is especially interesting because it is a major source of revenue for local government. This study finds that state-level fiscal policies affect economic growth, but county-level fiscal policies do not. Alinaghi and Reed (2021) study the same effects for the Economic Cooperation and Development (OECD) countries. The authors use the taxonomy from Gemmell et al. (2011) that predicts the growth effects from various tax-spending-deficit combinations, and find that a 10% increase in taxes is associated with a decrease in annual gross domestic product (GDP) growth of approximately -0.2%, when bundled as part of a tax negative tax-spending-deficit combination. A similar study was conducted by Baiardi et al. (2019), finding results similar to those of Alinaghi and Reed (2021), but in this case, finding greater significance and consistency in the long-term effects.

Some research has innovated the methodology to observe this relationship, and two studies are examples of this. On the one hand, Segura (2017) implements a general method of moments spatial dynamic panel data model estimation procedure to arrive at a more refined set of estimates for the growth effects attributed to state and local fiscal policy. The author finds that their own source taxes as the sum of property tax, sales tax, individual income tax, corporate income tax, and general charges have a negative and significant effect on Gross State Growth. On the other hand, Luo (2020) presents an interesting perspective on how population aging can spur economic growth through the increase in consumption taxes concerning the income taxes generated by the generational change. Both articles give force to what Jaimovich and Rebelo (2017) established: First, the tax rates adopted by different countries are generally uncorrelated with their growth performance, and second, countries that drastically reduce private incentives to invest severely hurt their growth performance. In their model, the effects of taxation on growth are highly nonlinear. Low tax rates have a small impact on long-run growth rates. However, as tax rates rise, their negative impact on growth rises dramatically. This suggests that the relationship between taxes and economic growth, such as GDP, is more complex than it seems and requires further study.

The literature has shown that GNI, NBD, and Gross Fixed Capital Formation are key determinants of economic growth (Diacon & Maha, 2015; Fritsch, 2004; Fritsch & Mueller, 2008; Kohli, 2003; Meyer & Meyer, 2019; Tyler, 1981). Therefore, we will review their relationship with taxes. First, Iwamoto and Shibata (2008) discuss how capital income taxation affects economic growth (also as GNI) and welfare in an endogenously growing world economy with perfect capital mobility and worldwide externalities; we find intergenerational conflicts arising from the change in the growth rate caused by a change in the source tax rate of the foreign country. Second, further literature can be found on the effects of taxation on entrepreneurship as business creation. In this way, Belitski et al. (2016) investigate how tax rates, and the interaction between corruption and tax rates, influence variations in entry across a panel of 72 countries in the period 2005–2011. The authors use panel estimations as well as several robustness checks to test these effects, using controls for economic development, the size of the state, and other regulatory and tax policy measures. They find that higher tax rates consistently discourage entry. Further, the authors find that although the direct influence of corruption on entry is also consistently negative, the interaction influence of corruption and tax rate is positive. Finally, Alves (2019) evaluates the share of tax revenues in GDP and investment outcomes, making use of Gross Fixed Capital Formation as a proxy for investment. This author concludes that there is a maximizing effect of income taxation on investment growth when revenues from this tax source are about 10.7%, thus indicating a negative effect of income taxes on investment such as Gross Fixed Capital Formation. Therefore, this detailed review of the literature on the effects of tax structures leads us to propose that:

Hypothesis 2: Taxes, such as those on profits on income and capital gains, have a negative effect on economic growth determinants such as GNI, NBD, and Gross Fixed Capital Formation.

6.3 Methodology

6.3.1 Data

To examine the previous hypotheses, we use the World Development Indicators to create an unbalanced (due to the fact that data from developing countries is often remarkably poor and often missing) panel data with a maximum of 4,749 observations from 2000 to 2018. The World Development Indicators is a compilation of relevant, high-quality, and internationally comparable statistics about global development and the fight against poverty. The database contains 1,400 time series indicators for 217 economies and more than 40 country groups, with data for many indicators going back more than 50 years (World Bank, 2020). Thanks to this dataset, important research has been conducted to understand different aspects such as the individual, family, and municipality-level predictors of economic growth around the world (Easterly, 1999; King & Levine, 1993), which are useful to inform prevention and intervention strategies.

For this research, the unbalanced panel data allows us to identify economic growth determinants (dependent variables that represent economic growth such as GNI, NBD, and Gross Fixed Capital Formation), as well as taxes (taxes on income, profits, and capital gains [% of total taxes]), government institution performance (such as central government debt [as a percentage of GDP] and claims on central government [annual growth as a percentage of broad money]), and entrepreneurship (such as NBD) taken as the independent variables. Based on the structure of this information at the country level, we complement the analysis by controlling for regional characteristics (for instance, inflation, labor force participation rate, livestock production index, industry value, and self-employment among others).

6.3.2 Empirical Strategy

To support the suggested hypotheses, a multi-level model (specifically simultaneous equations) is used to observe the direct effect that income taxes have on economic growth determinants, respectively, of country *i* in survey year *t*:

$$Growth_{it} = \alpha + \beta_1 \widehat{Taxes}_{it} + \beta_2 CC_{it} + \varepsilon_{it} \quad (3)$$

$$Taxes_{it} = \alpha + \beta_1 GD_{it} + \beta_2 NBD_{it} + \beta_3 CCG_{it} + \varepsilon_{it} \quad (2)$$

In Equation (2), tax outcomes are shown by $Taxes_{it}$, while this is directly affected by government performance such as government total debt (GD_{it}) and claims on central government (CCG_{it}), as well as entrepreneurship conditions such as New Business Density (NBD_{it}). However, Equation (1) is our main outcome and reveals the direct effect that the estimated taxes ($Taxes_{it}$) exert on economic growth at the country level ($Growth_{it}$), conditioned by CC_{it}, which contains variant controls over time, such as inflation consumer prices, livestock production index, bank liquid reserves, labor force participation, industry value, self-employment, and oil, natural gas, and mineral rent.

To embrace the simultaneity between Equations (1) and (2), we used a three-stage estimation (3SLS) (Wooldridge, 2002) that considers both the direct effect of taxes on economic growth determinants and the direct and indirect effects that government performance and entrepreneurship have on a country's economic growth. Specifically, Zellner and Theil (1962) developed the three-stage estimation method, and went one step further, by using the two-stage least squares estimated moment matrix of the structural disturbances to estimate all coefficients of the entire system simultaneously. This is what enables the technique to be a full information method, which is able to take into account the constraints of the parameters in different structural equations. The first advantage of the specification by 3SLS over OLS is that it has characteristics of total information. However, one could think that through the steps performed in this methodology the mean-square errors can increase, which would allow the OLS estimation to have a point in favor. Nevertheless, Greene

(2012) presents limited and full information estimates for Klein's Model I, and demonstrates that intuition suggests using system methods such as 3SLS, generalized methods of moments (GMM), and Full Information Maxime Likelihood (FILM) over single-equation methods, such as 2SLS and the Limited Information Maximum Likelihood (LIML). Moreover, Greene (2012) suggests that the only reason to use the latter methods is disappearing due to the computational advances of the software used for these estimates.

6.4 Results

Table 6.1 displays the descriptive statistics for all variables used in our models. In Table 6.1, we can see that the Gross National Income growth is around 4% on average annually, an expected mean value without any doubt (Miglietta et al. 2017). Another interesting fact is the average of NBD (3.141). Although the research of Carbonara et al. (2016) is cross-sectional, this value shows the discouragement that the sector in charge of business creation has received. Although the Gross Fixed Capital Formation shows a good average performance (6.402), we can observe that its standard deviation is high, and therefore must be careful when interpreting our results. Perhaps the crucial value to note in Table 6.1 is the mean of the taxes on income, profits, and capital gains as a percentage of total taxes, which is a high value given that the literature mentions the high probability that this type of tax is distorting. Regarding the other variables, it can be observed that the mean inflation is somewhat high. Some values are reassuring, such as self-employment (43.83), which is a strong proxy for entrepreneurship (Blanchflower et al., 2001), and it can boost the economic growth of a region under a labor system that provides guarantees. The mean value of oil, mineral, and gas rent does not appear to be very high, indicating the low dependence of countries on these products. Finally, a highly reassuring fact is the value of the industry (27.036 [as a percentage of GDP]) in the countries, as it reveals where the countries' production is going.

Focusing on our results, Table 6.2 shows our models through 3SLS regression, which has three clear advantages over multivariate regressions.

Table 6.1 Summary statistics

Variable	Mean	SD	Min	Max	P50	p99	N
GNI growth annual	3.940	4.481	–36.160	47.977	3.975	16.764	3512
New Business Density	3.141	4.317	0.006	39.039	1.601	21.737	1867
Gross Fixed Capital Formation	6.402	43.094	–65.689	2357.678	4.572	62.060	3420
Taxes	34.966	17.538	–4.469	95.424	34.384	90.212	2159
Inflation consumer prices	5.488	14.125	–30.243	513.906	3.550	36.522	4189
Labor force participation rate	38.794	15.854	4.582	83.412	37.106	76.899	4427
Livestock production index	106.818	20.590	32.64	364.86	103.07	182.34	4090
Industry value	27.036	12.089	1.305	87.7968	25.275	66.579	4435
Bank liquid reserves	21.147	20.744	0.204	390.11	17.361	100.485	3188
Self-employed total	43.833	27.087	0.408	94.833	38.864	93.345	4427
Real interest rate	6.409	9.368	-60.781	93.915	5.580	41.252	2467
Oil rent	4.178	9.512	0	78.541	0.083	48.432	4546
Natural gas rent	0.648	2.649	0	66.946	0.0147	8.508	4460
Mineral rent	1.135	3.246	0	46.624	0.046	18.011	4749
Central government debt	53.133	32.202	0.018	197.284	49.874	158.874	839
Claims on central government	0.604	24.537	–571.260	346.476	0.715	47.523	3014

N = observations; P = percentiles; SD = standard deviation

Table 6.2 Income taxes' effects on economic growth

	GNI growth					
	3SLS		2SLS		OLS	
	(1)	(2)	(3)	(4)	(5)	(6)
EQ1: Growth						
Taxes on income profits	-0.412**	-0.295*	-0.499**	-0.338*	-0.089	-0.089
	(0.158)	(0.143)	(0.165)	(0.147)	(0.066)	(0.066)
Inflation consumer prices	-0.402**	-0.348**	-0.523***	-0.422**	-0.265*	-0.265*
	(0.140)	(0.135)	(0.154)	(0.142)	(0.112)	(0.112)
Labor force participation rate	0.0217	0.025	0.270	0.170	0.015	0.015
	(0.128)	(0.122)	(0.139)	(0.128)	(0.095)	(0.095)
Livestock production index	-0.065	-0.069	-0.160*	-0.117	-0.051	-0.051
	(0.071)	(0.069)	(0.079)	(0.073)	(0.063)	(0.063)
Industry value	0.698***	0.630***	0.700***	0.624***	0.507***	0.507***
	(0.130)	(0.123)	(0.137)	(0.127)	(0.108)	(0.108)
Bank liquid reserves	0.097	0.084	0.055	0.058	0.062	0.062
	(0.077)	(0.077)	(0.086)	(0.081)	(0.079)	(0.079)
Self-employed total	0.114	0.136	0.247*	0.220*	0.179*	0.179*
	(0.089)	(0.087)	(0.097)	(0.092)	(0.086)	(0.086)
Oil rents (% of GDP)	0.576**	0.604**	0.527*	0.571**	0.639**	0.639**
	(0.208)	(0.201)	(0.221)	(0.210)	(0.200)	(0.200)
Natural gas rents (% of GDP)	-0.770***	-0.723**	-0.681**	-0.660**	-0.628**	-0.628**
	(0.221)	(0.220)	(0.246)	(0.233)	(0.225)	(0.225)
Mineral rents (% of GDP)	0.190*	0.169*	0.094	0.110	0.134	0.134
	(0.085)	(0.082)	(0.090)	(0.085)	(0.082)	(0.082)
Constant	-0.020	-0.005	0.099	0.065	0.012	0.012
	(0.097)	(0.093)	(0.103)	(0.097)	(0.090)	(0.090)

(*continued*)

Table 6.2 (continued)

	GNI growth					
	3SLS		2SLS		OLS	
	(1)	(2)	(3)	(4)	(5)	(6)
EQ2: Taxes						
Central government debt total	0.328***	0.338***	0.322***	0.325***	0.322***	0.325***
	(0.050)	(0.050)	(0.052)	(0.053)	(0.052)	(0.053)
New Business Density	0.440***	0.475***	0.486***	0.498***	0.486***	0.498***
	(0.068)	(0.069)	(0.072)	(0.073)	(0.072)	(0.073)
Claims on central government	0.464***	0.435**	0.331*	0.371*	0.331*	0.371*
	(0.133)	(0.141)	(0.146)	(0.152)	(0.146)	(0.152)
Industry value	0.892***	0.883***	0.883***	0.868***	0.883***	0.868***
	(0.099)	(0.100)	(0.101)	(0.105)	(0.101)	(0.105)
Oil rents (% of GDP)	-0.445**	-0.472**	-0.452**	-0.485**	-0.452**	-0.485**
	(0.146)	(0.145)	(0.149)	(0.152)	(0.149)	(0.152)
Mineral rents (% of GDP)	0.242**	0.220**	0.220**	0.187*	0.220**	0.187*
	(0.075)	(0.076)	(0.078)	(0.080)	(0.078)	(0.080)
Real interest rate (%)	0.184**	0.201**	0.178**	0.216**	0.178**	0.216**
	(0.063)	(0.066)	(0.068)	(0.071)	(0.068)	(0.071)
Constant	-0.124	-0.021	-0.121	0.048	-0.121	0.048
	(0.077)	(0.238)	(0.079)	(0.256)	(0.079)	(0.256)
FE	**NO**	**YES**	**NO**	**YES**	**NO**	**YES**
Observations	213	213	213	213	213	213
R-squared	0.220	0.286	0.201	0.282	0.328	0.328
	New Business Density					
	3SLS		**2SLS**		**OLS**	
	(7)	(8)	(9)	(10)	(11)	(12)

EQ1: Growth						
Taxes on income profits	-1.017**	-0.772**	-1.156**	-0.757**	0.105	0.105
	(0.355)	(0.245)	(0.370)	(0.252)	(0.061)	(0.061)
Inflation consumer prices	-0.404	-0.383*	-0.941**	-0.683**	-0.125	-0.125
	(0.246)	(0.189)	(0.290)	(0.211)	(0.107)	(0.107)
Labor force participation rate	0.430*	0.463***	0.927***	0.760***	0.398***	0.398***
	(0.169)	(0.122)	(0.183)	(0.132)	(0.064)	(0.064)
Livestock production index	-0.177	-0.201**	-0.395***	-0.314***	-0.140**	-0.140**
	(0.091)	(0.073)	(0.111)	(0.0838)	(0.051)	(0.051)
Industry value	0.351	0.237	0.446	0.244	-0.193*	-0.193*
	(0.214)	(0.159)	(0.228)	(0.166)	(0.085)	(0.085)
Bank liquid reserves	-0.006	-0.016	0.006	-0.012	-0.054	-0.054
	(0.079)	(0.070)	(0.111)	(0.090)	(0.066)	(0.066)
Self-employed total	-0.378***	-0.360***	-0.246	-0.291**	-0.388***	-0.388***
	(0.094)	(0.080)	(0.127)	(0.102)	(0.073)	(0.073)
Oil rents (% of GDP)	0.019	0.092	0.287	0.254	0.184	0.184
	(0.189)	(0.157)	(0.210)	(0.171)	(0.127)	(0.127)
Natural gas rents (% of GDP)	-0.450	-0.422*	-0.706*	-0.527	-0.139	-0.139
	(0.254)	(0.214)	(0.342)	(0.268)	(0.184)	(0.184)
Mineral rents (% of GDP)	0.216***	0.197***	0.162*	0.157**	0.146***	0.146***
	(0.065)	(0.053)	(0.0701)	(0.057)	(0.042)	(0.042)
Constant	-0.025	-0.009	0.175	0.098	-0.066	-0.066
	(0.122)	(0.096)	(0.132)	(0.103)	(0.069)	(0.069)

(continued)

Table 6.2 (continued)

	GNI growth					
	3SLS		**2SLS**		**OLS**	
	(1)	(2)	(3)	(4)	(5)	(6)
EQ2: Taxes						
Central government debt total	0.209***	0.238***	0.155***	0.162***	0.155***	0.162***
	(0.040)	(0.040)	(0.046)	(0.047)	(0.046)	(0.047)
New Business Density						
Claims on central government	0.168	0.245*	0.309*	0.355*	0.309*	0.355*
	(0.114)	(0.118)	(0.140)	(0.147)	(0.140)	(0.147)
Industry value	0.567***	0.584***	0.594***	0.600***	0.594***	0.600***
	(0.082)	(0.081)	(0.084)	(0.085)	(0.084)	(0.085)
Oil rents (% of GDP)	-0.266*	-0.285*	-0.348**	-0.375**	-0.348**	-0.375**
	(0.125)	(0.125)	(0.130)	(0.132)	(0.130)	(0.132)
Mineral rents (% of GDP)	0.111*	0.109*	0.094*	0.090	0.094*	0.090
	(0.046)	(0.045)	(0.047)	(0.048)	(0.047)	(0.048)
Real interest rate (%)	0.137**	0.187***	0.207**	0.243***	0.207**	0.243***
	(0.049)	(0.054)	(0.065)	(0.067)	(0.065)	(0.067)
Constant	0.000	0.130	-0.019	0.034	-0.019	0.034
	(0.065)	(0.167)	(0.067)	(0.208)	(0.067)	(0.208)
FE	**NO**	**YES**	**NO**	**YES**	**NO**	**YES**
Observations	260	260	260	260	260	260
R-squared	-0.712	-0.257	-0.709	-0.136	0.368	0.368
	Gross Fixed Capital Formation					
	3SLS		**2SLS**		**OLS**	
	(13)	(14)	(15)	(16)	(17)	(18)

EQ1: Growth						
Taxes on income profits	–0.159*	–0.125*	–0.233**	–0.161**	–0.043*	–0.043*
	(0.067)	(0.0588)	(0.071)	(0.060)	(0.022)	(0.022)
Inflation consumer prices	–0.100	–0.0890	–0.187**	–0.140*	–0.062	–0.062
	(0.055)	(0.0520)	(0.062)	(0.055)	(0.038)	(0.038)
Labor force participation rate	0.015	0.0185	0.087*	0.058	0.010	0.010
	(0.034)	(0.0323)	(0.039)	(0.034)	(0.024)	(0.024)
Livestock production index	–0.047	–0.0548*	–0.104***	–0.085**	–0.054*	–0.054*
	(0.026)	(0.0257)	(0.030)	(0.027)	(0.021)	(0.021)
Industry value	0.178***	0.162***	0.219***	0.181***	0.118***	0.118***
	(0.050)	(0.0462)	(0.054)	(0.048)	(0.035)	(0.035)
Bank liquid reserves	0.032	0.0265	0.024	0.021	0.016	0.016
	(0.025)	(0.0251)	(0.029)	(0.027)	(0.025)	(0.025)
Self-employed total	0.003	0.0118	0.044	0.038	0.027	0.027
	(0.028)	(0.0278)	(0.032)	(0.030)	(0.028)	(0.028)
Oil rents (% of GDP)	–0.076	–0.0678	–0.037	–0.044	–0.055	–0.055
	(0.049)	(0.0462)	(0.052)	(0.048)	(0.045)	(0.045)
Natural gas rents (% of GDP)	–0.064	–0.0546	–0.118	–0.084	–0.028	–0.028
	(0.070)	(0.0690)	(0.082)	(0.075)	(0.066)	(0.066)
Mineral rents (% of GDP)	0.084**	0.0787**	0.073*	0.071**	0.068**	0.068**
	(0.028)	(0.0264)	(0.030)	(0.027)	(0.025)	(0.025)
Constant	–0.082*	–0.0769*	–0.034	–0.048	–0.071*	–0.071*
	(0.032)	(0.0303)	(0.034)	(0.031)	(0.027)	(0.027)

(continued)

Table 6.2 (continued)

	GNI growth					
	3SLS		2SLS		OLS	
	(1)	(2)	(3)	(4)	(5)	(6)
EQ2: Taxes						
Central government debt total	0.296***	0.310***	0.310***	0.308***	0.310***	0.308***
	(0.046)	(0.0476)	(0.050)	(0.051)	(0.050)	(0.051)
New Business Density	0.379***	0.402***	0.416***	0.420***	0.416***	0.420***
	(0.058)	(0.0601)	(0.063)	(0.064)	(0.063)	(0.064)
Claims on central government	0.481***	0.479***	0.378**	0.413**	0.378**	0.413**
	(0.124)	(0.135)	(0.141)	(0.148)	(0.141)	(0.148)
Industry value	0.892***	0.888***	0.886***	0.884***	0.886***	0.884***
	(0.095)	(0.0968)	(0.097)	(0.101)	(0.097)	(0.101)
Oil rents (% of GDP)	-0.348**	-0.345**	-0.312*	-0.335**	-0.312*	-0.335**
	(0.122)	(0.122)	(0.126)	(0.128)	(0.126)	(0.128)
Mineral rents (% of GDP)	0.245***	0.240**	0.250**	0.226**	0.250**	0.226**
	(0.073)	(0.0739)	(0.076)	(0.078)	(0.076)	(0.078)
Real interest rate (%)	0.227***	0.232***	0.192**	0.227***	0.192**	0.227***
	(0.056)	(0.0615)	(0.064)	(0.067)	(0.064)	(0.067)
Constant	-0.111	-0.131	-0.104	-0.050	-0.104	-0.050
	(0.069)	(0.211)	(0.070)	(0.233)	(0.070)	(0.233)
FE	**NO**	**YES**	**NO**	**YES**	**NO**	**YES**
Observations	227	227	227	227	227	227
R-squared	-0.011	0.066	-0.156	0.023	0.135	0.135

Standard errors in parentheses: * p<0.05; ** p<0.01; *** p<0.001.

First, it fits the data better than OLS (Wooldridge, 2002). Second, it captures the indirect effects of our independent variables (central government debt, claims on central government, and NBD) in Equation (2) on economic growth (Equation [1]) through taxes, such as taxes on income, profits, and capital gains. The latter, related to above, shows us the dependence of tax decisions on government performance, which ultimately influences economic growth. Therefore, our analysis relies on Table 6.2.

Table 6.2 displays the estimation results for the relationships outlined in the hypotheses development. Models 1–18 are composed of two equations, the first one shows the effects of taxes on income, profits, and capital gain; control variables on sector activity such as oil, mineral, and gas rents; and control variables on economic performance, such as real interest rate, inflation consumer prices, industry value, among others. The second equation shows the effects of government performance, such as government debt and claims on government, and the entrepreneurship context, such as NBD on taxes on income, profits, and capital gain. The effects of taxes on income, profits, and capital gain on economic growth, such as GNI growth, are shown in models 1–6, NBD in models 7–12, and Gross Fixed Capital Formation in models 13–18. It should be noted that in models 1–6 and 13–18 there is no modification in the second equation, but in models 7–12 we use the NBD as a dependent variable; it is removed from Equation (2). Table 6.2 shows the results with different estimation methods, and each method shows the effects with and without fixed effects. On the one hand, focusing on the results of OLS estimation, we can conclude that this type of estimation does not adequately capture the effects of our relationship (see models 5, 6 and 11, 12), as Wooldridge (2002) states, in our case due to the effects of taxes on economic growth. On the other hand, estimates by the 2SLS method adequately capture the expected effects in both equations. However, this method does not pick up the errors in Equation (2) and transforms them into an estimation tool for Equation (1), as does the 3SLS method. Even so, this method serves as robustness to indicate that the established relationships are adequate. Another thing to consider is that when we introduce fixed effects, the R^2 of most models improves, but we also lose explanatory power in key estimators, such as taxes.

Concerning the hypothesis testing, we suggest in Hypothesis 1 that government performance, such as total central government debt and claims on central government, have a positive and significant effect on taxes (income profits and capital gains). All models support this hypothesis. When government performance, such as total central government debt and claims on central government, increases by 1% in taxes, income profits and capital gains increase by 0.32% and 0.46%, respectively (model 1 fits the data better). This complements what Bassetto and Kocherlakota (2004) have found about the significant positive effect of government performance on taxes. If we focus on Equation (2) (model 1), it can be observed that both effects have a significance of 0.01%. This indicates that it appears that short-term and long-term decisions to cover some expenditures play a fundamental role in tax burden decisions. An interesting result in models 1, 6, and 13–18 (Equation [2]) is the tautological effect of business creation on tax revenues of income, profits, and gain. When there is a 1% increase in NBD, the value of income taxes increases by 0.44%. This is more than interesting because it initiates an important debate on the use of these taxes, and whether taxes have a negative effect on business creation (Belitski et al., 2016), but business creation has a positive effect on taxes. This implies that there should be more incentives for business creation; however, we will discuss this in the conclusions.

Hypothesis 2 has stated that tax revenues, such as taxes on income profits and capital gains, have a negative effect on economic growth determinants such as GNI, NBD, and Gross Fixed Capital Formation. All models (except the OLS estimation method for NBD) support this hypothesis. When taxes on income, profits, and gain increase by 1%, economic growth determinants such as GNI growth, NBD, and Gross Fixed Capital Formation decrease by 0.41%, 1.01%, and 0.15%, respectively. These findings confirm the knowledge in current literature (e.g., Alves, 2019; Belitski et al., 2016; Iwamoto & Shibata, 2008), showing tax's effects on economic growth determinants. These results show that the economic growth determinant that suffers most from the effect of taxes on income is the NBD, which leads us to think that taxes are stifling the creation of companies that drive innovation, which spurs economic development (Nelson & Pack, 1999).

It is also important to observe what happens with the utilized controls. If we focus on model 1, we can observe that we find some expected behaviors such as the GNI growth decrease by 0.40% when there is a 1% increase in inflation consumer prices. Some positive results show that a 1% increase in the value of industry (including construction) generates a GNI growth increase by 0.69%, supporting the idea that industrialized processes and entrepreneurship are crucial for economic growth (Opoku & Yan, 2019; Van Praag & Versloot, 2007; Yerrabati, 2021). However, we still find discouraging results, such as the positive effect of oil rents and mineral rents on economic growth. If we look at what happens with NBD, we find that with a 1% increase in female labor participation the NBD increases by 0.43%. Still, the crucial result in models 7–12 and 13–18 is the negative effect of taxes on NBD and Gross Fixed Capital Formation, thus complementing the literature (Braunerhjelm et al., 2021).

6.5 Discussion and Conclusions

The bulk of the literature attempting to explain the relationship between tax structure (in particular income, profit, sales, gain, consumption) and economic growth has been focused on analyzing direct effects, most of the time not taking into account the determinants of such growth (Lee & Gordon, 2005; Sabir, 2019) and the direct effects of government performance on such taxes and the indirect effect of such performance on the determinants of economic growth. That is why this research has tried to fill some gaps by exploring how the relationship between taxes on income, profits, and gain, and economic growth determinants outcomes is conditioned by government performance, such as government total debt. In this regard, we have derived theoretical support from North (1990) and Steinmo (1989), who inspired Bassetto and Kocherlakota (2004) to suggest that government institutions are key factors in determining the taxes that negatively influence economic growth.

Using North (2005) and Steinmo's (1989) theoretical bases, as well as a 3SLS empirical strategy, we arrived at three important findings. The first result confirms that taxes on income, profit, and gain have a negative and significant effect on economic growth determinants such as GNI growth, NBD, and Gross Fixed Capital Formation, thus reinforcing the lack of literature in this area (Alves, 2019; Belitski et al., 2016; Iwamoto & Shibata, 2008). However, an interesting behavior is observed based on this result. The determinant of economic growth that suffers most from the effect of taxes is Gross Fixed Capital Formation, demonstrating the strong discouraging nature of taxes to industrialization and innovation. This opens the possibility for a new research agenda in which there is synergy between taxes and capital formation.

The second result argues in a tautologous way that government performance, such as central government debt and claims on central government, has a significant positive effect, respectively, on taxes (income, profits, and gain), as supported in a small quantity of literature (Bassetto & Kocherlakota, 2004). This result fills a gap in the literature on this relationship. Although the most important part of this result lies in the mechanism of the indirect effects of government performance on economic growth, given that taxes on income negatively affect the determinants of economic growth, it can be concluded that government performance is crucial for the impact of these taxes.

The third result reflects the scarcity of literature on the effects of NBD on taxes revenues. This result opens a broad discussion on the endogeneity problems faced by government decisions on taxation, given that even though new ventures represent an increase in tax revenue, it is certain that taxes negatively affect the determinants of economic growth. This creates major challenges for policymakers.

6.5.1 Theoretical Implications

The results of this research allow us to establish theoretical implications about tax structure and its relationship to economic growth and government institutions. Two important theoretical implications will be shown below.

First, there is bulk literature on the various effects of taxes on economic growth (Easterly & Rebelo, 1993; Stokey & Rebelo, 1995). Key research like Sabir (2019) and Denaux (2007) examines the impact of fiscal policy (tax structure) on the growth process of economies. However, these studies support the direct effects of taxes on economic growth such as GDP. This research addresses the gap in the literature, in which the tax structure has direct effects on the determinants of economic growth such as GNI, NBD, and capital formation. These determinants have effects on economic growth (Diacon & Maha, 2015; Fritsch, 2004; Fritsch & Mueller, 2008; Kohli, 2003; Meyer & Meyer, 2019; Tyler, 1981), but they also play a key role in the process of economic development.

The second theoretical implication is aimed at assessing how tautological the relationship between government and tax structure is. This supports the idea that although taxes are the main source of distortion to economic growth, there is a government action that can control the magnitude of this tax structure. Therefore, this research helps to reinforce the ideas proposed by Bassetto and Kocherlakota (2004) for understanding the relationship between government performance and taxation. Authors consider a government that can only raise funds by levying distortionary taxes. They allow the government to collect taxes in each period that are based on incomes earned in previous periods. The results show that once they do so, given any debt path, the government can adjust its tax policy to attain that debt path without affecting equilibrium allocations or prices. This indicates the importance of fiscal policies and policymakers' decisions, as they can positively or negatively influence the country's economic growth.

6.5.2 Policy Implications

A major challenge of this research is being able to make clear recommendations to policymakers, applicable to the policy framework of the countries. We believe our study enables policymakers to pay greater attention to their performance in debt, the support for the creation of new businesses, and the way tax revenues are used. Ghourchian and Yilmazkuday (2020) compare the effects of government consumption and government debt on economic growth using data from 83 countries, including both developed and developing markets, over the period between 1960 and 2014. Authors suggest that the restrictions on government expenditure to prevent negative growth are more important for countries with lower trade openness, lower inflation, or greater financial depth, whereas the restrictions on government debt are shown to be more important for countries with higher trade openness, lower inflation, and greater financial depth. Although this research presents direct effects of government performance on economic growth, it shows us the importance of policy decisions.

An important result of this research is the clear effect of NBD on tax revenue. However, the literature has shown the discouragement generated by taxes on business creation and entry (Belitski et al., 2016). This presents an interesting challenge for policymakers, who must find an optimal tax on income, profits, and gain for new ventures that do not create discouragement that could lead to tax evasion (Alm, 2012; Bame-Aldred et al., 2013). An interesting point to consider is how the revenues from this type of tax are used, given that if they are used in the wrong way, it not only discourages the creation of companies but also produces a huge fiscal gap for the country's finances. This indicates that the best option is to try to reduce income on taxes, profits, and gain, and replace them with sales taxes, which have positive effects on growth in some regions (Hall & Kanaan, 2020).

6.5.3 Limitations and Future Research

It should be noted that the results, as well as theoretical and policy implications obtained in this research, play an important role in the literature on tax structure, government institutions, and economic growth, but undoubtedly future lines of research emerge from the limitations observed in this chapter. The first limitation refers to the impossibility of determining what role government institutions play in economic growth, as we were able to determine its effect, but not its path, especially the mechanism of transmission. The second limitation arises when we observe that taxes on income, profit, and gain have a significant effect on economic growth determinants, given that through this methodology we cannot observe a substitution effect of migrating to other types of taxes to boost economic growth. The third limitation is related to the fact that the panel is unbalanced, which reduces the consistency of the results, given the number of observations at the time the estimations were made. In this sense, future research should focus on obtaining substitution effects within tax rates and their effects on economic growth.

References

Alinaghi, N., & Reed, W. R. (2021). Taxes and Economic Growth in OECD Countries: A Meta-analysis. *Public Finance Review, 49*(1), 3–40. https://doi.org/10.1177/1091142120961775

Alm, J. (2012). Measuring, explaining, and controlling tax evasion: Lessons from theory, experiments, and field studies. *International Tax and Public Finance, 19*(1), 54–77. https://doi.org/10.1007/s10797-011-9171-2

Alt, J. E., & Lowry, R. C. (1994). Divided Government, Fiscal Institutions, and Budget Deficits: Evidence from the States. *American Political Science Review, 88*(4), 811–828. https://doi.org/10.2307/2082709

Alves, J. (2019). The impact of tax structure on investment: An empirical assessment for OECD countries. *Public Sector Economics, 43*(3), 291–309. https://doi.org/10.3326/pse.43.3.4

Androniceanu, A., Gherghina, R., & Ciobănașu, M. (2019). The interdependence between fiscal public policies and tax evasion. *Administratie Si Management Public, 2019*(32), 32–41. https://doi.org/10.24818/amp/2019.32-03

Aparicio, S., Urbano, D., & Audretsch, D. (2016). Institutional factors, opportunity entrepreneurship and economic growth: Panel data evidence. *Technological Forecasting and Social Change, 102*, 45–61.

Arbel, Y., Fialkoff, C., & Kerner, A. (2019). Public policy for reducing tax evasion: implications of the Yule–Simpson paradox. *Applied Economics Letters, 26*(13), 1092–1099. https://doi.org/10.1080/13504851.2018.1537471

Arnold, J. M., Brys, B., Heady, C., Johansson, Å., Schwellnus, C., & Vartia, L. (2011). Tax Policy for Economic Recovery and Growth. *Economic Journal, 121*(550), 1. https://doi.org/10.1111/j.1468-0297.2010.02415.x

Auerbach, A. J., & Gorodnichenko, Y. (2012). Measuring the output responses to fiscal policy. *American Economic Journal: Economic Policy, 4*(2), 1–27. https://doi.org/10.1257/pol.4.2.1

Baiardi, D., Profeta, P., Puglisi, R., & Scabrosetti, S. (2019). Tax policy and economic growth: does it really matter? *International Tax and Public Finance, 26*(2), 282–316. https://doi.org/10.1007/s10797-018-9494-3

Bame-Aldred, C. W., Cullen, J. B., Martin, K. D., & Parboteeah, K. P. (2013). National culture and firm-level tax evasion. *Journal of Business Research, 66*(3), 390–396. https://doi.org/10.1016/j.jbusres.2011.08.020

Barro, R. J. (1974). Are government bonds net wealth? *Journal of Political Economy, 82*(6), 1095–1117. https://doi.org/10.1086/260266

Bassetto, M., & Kocherlakota, N. (2004). On the irrelevance of government debt when taxes are distortionary. *Statistics and Probability Letters, 66*(4), 299–304. https://doi.org/10.1016/j.jmoneco.2002.12.001

Belitski, M., Chowdhury, F., & Desai, S. (2016). Taxes, corruption, and entry. *Small Business Economics, 47*(1), 201–216. https://doi.org/10.1007/s11187-016-9724-y

Blakely, T., Cleghorn, C., Mizdrak, A., Waterlander, W., Nghiem, N., Swinburn, B., et al. (2020). The effect of food taxes and subsidies on population health and health costs: a modelling study. *The Lancet Public Health, 5*(7), e404–e413. https://doi.org/10.1016/S2468-2667(20)30116-X

Blanchflower, D. G., Oswald, A., & Stutzer, A. (2001). Latent entrepreneurship across nations. *European Economic Review, 45*(4–6), 680–691. https://doi.org/10.1016/S0014-2921(01)00137-4

Braunerhjelm, P., Eklund, J. E., & Thulin, P. (2021). Taxes, the tax administrative burden and the entrepreneurial life cycle. *Small Business Economics, 56*(2), 681–694. https://doi.org/10.1007/s11187-019-00195-0

Bruno, R. L. (2019). Tax enforcement, tax compliance and tax morale in transition economies: A theoretical model. *European Journal of Political Economy, 56*, 193–211. https://doi.org/10.1016/j.ejpoleco.2018.08.006

Carbonara, E., Santarelli, E., & Tran, H. T. (2016). De jure determinants of new firm formation: how the pillars of constitutions influence entrepreneurship. *Small Business Economics, 47*(1), 139–162. https://doi.org/10.1007/s11187-016-9715-z

Cox, J. C., Rider, M., & Sen, A. (2018). Tax Incidence: Do Institutions Matter? *An Experimental Study. Public Finance Review, 46*(6), 899–925. https://doi.org/10.1177/1091142117700720

Darnihamedani, P., Block, J. H., Hessels, J., & Simonyan, A. (2018). Taxes, start-up costs, and innovative entrepreneurship. *Small Business Economics, 51*(2), 355–369. https://doi.org/10.1007/s11187-018-0005-9

De Miglietta, P., Leo, F., & Toma, P. (2017). Environmental Kuznets curve and the water footprint: an empirical analysis. *Water and Environment Journal, 31*(1), 20–30. https://doi.org/10.1111/wej.12211

Denaux, Z. S. (2007). Endogenous growth, taxes and government spending: Theory and evidence. *Review of Development Economics, 11*(1), 124–138. https://doi.org/10.1111/j.1467-9361.2007.00377.x

Diacon, P. E., & Maha, L.-G. (2015). The Relationship between Income, Consumption and GDP: A Time Series, Cross-Country Analysis. *Procedia Economics and Finance, 23*, 1535–1543. https://doi.org/10.1016/s2212-5671(15)00374-3

Djankov, S., Ganser, T., McLiesh, C., Ramalho, R., & Shleifer, A. (2010). The effect of corporate taxes on investment and entrepreneurship. *American Economic Journal: Macroeconomics, 2*(3), 31–64. https://doi.org/10.1257/mac.2.3.31

Easterly, W. (1999). Life during growth. *Journal of Economic Growth, 4*(3), 239–276. https://doi.org/10.1023/A:1009882702130

Easterly, W., & Rebelo, S. (1993). Fiscal policy and economic growth. *Journal of Monetary Economics, 32*(3), 417–458. https://doi.org/10.1016/0304-3932(93)90025-B

Eissa, N., & Liebman, J. B. (1996). Labor supply response to the earned income tax credit. *Quarterly Journal of Economics, 111*(2), 605–637. https://doi.org/10.2307/2946689

Faria-e-Castro, M. (2021). Fiscal policy during a pandemic. *Journal of Economic Dynamics and Control, 125*, 1. https://doi.org/10.1016/j.jedc.2021.104088

Fritsch, M. (2004). Entrepreneurship, entry and performance of new business compared in two growth regimes: East and West Germany. *Journal of Evolutionary Economics, 14*, 525–542. https://doi.org/10.1007/s00191-004-0230-z

Fritsch, M., & Mueller, P. (2008). The effect of new business formation on regional development over time: The case of Germany. *Small Business Economics, 30*(1), 15–29. https://doi.org/10.1007/s11187-007-9067-9

Gemmell, N., Kneller, R., & Sanz, I. (2011). The timing and persistence of fiscal policy impacts on growth: evidence from OECD countries. *The Economic Journal, 121*(550), F33–F58.

Ghourchian, S., & Yilmazkuday, H. (2020). Government consumption, government debt and economic growth. *Review of Development Economics, 24*(2), 589–605. https://doi.org/10.1111/rode.12661

Gokalp, O. N., Lee, S. H., & Peng, M. W. (2017). Competition and corporate tax evasion: An institution-based view. *Journal of World Business, 52*(2), 258–269. https://doi.org/10.1016/j.jwb.2016.12.006

Greene, W. H. (2012). *Econometric Analysis* (7th ed.). Prentice Hall.

Hall, J. L., & Kanaan, D. Z. (2020). State Tax Policy, Municipal Choice, and Local Economic Development Outcomes: A Structural Equation Modeling Approach to Performance Assessment. *Public Administration Review*. https://doi.org/10.1111/puar.13165

Iwamoto, Y., & Shibata, A. (2008). International and intergenerational aspects of capital income taxation in an endogenously growing world economy. *Review of International Economics, 16*(2), 383–399. https://doi.org/10.1111/j.1467-9396.2007.00719.x

Jaimovich, N., & Rebelo, S. (2017). Nonlinear effects of taxation on growth. *Journal of Political Economy, 125*(1), 265–291. https://doi.org/10.1086/689607

Johnston, A. C. (2021). Unemployment Insurance Taxes and Labor Demand: Quasi-Experimental Evidence from Administrative Data. *American Economic Journal: Economic Policy, 13*(1), 266–293. https://doi.org/10.1257/pol.20190031

King, R. G., & Levine, R. (1993). Finance and growth: Schumpeter might be right. *Quarterly Journal of Economics, 108*(3), 717–737. https://doi.org/10.2307/2118406

Kohli, U. (2003). GDP growth accounting: A national income function approach. *Review of Income and Wealth, 49*(1), 23–34. https://doi.org/10.1111/1475-4991.00072

Kormendi, R. C. (1983). Government Debt, Government Spending, and Private Sector Behavior. *The American Economic Review, 73*(5), 994–1010.

Lee, Y., & Gordon, R. H. (2005). Tax structure and economic growth. *Journal of Public Economics, 89*(5–6), 1027–1043. https://doi.org/10.1016/j.jpubeco.2004.07.002

Lucas, R. E., & Stokey, N. L. (1983). Optimal fiscal and monetary policy in an economy without capital. *Journal of Monetary Economics, 12*(1), 55–93. https://doi.org/10.1016/0304-3932(83)90049-1

Luo, W. (2020). Demography and economic growth: the effect of tax composition. *Applied Economics Letters, 27*(20), 1629–1634. https://doi.org/10.1080/13504851.2019.1707761

Meyer, N., & Meyer, D. F. (2019). Examining the impact of entrepreneurial activity on employment and economic growth: The case of the visegrád countries. *Polish Journal of Management Studies, 20*(1), 277–292. https://doi.org/10.17512/pjms.2019.20.1.25

Nelson, R. R., & Pack, H. (1999). The Asian miracle and modern growth theory. *Economic Journal, 109*(457), 416–436. https://doi.org/10.1111/1468-0297.00455

Neog, Y., & Gaur, A. K. (2020). Tax structure and economic growth: a study of selected Indian states. *Journal of Economic Structures, 9*(1), 1. https://doi.org/10.1186/s40008-020-00215-3

North, D. C. (1990). *Institutions, institutional change and economic performance.* Cambridge University Press.

North, D. C. (2005). *Understanding the process of economic change.* Princeton University Press.

North, D. C., & Weingast, B. R. (1989). Constitutions and Commitment: The Evolution of Institutions Governing Public Choice in Seventeenth-Century England. *The Journal of Economic History, 49*(4), 803–832. https://doi.org/10.1017/S0022050700009451

Opoku, E. E. O., & Yan, I. K. M. (2019). Industrialization as driver of sustainable economic growth in Africa. *Journal of International Trade and Economic Development, 28*(1), 30–56. https://doi.org/10.1080/09638199.2018.1483416

Oyarzo, M., & Paredes, D. (2021). The impact of mining taxes on public education: Evidence for mining municipalities in Chile. *Resources Policy, 70*, 1. https://doi.org/10.1016/j.resourpol.2018.05.018

Ricciuti, R., Savoia, A., & Sen, K. (2019). How do political institutions affect fiscal capacity? Explaining taxation in developing economies. *Journal of Institutional Economics, 15*(2), 351–380. https://doi.org/10.1017/S1744137418000097

Romero-Jordán, D., Sanz-Labrador, I., & Sanz-Sanz, J. F. (2020). Is the corporation tax a barrier to productivity growth? *Small Business Economics, 55*(1), 23–38. https://doi.org/10.1007/s11187-019-00136-x

Room, R. Babor, T., & Rehm, J. (2005). Alcohol and public health. Lancet. Elsevier B.V. https://doi.org/10.1016/S0140-6736(05)70276-2

Sabir, S. (2019). Fiscal policy, institutions and inclusive growth: evidence from the developing Asian countries. *International Journal of Social Economics, 46*(6), 822–837. https://doi.org/10.1108/IJSE-08-2018-0419

von Schiller, A. (2016). Business Organisations, Party Systems and Tax Composition in Developing Countries: A Comparison between Colombia and Peru. *Journal of Development Studies, 52*(12), 1722–1743. https://doi.org/10.1080/00220388.2016.1153074

Segura, J. (2017). The effect of state and local taxes on economic growth: A spatial dynamic panel approach. *Papers in Regional Science, 96*(3), 627–645. https://doi.org/10.1111/pirs.12221

Steinmo, S. (1989). Political Institutions and Tax Policy in the United States, Sweden, and Britain. *World Politics, 41*(4), 500–535. https://doi.org/10.2307/2010528

Stokey, N. L., & Rebelo, S. (1995). Growth effects of flat-rate taxes. *Journal of Political Economy, 103*(3), 519–550. https://doi.org/10.1086/261993

Tyler, W. G. (1981). Growth and export expansion in developing countries. Some empirical evidence. *Journal of Development Economics, 9*(1), 121–130. https://doi.org/10.1016/0304-3878(81)90007-9

Van Praag, C. M., & Versloot, P. H. (2007). What is the value of entrepreneurship? A review of recent research. *Small Business Economics, 29*(4), 351–382. https://doi.org/10.1007/s11187-007-9074-x

Wooldridge, J. M. (2002). *Econometric Analysis of Cross Section and Panel Data.* MIT Press.

World Bank. (2020). World development indicators | data. World Development Indicators, (July), 1–4. Retrieved from https://databank.worldbank.org/data/download/GDP.pdf

Yerrabati, S. (2021). Self-employment and economic growth in developing countries: is more self-employment better? Journal of Economic Studies. https://doi.org/10.1108/JES-08-2020-0419

Zellner, A., & Theil, H. (1962). Three-Stage Least Squares: Simultaneous Estimation of Simultaneous Equations. *Econometrica, 30*(1), 54–78.

7

The Effects of the Internal Rate of Return on Economic Development: A Country-Level Study

Diego Gomez, Sebastian Aparicio, David Urbano, and Diego Martinez-Moya

7.1 Introduction

Investment decisions are a fundamental part of a company's structure since they determine how profitable a project or business initiative is (Khresiat, 2019). Even so, few studies have investigated the macroeconomic effects of such decisions; this literature becomes non-existent if we inquire about the effects that investment decision measures such as the internal rate of return (IRR) or the return on equity (ROE) have on

---

D. Gomez • D. Martinez-Moya
Fundación ECSIM, Medellin, Colombia

S. Aparicio (✉) • D. Urbano
Department of Business, Universitat Autònoma de Barcelona, Cerdanyola del Vallés, Barcelona, Spain

Centre for Entrepreneurship and Social Innovation Research (CREIS), Universitat Autònoma de Barcelona, Sabadell, Barcelona, Spain
e-mail: Sebastian.Aparicio@uab.cat

D. Gomez et al. (eds.), *Driving Complexity in Economic Development*,
https://doi.org/10.1007/978-3-031-34386-5_7

economic development such as GDP per capita (Combey & Togbenou, 2017; de Leon, 2020; Yassin & Derar, 2014). Very little research has attempted to unravel this relationship, which is why this study attempts to fill this gap in the literature, in addition to trying to identify the main determinants of IRR.

To achieve this, we use a theoretical basis focused on observing the potential effects that certain financial variables have on the economic growth of nations. The literature studying economic development is extensive, and the effects of financial behavior on economic development have been extensively studied. However, observing the effects of the proposed relationships is more than interesting, as there are challenges such as the limited literature and the choice of a consistent variable to measure investment decisions. Based on the theoretical framework of economic growth (Acemoglu, 2008; Lucas, 1988) and its relationship with the financial world, we proceed to propose two hypotheses that support the positive effect of decision investment measures such as IRR and ROE on economic growth such as GDP per capita, in addition to observing the determinants of IRR and variables related to country risk, such as the lending interest rate, taxes and contribution rates, cost of construction permits, electricity cost, and exporting cost. To test these hypotheses, we use the World Development Indicators to create unbalanced panel data with a maximum of 2395 observations from 2005 to 2018 and also use a multilevel equation model (i.e., simultaneous equations) to develop a three-stage estimation (3SLS) (Wooldridge, 2002). We use this 3SLS estimation to consider both the direct effect of IRR and the direct and indirect effects that the lending interest rate, taxes and contribution rates, the cost of construction permits, electricity costs, and exporting costs have on IRR and country economic growth, respectively. To develop these estimations, we use the IRR variable proposed by Feenstra et al. (2015), and also create our measure of ROE so that its effects on economic growth can be compared with the dependent variable IRR.

The results reveal that country risk factors such as the lending interest rate, taxes and contribution rates, the cost of construction permits, electricity costs, and exporting costs harm investment decision measures such as IRR. More importantly, they support the hypothesis that IRR has a positive effect on economic growth through GDP per capita. When investment decision measures such as IRR and ROE each increase by

1%, economic growth such as GDP per capita increases by 1.839% and 6.717%, respectively. These results strengthen the current literature (Yassin & Derar, 2014). Furthermore, they also clarify the positive effect of investment decision measures such as IRR and ROE on economic growth; however, they highlight that the ROE variable was more significant and had a greater impact on growth.

These results not only prompt further discussion on the macroeconomic effects of investment decision measures such as IRR and ROE but also establish the importance of companies for the proper development of society. Companies are in charge of gearing the knowledge of economic agents and transforming it into added value; even so, if we affect investment decisions through impositions such as increasing taxes or interest rates, we discourage companies from increasing their production and plans for expansion.

This research is structured as follows. The next section presents the theoretical framework, in which we establish economic development and its relationship with finances as the main axis of the research. Afterward, we explain the methodology, involving the source of the data and the empirical strategy. The results are subsequently presented. Finally, we conclude and discuss the study's theoretical and policy implications.

7.2 Conceptual Framework

Economic development is widely studied. Indeed, the literature focuses on how it is generated (Lucas, 1988; Nelson, 2007), its externalities (Azariadis & Drazen, 1990; Helmsing, 2001), and the fundamental factors to generate economic development (Acs et al., 2008; Fagerberg & Srholec, 2018; Moschos, 1989), among many other research questions that illustrate the complexity of economic development. Among the theories of economic development, the mainstream tries to explain this phenomenon through economic growth employing internal factors to the system, endogenous growth (Howitt, 2010). There are many factors in the literature through which to drive such growth, such as institutions (Bosma et al., 2018; Glaeser et al., 2004), entrepreneurship (Acs et al., 2009; Aparicio et al., 2016; Wennekers & Thurik, 1999), innovation (Acs et al., 2002; Feldman & Audretsch, 1999), environment (Beckerman,

1992; Grossman & Krueger, 1995), education (Easterly, 2001; Fleisher et al., 2010), financial development (King & Levine, 1993; Levine, 1997; Stiglingh & Vijloen, 2018), foreign direct investment (Abdouli & Hammami, 2020; Duarte et al., 2017), and migration (Beine et al., 2001; Peri, 2012; Rebelo, 1991).

The financial factors affecting economic growth and thus development are varied, leading to the expansion of this literature at the end of the twentieth century. Jayaratne and Strahan (1996) studied the finance-growth nexus and provided evidence that financial markets can directly affect economic growth (Demetriades & Hussein, 1996) by studying the relaxation of bank branch restrictions in a study for the United States. The authors identified that the rates of real per capita growth in income and output significantly increased following intrastate branch reforms. This research was crucial to give value to this relationship previously established by important authors such as King and Levine (1993). Moreover, Rajan and Zingales (1998) examine whether financial development facilitates economic growth by reducing the costs of external finance to firms. In this research, the authors question whether industrial sectors that are relatively more in need of external finance develop disproportionately faster in countries with more developed financial markets, and they confirmed this hypothesis in a large sample of countries over the 1980s. In a study on the finance system and the sources of growth, Beck et al. (2000) evaluated the relation between the level of financial intermediary development and economic growth, total factor productivity growth, physical capital accumulation, and private savings rates. The authors arrived at two key findings. First, financial intermediaries exert a positive impact on total factor productivity growth, which feeds through to overall GDP growth; second, the long-run links between financial intermediary development and both physical capital growth and private savings rates are tenuous. In a deeper analysis, Beck et al. (2007) stated that financial development boosts the incomes of the poorest quintile and reduces income inequality, emphasizing the importance of the financial system for the poor.

In more recent studies, Rioja and Valev (2004) re-examined the finance and growth relationship. The authors proposed that this relationship may vary in compliance with the level of financial development (divided into three regions), determining that improvements in financial markets have an uncertain effect on growth in low regions, a large positive effect in intermediate regions, and a positive but smaller effect in high regions. However, in an even more recent study, Arcand et al. (2015) inquired whether the finance-growth relationship was still positive, showing that financial depth started harming output growth when credit to the private sector reached 100% of GDP. This shows that although financial factors have positive effects on economic growth, policymakers must be careful when implementing policies. In analyzing this literature, we realize that the only way in which corporate decisions intervene in the relationship between financial development and the economic growth of a country is through credit or cost reduction. But what happens to the profitability of companies? Here lies a gap in the literature, since the relationship between the profitability of companies (an important agent within an economic system capable of transforming knowledge into innovation and development) and the economic growth at the country level has received little exploration.

The two main measures of a company's profitability are the ROE and IRR, terms developed by Smith (1987) and Lombardi (1988), respectively. In this research, we will focus specifically on these two measures, with more emphasis on the IRR. The IRR is the discount rate that yields net present value (NPV) = 0 for a stream of positive and negative cash flows, including at least one of each sign and with no explicit financing payments (Mellichamp, 2017). The literature studying IRR is extensive, ranging from new ways of measuring it (Vance, 2018), its differences with respect to other measures (Beal, 2000), to its effects on agents' investment decisions (Patrick & French, 2016).

On the one hand, there is research proposing new measures. Percoco and Borgonovo (2012) discussed the sensitivity analysis of the IRR and showed that the use of partial derivatives can be misleading in the identification of key drivers of an investment project's performance. Trying to solve this, the authors propose the use of an alternative sensitivity measure called the differential importance measure, finding that the sensitivity analysis results for the two indicators (NPV or the IRR) may differ. Roenganan et al. (2021) proposed a mathematical model with applications for investment decisions (extension of IRR) and taking into account the life probability, considering different types of life insurance policies, and other factors specified within life insurance investments. The results show that the sensitivity analyses of the life IRR perform the natural characteristics of life insurance. Magni (2010) offered a solution to the serious flaws of IRR ("multiple real-valued IRRs may arise; complex-valued IRRs may arise; incompatible with the net present value (NPV) in accepting/rejecting decisions; the IRR ranking is, in general, different from the NPV ranking; the IRR criterion is not applicable with variable costs of capital"), introducing the average IRR to solve these problems. This new measure was supported and extended a few years later by the same author (Magni, 2013).

On the other hand, some research has attempted to solve the problem of multiple IRR. First, Hazen (2003) demonstrated that when there are multiple internal rates, each has a meaningful interpretation as a rate of return on its underlying investment stream. The author affirmed that it does not matter which rate is used to accept or reject the cash flow stream, as long as one identifies the underlying investment stream as a net investment or net borrowing. Second, Speranda and Speranda (2019) proposed a new integral method of calculating IRR and a redefinition (as a rate that does not make the NPV equal to zero), facilitating the calculation of the central rate and the corresponding central NPV. Although this literature shows the importance of IRR and its importance in investment decisions, the relationship between this measure with economic growth is almost non-existent. This gap in the literature may be because it is difficult to calculate the IRR at the country level, making it a challenge for this research. Thus, we will use some approximations for IRR and even our calculation for ROE to look at the factors that have effects on these measures, and to finally observe their effects on economic growth.

7.3 Hypothesis Development

The IRR is fundamental in making investment decisions or evaluating the acceptability of a project (Hartman & Schafrick, 2004). However, in the literature exploring this measure, research on the factors that influence its behavior is almost non-existent. Since IRR is recurrently used for project acceptability within a company, it can be assumed that factors affecting a company's operating or financial costs may also affect IRR. Our research involves the challenge of taking this measure to the country level, which encourages us to use the country risk in the analysis. The literature agrees that country risk is the result of political, social, and economic factors that affect investment decisions (Oetzel et al., 2001); we will thus review which of these factors encourage or discourage the IRR.

Eaton et al. (1986) provided the first pure theory based on country risk; in their research, the authors punished solvency and liquidity as determinants of sovereign debt, as they claimed that it is more important to have information on moral hazard and the adverse selection of lenders. However, the study of country risk has changed over the years, since most of the literature exploring this measure seeks to explain its direct relationship with foreign direct investment (Vijayakumar et al., 2009). Meldrum (2000) developed research that concludes that company analysts may improve the performance of risk measures available from commercial services by adjusting risk measurement to fit the company's specific type of foreign direct investment. Sanjo (2012) studied the tax competition for foreign direct investment with country risk using a two-country model with different market sizes; the author argued that the trade-off between country size as a locational advantage and country risk as a locational disadvantage affects the location choice of a foreign firm. In a study of post-socialist central and eastern European economies, Săvoiu and Ţaicu (2014) identified several econometric models of foreign direct investment (FDI) focused on the country risk (Carstensen & Toubal, 2004), and ascertained that this can also affect other macroeconomic indicators. In contrast to the aforementioned research, Damodaran (2003) evaluated whether country risk should be considered explicitly in valuations, in addition to how to assess a company's exposure to country risk. The author explained that assessing and dealing with country risk can be important even for companies that trade in developed markets if they receive a significant portion of their revenues from emerging markets.

This literature sheds light on the significance of country risk in investment decisions. However, it does not yet allow us to hypothesize about the effects of country risk on IRR. For this, we will use economic factors (of the country risk) such as interest rates, taxes, and certain costs that affect business decisions. The first factor to consider is the interest rate. Lin (1976) made a first approximation by developing a modified internal rate of return (MIRR), which is advantageous in that it provides a single solution consistent with the NPV and the cost-benefit decision rules. In addition, this rate also measures the rate of return for investment using both intermediate costs and benefits, when the borrowing and the lending rates differ for the firm. This highlights the direct relationship that a good IRR measure has with interest lending rates. Subsequently, Eichengreen (1991) developed historical research on international loans and debt, concluding the importance of lending rates on investment decisions, specifically on IRR; he discusses the importance of lending rates in the macroeconomic effects triggered by investment incentives or disincentives. In a study focused on the present value criterion, Liu et al. (2004) investigated this measure using the concepts of neutralizing and generating present value in a capital market with differing borrowing and lending rates. This allows authors to present an economic explanation of why the traditional NPV may exhibit the anomalous behavior of either increasing or decreasing as the market interest rates go up, affecting investment decisions based on IRR. In recent research, Chen et al. (2022) used more than 750,000 loan records from LendingClub issued from 2015 through 2018 and attempted to estimate the gross rates of return (ROR) for each loan, assuming the borrowers stopped paying their loans once a default occurred. The results showed that borrowers' credit rating, interest rates, loan status, and paid months are the most critical factors to influence investors' ROR. This literature supports the relationship between one of the factors of country risk such as interest rates and the IRR.

The second factor to consider is taxes. The relationship between taxes and the IRR was explored around the mid-twentieth century. Johansson (1969) studied investment decisions such as IRR with and without considering taxes as income. The author concluded that increases in income taxes decrease the IRR, so he is pessimistic about policymakers who want to impose a neutral income tax system on investment decisions. Johansson's conclusions concerning this relationship were strengthened a few years later when Askari (1972) calculated the IRR on owner-occupied housing for people in different tax brackets and under a range of values of the relevant parameters. The author concluded that policymakers should decrease taxation to increase the IRR for people in the lowest income brackets. This relationship was subsequently taken to the private field, with Cymrot (1980) evaluating the extent to which tax sheltering increases the after-tax rate of return of private pensions. The results illustrated that postponing tax payments is good for the taxpayers by deriving a measure of the differential in the after-tax rate of return of a pension contribution over alternative forms of saving. Finally, in recent studies, Heckman et al. (2008) calculated the IRR for different schooling levels, finding that taxation decrease this measure.

Other factors such as the cost of construction permits, electricity, and export are taken into account in the country risk. First, Prol and Steininger (Prol & Steininger, 2020) explored the impact of the new photovoltaic self-consumption (PVSC) regulation on residential, commercial, and industrial prosumers' profitability (IRR). The authors concluded that residential, commercial, and industrial prosumers obtain positive profitability in average conditions and better results when electricity costs are reduced. A similar result was found by Bonazzi and Iotti (2014) when calculating the IRR for biogas plants with renewable energy, finding that these plants obtain a higher IRR than with traditional electricity, thus reducing costs. Talavera et al. (2010) developed a comprehensive sensitivity analysis that identified that photovoltaic electricity unitary price has a high impact on IRR. Second, in a seminal article written for the World Bank, Warr (1989) studied the benefits and costs of export processing zones (EPZS) in Indonesia, the Republic of Korea, Malaysia, and the Philippines, in addition to reviewing the relationship between the welfare effects of EPZS and the host country's economic policies. The authors found that electricity, administrative, and infrastructure costs have a negative effect on the IRR, affecting exports. This extensive literature allows us to establish the following hypothesis:

Hypothesis 1 : Country risk factors (i.e., lending interest rate, taxes, cost of construction permits, electricity, and export) harm investment decision measures such as IRR.

We have already reviewed the effects of some country risk factors on the IRR; however, we need to observe what happens to the effect this measure has on a country's economy. The literature that studies this relationship is almost non-existent, but three key research studies have made some progress. First, Jorgenson and Nishimizu (1978) provided an international comparison of aggregate economic growth in the United States and Japan during the period 1952–1974. The authors discussed four significant events for the transition in the relative growth of the United States and Japanese economies; one of these events was in 1956 concerning the own rate of return in

Japan, which revealed that the marginal product of all capital in the business sector surpassed the United States. The increase in the IRR resulted in Japan generating higher annual total output growth rates than the United States from 1956 to 1961. Second, Ohanian and Wright (2007) studied the capital flow locations for 200 countries between 1950 and 2005, based on the marginal product/internal rate of return. The authors found a direct relationship between the performance of economies and IRR. However, the most fundamental finding focuses on understanding why capital has not flowed from low return to high return countries. Finally, Inklaar et al. (2019) from Penn World Table (PWT) proposed an IRR at the country level, finding significance for high-, middle-, and low-income countries, except for the United States. This key study facilitates future investigations to study this important relationship. Although there is little literature on this subject, this research allows us to establish the following hypothesis:

Hypothesis 2 : Improvements in investment decision measures such as IRR spur economic growth.

7.4 Methodology

7.4.1 Data

To examine the previous hypotheses, we use two data sources. First, we use the PWT version 10.0 database created by Feenstra et al. (2015), which is used in key research such as Acemoglu et al. (2019) and Feenstra and Romalis (2014). Second, we use the World Development Indicators (WDI) from the World Bank to create an unbalanced (because data in developing countries is often remarkably poor or missing entirely) panel data with a maximum of 2395 observations from 2005 to 2018. The WDI is a compilation of relevant, high-quality, and internationally comparable statistics about global development and the fight against poverty. This database contains 1400 time series indicators for 217 economies and more than 40 country groups, with data for many indicators going back more than 50 years (World Bank, 2020).

This unbalanced panel data allows us to identify some key variables for the research. The real IRR variable is extracted from Feenstra et al. (2015); here, the authors used the asset-specific investment price for the current year instead of the previous year in the denominator for the calculation of the real IRR. This greatly facilitates the estimation work, since this variable can be compared with countries' macroeconomic variables (specifically GDP). In addition, for the dependent variable, we also performed a calculation that allows us to obtain a return on equity (ROE) at the country level. To achieve this, we assume a capital stock of \$100 million, sales of \$300 million, indebtedness of 30% of the capital stock, and a production cost of 60% of sales. Thus, the ROE would be the net earnings on the capital stock; this percentage would vary for each country depending on its lending interest rate and taxes. The rest of the variables are extracted from the WDI. To analyze the growth of an economy, we use GDP per capita. Other variables relevant to our analysis are: population growth, expressed as an annual percentage; gross savings, expressed as a percentage of GDP; New Business Density (NBD), expressed as the total number of businesses registered per 1000 people at ages 15–64; central government debt, expressed as a percentage of GDP; total taxes as contribution rates, expressed as a percentage of company profits; interest rate, expressed as a percentage of GDP; lending interest rate, the bank rate that usually meets the short- and medium-term financing needs of the private sector, this variable is also expressed as a percentage; construction permits cost as a percentage of warehouse value; electricity cost as a percentage of per capita income; and, finally, export cost expressed as a dollar value per container. These variables will allow us to develop an appropriate econometric model to support the hypotheses proposed.

7.4.2 Empirical Strategy

To support the suggested hypotheses, a multilevel model (i.e., simultaneous equations) is used to observe the direct effect that the IRR has on economic growth (GDP pc), respectively, of country *i* in survey year *t*:

$$Growth_{it} = \alpha + \beta_1 \widehat{IRR}_{it} + \beta_2 CV_{it} + \varepsilon_{it} \tag{7.1}$$

$$IRR_{it} = \alpha + \beta_1 LIR_{it} + \beta_2 T_{it} + \beta_3 CCP_{it} + \beta_4 CE_{it} + \beta_5 CX_{it} + \varepsilon_{it} \quad (7.2)$$

In Eq. (7.2), the IRR outcomes are shown by IRR_{it}. This variable is directly affected by the lending interest rate (LIR_{it}), taxes and contribution rate (T_{it}), cost of construction permits (CCP_{it}), cost of electricity (CE_{it}), as well as the cost to export (CX_{it}). However, Eq. (7.1) is the main outcome, which reveals the direct effect that the estimated IRR (IRR_{it}) exerts on economic growth at the country level ($Growth_{it}$), conditioning by CV_{it}, which contains several control variables over time such as population growth, gross saving, NBD, central government debt, and the total taxes and contribution rate.

To enfold the simultaneity between Eqs. 7.1 and 7.2, we used a 3SLS (Wooldridge, 2002), a full information method developed by Zellner and Theil (1962) and used in key research like Bosma et al. (2018) and Ramírez-Hassan (2021). Our decision to utilize this methodology is based on the gain in statistical efficiency; although some years ago 2SLS meant a gain in computational cost, today this is not a problem (Belsley, 1988). The 3SLS allows us to have excellent results in terms of cross-equation correlation coefficients, so it is worthwhile using this methodology with the number of observations available (see Table 7.1).

7.5 Results

7.5.1 Main Results

Table 7.1 presents the descriptive statistics of all the variables used in the model. In this, we can observe some interesting facts, as the IRR calculated by Feenstra et al. (2015) has a mean of 0.109, while our ROE calculations have a mean of 0.648. Our calculation, although drastic, meets the objective of exposing countries that are not profitable to receive FDI flows. Clear examples are Argentina and Burundi, countries whose economies have been in decline in recent years, but whose IRR does not behave accordingly. Cases such as Colombia indicate that for some countries these variables do not differ by more than 0.15 percentage points, since its IRR is 12% while its ROE is 23%. Another interesting fact from

Table 7.1 Descriptive statistics

Variable	Mean	SD	Min	Max	P50	p99	N
GDP pc	15*	21*	210.804	110*	5919.210	93*	2309
HDI	0.701	0.160	0.294	0.956	0.734	0.943	2037
IRR	0.109	0.068	0.010	0.465	0.096	0.325	1918
ROE	0.648	0.392	-2.555	1.089	0.712	1.052	2154
Population growth	1.474	1.614	-4.537	17.511	1.290	6.264	2395
Gross savings	22.206	12.529	-70.263	66.884	21.345	56.942	2042
New business density (NBD)	3.353	4.332	0.007	39.040	1.673	20.090	1471
Central government debt	54.452	35.315	0.018	197.284	48.948	177.961	522
Total tax and contribution rate	44.968	33.940	7.400	339.100	39.300	235.200	2154
Lending interest rate	12.110	8.110	0.000	67.718	10.260	46.011	1645
Cost of construction permits	8.556	18.345	0.000	278.200	3.100	95.600	2154
Cost of electricity	1642.212	3317.467	0.000	43*	447.300	15*	1511
Cost to export	1907.578	1696.467	416.180	18*	1352.744	9026.514	1658

Note: *values in thousands; N = observations; P = percentiles; SD = standard deviation

Table 7.1 is that the mean of savings has remained “constant,” as in 2005 it was 22.30% of GDP and in 2018 it is 22.26% of GDP. Crucially, the mean NBD has grown over time, totaling 3.26 in 2005 and 3.76 in 2018; although the growth has not been significant, this demonstrates the importance of business creation worldwide. In addition to our dependent variables, taxes play a crucial role in our research, since they determine the percentage of profits that a company must allocate to cover this item. Although the statistics are encouraging given that taxes have decreased by 32% from 2005 to 2018, some countries such as Colombia and Argentina still maintain high tax rates, reaching 71.9% and 106% for 2018, respectively, statistics well above the world mean (40.35%).

Table 7.2 shows several significant correlations at the 99% level for all the variables in the model. These correlations give us indications of the expected estimators for the model results. A preview of the results could be the positive correlation between GDP pc and ROE, and the negative correlation between IRR and taxes, lending interest rate, and country risk variables.

Concentrating on results, Table 7.3 presents our model through 3SLS regression, which has two clear advantages over multivariate regressions. First, it fits the data better than OLS (Wooldridge, 2002). Second, it captures the indirect effects of our independent variables (lending interest rate, taxes and contribution rate, cost of construction permits, electricity cost, and export cost) in Eq. (7.2) on economic growth (Eq. 7.1) through investment decision measures such as IRR and ROE. Thus, our analysis relies on Table 7.3.

Table 7.3 reports the estimation results for the relationships outlined in the hypotheses development and the proposed model. Models 1–4 are composed of two equations; the first shows the effects of country risk variables such as lending interest rate, taxes and contribution rate, cost of construction permits, electricity cost, and export cost on investment decision measures such as IRR and ROE; on the other hand, the second equation shows the effects of these investment decision measures on economic growth such as GDP pc. Models 1 and 2 show the effects of the relationships proposed with the IRR variable, while Models 3 and 4 present these relationships with the ROE variable. Another thing to note is that Models 2 and 4 contain year fixed effects, attempting to control for

Table 7.2 Correlation matrix

Variables	(1)	(2)	(3)	(4)	(5)	(6)	(7)
(1) GDP pc	1.000						
(2) HDI	0.699*	1.000					
(3) IRR	-0.029	-0.153*	1.000				
(4) ROE	0.186*	0.250*	0.028	1.000			
(5) Pop. growth	-0.028	-0.332*	0.252*	-0.043	1.000		
(6) Gross saving	0.283*	0.246*	0.097*	0.189*	0.031	1.000	
(7) NBD	0.439*	0.477*	-0.054	0.224*	-0.141*	-0.025	1.000
(8) Cent. gov. debt	0.185*	0.239*	-0.077	-0.050	-0.129*	-0.165*	-0.092
(9) Taxes	-0.170*	-0.236*	-0.030	-0.999*	0.043	-0.182*	-0.213*
(10) Interest rate	-0.385*	-0.333*	-0.098*	-0.271*	0.090*	-0.178*	-0.242*
(11) Construction permits cost	-0.233*	-0.437*	-0.062	-0.252*	0.177*	-0.240*	-0.209*
(12) Electricity cost	-0.311*	-0.638*	0.023	-0.242*	0.290*	-0.247*	-0.281*
(13) Export cost	-0.265*	-0.379*	-0.106*	-0.226*	0.130*	0.021	-0.216*
Variables	(8)	(9)	(10)	(11)	(12)	(13)	
(8) Cent. gov. debt	1.000						
(9) Taxes	0.057	1.000					
(10) Interest rate	-0.134*	0.247*	1.000				
(11) Construction permits cost	-0.078	0.245*	0.174*	1.000			
(12) Electricity cost	-0.186*	0.233*	0.201*	0.459*	1.000		
(13) Export cost	-0.298*	0.216*	0.294*	0.178*	0.353*	1.000	

Table 7.3 Rates of return effects on GDP

	(1)	(2)	(3)	(4)
EQ1: Growth				
IRR	1.839***	1.862***		
	(0.354)	(0.354)		
ROE			6.717***	6.748***
			(1.060)	(1.060)
Population growth	-0.063	-0.065	-0.004	-0.004
	(0.072)	(0.073)	(0.027)	(0.027)
Gross saving	0.195***	0.194***	0.201***	0.201***
	(0.030)	(0.030)	(0.028)	(0.028)
New business density	0.465***	0.466***	0.421***	0.421***
	(0.039)	(0.039)	(0.036)	(0.036)
Central government debt	0.261***	0.262***	0.209***	0.210***
	(0.049)	(0.050)	(0.047)	(0.047)
Total tax and contribution rate	-0.099	-0.101	6.883***	6.914***
	(0.056)	(0.057)	(1.102)	(1.101)
Constant	0.066	0.120	0.056*	0.078
	(0.047)	(0.079)	(0.028)	(0.063)
EQ2: Rate of return				
Lending interest rate	-0.068**	-0.067**	-0.030***	-0.030***
	(0.022)	(0.022)	(0.001)	(0.001)
Total tax and contribution rate	0.026	0.026	-1.035***	-1.035***
	(0.033)	(0.033)	(0.001)	(0.001)
Cost of construction permits	-0.035	-0.035	-0.007***	-0.007***
	(0.025)	(0.025)	(0.002)	(0.002)
Cost of electricity	-0.030	-0.031	-0.000	-0.000
	(0.018)	(0.018)	(0.001)	(0.001)
Cost to export	-0.052	-0.052	-0.004**	-0.004**
	(0.028)	(0.028)	(0.001)	(0.001)
Constant	-0.060*	-0.060*	-0.015***	-0.015***
	(0.025)	(0.025)	(0.001)	(0.001)
Year FE	**NO**	**YES**	**NO**	**YES**
Observations	1002	1002	912	912
R-squared	-2.706	-2.772	0.347	0.348
AIC	4630	4640	-1700	-1691
BIC	4694	4728	-1638	-1604

Note: Standard errors in parentheses: *p<0.05; **p<0.01; ***p<0.001. AIC and BIC refer to the criteria information

factors changing annually that are common to all countries for a given year. Paying attention to how well the data fit the model, we can observe that for Models 1 and 2 we have a negative R^2, and since the R^2 is a goodness-of-fit measure that does not make much sense in 3SLS estimates (Wooldridge, 2002), we take into account the information criteria proposed by Akaike (1974). In summary, the so-called Akaike information criterion (AIC) is a metric used to compare the fit of different regression models; put simply, the smaller the AIC value, the better the fit (this also applies to the Bayesian information criterion [BIC]). Taking these values into account, we will now explain the results with Models 1 and 3.

Regarding the hypothesis testing, we suggest in hypothesis 1 that country risk factors (lending interest rate, taxes, cost of construction permits, electricity, and export) harm investment decision measures such as IRR. Models 1 and 2 support this hypothesis, as most country risk factors have a negative effect on IRR, and if we look at what happens with Model 3 we reach the same interpretation for ROE. We will subsequently inspect what happens with each of these factors. First, when country risk factors such as the lending interest rate increase by 1%, investment decision measures (IRR and ROE) decrease by 0.068% and 0.030% respectively, with the effect on ROE being more significant. Second, when country risk factors such as total taxes and contribution rates increase by 1%, investment decision measures (IRR and ROE) increase by 0.026% and decrease by 1.035%, respectively, finding significance in Model 3. Third, when country risk factors such as the cost of construction permits increase by 1%, investment decision measures (IRR and ROE) decrease by 0.035% and 0.007%, respectively (being more significant in the ROE model). Fourth, although the effect of electricity costs on investment decision measures such as IRR and ROE is negative, no significance is found in either model. Finally, when country risk factor such as export cost increases by 1%, investment decision measures such as ROE decrease by 0.004%, and the effect, although negative, on IRR (Model 1) is not significant. If we focus on the results in Eq. 2, we can observe that we obtain more significant estimators in the effects on ROE (Model 3); this coincides with the fact that the information criteria already dictated that this model was a better fit for the data. Thus, the results support research such as Chen et al. (2022), Heckman et al. (2008), Prol and Steininger (2020), and Talavera et al. (2010).

Hypothesis 2 states that improvements in investment decision measures such as IRR spur economic growth. Again, we inspect Models 1 and 3 to observe what happens when our independent variable is ROE, with their results supporting hypothesis 2. When investment decision measures such as IRR and ROE increase by 1%, economic growth such as GDP per capita increases by 1.839% and 6.717%, respectively. These results strengthen the thoughts in current literature (Yassin & Derar, 2014) regarding the macroeconomic effects of ROR. In the results, the effect of the NBD on the economy should also be highlighted, since a 1% increase in NBD results in economic growth such as GDP per capita increasing by 0.465% and 0.421% in Models 1 and 3, respectively.

7.5.2 Robustness Checks

The results of the present study show that investment decision measures such as IRR and ROE spur economic growth such as GDP pc. However, we want to identify whether the results vary if we take into account another variable that is a proxy for economic growth or development. We performed additional types of robustness checks by estimating our model using a different proxy for economic performance and other estimation methods.

On the one hand, Table 7.4 displays the effects of IRR and ROE on an economic development proxy such as the Human Development Index (HDI) (Roy & Mohanty, 2020; Viddy & Asniwati, 2019). Model 1 indicates that the effect of IRR on economic performance increases because when IRR increases by 1%, economic development such as HDI increases by 3.352%; however, the effect continues to be greater when the investment decision measure is ROE since when this variable increases by 1%, economic development such as HDI increases by 6.864%. These results imply consistency with the baseline results in Table 7.3. On the other hand, focusing on the results using other estimation methods (OLS and 2SLS [Tables 7.5 and 7.6]), we can conclude that this type of estimation does not adequately capture the effects of our relationship for several reasons. First, in Table 7.5 the effects of IRR on economic growth such as GDP per capita are negative and significant, resulting in the use of

Table 7.4 Rate of return effects on HDI

	(1)	(2)	(3)	(4)
EQ1: Growth				
IRR	3.352***	3.354***		
	(0.576)	(0.578)		
ROE			6.864***	6.904***
			(1.053)	(1.053)
Population growth	-0.450***	-0.451***	-0.350***	-0.349***
	(0.105)	(0.106)	(0.028)	(0.028)
Gross saving	0.121***	0.121***	0.224***	0.224***
	(0.035)	(0.035)	(0.029)	(0.029)
New business density	0.347***	0.348***	0.348***	0.348***
	(0.047)	(0.047)	(0.037)	(0.037)
Central government debt	0.231***	0.233***	0.179***	0.176***
	(0.067)	(0.067)	(0.048)	(0.048)
Total tax and contribution rate	-0.049	-0.051	7.055***	7.098***
	(0.097)	(0.096)	(1.107)	(1.106)
Constant	0.261***	0.316**	0.137***	0.120
	(0.076)	(0.114)	(0.030)	(0.067)
EQ2: Rate of return				
Lending interest rate	-0.020	-0.020	-0.032***	-0.032***
	(0.017)	(0.017)	(0.001)	(0.001)
Total tax and contribution rate	0.009	0.009	-1.047***	-1.047***
	(0.038)	(0.038)	(0.001)	(0.001)
Cost of construction permits	-0.062**	-0.062**	-0.007***	-0.007***
	(0.021)	(0.021)	(0.002)	(0.002)
Cost of electricity	-0.109***	-0.109***	-0.002*	-0.002*
	(0.014)	(0.014)	(0.001)	(0.001)
Cost to export	-0.016	-0.016	-0.002	-0.002
	(0.031)	(0.031)	(0.001)	(0.001)
Constant	-0.058*	-0.058*	-0.015***	-0.015***
	(0.026)	(0.026)	(0.001)	(0.001)
Year FE	**NO**	**YES**	**NO**	**YES**
Observations	857	857	823	823
R-squared	-6.509	-6.510	0.398	0.398
AIC	3733	3745	-1733	-1724
BIC	3794	3830	-1672	-1639

Note: Standard errors in parentheses: *p<0.05; **p<0.01; ***p<0.001. AIC and BIC refer to the criteria information

Table 7.5 Rate of return effects on GDP with 2SLS estimation

	(1)	(2)	(3)	(4)
EQ1: Growth				
IRR	1.336***	1.348***		
	(0.366)	(0.368)		
ROE			6.695***	6.728***
			(1.064)	(1.067)
Population growth	-0.259**	-0.262**	-0.004	-0.004
	(0.081)	(0.082)	(0.027)	(0.027)
Gross saving	0.214***	0.213***	0.203***	0.202***
	(0.049)	(0.050)	(0.029)	(0.029)
New business density	0.516***	0.516***	0.424***	0.424***
	(0.062)	(0.063)	(0.036)	(0.036)
Central government debt	0.323***	0.325***	0.209***	0.210***
	(0.079)	(0.080)	(0.047)	(0.047)
Total tax and contribution rate	-0.088	-0.091	6.860***	6.893***
	(0.057)	(0.058)	(1.106)	(1.109)
Constant	0.039	0.129	0.056*	0.078
	(0.047)	(0.114)	(0.028)	(0.063)
EQ2: Rate of return				
Lending interest rate	-0.058	-0.058	-0.030***	-0.030***
	(0.034)	(0.034)	(0.001)	(0.001)
Total tax and contribution rate	-0.002	-0.002	-1.035***	-1.035***
	(0.033)	(0.033)	(0.001)	(0.001)
Cost of construction permits	-0.044	-0.044	-0.007***	-0.007***
	(0.039)	(0.039)	(0.002)	(0.002)
Cost of income per capita	0.070*	0.070*	-0.000	-0.000
	(0.028)	(0.028)	(0.001)	(0.001)
Cost to export	-0.089**	-0.089**	-0.004**	-0.004**
	(0.034)	(0.034)	(0.001)	(0.001)
Constant	-0.074**	-0.074**	-0.015***	-0.015***
	(0.026)	(0.026)	(0.001)	(0.001)
Year FE	**NO**	**YES**	**NO**	**YES**
Observations	1002	1002	912	912
R-squared	-1.328	-1.352	0.347	0.348

Note: Standard errors in parentheses: *p<0.05; **p<0.01; ***p<0.001

simultaneous equations. Second, Table 7.6 estimates using the 2SLS method adequately capture the expected effects in both equations; however, this method does not pick up the errors in Eq. 7.2 and transform them into an estimation tool for Eq. 7.1, as the 3SLS method does. Even so, this method serves as a robustness check to indicate that the established relationships are adequate.

Table 7.6 Rate of return effects on GDP with OLS estimation

	(1)	(2)	(3)	(4)
EQ1: Growth				
IRR	-0.132***	-0.132***		
	(0.031)	(0.031)		
ROE			7.124***	7.122***
			(0.652)	(0.654)
Population growth	0.001	0.001	-0.002	-0.003
	(0.028)	(0.028)	(0.027)	(0.027)
Gross saving	0.243***	0.243***	0.199***	0.199***
	(0.027)	(0.027)	(0.028)	(0.028)
New business density	0.494***	0.494***	0.419***	0.419***
	(0.035)	(0.035)	(0.035)	(0.035)
Central government debt	0.284***	0.285***	0.207***	0.208***
	(0.044)	(0.044)	(0.047)	(0.047)
Total tax and contribution rate	-0.100**	-0.101**	7.306***	7.303***
	(0.032)	(0.032)	(0.679)	(0.681)
Constant	-0.033	-0.021	0.061*	0.083
	(0.024)	(0.060)	(0.026)	(0.063)
EQ2: Rate of return				
Lending interest rate	-0.058	-0.058	-0.030***	-0.030***
	(0.034)	(0.034)	(0.001)	(0.001)
Total tax and contribution rate	-0.002	-0.002	-1.035***	-1.035***
	(0.033)	(0.033)	(0.001)	(0.001)
Cost of construction permits	-0.044	-0.044	-0.007***	-0.007***
	(0.039)	(0.039)	(0.002)	(0.002)
Cost of income per capita	0.070*	0.070*	-0.000	-0.000
	(0.028)	(0.028)	(0.001)	(0.001)
Cost to export	-0.089**	-0.089**	-0.004**	-0.004**
	(0.034)	(0.034)	(0.001)	(0.001)
Constant	-0.074**	-0.074**	-0.015***	-0.015***
	(0.026)	(0.026)	(0.001)	(0.001)
Year FE	**NO**	**YES**	**NO**	**YES**
Observations	1002	1002	912	912
R-squared	0.274	0.274	0.348	0.348
AIC	4679	4689	-1700	-1690
BIC	4743	4777	-163	-1604

Note: Standard errors in parentheses: *p<0.05; **p<0.01; ***p<0.001

7.6 Discussion and Conclusions

The literature studying the relationship between investment decision variables such as IRR and economic growth is sparse. Therefore, this research is crucial because it fills gaps in the literature. We rely on key research (Yassin & Derar, 2014) to identify the macroeconomic implications of the IRR, and to explain the effect it has on GDP. Thus, using unbalanced panel data and a 3SLS empirical strategy, we arrived at two important findings.

First, the result supports that some country risk factors such as lending interest rates, taxes and contribution rate, the cost of construction permits, the cost of electricity, and the cost of exporting have a negative effect on the IRR (Bonazzi & Iotti, 2014; Chen et al., 2022; Heckman et al., 2008; Liu et al., 2004; Prol & Steininger 2020). Although these negative effects support hypothesis 1, the effects of two of these factors are highly interesting to observe. The lending interest rate and taxes turned out to be the factors that have the greatest effect on the IRR. Therefore, the domestic IRR is greatly affected due to the high taxes (as a percentage of their profits) that firms have to pay and the high lending interest rate, which also affects firms directly.

The second result supports hypothesis 2, as it proves that measures of investment decisions such as IRR and ROE have a positive and significant effect on economic growth as GDP per capita (Yassin & Derar, 2014). This result is fundamental, as it paves the way for future research to study this relationship and its transmission mechanisms in greater depth. In addition, this result generates wide-ranging discussions on theoretical and policy implications.

7.6.1 Theoretical Implications

The results of this research allow us to establish theoretical implications about the importance of measures of decision investment such as IRR and ROE, as well as their effect on economic growth. Four important theoretical implications will be discussed.

First, the relationship between IRR and economic growth as GDP per capita is unexplored. With the exception of Yassin and Derar (2014), few studies have been concerned with unveiling the macroeconomic effects of IRR. This is because IRR is a measure of corporate and project investment decisions, that is, at the firm level; which could lead to studies of spurious relationships such as GDP on IRR or ROE (Combey & Togbenou, 2017; de Leon, 2020). With this research, we hope to fill this gap in the literature, raising interest in studying this relationship in-depth, after having demonstrated the positive and significant effect of IRR and ROE on GDP per capita. Second, tied to the previous implication, this research encourages the use of investment decision variables not only for the analysis of foreign investment or capital inflows but also for the study of their macroeconomic effects.

The third implication is linked to the first hypothesis, as this research encourages the use of country risk factors to study measures of investment decisions such as IRR and ROE. This implication is of significant importance, given that these country risk factors are variables that directly affect the decisions of firms in a given country (Harvey, 2005). Companies play a fundamental role in society since they are responsible for combining knowledge with innovation (Zieba et al., 2017), and if variables such as lending interest rate, taxes they have to pay, and the increase of certain operational costs affect them, then the economy of a country is indirectly affected.

Finally, the last theoretical implication is focused on highlighting that our measure of ROE showed a greater significance in the expected relationships and a greater effect on the variables. Although Feenstra et al. (2015) did an outstanding job of obtaining an IRR at the country level, we believe that there is still a long way to go to create a consistent variable that is able to be used to observe its effects on macroeconomic variables.

7.6.2 Policy Implications

One of the greatest challenges of this research is to generate a discussion on policy decisions that would help to spur economic growth from measures of investment decisions such as IRR and ROE, and country risk factors like lending interest rate, taxes and contribution rate, cost of construction permits, electricity cost, and exporting cost. Through this research, we generated three vital policy implications.

The first implication encourages policymakers to generate improvements in country risk factors. For example, generating a decrease in interest rates would mean that companies would have the borrowing facilities needed to be able to carry out their operations and market expansions; decreasing tax rates for companies, since some countries' high rates hinder the profitability of projects or businesses; reducing the costs derived from the construction permit process (warehouse costs), as this will increase foreign investors' interest in the country that implements such policies; reduce electricity costs, as it is one of the highest operational costs within the cost item of the companies; and finally, reduce export costs, as these prevent companies from expanding worldwide.

Second, we propose the inclusion of companies in the macroeconomic decisions of countries, since they are responsible for creating value and innovation. Policymakers should at least take into account the effects of some decisions on variables that affect companies' operating costs and investment decisions. Finally, these implications indicate the importance of companies within society. Therefore, policymakers should also make an effort to lower the barriers or costs in the creation of new businesses. The literature showing the positive and significant effect that the creation of new businesses has on economic growth/development is extensive.

7.6.3 Limitations and Future Research

This research led to interesting results since the relationships studied pave the way for future research to comprehensively investigate their functioning and transmission mechanisms. However, there were two major limitations in carrying out this study. First, the IRR variable, although consistent for most countries, showed some deficiencies and oscillations in crucial countries such as the United States. However, this led us to perform our calculations (ROE) to test the dependent variable IRR. Second, although sometimes it can be seen as an advantage, there is no existing literature that talks about the causal relationships raised in this research, and this is due to the first major limitation since there are no corporate decision variables at the country level that allow us to evaluate their macroeconomic effects. Thus, we hope that this research will be the first step to encourage the study of these fundamental relationships.

References

Abdouli, M., & Hammami, S. (2020). Economic growth, environment, FDI inflows, and financial development in middle East countries: Fresh evidence from simultaneous equation models. *Journal of the Knowledge Economy, 11*(2), 479–511. https://doi.org/10.1007/s13132-018-0546-9

Acemoglu, D. (2008). *Introduction to modern economic growth*. Princeton University Press. https://doi.org/10.1111/j.1475-4932.2011.00816.x

Acemoglu, D., Naidu, S., Restrepo, P., & Robinson, J. A. (2019). Democracy does cause growth. *Journal of Political Economy, 127*(1), 47–100. https://doi.org/10.1086/700936

Acs, Z. J., Anselin, L., & Varga, A. (2002). Patents and innovation counts as measures of regional production of new knowledge. *Research Policy, 31*(7), 1069–1085. https://doi.org/10.1016/S0048-7333(01)00184-6

Acs, Z. J., Desai, S., & Hessels, J. (2008). Entrepreneurship, economic development and institutions. *Small Business Economics, 31*(3), 219–234. https://doi.org/10.1007/s11187-008-9135-9

Acs, Z. J., Braunerhjelm, P., Audretsch, D. B., & Carlsson, B. (2009). The knowledge spillover theory of entrepreneurship. *Small Business Economics, 32*(1), 15–30. https://doi.org/10.1007/s11187-008-9157-3

Akaike, H. (1974). A new look at the statistical model identification. *IEEE Transactions on Automatic Control, 19*(6), 716–723.

Aparicio, S., Urbano, D., & Audretsch, D. (2016). Institutional factors, opportunity entrepreneurship and economic growth: Panel data evidence. *Technological Forecasting and Social Change, 102*, 45–61. https://doi.org/10.1016/j.techfore.2015.04.006

Arcand, J. L., Berkes, E., & Panizza, U. (2015). Too much finance? *Journal of Economic Growth, 20*(2), 105–148. https://doi.org/10.1007/s10887-015-9115-2

Askari, H. (1972). Federal taxes and the internal rate of return on owner-occupied housing. *National Tax Journal, 25*(1), 101–105. https://doi.org/10.1086/ntj41791783

Azariadis, C., & Drazen, A. (1990). Threshold externalities in economic development. *Quarterly Journal of Economics, 105*(2), 501–526. https://doi.org/10.2307/2937797

Beal, R. W. (2000). Bridging the gap between roe and IRR. *North American Actuarial Journal, 4*(4), 1–11. https://doi.org/10.1080/10920277.2000.10595934

Beck, T., Levine, R., & Loayza, N. (2000). Finance and the sources of growth. *Journal of Financial Economics, 58*(1–2), 261–300. https://doi.org/10.1016/s0304-405x(00)00072-6

Beck, T., Demirgüç-Kunt, A., & Levine, R. (2007). Finance, inequality and the poor. *Journal of Economic Growth, 12*(1), 27–49. https://doi.org/10.1007/s10887-007-9010-6

Beckerman, W. (1992). Economic growth and the environment: Whose growth? whose environment? *World Development, 20*(4), 481–496. https://doi.org/10.1016/0305-750X(92)90038-W

Beine, M., Docquier, F., & Rapoport, H. (2001). Brain drain and economic growth: Theory and evidence. *Journal of Development Economics, 64*(1), 275–289. https://doi.org/10.1016/S0304-3878(00)00133-4

Belsley, D. A. (1988). Two- or three-stage least squares? *Computer Science in Economics and Management, 1*(1), 21–30. https://doi.org/10.1007/BF00435200

Bonazzi, G., & Iotti, M. (2014). Evaluation of biogas plants by the application of an internal rate of return and debt service coverage approach. *American Journal of Environmental Sciences, 11*(1), 35–45. https://doi.org/10.3844/ajessp.2015.35.45

Bosma, N., Content, J., Sanders, M., & Stam, E. (2018). Institutions, entrepreneurship, and economic growth in Europe. *Small Business Economics, 51*(2), 483–499. https://doi.org/10.1007/s11187-018-0012-x

Carstensen, K., & Toubal, F. (2004). Foreign direct investment in Central and Eastern European countries: A dynamic panel analysis. *Journal of Comparative Economics, 32*(1), 3–22. https://doi.org/10.1016/j.jce.2003.11.001

Chen, P. F., Lo, S., & Tang, H. Y. (2022). What if borrowers stop paying their loans? Investors' rates of return on a peer-to-peer lending platform. *International Review of Economics and Finance, 77*, 359–377. https://doi.org/10.1016/j.iref.2021.10.011

Combey, A., & Togbenou, A. (2017). The bank sector performance and macroeconomics environment: Empirical evidence in Togo. *International Journal of Economics and Finance, 9*(2), 180. https://doi.org/10.5539/ijef.v9n2p180

Cymrot, D. J. (1980). Private pension saving: The effect of tax incentives on the rate of return. *Southern Economic Journal, 47*(1), 179. https://doi.org/10.2307/1057071

Damodaran, A. (2003). Country risk and company exposure: Theory and practice. *Journal of Applied Finance, 13*(2), 63–76.

Demetriades, P. O., & Hussein, K. A. (1996). Does financial development cause economic growth? Time-series evidence from 16 countries. *Journal of Development Economics, 51*(2), 387–411. https://doi.org/10.1016/S0304-3878(96)00421-X

Duarte, L. D. R. V., Kedong, Y., & Xuemei, L. (2017). The relationship between FDI, economic growth and financial development in Cabo Verde. *International Journal of Economics and Finance, 9*(5), 132. https://doi.org/10.5539/ijef.v9n5p132

Easterly, W. (2001). The lost decades: Developing countries' stagnation in spite of policy reform 1980–1998. *Journal of Economic Growth, 6*(2), 135–157. https://doi.org/10.1023/A:1011378507540

Eaton, J., Gersovitz, M., & Stiglitz, J. E. (1986). The pure theory of country risk. *European Economic Review, 30*(3), 481–513. https://doi.org/10.1016/0014-2921(86)90004-8

Eichengreen, B. (1991). Historical research on international lending and debt. *Journal of Economic Perspectives, 5*(2), 149–169. https://doi.org/10.1257/jep.5.2.149

Fagerberg, J., & Srholec, M. (2018). National innovation systems, capabilities and economic development. In *Innovation, Economic Development and Policy: Selected Essays* (pp. 259–277). Edward Elgar Publishing Ltd.. https://doi.org/10.1016/j.respol.2008.06.003

Feenstra, R. C., & Romalis, J. (2014). International prices and endogenous quality. *Quarterly Journal of Economics, 129*(2), 477–527. https://doi.org/10.1093/qje/qju001

Feenstra, R. C., Inklaar, R., & Timmer, M. P. (2015). The next generation of the Penn world table. *American Economic Review, 105*(10), 3150–3182. https://doi.org/10.1257/aer.20130954

Feldman, M. P., & Audretsch, D. B. (1999). Innovation in cities: Science-based diversity, specialization and localized competition. *European Economic Review, 43*(2), 409–429. https://doi.org/10.1016/S0014-2921(98)00047-6

Fleisher, B., Li, H., & Zhao, M. Q. (2010). Human capital, economic growth, and regional inequality in China. *Journal of Development Economics, 92*(2), 215–231. https://doi.org/10.1016/j.jdeveco.2009.01.010

Glaeser, E. L., La Porta, R., Lopez-de-Silanes, F., & Shleifer, A. (2004). Do institutions cause growth? *Journal of Economic Growth, 9*(3), 271–303. https://doi.org/10.1023/B:JOEG.0000038933.16398.ed

Grossman, G. M., & Krueger, A. B. (1995). Economic growth and the environment. *Quarterly Journal of Economics, 110*(2), 353–377. https://doi.org/10.2307/2118443

Hartman, J. C., & Schafrick, I. C. (2004). The relevant internal rate of return. *Engineering Economist, 49*(2), 139–158. https://doi.org/10.1080/00137910490453419

Harvey, C. R. (2005). Country risk components, the cost of capital, and returns in emerging markets. *SSRN Electronic Journal.* https://doi.org/10.2139/ssrn.620710

Hazen, G. B. (2003). A new perspective on multiple internal rates of return. *Engineering Economist.* https://doi.org/10.1080/00137910308965050

Heckman, J. J., Lochner, L. J., & Todd, P. E. (2008). Earnings functions and rates of return. *Journal of Human Capital, 2*(1), 1–31. https://doi.org/10.1086/587037

Helmsing, A. H. J. (2001). Externalities, learning and governance: New perspectives on local economic development. *Development and Change, 32*(2), 277–308. https://doi.org/10.1111/1467-7660.00206

Howitt, P. (2010). Endogenous growth theory. In *Economic growth* (pp. 68–73). Palgrave Macmillan.

Inklaar, R., Woltjer, P., Albarrán, D. G., & Gallardo, D. (2019). The composition of capital and cross-country productivity comparisons. *International Productivity Monitor, 36*(36), 34–52.

Jayaratne, J., & Strahan, P. E. (1996). The finance-growth nexus: Evidence from bank branch deregulation. *Quarterly Journal of Economics, 111*(3), 639–670. https://doi.org/10.2307/2946668

Johansson, S. E. (1969). Income taxes and investment decisions. *The Swedish Journal of Economics, 71*(2), 104. https://doi.org/10.2307/3438990

Jorgenson, D. W., & Nishimizu, M. (1978). U.S. and Japanese economic growth, 1952–1974: An international comparison. *The Economic Journal, 88*(352), 707. https://doi.org/10.2307/2231974

Khresiat, O. M. (2019). Impact of investment decisions on the profits of Jordanian insurance companies listed on the Amman stock exchange. *Academy of Accounting and Financial Studies Journal, 23*(5), 1–12.

King, R. G., & Levine, R. (1993). Finance and growth: Schumpeter might be right. *Quarterly Journal of Economics, 108*(3), 717–737. https://doi.org/10.2307/2118406

de Leon, M. V. (2020). The impact of credit risk and macroeconomic factors on profitability: The case of the ASEAN banks. *Banks and Bank Systems, 15*(1), 21–29. https://doi.org/10.21511/bbs.15(1)0.2020.03

Levine, R. (1997). Financial development and economic growth: Views and agenda. *Journal of Economic Literature, 35*(2), 688–726. https://doi.org/10.1596/1813-9450-1678

Lin, S. A. Y. (1976). The modified internal rate of return and investment criterion. *Engineering Economist, 21*(4), 237–247. https://doi.org/10.1080/00137917608902796

Liu, L., Rettenmaier, A. J., & Saving, T. R. (2004). Present value criterion: The case of differing borrowing and lending rates. *Economics Letters, 84*(3), 427–432. https://doi.org/10.1016/j.econlet.2004.03.013

Lombardi, L. J. (1988). Relationships between statutory and generally accepted accounting principles (GAAP). *TSA, 40*, 485–508.

Lucas, R. E. (1988). On the mechanics of economic development. *Journal of Monetary Economics, 22*(1), 3–42. https://doi.org/10.1016/0304-3932(88)90168-7

Magni, C. A. (2010). Average internal rate of return and investment decisions: A new perspective. *Engineering Economist, 55*(2), 150–180. https://doi.org/10.1080/00137911003791856

Magni, C. A. (2013). The internal rate of return approach and the Airr paradigm: A refutation and a corroboration. *Engineering Economist, 58*(2), 73–111. https://doi.org/10.1080/0013791X.2012.745916

Meldrum, D. (2000). Country risk and foreign direct investment. *Business Economics, 35*(1), 33–40. Retrieved from http://citeseerx.ist.psu.edu/viewdoc/download?doi=10.1.1.195.9987&rep=rep1&type=pdf

Mellichamp, D. A. (2017). Internal rate of return: Good and bad features, and a new way of interpreting the historic measure. *Computers and Chemical Engineering, 106*, 396–406. https://doi.org/10.1016/j.compchemeng.2017.06.005

Moschos, D. (1989). Export expansion, growth and the level of economic development. An empirical analysis. *Journal of Development Economics, 30*(1), 93–102. https://doi.org/10.1016/0304-3878(89)90052-7

Nelson, R. R. (2007). Economic development from the perspective of evolutionary economic theory. *Oxford Development Studies, 36*(1), 9–21. https://doi.org/10.1080/13600810701848037

Oetzel, J. M., Bettis, R. A., & Zenner, M. (2001). Country risk measures: How risky are they? *Journal of World Business, 36*(2), 128–145. https://doi.org/10.1016/S1090-9516(01)00049-9

Ohanian, L. E., & Wright, M. L. (2007). *Where did capital flow? Fifty years of international rate of return differentials and capital flows*. Federal Reserve Bank of Minneapolis Research Department Staff Report.

Patrick, M., & French, N. (2016). The internal rate of return (IRR): Projections, benchmarks and pitfalls. *Journal of Property Investment and Finance*. Emerald Group Publishing Ltd. https://doi.org/10.1108/JPIF-07-2016-0059

Percoco, M., & Borgonovo, E. (2012). A note on the sensitivity analysis of the internal rate of return. *International Journal of Production Economics*. Elsevier B.V. https://doi.org/10.1016/j.ijpe.2011.09.002

Peri, G. (2012). The effect of immigration on productivity: Evidence from U.S. states. *Review of Economics and Statistics, 94*(1), 348–358. https://doi.org/10.1162/REST_a_00137

Prol, J. L., & Steininger, K. W. (2020). Photovoltaic self-consumption is now profitable in Spain: Effects of the new regulation on prosumers' internal rate of return. *Energy Policy, 146*, 111793.

Rajan, R. G., & Zingales, L. (1998). Financial dependence and growth. *American Economic Review, 88*(3), 559–586. https://doi.org/10.2307/116849

Ramírez-Hassan, A. (2021). Bayesian estimation of the exact affine Stone index demand system: Replicating the Lewbel and Pendakur (2009) results. *Journal of Applied Econometrics, 36*(4), 484–491. https://doi.org/10.1002/jae.2814

Rebelo, S. (1991). Long-run policy analysis and long-run growth. *Journal of Political Economy, 99*(3), 500–521. https://doi.org/10.1086/261764

Rioja, F., & Valev, N. (2004). Does one size fit all?: A reexamination of the finance and growth relationship. *Journal of Development Economics, 74*(2), 429–447. https://doi.org/10.1016/j.jdeveco.2003.06.006

Roenganan, S., Misran, M., & Phewchean, N. (2021). A study of life internal rate of return. *WSEAS Transactions on Mathematics, 20*, 122–133. https://doi.org/10.37394/23206.2021.20.13

Roy, S., & Mohanty, R. P. (2020). Microfinance models in improving "quality of life": Empirical analysis on Indian perspective. *International Journal of Business Innovation and Research*. Inderscience Publishers. https://doi.org/10.1504/IJBIR.2020.104031

Sanjo, Y. (2012). Country risk, country size, and tax competition for foreign direct investment. *International Review of Economics and Finance, 21*(1), 292–301. https://doi.org/10.1016/j.iref.2011.08.002

Săvoiu, G., & Ţaicu, M. (2014). Foreign direct investment models, based on country risk for some post-socialist Central and Eastern European economies. *Procedia Economics and Finance, 10*, 249–260. https://doi.org/10.1016/s2212-5671(14)00300-1

Smith, B. (1987). Pricing in a return-on-equity environment. *TSA, 39*, 257–293.

Speranda, I. V. O., & Speranda, Z. (2019). The comprehensive method of solving the multiple internal rate of return problem. *Montenegrin Journal of Economics, 15*(1), 73–86. https://doi.org/10.14254/1800-5845/2019.15-1.6

Stiglingh, A., & Vijloen, D. (2018). An analysis of the relationship between economic growth and financial development for BRICS countries. *International Journal of Economics and Finance Studies, 10*(1), 81–95.

Talavera, D. L., Nofuentes, G., & Aguilera, J. (2010). The internal rate of return of photovoltaic grid-connected systems: A comprehensive sensitivity analysis. *Renewable Energy, 35*(1), 101–111. https://doi.org/10.1016/j.renene.2009.07.006

Vance, D. E. (2018). A new algorithm for internal rate of return. *Journal of Economics, Management and Trade, 21*(8), 1–9. https://doi.org/10.9734/jemt/2018/43914

Viddy, A. R., & Asniwati, B. (2019). The determinants of human development index and economic growth in Indonesia. *International Journal of Scientific and Technology Research, 8*(12), 661–665.

Vijayakumar, J., Rasheed, A. A., & Tondkar, R. H. (2009). Foreign direct investment and evaluation of country risk: An empirical investigation. *Multinational Business Review*. https://doi.org/10.1108/1525383X200900023

Warr, P. G. (1989). Export processing zones: The economics of enclave manufacturing. *World Bank Research Observer, 4*(1), 65–88. https://doi.org/10.1093/wbro/4.1.65

Wennekers, S., & Thurik, R. (1999). Linking entrepreneurship and economic growth. *Small Business Economics, 13*(1), 27–56. https://doi.org/10.1023/A:1008063200484

Wooldridge, J. M. (2002). *Econometric analysis of cross section and panel data*. MIT Press.

World Bank. (2020). World development indicators | data. *World Development Indicators*, (July), 1–4. Retrieved from https://databank.worldbank.org/data/download/GDP.pdf

Yassin, E. T., & Derar, E. O. (2014). Internal rate of return: A suggested alternative formula and its macro-economics implications. *Journal of American Science, 10*(11), 216–221.

Zellner, A., & Theil, H. (1962). Three-stage least squares: Simultaneous estimation of simultaneous equations. *Econometrica, 30*(1), 54–78.

Zieba, M., Bolisani, E., Paiola, M., & Scarso, E. (2017). Searching for innovation knowledge: Insight into KIBS companies. *Knowledge Management Research and Practice, 15*(2), 282–293. https://doi.org/10.1057/s41275-017-0050-1

8

Entrepreneurship Crossing Borders: The Multilevel Relationship Between Institutional Obstacles and Firm's Export

Diego Gomez, Sebastian Aparicio, David Urbano, and Diego Martinez-Moya

8.1 Introduction

Entrepreneurship has been widely studied by scholars (Audretsch et al., 2022a; Packard & Burnham, 2021; Solomon et al., 2021), from the types of entrepreneurship (Baumol, 1996; Lucas & Fuller, 2017), its relationship with informality (Ault & Spicer, 2020; Omri, 2020), migration (Muñoz-Mora et al., 2022; Wassink, 2020), and other fundamental concepts in the economy. Even so, its relationship with variables that

D. Gomez • D. Martinez-Moya
Fundación ECSIM, Medellin, Colombia

S. Aparicio (✉) • D. Urbano
Department of Business, Universitat Autònoma de Barcelona, Cerdanyola del Vallés, Barcelona, Spain

Centre for Entrepreneurship and Social Innovation Research (CREIS), Universitat Autònoma de Barcelona, Sabadell, Barcelona, Spain
e-mail: Sebastian.Aparicio@uab.cat

D. Gomez et al. (eds.), *Driving Complexity in Economic Development*, https://doi.org/10.1007/978-3-031-34386-5_8

compromise the international growth of firms such as international business still has a long way to go (Nguyen, Nguyen, & Thanh, 2022b). However, this research plans to go a step further by considering the fundamental role played by institutions (as rules of the game—North, 1990) in the interaction between economic agents (in this case, firms) and their intention to expand internationally.

Thus, this chapter has a threefold purpose. First, it analyzes the triad between institutions, entrepreneurship, and international business by revealing the effect that some institutional obstacles have on the exports of initially formal or new companies. Second, the chapter seeks to demonstrate the importance of micro- and macrolevel analysis in the observed relationship. Finally, and as an addition, it examines whether the effect of these relationships is maintained when we look at firms when these were informal.

To achieve these objectives, we rely on North (1990) and Williamson (2000) to conduct a multilevel analysis that considers both the macrolevel and the microlevel factors, allowing us to propose hypotheses that study the effect of certain institutional obstacles at the firm, city, and country level on the exports of initially formal or new firms. To test these hypotheses, we built two pooled cross-sectional datasets using two databases (The World Bank' Enterprise Survey [WBES]—firm-level data and the World Development Indicators) during the 2006–2020 period. This information was useful to identify those initially formal or new firms (start-ups less than five years old) and those initially informal or new firms. Both databases allowed us to obtain a sample size of 16,923 and 3645, respectively. The results reveal the negative effect that institutional obstacles at the firm, city, and country levels have on the exports of initially formal or new firms. The findings are also useful to understand the behavior of these relationships for initially informal firms since they are indifferent to the negative effects at the city and country levels but not to the effects at the firm level. These results allow us to provide a rich discussion that leads to theoretical and policy implications, making it clear that there is still a long way to go and emphasizing the limitations of this research.

8.2 Theoretical Underpinning and Hypothesis Development

8.2.1 International Business

According to Buckley (2011), the history of international business theory is split in two, starting with the work of Hymer (1960). In his thesis, Hymer (1960) analyzed the main causes for the generation of international business, the main one being the appropriation of the return on their skills, or what is known today in economics as "competitive advantage." Buckley (2011), based on the literature, asserted that international business is the logical interception between industrial economics, international economics, and the theory of the firm. He also stated that two concepts have been key to the development of international business theory: international competitiveness (paving the way for exports) and foreign direct investment (FDI). However, much of the research that investigates international business takes FDI as the main measure.

The effects of FDI on key economic and social variables, such as education (Kheng, Sun, & Anwar, 2017; Lipsey & Sjöholm, 2004), employment (Blomström et al., 1997; Mcdonald et al., 2002; Wong & Tang, 2011), health (Burns et al., 2017; Smith, 2004), innovation (Fu, 2007; Hintošová et al., 2020), and economic growth (Cicea & Marinescu, 2021; Osei & Kim, 2020), have been widely analyzed. Even so, what about international competitiveness? It turns out that the beginnings of international business are rooted in the mercantilists' efforts to build up the "national treasure" by ensuring a surplus of exports over imports (Buckley, 2011). Therefore, international business can also be studied through the competitive advantage generated by some firms in their efforts to cross borders and export. Following Leonidou et al. (2010), exporting is the most common way for many firms (particularly those of small-to-medium size) to enter international markets. Despite this, the author stressed that there is still some way to go before it reaches the level of maturity attained by other fields within the international business domain.

8.2.2 Institutional Economics

Almost a century ago, Coase (1937) stated that a firm consists of the system of relationships that comes into existence when the direction of resources is dependent on an entrepreneur within a specialized price-determined exchange economy. However, economic agents, such as entrepreneurs, buyers, and firms, are constrained by institutions since these are the ones that set the rules of the game in the agents' exchange (North, 1990), also considering that these institutions can be both formal and informal (North, 2005). Based on these theoretical aspects, we can assure that international business, approached through exports, depends to a great extent on the behavior of institutions.

Given the importance of institutions in the performance of firms (Aparicio et al., 2021; Fuentelsaz et al., 2019, 2020; Sahasranamam & Nandakumar, 2020) and their ability to grow through exports, vast literature has focused on studying this relationship. For example, Araujo et al. (2016) studied how contract enforcement and export experience shape firm export dynamics in an environment with incomplete information, showing that exporters start with higher volumes and sell for longer periods in countries with better contracting institutions and when they have prior foreign experience. However, conditional on survival, firm export growth decreases with the quality of the country's institutions. In research on transition economies, Hernández et al. (2022) analyzed the relationship between home-country governance imperfections and the export intensity of firms, concluding that although firms from transition economies face difficulties to export due to the regulatory constraints of their home countries, a strategy based on innovation represents a viable way to overcome these limitations.

Other important research mixes the relationship between exports and institutions with information barriers (Martincus et al., 2010), gender (Audretsch et al., 2022b), and innovation (Bierut & Dybka, 2021), among other factors, and although through this literature we are able to analyze that institutions can be facilitators or obstacles to firm exports (Faruq, 2011; Munemo, 2022), there are gaps in the literature concerning the methodologies used to observe to what extent and how institutions can present an obstacle to formal/informal firms' exports or new firms' exports.

8.2.3 Hypothesis Development

It has been suggested that firms are affected by changes in input prices (Hartman, 1975; Naylor & Soegaard, 2022), labor wages (Babecký et al., 2012; Harasztosi & Lindner, 2019), and other factors inherent to their production process at the firm level. However, they can also be affected by regional (Tojeiro-Rivero & Moreno, 2019; Weterings, 2014) and country conditions (Mertzanis et al., 2019; Sá & Pinho, 2019).

Empirical research analyzing the effect of some firm-level obstacles is emerging. Kahiya (2018) appraised rigorously the empirical literature on factors associated with export barriers. The author showed that between the period 2007–2016, around 43 barriers were found in export-related research. Regarding key institutional barriers, some of them were preparing/handling export documentation (10 studies), high tariff barriers (16 studies), excessive transportation/insurance costs (15 studies), and lack of government incentives/support (12 studies), among others. This uncovered the importance of institutional obstacles to firms' exports. Some institutional obstacles that affected firm exports were related to corruption, gender, justice, and institutional voids, among others.

For example, Carbonero et al. (2021) used firm-level data to assess whether the reform that introduced a gender-balancing quota on the boards of directors of Italian listed firms had any impact on a variety of measures related to exports, finding that the reform increased the probability of exporting and the value of exports. Continuing with the gender analysis, Audretsch et al. (2022b) evaluated the role-play of chief executive officers' (CEOs') gender in the relationship between home country corruption and firm exports. The authors found that women CEOs positively moderated the relationship between pervasive corruption and firm export intensity.

Other research has focused on observing the effects of variables such as corruption, justice, and other variables related to administrative aspects. Qi et al. (2020) examined the relationship between corruption and export in emerging economies. The authors found a U-shaped relationship between firms' corruption and exports, showing that in a business environment with high levels of political instability, regulatory burden, or threats of competition from the informal sector, the relationship between corruption and exportation was strengthened to varying degrees. In a study about court fairness, Kapri (2021) examined the causal relationship between court fairness and the firm-level export decisions (propensity and intensity), and through several specifications, the author showed that court fairness increased the export share as well as the likelihood that a firm will become an exporter. Ha et al. (2021) examined the effects of bribery on export decisions for firms facing institutional constraints ("greasing" and rent-seeking behavior). The authors found a positive effect, particularly sizable for large-sized firms or those facing no institutional constraints. In addition, in other important research, obstacles such as time to trade and institutional voids were found to harm firms' export performance (Goedhuys & Sleuwaegen, 2016; Hendy & Zaki, 2021).

Two other important relationships analyzed in this literature are the effect of financial access and informality on exports. First, some research has revealed the effect of financial access on exports. Nguyen, Almodóvar, and Wei (2022a) examined how financial capital affected the decision to export (export propensity) and the share of exports over total sales (export intensity) by the foreign subsidiaries of multinational enterprises. The authors found that intrafirm loans were positively related to arm's length export propensity and intensity. However, intrafirm loans had no significant relationship with intrafirm export propensity and export intensity. In an analysis of small and medium enterprises (SMEs), Rossi et al. (2021) analyzed the impact that innovation, financial constraints, and an efficient regulatory environment exerted on the probability of switching from the status of non-exporter to exporter and vice versa, finding that either the use of finance for innovation or undertaking product innovation increased the likelihood of starting to export and lowered the likelihood of stopping exporting, with these results being supported by Abor et al. (2014).

Second, there is research that has analyzed the effect of informality on firm exports. Bassetti et al. (2015) found that, in contrast to non-family firms, family firms were rather sensitive to corruption. In particular, the export share of family firms was positively associated with informal payments that aim to facilitate business operations. Escobar et al. (2021) studied how local firms in an emerging economy (Mexico) exploit institutional voids by sourcing inputs from industries with a large informal economy, allowing them to build a cost-related competitive advantage and leverage it both to export and to enhance export performance. However, this seems to be more related to issues of corruption than informality; so, what about informal competition? Krammer et al. (2018) developed a study for Brazil, China, India, and Russia, claiming that emerging economy firms (EEFs) are more likely to export when facing more uncertainty at home from greater political instability, substantial informal competition, and high corruption. Their results are supported by research analyzing the effects of the intensity of informal competition on the propensity to export (Deb et al., 2020). Even so, what happens when we analyze the effects on direct exports? One could suppose that under conditions of institutional weakness, the effect would not be positive but negative because the firms, apart from having institutional obstacles, compete with firms that benefit from the informal market or industry. And even more importantly, does the effect remain when we analyze new ventures? The literature analyzed indicates a positive answer since large firms have more room to maneuver than new ventures. Accordingly, with the literature, we hypothesize the following:

Hypothesis 1a : Under conditions of political instability, firm-level obstacles such as financial access negatively influence direct exports of formal or new firms.

Hypothesis 1b : Under conditions of political instability, firm-level obstacles such as competitors in the informal sector adversely affect direct exports of formal or new firms.

To this point, we have scrutinized the literature on firm-level effects. Yet, this research aims to go a step further and look at what happens with the city- and country-level effects. There are some key city determinants to understanding export behavior. Among them are environmental information disclosure (Xie et al., 2022), performance feedback (Dong et al., 2022a), transport (Tsekeris, 2017), geography (Losilla-Solano et al., 2019; Rodríguez-Pose et al., 2013), ethnic diversity (Parrotta et al., 2016), finance development (Chen et al., 2020), and property rights (Dong, Guo, & Hu, 2022b), and so on. However, we pay especial attention to some determinants that are necessary for business operations, such as some services like electricity and telecommunications, for which there is not much literature.

On the one hand, although there is little research that shows great interest in the effects of telecommunications on firms' exports, some are noteworthy. Zhou, Wen, and Lee (2022a) treated the pilot policy of the Broadband China strategy as a quasi-natural experiment and investigated how broadband infrastructure development affected export trade in Chinese cities. The authors showed that export trade in the pilot cities increased by 6.82–18.8% on average because of the Broadband China policy intervention, supporting the idea that this policy could effectively promote the use of internet facilities, and broadband infrastructure could significantly promote the growth of a city's export trade. The authors stated that the transmission mechanism was improving information efficiency, which in turn lowered logistics costs, promotes trade efficiency, and reduces trade barriers. In other research for China in the period from 1999 to 2007, Fernandes et al. (2019) examined how the internet rollout across Chinese provinces influenced manufacturing firms' export behavior. The authors showed that the internet rollout boosted firm manufacturing exports, even before the rise of major e-commerce platforms, supporting that the internet did not just enhance trade but improved overall firm performance. Even with modern methodologies, such as machine learning models, Shetewy et al. (2022) established that internet use increased China's exports in all the Chinese provinces. This literature helps us understand that just as telecommunications are an enabler, if they become an obstacle, they can affect firms' exports.

On the other hand, we also found limited literature on the city-level effect of electricity infrastructure (or electricity conditions) on firm exports, although again some key research can be highlighted. Montalbano and Nenci (2019) explored the relationship between energy efficiency, productivity, and exporting for a sample of firms located in 30 Latin American and Caribbean (LAC) countries. The authors found significant but heterogeneous results by firm size and industrial sector, clarifying that energy efficiency had a significant positive effect on large exporting companies and those in the chemical and mining sector. However, this research does not shed light on how electricity can become an obstacle for firms, as other research goes straight to the point. For example, Cole et al.

(2018) assessed the extent to which power outages affected the sales of firms across different African economies, finding evidence of a negative relationship between an unreliable electricity supply and firms' sales, with a stronger effect for firms that did not own a generator. In a similar investigation, where many enterprises from developing countries must contend with an insufficient and unreliable supply of electricity, researchers have analyzed the negative effects of these energy restrictions and looked for the second-best solution through generators, which enable firms to reduce the negative effects of these outages (Alby et al., 2013). Key research is that of Moyo (2012), who studied how geography and infrastructure variables such as customs, transport, electricity, and water affected trade performance (exports), finding negative effects on export intensity and participation. Through the findings of these investigations, we propose the following:

Hypothesis 2a : Under conditions of political instability, city-level obstacles such as telecommunications perception have a negative effect on direct exports of formal or new firms.

Hypothesis 2b : Under conditions of political instability, city-level obstacles such as electricity perception damage direct exports of formal or new firms.

We have already reviewed the literature that analyzes the effects of firm- and city-level institutional determinants on firm exports. Finally, looking at the effects of institutional variables at the country level on firms' exports, we have found a wide variety of determinants, such as economic freedom and its indexes (Söderlund & Tingvall, 2014), productivity and credit/financial constraints (Castellani et al., 2022; Laborda et al., 2020; Regis, 2018; Zhou, Li, Yan, & Li, 2022b), formal institutions (Aparicio et al., 2021; Hernández et al., 2022; Wang & Ma, 2018; Yang et al., 2020), international sanctions (Crozet et al., 2021), among others. Although there is a wide diversity of determinants at the country level, we focus on two institutional obstacles that are also key determinants: taxes and the cost of business start-up procedures, which help us draw comparisons with extant research (cf. Aparicio et al., 2021).

On the one hand, the literature analyzing the effects of taxes on firm performance is extensive (Chauvet & Ferry, 2021; Hasan et al., 2021; Khuong et al., 2020); however, the literature analyzing the effects of taxes at the country level on firm exports is somewhat scant. The first approach to this relationship was developed approximately 50 years ago when Horst (1971) explored the profit-maximizing strategy for a monopolistic firm selling to two national markets simultaneously. The choice of how much to export between the two rested on two key considerations: (1) whether the marginal costs of production were rising or falling, and (2) whether tariffs and tax rates were high enough for the firm to discriminate perfectly between its two national markets. In general, the author concluded that a sufficiently restrictive tax policy induced a decision not to import by firms in both countries, indicating a negative effect of taxes on exports. A similar study was recently conducted using a trade model, in which Flach et al. (2021) analyzed how exporters were affected by corporate tax reforms in destination markets. The authors showed that introducing tax policy in a trade model of multiproduct firms allowed producers to face tougher competition in export markets with lower corporate tax rates. Thus, the competitive effect induced firms to reduce the number of exported products and to skew their export sales toward the better performing varieties. Okafor et al. (2020) supported this idea by claiming that firms benefiting from tax financial incentives showed a better export performance compared to those that did not, regardless of the degree of access to credit and/or financial incentives in the country in which they operate. In a detailed analysis of Italy, Federici et al. (2020) analyzed the effect of home corporate taxes on a firm's decision to expand the scale of its activity through exports and found that the burden of home corporate taxes affected the Italian firm's participation in international trade.

On the other hand, there is little literature that has analyzed the role of procedure costs on firm export performance; even so, three research studies are worth mentioning. On a first attempt, Alessandria and Choi (2007) derived the discrete entry and exit decisions yielding exporter dynamics in an open economy business cycle model, assuming that firms face a sunk cost of entering foreign markets. The authors showed that although the model's business cycle exporter dynamics were consistent with those of the US exporters, the results revealed that export decisions had negligible aggregate effects, taking into account these sunk costs. A year later, Kneller et al. (2008) highlighted the importance of firm characteristics and trade costs for exports from a theoretical and empirical perspective. The authors found that improvements in the business environment of foreign countries, such as decreased export costs, led to an increase in the export intensity of exporters in the UK manufacturing sector and additional export market entry. Finally, Dennis and Shepherd (2011) showed that improved trade facilitation can help promote export diversification in developing countries. Thus, the authors found that a 10% reduction in the cost of international transport and domestic exporting costs (documentation, inland transport, port, and customs charges) were associated with export diversification gains of 4% and 3%. This literature has allowed us to suggest the following set of hypotheses:

Hypothesis 3a : Under conditions of political instability, country-level obstacles such as total taxes and contribution rate harm direct exports of formal or new firms.

Hypothesis 3b : Under conditions of political instability, country-level obstacles such as the cost of business start-up procedures damage direct exports of formal or new firms.

The suggested hypotheses are summarized in the conceptual framework of Fig. 8.1.

8.3 Methodology

8.3.1 Data

We combined firm-level and country-level data for our sample and built two pooled cross-sectional datasets. First, we used The World Bank Enterprise Survey (WBES) firm-level data collected between 2006 and 2020. There are several aspects of this database to be considered. Each

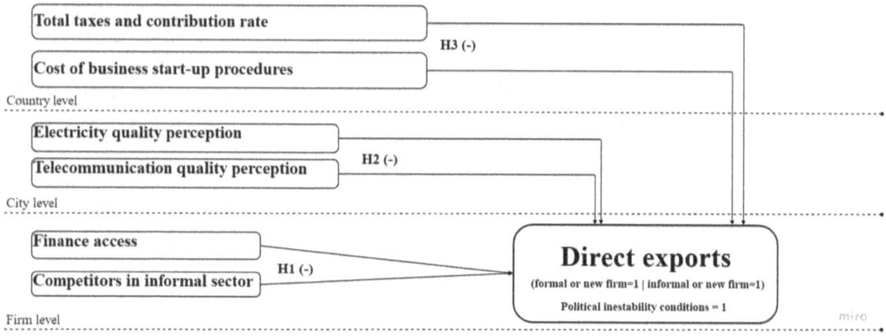

Fig. 8.1 Theoretical framework

country's survey may cover one, two, or three waves during the period mentioned. Also, the survey rounds and the number of interviews per country are conditional on the size of the economy. In addition, this survey is not country-specific; respondents in different countries were asked the same questions, and the sample was not repeated, so different firms were surveyed during the three periods (World Bank, 2021). A final comment on this database is that it allows us to build information at the city level, which is advantageous for our objectives. Second, we used the world development indicators from the World Bank between 2006–2020, allowing us to have information at the country level and to carry out a merge with the first database.

To obtain these two final databases, we carried out several steps. First, we kept the firms under political instability conditions (firms that consider political instability as a moderate, major, and a very severe obstacle to their current operations). Then, we bias by entrepreneurship and formality/informality firms. For this, in one database, we kept the initially formal or new firms (less than five years constituted) under conditions of political instability; and in the other database, we kept the initially informal or new firms under conditions of political instability. This was how we obtained our two databases. In the database that retained formal or new firms, we had a sample of 16,923 firms, 575 cities, and 111 countries; while for the database of informal or new firms we had a total of 3645 firms, 461 cities, and 111 countries. For more detailed information on the sample databases, please refer to Tables 8.4 and 8.5 in the Appendix.

To test our hypotheses, we used the firm's direct exports (% sales) as the dependent variable. This measure considered direct sales to a customer abroad, that is, sales in which firms carry out the entire process until the product reaches the customer's hands. We used two explanatory variables for each level: firm, city, and country level. At the firm level, we used two dummy variables which consisted of the firm's self-evaluation of the extent to which the access to finance and the practices of competitors in the informal sector were moderate, major, and very severe obstacles to the current operation of the establishment. At the city level, we used two variables representing the mean of the percentage of firms' self-perception that telecommunications and electricity were moderate, major, and very severe obstacles to their current operation. At the country level, we used the total taxes and contribution rate and the cost of business start-up procedures. For the control variables, we used one for each level: expenditure on research and development, time spent on government regulations, and gross capital formation. Table 8.1 shows a more detailed description of the variables.

Table 8.1 Variables' description

Variables	Description
Firm-level variables	
Direct export (% sales)	Firm's direct exports as a percentage of sales
Expenditure on R&D	During the last fiscal year, this establishment spent on research and development? 1=yes, no=0
Finance access	Access to finance is a moderate, major, and very severe obstacle to the current operation of this establishment? 1=yes, no=0
Competitors in the informal sector	Practices of competitors in the informal sector are a moderate, major, and very severe obstacle to the current operation of this establishment? 1=yes, no=0
City-level variables	
Time spent on government regulation	What percentage of senior management time was spent in dealing with government regulations? Mean at the city level
Electricity	Percentage of firms' self-perception of electricity as a moderate, major, and very severe obstacle to the current operation (at city level).
Telecommunications	Percentage of firms' self-perception of telecommunications as a moderate, major, and very severe obstacle to the current operation (at city level).

(continued)

Table 8.1 (continued)

Variables	Description
Country-level variables	
Gross capital formation (% GDP)	Gross capital formation (formerly gross domestic investment) consists of outlays on additions to the fixed assets of the economy plus net changes in the level of inventories
Total tax and contribution rate	The total tax rate measures the amount of taxes and mandatory contributions payable by businesses after accounting for allowable deductions and exemptions as a share of commercial profits. As % of profit
Cost of business start-up procedures	The cost to register a business is normalized by presenting it as a percentage of gross national income (GNI) per capita

Source: World development indicators and World Business Enterprise Survey

8.3.2 Empirical Strategy

A three-level model (with random intercepts [mixed effects]) was used to observe the effect that some institutional obstacles (at the firm, city, and country level) had on the direct exports of firm *i*, within city *j* nested in country *k*:

$$\boldsymbol{X}_{ijk} = \alpha + \boldsymbol{IO}_{ijk}\boldsymbol{\beta} + \boldsymbol{C}_{ijk}\theta + \boldsymbol{Z}^{3}_{ijk}\boldsymbol{u}^{3}_{k} + \boldsymbol{Z}^{2}_{ijk}\boldsymbol{u}^{2}_{jk} + \varepsilon_{ijk} \tag{8.1}$$

for which $i = 1, \ldots, n_{jk}$ (where n is equal to the observations; 16,923 for the formal or new firm's database and 3645 for the informal or new ones) firm-level observations nested within $j = 1, \ldots, M_k$ (where M_k is equal to the number of independent groups for the city) city-level groups, which are nested within $k = 1, \ldots, M$ country-level groups (where M is equal to the numbers of independent groups for the countries). Group j, k consists of n_{jk} observations, so $\boldsymbol{X}_{ijk}$, $\boldsymbol{IO}_{ijk}\boldsymbol{\beta}$, $\boldsymbol{C}_{ijk}\boldsymbol{\theta}$, and $\boldsymbol{\epsilon}_{ijk}$ each have a row dimension n_{jk}. Where $\boldsymbol{IO}_{ijk}$ is the design matrix for different institutional obstacles variables (i.e., explanatory variables) at the firm, city, and country levels, so $\boldsymbol{IO}_{ijk}$: {$\boldsymbol{IOfirm}_{ijk}$ [access to finance and competitors in the informal sector]; $\boldsymbol{IOcity}_{jk}$ [Electricity and telecommunication]; $\boldsymbol{IOcountry}_{k}$[Total tax and contribution rate and Cost of business start - up procedures]}. $\boldsymbol{C}_{ijk}\boldsymbol{\theta}$ is the design matrix for control variables.

X_{ijk} is the vector of responses for firms' direct exports. Z^3_{ijk} is the $n_{jk} \times 1$ design matrix for the third-level random effects u^3_k, while Z^2_{ijk} is the $n_{jk} \times 1$ design matrix for the second-level random effects u^2_{jk}. In addition, it is assumed that normal distribution for random effects is as follows:

$$u^3_k \sim N(0,\Sigma_3); u^2_{jk} \sim N(0,\Sigma_2); \varepsilon_{ijk} \sim N(0,\sigma^2_\varepsilon \mathbf{I}) \quad (8.2)$$

and that u^3_k, u^2_{jk}, and ϵ_{ijk} are independent. The variable list for the third-level random-effects equation is represented by Z^3_{ijk} and the second-level random-effects equation is represented by Z^2_{ijk}, with both set to the $n_{jk} \times 1$ column of ones. Finally, it is essential to mention that in our case $\Sigma_3 = \sigma^2_3$ and $\Sigma_2 = \sigma^2_2$ are both scalars (STATA, 2021).

To carry out the estimations, we first performed the xtmixed command at STATA 16, and developed different models depending on the level of the explanatory variable and whether the firms were formal/informal or new under political instability conditions. This empirical strategy enabled us to estimate the effects of our explanatory variables on direct exports considering the digital institutional bias of political instability conditions.

8.4 Results

8.4.1 Main Results

To approach the main results, Table 8.2 displays the descriptive statistics for the variables used in our models. There are some important aspects to highlight in this table. First, the average exports of initially formal or new firms were close to 12.8% of their sales, while those of initially informal or new firms were around 7.6%. This may be an indication that the path of formality had led to rapid growth for firms, while informality implied a delay in such growth. Second, if we observe the variables at the firm level, we can see that for a higher percentage of initially informal or new firms, access to finance and competition in the informal sector was a moderate, major, and very severe obstacle to their operations, 56% and

Table 8.2 Descriptive statistics

	Initially formal | new firms							Initially informal | new firms						
Variables	Mean	SD	Min	Max	P50	P75	N	Mean	SD	Min	Max	P50	P75	N
Direct export (% sales)	12.733	27.111	0.000	100.000	0.000	10.000	16,923	7.553	21.333	0.000	100.000	0.000	0.000	3645
Expenditure on R&D	0.296	0.457	0.000	1.000	0.000	1.000	16,923	0.235	0.424	0.000	1.000	0.000	0.000	3645
Finance access	0.531	0.499	0.000	1.000	1.000	1.000	16,923	0.562	0.496	0.000	1.000	1.000	1.000	3645
Competitors in informal sector	0.532	0.499	0.000	1.000	1.000	1.000	16,923	0.571	0.495	0.000	1.000	1.000	1.000	3645
Time spent on government regulation	10.528	7.308	0.000	60.700	11.168	15.065	16,923	9.591	6.978	0.000	60.700	9.606	13.562	3645
Electricity	0.538	0.219	0.000	1.000	0.547	0.693	16,923	0.550	0.225	0.000	1.000	0.567	0.708	3645
Telecommunications	0.175	0.154	0.000	1.000	0.158	0.276	16,923	0.189	0.170	0.000	1.000	0.161	0.309	3645
Gross capital formation (% GDP)	25.405	7.172	7.224	50.797	24.143	28.536	16,923	24.920	7.564	7.224	50.797	23.861	28.536	3645
Total tax and contribution rate	48.074	27.699	8.000	272.100	43.800	54.600	16,575	49.010	36.983	8.000	272.100	41.524	49.000	3637
Cost of business start-up procedures	26.310	41.738	0.200	235.300	12.400	32.391	16,575	28.954	47.162	0.200	235.300	12.400	32.967	3637

Note: N is equal to the observation. P50 and P75 are the respective percentiles

57% (formal or new firms), respectively, while at the city level, the perception of electricity and telecommunications as an obstacle was similar for both initially formal/informal and new firms.

In order to test our research hypotheses, we estimated Eq. (8.1). Table 8.3 below illustrates our main findings. Our results are robust across all twelve specifications, including and excluding firm, city, and country-level explanatory variables. Also, it can be seen that the estimates from 9–12 specifications with the country-level explanatory variables present a better fit to the data than the 1–8 specification since the Akaike Information Criterion f(AIC) and Bayesian Information Criterion (BIC) information criteria were much lower. In addition, it should be noted that the specifications that considered initially informal or new firms had a smaller number of observations, so their AIC and BIC will be lower (Akaike, 1974).

First, we found support for hypotheses 1a and 1b, which predicted that under conditions of political instability the finance access and competitors in the informal sector would negatively affect the direct exports of formal or new firms. Thus, under these conditions of political instability, direct exports decreased by 0.043% ($p < 0.001$) and 0.136% ($p < 0.001$) for formal or new firms that considered financial access and competition from the informal sector a moderate, major, or a very severe obstacle to their operations, respectively. These results support what Rossi et al. (2021) stated. Second, we also found support for hypotheses 2a and 2b, which predicted that under conditions of political instability the electricity and telecommunications institutional obstacles would harm formal or new firms' exports. In consequence, when the percentage of firms (at the city level) that consider electricity and telecommunications a moderate, major, or a very severe obstacle to their current operations increased by 1%, the formal or new firms' exports decreased by 0.062% ($p < 0.01$) and 0.052% ($p < 0.01$) respectively, thus supporting research such as that of Fernandes et al. (2019) and Moyo (2012). Finally, at the country level, we found support for hypotheses 3a and 3b, which predicted that under conditions of political instability institutional obstacles such as the total taxes and contribution rate and the cost of business start-up procedures would affect formal or new firms' export. Accordingly,

Table 8.3 Institutional obstacles' effect on firms' export

	Dependent variable: direct exports (% sales)											
	(1)	(2)	(3)	(4)	(5)	(6)	(7)	(8)	(9)	(10)	(11)	(12)
	New firms | initially formal	New firms | initially informal	New firms | initially formal	New firms | initially informal	New firms | initially formal	New firms | initially informal	New firms | initially formal	New firms | initially informal	New firms | initially formal	New firms | initially informal	New firms | initially formal	New firms | initially informal
Obstacle at the firm level												
Finance access	-0.043***	-0.044**										
	(0.008)	(0.014)										
Competitors in the informal sector			-0.136***	-0.072***								
			(0.008)	(0.015)								
Obstacle at the city level												
Telecomm-unication					-0.052**	-0.005						
					(0.019)	(0.022)						
Electricity							-0.062**	-0.063*				
							(0.023)	(0.025)				
Obstacle at the country level												
Total tax and contribution rate									-0.078**	0.006		
									(0.028)	(0.029)		

Cost of business start-up procedures											-0.107**	-0.014
											(0.041)	(0.057)
Constant	0.127**	-0.026	0.132***	-0.027	0.134***	-0.031	0.128***	-0.027	0.106**	-0.046	0.095*	-0.049
	(0.039)	(0.037)	(0.038)	(0.036)	(0.038)	(0.038)	(0.038)	(0.036)	(0.039)	(0.038)	(0.040)	(0.039)
Controls: firm level	**YES**	**YES**	**YES**	**YES**	**YES**	**YES**	**YES**	**YES**	**YES**	**YES**	**YES**	**YES**
Controls: regional level	**YES**	**YES**	**YES**	**YES**	**YES**	**YES**	**YES**	**YES**	**YES**	**YES**	**YES**	**YES**
Controls: country level	**YES**	**YES**	**YES**	**YES**	**YES**	**YES**	**YES**	**YES**	**YES**	**YES**	**YES**	**YES**
Observations	**16,923**	**3645**	**16,923**	**3645**	**16,923**	**3645**	**16,923**	**3645**	**16,575**	**3537**	**16,575**	**3537**
R-squared												
AIC	**48,019.614**	**8832.234**	**47,776.791**	**8817.669**	**48,040.683**	**8842.091**	**48,040.685**	**8836.557**	**46,914.195**	**8479.218**	**46,915.295**	**8479.203**
BIC	**48,081.505**	**8881.843**	**47,838.682**	**8867.278**	**48,102.575**	**8891.700**	**48,102.576**	**8886.166**	**46,975.920**	**8528.586**	**46,977.021**	**8528.572**

Note: Standard errors in parentheses: *$p<0.05$; **$p<0.01$; ***$p<0.001$. Control variables at the firm level: spent On R&D. At the regional level: time spent on government regulation. At the country level: gross capital formation (% GDP). AIC and BIC are the respective information criteria

under conditions of political instability when institutional obstacles such as the total taxes and contribution rate and the cost of business start-up procedures increased by 1%, the formal or new firms' exports decreased by 0.078% ($p < 0.01$) and 0.107% ($p < 0.01$), respectively.

If we look at the columns corresponding to the estimates that consider initially informal or new firms (even columns of Table 8.3), we can see that the effects at the city and country level lost significance, so we can deduce that the exports of this kind of firms were not significantly affected by the institutional obstacles at the city and country level, which makes a lot of sense. However, at the firm level, it did retain significance, as the exports of firms that considered financial access and competition from the informal sector as a moderate, major, or very severe obstacle to their operations decreased by 0.044% ($p < 0.01$) and 0.072% ($p < 0.001$), respectively.

8.4.2 Robustness Check

For this robustness check, we observed the change in the estimators when we modified the institutional condition bias from political instability to macroeconomic instability. Table 8.6 (in the Appendix) shows the estimates developed for the robustness check. As in our main results, the odd columns show the estimators for initially formal or new firms, while the even columns show the estimators for initially informal or new firms. The rows show the institutional barriers at the firm, city, and country levels.

First, through odd columns, we can identify that the negative and significant effect of institutional obstacles at the firm, regional, and country level on firms' direct exports was maintained when we performed the same mixed-effects (with random intercepts) estimation. Second, if we focus on the even columns, we can see that under institutional conditions of macroeconomic instability, significance was lost in most of the estimators except at the firm level, presenting consistency with the relationships and significances found in the main results of Table 8.3. Therefore, these robustness check analyses allow us to establish that the empirical strategy and the structure of the baseline models were consistent.

8.5 Discussion and Conclusions

Motivated by feeding the theory of international business, this chapter has a mix of concepts, such as entrepreneurship (new firms less than five years old), informality (through formally or informally constituted companies), and institutions (institutional obstacles), due to the wide transmission mechanisms that induce firms to carry out an exporting process. Thus, this chapter has a threefold purpose. First, it analyzes the triad between institutions, entrepreneurship, and international business by revealing the effect that some institutional obstacles have on the exports of initially formal or new companies. Second, the chapter seeks to demonstrate the importance of micro- and macrolevel analysis in the observed relationship. Finally, and as an addition, it examines whether the effect of these relationships is maintained when we look at firms which were informal.

Using institutional economics (North, 1990), we have reached three key conclusions that allow us to fill gaps in the literature on international business, entrepreneurship, and institutions. First, our research improves the understanding of the relationship between institutional barriers and international business such as firm exports, given that some research claims that complex institutional contexts contribute to firm growth through exports (Escobar et al., 2021; Krammer et al., 2018). Second, the negative effects of institutional barriers are more significant on formal or new firms, while these barriers lose significance when we analyze what happens with informal or new firms, which makes sense since informal firms move in the shadows many times, thus evading government procedures (Fan et al., 2020; Ferrantino et al., 2012) or benefiting from the advantage of the informality sector. Finally, it is important to emphasize that many determinants influence the export decision of firms (Haddoud et al., 2021), which is why adopting a multilevel methodology is important since it allows us to reveal the role of variables not only at the firm level but also at the city and country level; an example is what happens with informal or new firms in our results because although institutional barriers lose significance at the city and country level, barriers at the firm level still affect their international business, such as the firm's exports.

8.5.1 Theoretical and Policy Implications

The literature on international business and entrepreneurship is extensive (Cristea, 2011; Glavas & Mathews, 2014; Laborda et al., 2020; Nyu et al., 2022). Nonetheless, this research is able to find gaps in the triad of international business, entrepreneurship, and institutions, converging to three theoretical and two policy implications.

Firstly, we deal with the theoretical implications. We provide fresh insight into how institutional obstacles harm international businesses, such as exports of formal or new firms (start-ups). Although some research claims that institutional barriers drive exports, in this research we have found that firms need not feel threatened by financial access and competition from the informal sector, from services such as electricity and telecommunications, and national taxes or costs related to entrepreneurship. Second, perhaps these investigations that support a positive effect of institutional obstacles on the firm's exports do not take into account the fundamental role of informality in the countries; thus, our research points to differences in the effects that these obstacles have both on informal and formal start-ups. This allows us to understand that the ability of initially informal firms to evade some institutional barriers may allow them to do better locally than abroad. Third, and perhaps most importantly, this paper develops a micro- and macrolevel analysis of the relationship between institutions, entrepreneurship, and international business, accompanied by the informality bias, a methodology never used to analyze this complex set of literature. Scholars have long called for deeper analysis and research into institutional economics and entrepreneurship (Ha et al., 2021), but until now it has never been accompanied by international business and an important bias such as informality.

Next, we focus on the policy implications by providing recommendations to the policymakers of the countries and cities considered in this chapter. First, it is necessary to reduce taxes on company profits, which will generate a more accelerated growth of firms, leading them to international markets, in addition to reducing the costs of procedures related to business start-ups. Second, the cities' policymakers must provide adequate electrical and telecommunications services so that companies do not worry about power outages or failures in the internet or satellite signals, as this can affect productivity, leading to decreases in exports. Third, policymakers must provide easy access to credit and provide guarantees of competition in the sector in which these companies operate. Finally, it is necessary to generate programs for the formalization of companies as this will lead them to generate high growth rates and possible international expansion.

8.5.2 Limitations and Future Research

Although this research makes important contributions to the literature on entrepreneurship, institutional economics, and international business theory, it has two limitations that should be addressed in future research. The first limitation concerns the methodology. Although this methodology allowed us to carry out a multilevel analysis, the estimation method is sensitive to a greater number of variables; that is, the simpler the specification, the better. This methodology does not allow exploiting the amount of information that the database has at the signature level. Second, the structure of the database does not allow carrying out a dynamic cross-border analysis. Although there are countries that have two waves of data, there are countries that only have one, which leads to analyses focused on a single country or a specific region.

Appendix

Table 8.4 Number of firms and cities by country and region (initially informal)

Region and countries	# Cities	# Firms
Africa	86	571
Benin	2	5
Burundi	1	5
Cameroon	3	11
Chad	1	21
Congo, Dem. Rep.	4	65
Côte d'Ivoire	2	5

(continued)

Table 8.4 (continued)

Region and countries	# Cities	# Firms
Eswatini	1	6
The Gambia	1	17
Ghana	4	40
Guinea	1	1
Kenya	12	51
Lesotho	1	6
Liberia	2	8
Malawi	1	2
Mali	2	10
Mozambique	7	40
Nigeria	16	85
Rwanda	3	25
Senegal	2	11
Sierra Leone	3	16
South Sudan	3	30
Tanzania	4	23
Togo	1	6
Uganda	5	27
Zambia	4	55
East Asia Pacific	**65**	**537**
Cambodia	5	19
China	19	53
Indonesia	9	153
Lao PDR	5	16
Malaysia	5	74
Mongolia	5	16
Myanmar	5	128
Papua New Guinea	1	1
Philippines	5	21
Solomon Islands	1	10
Timor-Leste	1	5
Vietnam	4	41
Europe and Central Asia	**169**	**660**
Albania	4	9
Azerbaijan	1	1
Belarus	6	19
Bosnia and Herzegovina	2	5
Bulgaria	3	4
Croatia	4	6
Cyprus	1	2
Czech Republic	4	13
Denmark	5	10

(*continued*)

Table 8.4 (continued)

Region and countries	# Cities	# Firms
Estonia	3	5
Finland	4	16
Georgia	8	27
Greece	4	16
Hungary	3	3
Italy	4	17
Kazakhstan	13	80
Kosovo	5	10
Kyrgyz Republic	3	6
Lithuania	2	3
Luxembourg	1	1
Montenegro	2	5
North Macedonia	4	9
Poland	5	11
Portugal	5	45
Romania	10	16
Russian Federation	23	104
Serbia	2	5
Slovak Republic	3	8
Slovenia	2	3
Sweden	4	7
Tajikistan	1	2
Turkey	6	25
Ukraine	11	80
Uzbekistan	11	87
Latin America and Caribbean	**67**	**1236**
Antigua and Barbuda	1	4
Argentina	6	103
The Bahamas	1	4
Barbados	1	8
Belize	1	9
Bolivia	3	69
Chile	6	45
Colombia	5	323
Dominican Republic	3	17
El Salvador	6	164
Grenada	1	4
Guatemala	5	78
Guyana	1	11
Jamaica	2	9
Mexico	9	193
Paraguay	2	16

(*continued*)

Table 8.4 (continued)

Region and countries	# Cities	# Firms
Peru	4	117
St. Kitts and Nevis	1	2
St. Lucia	1	2
St. Vincent and the Grenadines	1	7
Suriname	2	3
Trinidad and Tobago	2	18
Uruguay	2	28
Venezuela, RB	1	2
Middle East/North Africa	**39**	**221**
Israel	2	5
Jordan	7	34
Lebanon	7	67
Malta	1	2
Morocco	10	47
Tunisia	7	23
West Bank and Gaza	3	28
Yemen, Rep.	2	15
South Asia Region	**35**	**431**
Bangladesh	4	163
Bhutan	3	5
India	22	199
Nepal	3	16
Pakistan	3	48
Total	**461**	**3656**

Table 8.5 Number of firms and cities by country and region (initially formal)

Region and countries	# Cities	# Firms
Africa	**96**	**1369**
Benin	2	25
Burundi	1	24
Cameroon	3	29
Chad	1	31
Congo, Dem. Rep.	4	53
Côte d'Ivoire	2	31
Eswatini	1	11
The Gambia	1	36
Ghana	4	74
Guinea	1	4
Kenya	12	357
Lesotho	1	18
Liberia	2	17
Malawi	4	15
Mali	2	37
Mauritania	2	9
Mozambique	7	112
Nigeria	17	106
Rwanda	3	29
Senegal	3	48
Sierra Leone	4	52
South Sudan	3	35
Sudan	1	1
Tanzania	5	75
Togo	1	14
Uganda	5	24
Zambia	4	102
East Asia Pacific	**77**	**1391**
Cambodia	5	50
China	25	243
Indonesia	9	201
Lao PDR	7	66
Malaysia	5	155
Mongolia	8	115
Myanmar	5	254
Papua New Guinea	2	16
Philippines	5	112
Solomon Islands	1	21
Timor-Leste	1	30
Vietnam	4	128

(*continued*)

Table 8.5 (continued)

Region and countries	# Cities	# Firms
Europe and Central Asia	**246**	**3936**
Albania	6	61
Azerbaijan	1	1
Belarus	8	100
Bosnia and Herzegovina	7	77
Bulgaria	8	90
Croatia	5	128
Cyprus	1	22
Czech Republic	5	178
Denmark	5	10
Estonia	7	52
Finland	4	16
Georgia	8	73
Greece	4	259
Hungary	8	77
Italy	5	147
Kazakhstan	14	247
Kosovo	9	53
Kyrgyz Republic	7	81
Lithuania	7	62
Luxembourg	1	1
Montenegro	4	13
North Macedonia	5	73
Poland	9	126
Portugal	6	301
Romania	11	353
Russian Federation	38	423
Serbia	5	71
Slovak Republic	8	127
Slovenia	4	78
Sweden	4	7
Tajikistan	4	12
Turkey	6	135
Ukraine	11	358
Uzbekistan	11	124
Latin America and Caribbean	**72**	**6312**
Antigua and Barbuda	1	13
Argentina	6	848
The Bahamas	1	9
Barbados	1	17
Belize	1	46
Bolivia	3	214

(continued)

Table 8.5 (continued)

Region and countries	# Cities	# Firms
Chile	6	560
Colombia	5	1014
Dominica	1	3
Dominican Republic	4	59
El Salvador	6	345
Grenada	1	4
Guatemala	5	420
Guyana	1	31
Jamaica	2	45
Mexico	9	1324
Paraguay	2	184
Peru	5	802
St. Kitts and Nevis	1	9
St. Lucia	1	16
St. Vincent and the Grenadines	1	20
Suriname	2	69
Trinidad and Tobago	2	50
Uruguay	2	184
Venezuela, RB	3	26
Middle East/North Africa	**45**	**1017**
Israel	3	13
Jordan	7	126
Lebanon	7	234
Malta	1	23
Morocco	13	196
Tunisia	9	264
West Bank and Gaza	3	124
Yemen, Rep.	2	37
South Asia Region	**39**	**2898**
Bangladesh	4	861
Bhutan	4	28
India	23	1701
Nepal	3	191
Pakistan	5	117
Total	**575**	**16,923**

Table 8.6 Macroeconomics instability robustness check

	Dependent variable: direct exports (% sales)											
	(1)	(2)	(3)	(4)	(5)	(6)	(7)	(8)	(9)	(10)	(11)	(12)
	New firms | initially formal	New firms | initially informal	New firms | initially formal	New firms | initially informal	New firms | initially formal	New firms | initially informal	New firms | initially formal	New firms | initially informal	New firms | initially formal	New firms | initially informal	New firms | initially formal	New firms | initially informal
Obstacle at the firm level												
Finance Access	-0.042***	-0.040**										
	(0.007)	(0.012)										
Competitors in the informal sector			-0.130***	-0.075***								
			(0.007)	(0.013)								
Obstacle at the city level												
Telecomm-unication					-0.040*	-0.018						
					(0.017)	(0.020)						
Electricity							-0.050*	-0.077**				
							(0.020)	(0.024)				
Obstacle at the country level												
Total tax and contribution rate									-0.064*	0.002		
									(0.025)	(0.028)		
Cost of business start-up procedures											-0.098**	-0.029
											(0.037)	(0.055)

Constant	0.109** (0.037)	−0.033 (0.036)	0.108** (0.036)	−0.034 (0.035)	0.117** (0.037)	−0.034 (0.037)	0.111** (0.037)	−0.032 (0.035)	0.095* (0.038)	−0.050 (0.037)	0.085* (0.039)	−0.054 (0.038)
Controls: firm level	**YES**	**YES**	**YES**	**YES**	**YES**	**YES**	**YES**	**YES**	**YES**	**YES**	**YES**	**YES**
Controls: regional level	**YES**	**YES**	**YES**	**YES**	**YES**	**YES**	**YES**	**YES**	**YES**	**YES**	**YES**	**YES**
Controls: country level	**YES**	**YES**	**YES**	**YES**	**YES**	**YES**	**YES**	**YES**	**YES**	**YES**	**YES**	**YES**
Observations	**24,159**	**4518**	**24,159**	**4518**	**24,159**	**4518**	**24,159**	**4518**	**23,758**	**4405**	**23,758**	**4405**
R-squared												
AIC	**67,906.964**	**10,669.544**	**67,598.793**	**10,645.458**	**67,940.205**	**10,679.378**	**67,939.640**	**10,670.145**	**66,665.213**	**10,312.249**	**66,664.718**	**10,311.982**
BIC	**67,971.703**	**10,720.870**	**67,663.532**	**10,696.784**	**68,004.944**	**10,730.704**	**68,004.380**	**10,721.472**	**66,729.818**	**10,363.373**	**66,729.323**	**10,363.106**

Note: Standard errors in parentheses: $^{*}p<0.05$; $^{**}p<0.01$; $^{***}p<0.001$. Control variables at the firm level: spent on R&D. At the regional level: time spent on government regulation. At the country level: gross capital formation (% GDP). AIC and BIC are the respective information criteria

References

Abor, J. Y., Agbloyor, E. K., & Kuipo, R. (2014). Bank finance and export activities of small and medium enterprises. *Review of Development Finance, 4*(2), 97–103. https://doi.org/10.1016/j.rdf.2014.05.004

Akaike, H. (1974). A new look at the statistical model identification. *IEEE Transactions on Automatic Control, 19*(6), 716–723. https://doi.org/10.1109/TAC.1974.1100705

Alby, P., Dethier, J. J., & Straub, S. (2013). Firms operating under electricity constraints in developing countries. *World Bank Economic Review, 27*(1), 109–132. https://doi.org/10.1093/wber/lhs018

Alessandria, G., & Choi, H. (2007). Do sunk costs of exporting matter for net export dynamics? *Quarterly Journal of Economics, 122*(1), 289–336. https://doi.org/10.1162/qjec.122.1.289

Aparicio, S., Audretsch, D., & Urbano, D. (2021). Why is export-oriented entrepreneurship more prevalent in some countries than others? Contextual antecedents and economic consequences. *Journal of World Business, 56*(3), 101,177.

Araujo, L., Mion, G., & Ornelas, E. (2016). Institutions and export dynamics. *Journal of International Economics, 98*, 2–20. https://doi.org/10.1016/j.jinteco.2015.08.004

Audretsch, D. B., Belitski, M., Caiazza, R., Günther, C., & Menter, M. (2022a). From latent to emergent entrepreneurship: The importance of context. *Technological Forecasting and Social Change. Elsevier Inc.* https://doi.org/10.1016/j.techfore.2021.121356

Audretsch, D. B., Belitski, M., Chowdhury, F., & Desai, S. (2022b). CEO gender, institutional context and firm exports. *International Business Review, 102*, 008.

Ault, J. K., & Spicer, A. (2020). The formal institutional context of informal entrepreneurship: A cross-national, configurational-based perspective. *Research Policy.* https://doi.org/10.1016/j.respol.2020.104160

Bassetti, T. D., Maso, L., & Lattanzi, N. (2015). Family businesses in Eastern European countries: How informal payments affect exports. *Journal of Family Business Strategy, 6*(4), 219–233. https://doi.org/10.1016/j.jfbs.2015.07.004

Baumol, W. J. (1996). Entrepreneurship: Productive, unproductive, and destructive. *Journal of Business Venturing, 11*(1), 3–22. https://doi.org/10.1016/0883-9026(94)00014-X

Bierut, B. K., & Dybka, P. (2021). Increase versus transformation of exports through technological and institutional innovation: Evidence from Bayesian model averaging. *Economic Modelling, 99*. https://doi.org/10.1016/j.econmod.2021.105501

Blomström, M., Fors, G., & Lipsey, R. E. (1997). Foreign direct investment and employment: Home country experience in the United States and Sweden. *Economic Journal, 107*(445), 1787–1797. https://doi.org/10.1111/j.1468-0297.1997.tb00082.x

Buckley, P. J. (2011). The theory of international business pre-Hymer. *Journal of World Business, 46*(1), 61–73. https://doi.org/10.1016/j.jwb.2010.05.018

Burns, D. K., Jones, A. P., Goryakin, Y., & Suhrcke, M. (2017). Is foreign direct investment good for health in low and middle income countries? An instrumental variable approach. *Social Science and Medicine, 181*, 74–82. https://doi.org/10.1016/j.socscimed.2017.03.054

Carbonero, F., Devicienti, F., Manello, A., & Vannoni, D. (2021). Women on board and firm export attitudes: Evidence from Italy. *Journal of Economic Behavior and Organization, 192*, 159–175. https://doi.org/10.1016/j.jebo.2021.10.011

Castellani, D., Giaretta, E., & Staglianò, R. (2022). Early-stage financing diversity and firms' export intensity: A cross-country analysis. *Finance Research Letters, 44*. https://doi.org/10.1016/j.frl.2021.102030

Chauvet, L., & Ferry, M. (2021). Taxation, infrastructure, and firm performance in developing countries. *Public Choice, 187*(3–4), 455–480. https://doi.org/10.1007/s11127-020-00788-4

Chen, Z., Poncet, S., & Xiong, R. (2020). Local financial development and constraints on domestic private-firm exports: Evidence from city commercial banks in China. *Journal of Comparative Economics, 48*(1), 56–75. https://doi.org/10.1016/j.jce.2019.09.005

Cicea, C., & Marinescu, C. (2021). Bibliometric analysis of foreign direct investment and economic growth relationship. A research agenda. *Journal of Business Economics and Management, 22*(2), 445–466. https://doi.org/10.3846/jbem.2020.14018

Coase, R. H. (1937). The nature of the firm. *Economica, 4*(16), 386–405. https://doi.org/10.1111/j.1468-0335.1937.tb00002.x

Cole, M. A., Elliott, R. J. R., Occhiali, G., & trobl, E. (2018). Power outages and firm performance in Sub-Saharan Africa. *Journal of Development Economics, 134*, 150–159. https://doi.org/10.1016/j.jdeveco.2018.05.003

Cristea, A. D. (2011). Buyer-seller relationships in international trade: Evidence from U.S. States' exports and business-class travel. *Journal of International Economics, 84*(2), 207–220. https://doi.org/10.1016/j.jinteco.2011.02.003

Crozet, M., Hinz, J., Stammann, A., & Wanner, J. (2021). Worth the pain? Firms' exporting behaviour to countries under sanctions. *European Economic Review, 134*. https://doi.org/10.1016/j.euroecorev.2021.103683

Deb, R., Samalia, H. V., & Prusty, S. K. (2020). The role of informal competition in driving export propensity of emerging economy firms: An attention based approach. *International Journal of Sociology and Social Policy, 40*(1–2), 184–203. https://doi.org/10.1108/IJSSP-06-2019-0131

Dennis, A., & Shepherd, B. (2011). Trade facilitation and export diversification. *World Economy, 34*(1), 101–122. https://doi.org/10.1111/j.1467-9701.2010.01303.x

Dong, M., Wang, L., Yang, D., & Zhou, K. Z. (2022a). Performance feedback and export intensity of Chinese private firms: Moderating roles of institution-related factors. *International Business Review, 31*(3). https://doi.org/10.1016/j.ibusrev.2021.101948

Dong, B., Guo, Y., & Hu, X. (2022b). Intellectual property rights protection and export product quality: Evidence from China. *International Review of Economics and Finance, 77*, 143–158. https://doi.org/10.1016/j.iref.2021.09.006

Babecký, J., Du Caju, P., Kosma, T., Lawless, M., Messina, J., & Rõõm, T. (2012). How do European firms adjust their labour costs when nominal wages are rigid? *Labour Economics, 19*(5), 792–801. https://doi.org/10.1016/j.labeco.2012.03.010

Escobar, O., Lamotte, O., Colovic, A., & Meschi, P. X. (2021). Impact of sourcing from the informal economy on the export likelihood and performance of emerging economy firms. *Industrial and Corporate Change*. https://doi.org/10.1093/icc/dtab068

Fan, H., Liu, Y., Qiu, L. D., & Zhao, X. (2020). Export to elude. *Journal of International Economics, 127*. https://doi.org/10.1016/j.jinteco.2020.103366

Faruq, H. A. (2011). How institutions affect export quality. *Economic Systems, 35*(4), 586–606. https://doi.org/10.1016/j.ecosys.2011.05.001

Federici, D., Parisi, V., & Ferrante, F. (2020). Heterogeneous firms, corporate taxes and export behavior: A firm-level investigation for Italy. *Economic Modelling, 88*, 98–112. https://doi.org/10.1016/j.econmod.2019.09.012

Fernandes, A. M., Mattoo, A., Nguyen, H., & Schiffbauer, M. (2019). The internet and Chinese exports in the pre-Ali Baba era. *Journal of Development Economics, 138*, 57–76. https://doi.org/10.1016/j.jdeveco.2018.11.003

Ferrantino, M. J., Liu, X., & Wang, Z. (2012). Evasion behaviors of exporters and importers: Evidence from the U.S.-China trade data discrepancy. *Journal of International Economics, 86*(1), 141–157. https://doi.org/10.1016/j.jinteco.2011.08.006

Flach, L., Irlacher, M., & Unger, F. (2021). Corporate taxes and multi-product exporters: Theory and evidence from trade dynamics. *Journal of International Economics, 132*. https://doi.org/10.1016/j.jinteco.2021.103515

Fu, X. (2007). Foreign direct investment, absorptive capacity and regional innovation capabilities: Evidence from China. *Oxford Development Studies, 36*(1), 89–110. https://doi.org/10.1080/13600810701848193

Fuentelsaz, L., González, C., & Maicas, J. P. (2019). Formal institutions and opportunity entrepreneurship. The contingent role of informal institutions. *BRQ Business. Research Quarterly, 22*(1), 5–24. https://doi.org/10.1016/j.brq.2018.06.002

Fuentelsaz, L., Garrido, E., & Maicas, J. P. (2020). The effect of informal and formal institutions on foreign market entry selection and performance. *Journal of International Management, 26*(2). https://doi.org/10.1016/j.intman.2020.100735

Glavas, C., & Mathews, S. (2014). How international entrepreneurship characteristics influence Internet capabilities for the international business processes of the firm. *International Business Review, 23*(1), 228–245. https://doi.org/10.1016/j.ibusrev.2013.04.001

Goedhuys, M., & Sleuwaegen, L. (2016). International standards certification, institutional voids and exports from developing country firms. *International Business Review, 25*(6), 1344–1355. https://doi.org/10.1016/j.ibusrev.2016.04.006

Ha, L. T., Thanh, T. T., Thang, D. N., & Anh, P. T. H. (2021). Bribery, export decisions, and institutional constraints: Evidence from cross-country firm-level data. *Economic Analysis and Policy, 69*, 585–612. https://doi.org/10.1016/j.eap.2021.01.010

Haddoud, M. Y., Onjewu, A. K. E., Nowiński, W., & Jones, P. (2021). The determinants of SMEs' export entry: A systematic review of the literature. *Journal of Business Research. Elsevier Inc.* https://doi.org/10.1016/j.jbusres.2020.12.017

Harasztosi, P., & Lindner, A. (2019). Who pays for the minimum wage? *American Economic Review, 109*(8), 2693–2727. https://doi.org/10.1257/aer.20171445

Hartman, R. (1975). Competitive firm and the theory of input demand under price uncertainty: Comment. *Journal of Political Economy, 83*(6), 1289–1290. https://doi.org/10.1086/260399

Hasan, M. M., Lobo, G. J., & Qiu, B. (2021). Organizational capital, corporate tax avoidance, and firm value. *Journal of Corporate Finance, 70*. https://doi.org/10.1016/j.jcorpfin.2021.102050

Hendy, R., & Zaki, C. (2021). Trade facilitation and firms exports: Evidence from customs data. *International Review of Economics and Finance, 75*, 197–209. https://doi.org/10.1016/j.iref.2021.03.023

Hernández, V., Nieto, M. J., & Rodríguez, A. (2022). Home country institutions and exports of firms in transition economies: Does innovation matter? *Long Range Planning, 55*(1). https://doi.org/10.1016/j.lrp.2021.102087

Hintošová, A. B., Bruothová, M., & Vasková, I. (2020). Does foreign direct investment boost innovation? The case of the Visegrad and Baltic countries. *Quality Innovation Prosperity, 24*(3), 106–121. https://doi.org/10.12776/QIP.V24I3.1519

Horst, T. (1971). The theory of the multinational firm: Optimal behavior under different tariff and tax rates. *Journal of Political Economy, 79*(5), 1059–1072. https://doi.org/10.1086/259814

Hymer, S. H. (1960). The international operations of national firms, a study of direct foreign investment (Doctoral dissertation, Massachusetts Institute of Technology).

Kahiya, E. T. (2018). Five decades of research on export barriers: Review and future directions. *International Business Review, 27*(6), 1172–1188. https://doi.org/10.1016/j.ibusrev.2018.04.008

Kapri, K. (2021). Court fairness and firm level export decisions. *International Review of Economics & Finance, 75*, 269–277. https://doi.org/10.1016/j.iref.2021.04.016

Kheng, V., Sun, S., & Anwar, S. (2017). Foreign direct investment and human capital in developing countries: A panel data approach. *Economic Change and Restructuring, 50*(4), 341–365. https://doi.org/10.1007/s10644-016-9191-0

Khuong, N. V., Liem, N. T., Thu, P. A., & Khanh, T. H. T. (2020). Does corporate tax avoidance explain firm performance? Evidence from an emerging economy. *Cogent Business and Management, 7*(1). https://doi.org/10.1080/23311975.2020.1780101

Kneller, R., Pisu, M., & Yu, Z. (2008). Overseas business costs and firm export performance. *Canadian Journal of Economics, 41*, 639–669. https://doi.org/10.1111/j.1540-5982.2008.00480.x

Krammer, S. M. S., Strange, R., & Lashitew, A. (2018). The export performance of emerging economy firms: The influence of firm capabilities and institutional environments. *International Business Review, 27*(1), 218–230. https://doi.org/10.1016/j.ibusrev.2017.07.003

Laborda, J., Salas, V., & Suárez, C. (2020). Manufacturing firms' export activity: Business and financial cycles overlaps! *International Economics, 162*, 1–14. https://doi.org/10.1016/j.inteco.2020.03.001

Leonidou, L. C., Katsikeas, C. S., & Coudounaris, D. N. (2010). Five decades of business research into exporting: A bibliographic analysis. *Journal of International Management, 16*(1), 78–91. https://doi.org/10.1016/j.intman.2009.06.001

Lipsey, R. E., & Sjöholm, F. (2004). Foreign direct investment, education and wages in Indonesian manufacturing. *Journal of Development Economics, 73*(1), 415–422. https://doi.org/10.1016/j.jdeveco.2002.12.004

Losilla-Solano, L. V., Brümmer, B., Engler, A., & Otter, V. (2019). Effects of intra- and inter-regional geographic diversification and product diversification on export performance: Evidence from the Chilean fresh fruit export sector. *Food Policy, 86*. https://doi.org/10.1016/j.foodpol.2019.101730

Lucas, D. S., & Fuller, C. S. (2017). Entrepreneurship: Productive, unproductive, and destructive—Relative to what? *Journal of Business Venturing Insights, 7*, 45–49. https://doi.org/10.1016/j.jbvi.2017.03.001

Martincus, C. V., Estevadeordal, A., Gallo, A., & Luna, J. (2010). Information barriers, export promotion institutions, and the extensive margin of trade. *Review of World Economics, 146*(1), 91–111. https://doi.org/10.1007/s10290-009-0043-0

Mcdonald, F., Tüselmann, H. J., & Heise, A. (2002). Foreign direct investment and employment in host regions. *European Business Review*. https://doi.org/10.1108/09555340210414232

Mertzanis, C., Basuony, M. A. K., & Mohamed, E. K. A. (2019). Social institutions, corporate governance and firm-performance in the MENA region. *Research in International Business and Finance, 48*, 75–96. https://doi.org/10.1016/j.ribaf.2018.12.005

Montalbano, P., & Nenci, S. (2019). Energy efficiency, productivity and exporting: Firm-level evidence in Latin America. *Energy Economics, 79*, 97–110. https://doi.org/10.1016/j.eneco.2018.03.033

Moyo, B. (2012). Infrastructure quality and manufacturing exports in Africa: A firm-level analysis. *South African Journal of Economics, 80*(3), 367–386. https://doi.org/10.1111/j.1813-6982.2011.01315.x

Munemo, J. (2022). Export entrepreneurship promotion: The role of regulation-induced time delays and institutions. *International Review of Economics and Finance, 77*, 262–275. https://doi.org/10.1016/j.iref.2021.10.009

Muñoz-Mora, J. C., Aparicio, S., Martinez-Moya, D., & Urbano, D. (2022). From immigrants to local entrepreneurs: Understanding the effects of migration on entrepreneurship in a highly informal country. *International Journal of Entrepreneurial Behavior & Research, 28*(9), 78–103.

Naylor, R., & Soegaard, C. (2022). Profit-raising entry under oligopolistic trade with endogenous input prices. *World Economy.* https://doi.org/10.1111/twec.13242

Nguyen, Q. T. K., Almodóvar, P., & Wei, Z. (2022a). Intra-firm and arm's length export propensity and intensity of MNE foreign subsidiaries. *Journal of Business Research, 145*, 288–308. https://doi.org/10.1016/j.jbusres.2022.02.062

Nguyen, P. C., Nguyen, B., & Thanh, S. D. (2022b). The importance of export diversification for national entrepreneurship density. *Structural Change and Economic Dynamics., 62*, 114–129. https://doi.org/10.1016/j.strueco.2022.05.003

North, D. C. (1990). Institutions, institutional change, and economic performance. In *Institutions, Institutional Change and Economic Performance*. Cambridge University Press.

North, D. C. (2005). *Understanding the process of economic change*. Princeton University Press.

Nyu, V., Nilssen, F., & Kandemir, D. (2022). Small exporting firms' choice of exchange mode in international marketing channels for perishable products: A contingency approach. *International Business Review, 31*(1). https://doi.org/10.1016/j.ibusrev.2021.101919

Okafor, L. E., Bhattacharya, M., & Apergis, N. (2020). Bank credit, public financial incentives, tax financial incentives and export performance during the global financial crisis. *World Economy, 43*(1), 114–145. https://doi.org/10.1111/twec.12848

Omri, A. (2020). Formal versus informal entrepreneurship in emerging economies: The roles of governance and the financial sector. *Journal of Business Research, 108*, 277–290. https://doi.org/10.1016/j.jbusres.2019.11.027

Osei, M. J., & Kim, J. (2020). Foreign direct investment and economic growth: Is more financial development better? *Economic Modelling, 93*, 154–161. https://doi.org/10.1016/j.econmod.2020.07.009

Packard, M. D., & Burnham, T. A. (2021). Do we understand each other? Toward a simulated empathy theory for entrepreneurship. *Journal of Business Venturing, 36*(1). https://doi.org/10.1016/j.jbusvent.2020.106076

Parrotta, P., Pozzoli, D., & Sala, D. (2016). Ethnic diversity and firms' export behavior. *European Economic Review, 89*, 248–263. https://doi.org/10.1016/j.euroecorev.2016.08.001

Qi, G., Zou, H., Xie, X., Meng, X., Fan, T., & Cao, Y. (2020). Obedience or escape: Examining the contingency influences of corruption on firm exports. *Journal of Business Research, 106*, 261–272. https://doi.org/10.1016/j.jbusres.2018.09.004

Regis, P. J. (2018). The extensive and intensive margins of exports of firms in developing and emerging countries. *International Review of Economics and Finance, 56*, 39–49. https://doi.org/10.1016/j.iref.2018.03.016

Rodríguez-Pose, A., Tselios, V., Winkler, D., & Farole, T. (2013). Geography and the determinants of firm exports in Indonesia. *World Development, 44*, 225–240. https://doi.org/10.1016/j.worlddev.2012.12.002

Rossi, S. P. S., Bonanno, G., Giansoldati, M., & Gregori, T. (2021). Export starters and exiters: Do innovation and finance matter? *Structural Change and Economic Dynamics, 56*, 280–297. https://doi.org/10.1016/j.strueco.2020.11.004

Sá, E. S., & Pinho, J. C. M. R. de. (2019). Effect of entrepreneurial framework conditions on R&D transfer to new and growing firms: The case of European Union innovation-driven countries. *Technological Forecasting and Social Change, 141*, 47–58. https://doi.org/10.1016/j.techfore.2019.01.017

Sahasranamam, S., & Nandakumar, M. K. (2020). Individual capital and social entrepreneurship: Role of formal institutions. *Journal of Business Research, 107*, 104–117. https://doi.org/10.1016/j.jbusres.2018.09.005

Shetewy, N., Shahin, A. I., Omri, A., & Dai, K. (2022). Impact of financial development and internet use on export growth: New evidence from machine learning models. *Research in International Business and Finance, 61*. https://doi.org/10.1016/j.ribaf.2022.101643

Smith, R. D. (2004). Foreign direct investment and trade in health services: A review of the literature. *Social Science and Medicine, 59*(11), 2313–2323. https://doi.org/10.1016/j.socscimed.2004.03.021

Söderlund, B., & Tingvall, P. G. (2014). Dynamic effects of institutions on firm-level exports. *Review of World Economics, 150*(2), 277–308. https://doi.org/10.1007/s10290-013-0181-2

Solomon, S. J., Bendickson, J. S., Marvel, M. R., McDowell, W. C., & Mahto, R. (2021). Agency theory and entrepreneurship: A cross-country analysis. *Journal of Business Research, 122*, 466–476. https://doi.org/10.1016/j.jbusres.2020.09.003

STATA. (2021). *Multilevel mixed-effects reference manual.* Stata Press.

Tojeiro-Rivero, D., & Moreno, R. (2019). Technological cooperation, R&D outsourcing, and innovation performance at the firm level: The role of the regional context. *Research Policy, 48*(7), 1798–1808. https://doi.org/10.1016/j.respol.2019.04.006

Tsekeris, T. (2017). Domestic transport effects on regional export trade in Greece. *Research in Transportation Economics, 61*, 2–14. https://doi.org/10.1016/j.retrec.2016.08.006

Wang, W., & Ma, H. (2018). Export strategy, export intensity and learning: Integrating the resource perspective and institutional perspective. *Journal of World Business, 53*(4), 581–592. https://doi.org/10.1016/j.jwb.2018.04.002

Wassink, J. (2020). International migration experience and entrepreneurship: Evidence from Mexico. *World Development, 136*. https://doi.org/10.1016/j.worlddev.2020.105077

Weterings, A. (2014). What makes firms leave the neighbourhood? *Urban Studies, 51*(8), 1613–1633. https://doi.org/10.1177/0042098013498624

Williamson, O. E. (2000). The new institutional economics: Taking stock, looking ahead. *Journal of Economic Literature, 38*(3), 595–613.

Wong, K. N., & Tang, T. C. (2011). Foreign direct investment and employment in manufacturing and services sectors: Fresh empirical evidence from Singapore. *Journal of Economic Studies, 38*(3), 313–330. https://doi.org/10.1108/01443581111152427

World Bank. (2021). Survey methodology. Retrieved April 16, 2021, from https://www.enterprisesurveys.org/en/methodology

Xie, D., Li, X., & Zhou, D. (2022). Does environmental information disclosure increase firm exports? *Economic Analysis and Policy, 73*, 620–638. https://doi.org/10.1016/j.eap.2021.12.012

Yang, M. M., Li, T., & Wang, Y. (2020). What explains the degree of internationalization of early-stage entrepreneurial firms? A multilevel study on the joint effects of entrepreneurial self-efficacy, opportunity-motivated entrepreneurship, and home-country institutions. *Journal of World Business, 55*(6). https://doi.org/10.1016/j.jwb.2020.101114

Zhou, F., Wen, H., & Lee, C. C. (2022a). Broadband infrastructure and export growth. *Telecommunications Policy, 102*, 347. https://doi.org/10.1016/j.telpol.2022.102347

Zhou, T., Li, X., Yan, G., & Li, J. (2022b). How productivity and credit constraints affect exports differently? Firm-level evidence from China. *Structural Change and Economic Dynamics, 62*(C), 207–230.

9

From Micro to Macro: Entrepreneurial Choice and Economic Growth Across Cities in a Developing Country

Diego Gomez, Sebastian Aparicio, and David Urbano

9.1 Introduction

As mentioned in previous chapters, entrepreneurship plays a fundamental role in the economic growth of countries (Bosma et al., 2018; Wennekers & Thurik, 1999), which is why it has been widely examined and analyzed in the literature. Entrepreneurship begins once the individual decides to become an entrepreneur; this is called the entrepreneurial choice (Choi & Shepherd, 2004). Most of the literature studying the entrepreneurial decision employs different levels of analyses, with a focus on individual (Lévesque & Minniti, 2006; Sternberg and Stüber 2012)

D. Gomez
Fundación ECSIM, Medellin, Colombia

S. Aparicio (✉) • D. Urbano
Department of Business, Universitat Autònoma de Barcelona, Cerdanyola del Vallés, Barcelona, Spain

Centre for Entrepreneurship and Social Innovation Research (CREIS), Universitat Autònoma de Barcelona, Sabadell, Barcelona, Spain
e-mail: Sebastian.Aparicio@uab.cat

D. Gomez et al. (eds.), *Driving Complexity in Economic Development*,
https://doi.org/10.1007/978-3-031-34386-5_9

or regional (Stuetzer et al., 2014; Wennekers 2005) characteristics. However, little is known about the transition across these levels, where entrepreneurs are assumed to be a catalyst for income and employment generation, hence, increasing the level of regional development (Feldman, 2001; Mueller & Thomas, 2001). Although a wide range of literature exists on developed countries (Ghosh, 2017; Othman & Tengku Muda, 2018), limited analysis exists for regions in emerging economies (Bruton et al., 2008).

To fill these gaps in the literature, this chapter has three key purposes. First, it identifies the role that individual and regional characteristics play in the entrepreneurial choice. Second, it proposes a transmission mechanism through which the entrepreneur generates individual and social benefits. Third, it examines how the transmission mechanism boosts the economic growth of Colombian regions. To achieve this, we propose three-stage modeling using two different sources of information: the *Gran Encuesta Integrada de Hogares* (GEIH) from 2017 to 2019 and the *Indice de Competitividad de Ciudades* (ICC) from 2018 to 2019. With these two sources of information, we were able to create two data panels that helped us to construct entrepreneurship proxies (e.g., employer and self-employed), as well as individual and regional characteristics that enable entrepreneurial activity, which spurs the labor income (as the key transmission mechanism) and per capita GDP of the main Colombian cities. Considering a simultaneous approach, we propose a probit and two-stage probit least square (2SPLS) model, as well as linear regressions that aggregate individual results and variables at the regional level. These (fixed-effects) models are performed using a pooled dataset.

Three main results are obtained. First, when regional characteristics such as computer possession and company taxes appear in a particular city, the probability of becoming an employer increases and decreases, respectively, while the probability of becoming self-employed decreases. Similarly, individual characteristics increase the probability of being an employer or self-employed. Second, becoming an employer increases labor income, but becoming self-employed decreases this outcome. Third, when employers and the self-employed increase their income, the per capita GDP of the Colombian cities increases and decreases, respectively. These results strengthen the knowledge in current literature, leading to theoretical and policy implications that allow us to propose recommendations for policymakers on where to redirect efforts to obtain benefits for economic growth and to emphasize the fundamental role that the entrepreneurial decision plays in the development path of emerging economies.

The remainder of this chapter is structured as follows. The next section presents the theoretical framework. We then set out the hypothesis development. Then, we develop the methodology, involving the source of the data and the empirical strategy; this is followed by the presentation of the results. Finally, we conclude and generate a discussion on theoretical and policy implications.

9.2 Conceptual Framework

The literature on entrepreneurship is broad and covers clarification of the types of entrepreneurship (Baumol, 1996; Stenholm et al., 2013; Wennekers & Van Stel, 2017), entrepreneurial intentions (Krueger et al., 2000; Liñán & Chen, 2009), and the entrepreneurship effects on macro (Bosma et al., 2018; Wennekers & Thurik, 1999) and microeconomics (Baumol, 2010; Kirchhoff, 1992; Stull, 2014), as well as entrepreneurship in developed (Sternberg & Wennekers, 2005; Valliere & Peterson, 2009) and developing countries (Acs & Szerb, 2007; Mohamad et al., 2021; Naudé, 2010). The prior literature has also considered different forms of measuring entrepreneurship (Gartner & Shane, 1995; Henrekson & Sanandaji, 2020), involving the entrepreneurial decision (Choi & Shepherd, 2004; Eisenhauer, 1995) and decision-making (Dew et al., 2009; Long et al., 2021; Romano et al., 2001), among others. This research subscribes the literature focused on the entrepreneurial decision.

On the one hand, many definitions have been associated with entrepreneurship, from taking the risk of introducing new products to the market, identifying and exploiting opportunities, to the possibility of creating a company capable of generating value. Given the importance of entrepreneurship not only for the entrepreneur but also for the society and the economy in general, much effort has been put into identifying who is willing and committed to developing entrepreneurial activity (Kritikos, 2015). In general, the entrepreneurial decision is related to the idea of becoming an entrepreneur. The fundamental aspects of the entrepreneurial decision have already been studied. Eisenhauer (1995) offers a major contribution by suggesting a model with testable hypotheses that made it possible to identify the most significant determinants across the process of becoming an entrepreneur (self-employed). Eisenhauer (1995) finds that the probability of a worker choosing self-employment responds positively to wealth, the probability of unemployment, and hours of work in the wage sector, and responds negatively to increases in wages and income insurance provided to wage laborers. Other research has examined (individual) aspects such as age (Coduras et al., 2018), uncertainty (Rapp & Olbrich, 2020), and the role of personal capital (Elston & Audretsch, 2011). However, little research has analyzed individual and regional characteristics together as determinants of the entrepreneurial choice.

On the other hand, the extensive literature relating entrepreneurship to economic growth is well known (Acs et al., 2009; Audretsch et al., 2007; Stel et al., 2005; Urbano & Aparicio, 2016; Wennekers & Thurik, 1999), from research involving innovation (Hall et al., 2012; Wong et al., 2005), education (Guerrero & Urbano, 2012; Kuratko, 2005; Laukkanen, 2000), and institutions (Acs et al., 2018; Aparicio et al., 2016; Sobel, 2008), among other mechanisms to achieve economic growth. However, the relationship between the entrepreneurial decision (i.e., micro) and economic growth (i.e., macro) has been little explored, perhaps because a conducive mechanism that connects both levels has not been sufficiently explored.

Two key pieces of research help us address this gap. Audretsch (2009) explains why and how entrepreneurship has emerged as an engine of economic growth, employment creation, and competitiveness in global markets. He raises a fundamental question in his paper: what is the source of the entrepreneurial opportunity that endogenously generated the set-up of the new ventures? He then responds: "the spillover of knowledge that created the opportunities for the startup of a new firm" (p. 251). For Audretsch, it is clear that the mechanism through which the individual makes the decision to undertake an entrepreneurial project and, in turn, allows the creation of benefits through economic growth is knowledge. This mechanism supports Acs et al.'s (2013) knowledge spillover theory of entrepreneurship. It is at this point that we identify a limitation of the literature. What if other conducive mechanisms also exist? In this research, we therefore also seek to propose a mechanism related to monetary incentives that allows us to observe the effects of the entrepreneurial decision (micro) on economic growth (macro).

9.3 Hypothesis Development

From Leibenstein's (1968) theory of economics and entrepreneurship to the modern day, researchers have been concerned with showing the fundamental role of entrepreneurship in how societies develop. Studying its determinants is therefore of crucial importance. These determinants are heterogeneous and broad. For example, some research has examined the macro and micro determinants of entrepreneurship. Jabeur et al. (2022) use artificial intelligence to forecast the macro-level determinants of entrepreneurial opportunity and find that entrepreneurs prefer to exploit opportunities in countries with stable economic governance. Praag and Ophem (1995) develop an empirical model to separate the unobserved factors of "opportunity" and "willingness" in the decision of labor force participants to become self-employed or not. They find that although there is a great interest among young American people in becoming entrepreneurs, financing forms a barrier and is a fundamental determinant for the entrepreneurial choice. However, Grilo and Thurik (2008) decompose the entrepreneurial decision process into seven engagement levels ranging from "never thought about starting a business" to "gave up," "thinking about it," "taking steps for starting up," "having a young business," "having an older business," and "no longer being an entrepreneur." Unlike Van Praag and Ophem (1995), Grilo and Thurik (2008) find that the perception of lack of financial support has no negative effects across the various levels of entrepreneurial engagement, whereas the perception of administrative complexities plays a negative role only for high levels of engagement. Other types of research examine the determinants of the entrepreneurial decision from specific cases. Minniti and Naudé (2010) help clarify the motivations, constraints, and issues that confront female entrepreneurs, while Nkongolo-Bakenda and Chrysostome (2013) examine determinants such as level of altruistic motivation, the need for social recognition, entrepreneurial opportunities, friendliness, and receptivity of the home country for migrant entrepreneurs. This is how we can support the broad spectrum of the literature analyzing the determinants of the entrepreneurial decision. Even so, this literature is reduced if we look primarily at determinants such as regional and individual characteristics.

Important research has studied regional characteristics as determinants of the entrepreneurial decision (and entrepreneurship in general). Sternberg and Wennekers (2005) develop research on the determinants and effects of entrepreneurship based on the Global Entrepreneurship Monitor (GEM), and among their results, they find that entrepreneurship is again shown as a regional event that can only be understood if regional framework conditions, including networks and regional policies, are taken into consideration. Lasch et al. (2013) study the role of regional determinants in new entrepreneurs' location decisions, using data from new information and communication technology (ICT) firms in France from 1993 to 2001; they find that agglomeration, entrepreneurial capital, and human capital in the regions of France are key determinants of new entrepreneurs' location decisions. In a study of South Africa, Naudé et al. (2008) identify the determinants of start-up rates across different sub-national regions, finding that the most significant determinants are profit rates, educational levels, agglomeration as measured by the economic size of a district, and access to formal bank financing. Stuetzer et al. (2014), in a study of Western Germany with regional-level data, find no direct link between regional knowledge creation, the economic context, and entrepreneurial culture.

However, some regional characteristics require special attention, especially in a context such as Colombia. In this case, we refer to two regional characteristics: taxes and access to ICTs. First, high-quality literature has studied the significance and effect of taxes on the entrepreneurial decision (Baliamoune-Lutz & Garello, 2014). Some research has considered the effect on entrepreneurship such as self-employment or nascent entrepreneurs. Ngwaba and Azizi (2020) investigate the effects of tax reform on entrepreneurship decisions in South Africa, contrasting periods before and after tax reform, which allowed them to examine individuals in the formal and informal sector and measure the effectiveness of the reform on self-employment. They find that the tax reform had a positive and significant effect on the probability of becoming self-employed in South Africa. Baliamoune-Lutz (2015) examines how taxes and tax progressivity affect two different types of entrepreneurship—namely, established business ownership and nascent entrepreneurship in a large group of

OECD countries. She suggests that higher tax progressivity exerts a negative influence on nascent enterprises but appears to have no impact on established business ownership. This is crucial, because it reveals the difference in the effects of taxes depending on the definition of entrepreneurship. Finally, Venâncio et al. (2020) examine the impact of corporate taxation on entrepreneurship and find that the tax reform increased firm entry and new firm job creation. These findings suggest that corporate taxation is an imperative constraint for the entrepreneurial decision, particularly for high-quality entrepreneurs. This allows us to propose the following hypothesis:

Hypothesis 1a: Cities with less support for entrepreneurship (e.g., higher tax burden for entrepreneurs, i.e., regional characteristics) reduce the probability of an individual becoming either an employer or self-employed.

Second, the literature has also sought to identify the effects that ICTs have on entrepreneurship (Išoraitė, 2014; Zhang & Li, 2018). Felsenstein and Fleischer (2002) present an analysis of a public assistance program for small-scale entrepreneurship in peripheral areas. Some results indicate that ICTs have a potential role in increasing the visibility of small firms in remote locations and creating a more symmetrical flow of information. Chatterjee et al. (2020) support the idea that different types of access, such as mental, material, skill, and usage, contribute significantly toward the adoption of ICTs among rural women. ICT adoption leads to innovation and boosts entrepreneurial orientation which aids micro-entrepreneurship. In recent research, Asongu and Nwachukwu (2018) find that ICT complements openness to improve the conditions of doing business in Sub-Saharan Africa, and the effects are contingent on the dynamics of openness, ICT, and entrepreneurship. Wellalage et al. (2021) explore entrepreneurs' assessments of the role of ICT for their financial inclusion and its effects in Africa. The results confirm the significant role technological deepening plays in advancing financial inclusion in Africa, as well as its potential for wider applicability to other developing economies. Although there is not much evidence for the effects of ICT on entrepreneurship such as self-employment or becoming an employer, given the conditions of entrepreneurship in Colombia, where self-employment is associated with informality, the previous literature allows us to propose the following hypothesis:

> *Hypothesis 1b: Access to ICTs (i.e., computer possession across households) increases the probability of an individual becoming an employer, while the probability of an individual becoming self-employed is decreased.*

Some of the literature on entrepreneurship examines the effects of individual characteristics on the entrepreneurial decision. For example, Matos and Hall (2020) examine why impoverished people in Brazil may choose to engage in entrepreneurship, the characteristics that shape their entrepreneurial behavior, and the struggles they face, finding that temporal myopia, misjudgment of abilities, and counter-productive use of social networks result in non-productive entrepreneurship. The authors highlight that non-productive entrepreneurship is also a prevalent problem but is heavily shaped by the interactions between individual characteristics and the institutional environment. In a less theoretical exercise, Dileo and García Pereiro (2019) analyze the interplay between individual and context factors among nascent, young, and established entrepreneurs across 49 different countries, mixing data from different sources and applying multilevel binary logistic regression models. Focusing on the individual characteristics, the authors find that entrepreneurial activities are male-headed, irrespective of the entrepreneurial stage of their activities, and that highly educated entrepreneurs are more oriented toward starting up new ventures. In a study of Germany, Sternberg and Wagner (2004) examine the link of two stylized facts: the impact of the region and the impact of socio-demographic determinants such as gender and age on an individual's decision to start a new venture. They show that, ceteris paribus, region matters for the decision to start a new business, but controlling for gender, age, education, among other variables, is necessary. This literature elucidates that determinants such as individual characteristics (i.e., age and gender) are crucial to the entrepreneurial choice.

Two key pieces of research support this perspective. First, Lévesque and Minniti (2006) provide empirical evidence showing that younger individuals are more likely to start a new firm than older ones. They present a model in which individuals select a career path according to the dynamic interplay of age, wealth, and risk aversion. This suggests that, when considering employment status choice, younger individuals are more likely to start a new firm than older individuals, perhaps as a result of an age effect which, all else being equal, reduces the relative return to entrepreneurship as individuals become older. Second, Brixy et al. (2012) shed some light on the selection that takes place during the entrepreneurial process and explain empirically the demographic and cognitive characteristics of (potential) entrepreneurs. This research leads to important conclusions. For instance, the gender gap is a factor where politics is required. Women often do not even think of becoming self-employed, but those who do decide to start a firm do so with greater confidence than men, especially at a very young age. This leads us to propose the following hypothesis:

Hypothesis 1c: Being male and older age increase the probability of an individual becoming either an employer or self-employed.

As stated, knowledge spillover is a mechanism commonly identified in the prior literature, which is rooted in the knowledge spillover theory of entrepreneurship (Ghio et al., 2015). Audretsch (2005) presents this theoretical approach by suggesting that entrepreneurship is the missing link in the process of economic growth, because it facilitates the spillover of knowledge from universities and private firms, resulting in the commercialization of ideas that otherwise might remain uncommercialized. Acs et al. (2009) advance the microeconomic foundations of endogenous growth theory by developing a knowledge spillover theory of entrepreneurship, allowing entrepreneurs to identify and exploit opportunities. In a study in a developing economy, Iftikhar et al. (2020) use a novel dataset to measure knowledge stock and spillovers in ten major cities across Pakistan. They reveal that knowledge spillovers play a crucial role in the creation of new ventures and that the knowledge spillover theory of entrepreneurship holds at the city level in Pakistan. However, in our research, we want to establish a different mechanism, which serves as a connector with economic growth. We therefore use monetary incentives (e.g., income) as a mechanism, as some research has inquired into comparing earnings from entrepreneurship versus wage earning (cf. Åstebro, 2017) and the importance of these earnings as an incentive for the entrepreneurial decision (Markman et al., 2004).

Åstebro and Chen (2014) analyze why individuals become entrepreneurs when entrepreneurs, on average, earn less than employees. They explain that it is due to income underreporting by entrepreneurs. After correcting for income underreporting, the mean financial gain for entrepreneurship is positive and large, greater than 42%. Soon and Lim (2016) contribute to the empirical literature and focus on the issue of whether or not entrepreneurship education is significant in influencing earnings, employment probabilities, and types of job. They draw four main conclusions. First, graduate entrepreneurs' monthly earnings are higher than graduates employed in qualification-mismatched jobs but lower than those with qualification-matching jobs. Second, graduates with entrepreneurship degrees earn less than those with non-entrepreneurship degrees. Third, having an entrepreneurship degree has no significant influence on employment chances. Finally, an entrepreneurship degree also is insignificantly associated with any of the probabilities of landing a job that is either commensurate or incommensurate with one's degree, or with the probabilities of being unemployed. This research shows the importance of entrepreneurial knowledge for earning and employment.

Examining other research streams, some studies relate entrepreneurship choice and income to the individual characteristics of entrepreneurs. Budig (2006) explores how gender, family, and class alter the impact of self-employment on earnings. She finds that professionals receive the same self-employment earnings premium, regardless of gender. However, self-employment in non-professional occupations negatively affects women's earnings, with wives and mothers incurring the greatest penalties. Budig (2006) also states that the high concentration of non-professional self-employed women in child care accounts for much of these penalties. Marshall and Flaig (2014) focus on the relationship between marriage and women's self-employment earnings in the United States. They establish that marriage poses an additional constraint on women entrepreneurs, finding that marriage and children had a negative association with women's self-employment earnings.

Other researches have focused on the earnings structure of multiple jobholders. On the one hand, Schulz et al. (2017) demonstrate that engaging in self-employment as a second job significantly increases the probability of having higher average earnings in this second job, compared to being paid employed in both occupations. On the other hand, Alm and Erard (2016) have also developed a new approach for estimating the self-employment earnings of informal suppliers. Based on this literature and taking into account the labor structure in Colombia, we propose the following hypothesis:

Hypothesis 2: Becoming an employer increases labor income; however, becoming self-employed reduces it.

So far, we have reviewed the literature that strengthens the entrepreneurial choice depending on individual and regional characteristics, in addition to observing whether such a decision increases or decreases income. What about economic growth? Can labor income serve as a mechanism for identifying the effect of entrepreneurship on the growth process? This prior literature is helpful to clarify this. For example, some research has focused on explaining economic growth through income distribution, real income, and labor income share. Humphries and Weisdorf (2019) circumvent the problem that workers' annual incomes are inferred from day wage rates without knowing how many days of work laborers undertook per year. The results indicate that the current global downturn in labor share is not exceptional but fits within the range of historical fluctuations. Bilan et al. (2020) use structural analysis based on two forms of income (distribution-functional and household) to identify income inequality and inconsistencies in distributive strategies. They conclude that countries with the most stable and clear patterns in income distribution have distinct connections between the share of labor costs in GDP and successes in social and economic spheres, including human development level, property rights protection, and GDP growth. In a study of developing economies, De Gregorio (1992) considers growth determinants in 12 Latin American countries during the period 1950–1985, finding that share of labor in income was lower in the sample group than in developed countries, while factor productivity growth accounts for a larger proportion of growth in the fastest-growing countries. Using panel data, macroeconomic stability, in addition to investment (physical and human), is found to play a crucial role in growth.

However, very little has been documented about the interplay between the entrepreneurial decision, entrepreneur incomes, and economic growth in these countries, and especially in Colombia. Some literature on Colombia stands out in characterizing entrepreneurship (Mondragón-Vélez & Peña, 2010), entrepreneurship and growth (Aparicio et al., 2018), and determinants that influence the decision to become an employer (Aparicio et al., 2013). Although the literature studying entrepreneurship in Colombia has been growing (Cortés-Sánchez, 2018), there is still scarce research identifying the effect of entrepreneurs' earnings on economic growth. So, taking this limitation into account, and considering the structure of the labor market and informality in Colombia (Bernal, 2009; Cuesta & Bohorquez, 2014; Mondragón-Vélez et al., 2010), this literature allows us to establish labor income as an alternative mechanism, so that:

Hypothesis 3: Employers' income positively affects economic growth in cities; however, the income among the self-employed negatively affects economic growth.

9.4 Methodology

9.4.1 Data

To test our hypotheses, we use two different sources of information. First, we use the *Gran Encuesta Integrada de Hogares* (GEIH) from 2017 to 2019. This survey comes from the *Departamento Administrativo Nacional de Estadística* (DANE) and includes information about households in Colombia; it has a monthly frequency and is represented at the national and city levels, including information on the 13 biggest cities in Colombia. Important research such as Ferreira (2016) and Cuadros-Menaca and Gaduh (2020) have highlighted the use of this database to identify the behavior of the informal and child labor market in Colombia. Second, we use the *Indice de Competitividad de Ciudades* (ICC) from 2018 to

2019, which provide complementary information about taxes, exports, and murders, while information from DANE allows us to identify the behavior of GDP and unemployment in these major cities. With these sources of information, we created two datasets. The first contains individual information for the adult population with different characteristics at the individual (e.g., type of entrepreneurship [self-employed and employer], gender, age, schooling, labor income per month, economic activity), household (e.g., financial responsibility, computer possession), and city level (e.g., population, murder rate, company taxes). The second dataset contains panel data that aggregates information at the city level, with variables such as labor income, subsidies, and transfers, as well as health affiliation expenses.

9.4.2 Dependent Variables (Stage 1)

To test the first set of hypotheses, we have two dependent variables related to the type of entrepreneurship, employer and self-employed. An employer refers to an individual who creates jobs and has a labor income greater than two minimum legal salaries. This is represented by a dummy variable that takes the value 1 if the individual is an employer and 0 otherwise. Self-employed refers to an individual who employs him/herself and has a labor income less than or equal to two minimum legal salaries. This is a dummy variable equal to 1 if the respondent is self-employed and 0 otherwise. Some key studies have used similar variables, which allow us to understand individual determinants in the decision to become an entrepreneur (Aparicio et al., 2013; Farné & Vergara, 2015).

9.4.3 Independent Variables (Stage 1)

We used a set of four independent variables, one representing regional characteristics (company taxes), another one representing household characteristics (computer possession), and the other two (gender and age) representing the individual influences on the decision to become either an employer or self-employed. First, computer possession refers to families who have a computer in the house. This is a dummy variable that takes the value 1 if the household has a computer and 0 otherwise. This variable is a proxy for ICT possession. According to Aparicio et al. (2013), access to and use of ICTs allows the systematized organization of information as well as searches and strategic management in favor of productive projects. Second, for city-level variables, company taxes refer to taxes and contributions that a medium-sized company must pay in its second year of activity, on a scale from 0 (lowest performance) to 100 (the frontier). This variable is a proxy for governmental support of entrepreneurship. According to Hörisch et al. (2017), countries with a higher level of taxes are countries with a weaker environmental orientation toward entrepreneurs. Third, the gender (sex) variable is a dummy that takes the value 1 if the individual is a man and 0 otherwise. Finally, the age variable is a numerical variable that refers to the age of the individual. Both the gender and age variables are commonly used to identify individual characteristics (Aparicio et al., 2013; Hörisch et al., 2017).

9.4.4 Control Variables (Stage 1)

For the control variables, we used a set of four variables. First, the fiscal autonomy city variable refers to participation (percentage) of current revenues (tax and non-tax) of municipalities in the total resources of the city and is a proxy for the taxation level. Second, the financial responsibility variable refers to the number of people in the household compared to those employed in the household. This variable allows us to observe the economic dependence that occurs in households (Aparicio et al., 2013). Third, the unemployment variable refers to the rate of unemployment in the city. Finally, the export diversification variable refers to a diversification indicator (value between 0 and 1), where a lower value means a greater diversification of the export basket. According to Hörisch et al. (2017), earlier research has documented the possible influence of the unemployment rate and the technology export level on entrepreneurial activity (Bergmann & Sternberg, 2007).

9.4.5 Dependent and Independent Variables (Stage 2)

Some research has suggested that the income generation process depends on people's participation in the labor market (Budig, 2006; Garza-Rodríguez, 2016). In the second hypothesis, we wanted to identify if becoming an employer increases labor income, while becoming self-employed reduces it. The dependent variable is labor income, which refers to the income received by an individual due to his or her economic activity, while we use employer and self-employed (dependent variable in stage 1) as independent variables.

9.4.6 Control Variables (Stage 2)

For control variables, we used, first, the educational level variable, which refers to a dummy variable that takes the value 1 when the individual has a higher level of education and 0 otherwise. Some studies, most of them on poverty, posit that education level is a factor that affects the income levels (Bol et al., 2019; Darko & Abrokwa, 2020). Second, the potential know-how variable refers to a numerical factor that is calculated as age-years of schooling, where people with more potential know-how are expected to be more successful in self-employment due to their experience, networks, and endowment of physical capital, so its effect would be positive. However, older people claim to be more risk-averse, so the expected sign would be negative (Aparicio et al., 2013; Millán et al., 2010). Third, the population variable refers to the population at the city level. Fourth, the murder rate variable refers to the rate of murder in the city where the individual is living. This rate expresses the number of homicides in the city per 100,000 inhabitants. Finally, the economic activities variable is a dummy that takes the value 1 when the individual is working in a specific economic activity and 0 otherwise; we included 16 economic activities, as shown in Table 9.1.

Table 9.1 Variable's description: all stages

	Variable	Description	Source
Stage 1: Dependent variables			
	Employer	Dummy variable; takes the value 1 if the individual is employer or if is self-employed and has a labor income greater than two minimum legal salaries, and 0 otherwise.	GEIH 2017–2019
	Self-employed	Dummy variable; takes the value 1 if the individual is self-employed and has a labor income less than or equal to two minimum legal salaries, and 0 otherwise.	GEIH 2017–2019
Stage 1: Independent variables			
	Computer possession	Dummy variable; takes the value 1 if the household where the individual lives has a computer, and 0 otherwise.	GEIH 2017–2019
	City: company taxes	It records the taxes and contributions that a medium-sized company must pay in its second year of activity. Distance to frontier score, on a scale from 0 to 100 where 0 represents the lowest performance and 100 the frontier.	ICC 2018–2020
	Sex	Dummy variable; takes the value 1 if the individual is man, and 0 otherwise.	GEIH 2017–2019
	Age	Numerical variable; the age of the individual.	GEIH 2017–2019

Stage 1: Control variables	City: fiscal autonomy	Participation (percentage) of current revenues (tax and non-tax) of municipalities in the total resources of the city.	ICC 2018–2020
	Financial responsibility	Numerical variable; quotient of the number of people in the household and those employed in the household.	GEIH 2017–2019
	City: unemployment	Unemployment rate of 13 regions in the country.	DANE 2017–2019
	City: exports diversification	Diversification rate between 0 and 1, where a lower value means a greater diversification of the export basket.	ICC 2018–2020
Stage 2: Dependent variables			
	Labor income	Labor income per individual.	GEIH 2017–2019
Stage 2: Independent variables			
	Employer	Dummy variable; takes the value 1 if the individual is an employer or if is self-employed and has a labor income greater than two minimum legal salaries, and 0 otherwise.	GEIH 2017–2019
	Self-employed	Dummy variable; takes the value 1 if the individual is self-employed and has a labor income less than or equal to two minimum legal salaries, and 0 otherwise.	GEIH 2017–2019

(*continued*)

Table 9.1 (continued)

	Variable	Description	Source
Stage 2: Control variables			
	Educational level	Dummy variable; takes the value 1 if the individual has higher education, and 0 otherwise.	GEIH 2017–2019
	Potential know-how	Numerical variable; calculated as: age–years of schooling–6.	GEIH 2017–2019
	City: population	Population of 13 regions in the country.	DANE 2017–2019
	City: murder rate	Number of homicides in the metropolitan area per 100,000 inhabitants.	ICC 2018–2020
	Agriculture activities	Dummy variable; takes the value 1 if the individual is working in agriculture activities, and 0 otherwise.	DANE 2017–2019
	Fishing activities	Dummy variable; takes the value 1 if the individual is working in fishing activities, and 0 otherwise.	DANE 2017–2019
	Mining activities	Dummy variable; takes the value 1 if the individual is working in mining activities, and 0 otherwise.	DANE 2017–2019
	Industries activities	Dummy variable; takes the value 1 if the individual is working in industries activities, and 0 otherwise.	DANE 2017–2019
	Energy activities	Dummy variable; takes the value 1 if the individual is working in energy activities, and 0 otherwise.	DANE 2017–2019
	Commerce activities	Dummy variable; takes the value 1 if the individual is working in commerce activities, and 0 otherwise.	DANE 2017–2019
	Education activities	Dummy variable; takes the value 1 if the individual is working in education activities, and 0 otherwise.	DANE 2017–2019
	Transport activities	Dummy variable; takes the value 1 if the individual is working in transport activities, and 0 otherwise.	DANE 2017–2019
	Finances activities	Dummy variable; takes the value 1 if the individual is working in finances activities, and 0 otherwise.	DANE 2017–2019

	Construction activities	Dummy variable; takes the value 1 if the individual is working in construction activities, and 0 otherwise.	DANE 2017–2019
	Administration activities	Dummy variable; takes the value 1 if the individual is working in administration activities, and 0 otherwise.	DANE 2017–2019
	Extraterritorial activities	Dummy variable; takes the value 1 if the individual is working in extraterritorial activities, and 0 otherwise.	DANE 2017–2019
	Real estate activities	Dummy variable; takes the value 1 if the individual is working in real estate activities, and 0 otherwise.	DANE 2017–2019
	Health activities	Dummy variable; takes the value 1 if the individual is working in health activities, and 0 otherwise.	DANE 2017–2019
	Hotel activities	Dummy variable; takes the value 1 if the individual is working in hotel activities, and 0 otherwise.	DANE 2017–2019
	Community activities	Dummy variable; takes the value 1 if the individual is working in community activities, and 0 otherwise.	DANE 2017–2019
Stage 3: Dependent variable			
	GDP PC	GDP per capita, per city and economic activity.	DANE 2017–2019
Stage 3: Independent variable			
	Labor income	Collapsed labor income per city and economic activity.	GEIH 2017–2019

(*continued*)

Table 9.1 (continued)

	Variable	Description	Source
Stage 3: Control variable			
	Subsidies and transfers	Collapsed subsidies and transfers per city and economic activity.	GEIH 2017–2019
	Health affiliation expenses	Collapsed health affiliation expenses per city and economic activity.	GEIH 2017–2019
	Occupancy rate	Collapsed occupancy rate per city and economic activity.	GEIH 2017–2019
	Financial capital per year	Collapsed financial capital per year per city and economic activity.	GEIH 2017–2019
	Financial capital per month	Collapsed financial capital per month per city and economic activity.	GEIH 2017–2019
	Years of schooling	Collapsed years of schooling per city and economic activity.	GEIH 2017–2019
	Reading and writing ability	Collapsed reading and writing ability (dummy) per city and economic activity.	GEIH 2017–2019

9.4.7 Dependent and Independent Variables (Stage 3)

Moving to the macroeconomic level, we used the per capita gross domestic product (GDP PC) per city as a dependent variable because it demonstrates value added as a measure of economic efficiency and financial viability of a city, rather than the number of jobs created (Audretsch et al., 2015). In addition, per capita GDP is used in the extant literature as an indicator for economic wealth and growth at both the regional and country levels (Audretsch et al., 2015; Glaeser et al., 2010; Stam, 2014). The independent variable is labor income from employers and the self-employed (the dependent variable in stage 2), which is collapsed by city and economic activity.

9.4.8 Control Variables (Stage 3)

To control this stage, we used subsidies and transfers, health affiliation expenses, financial capital, and the occupancy rate, which are collapsed by city and economic activity. Concerning occupancy rate, conflicting hypotheses are posited in the economic literature regarding the impact of unemployment on regional growth, where higher unemployment indicates lower resilience and lower number of capabilities, but also higher labor reserve and market mobility (Audretsch et al., 2015). Also, a higher level of human capital is associated with higher economic growth and development (Lucas, 1988; Osiobe, 2019); this is the reason why we used the years of schooling variable as a human capital proxy, collapsed by city and economic activity.

Accordingly, the two datasets that contain this entire battery of variables allow us to develop an empirical approach with three stages and empirically examine our hypotheses. For a better understanding of these variables, Table 9.2 shows the descriptive statistics of each variable used in the research; Tables 9.3–9.5 show the correlation matrices, which make it possible to identify in advance the relationships between variables.

Table 9.2 Descriptive statistics: all stages

Stages 1 and 2	Variable	N	Mean	Std. dev.	Min	Max
1	Employer	804,909	0.036	0.186	0	1
2	Self-employed	804,909	0.211	0.408	0	1
3	Labor income	452,358	1,143,936	1,489,477	1000	100,000,000
4	Computer possession	804,909	0.463	0.499	0	1
5	City: company taxes	804,909	6.018	0.170	5.67	6.242
6	Sex	804,909	0.455	0.498	0	1
7	Age	804,909	43.204	17.663	18	108
8	City: fiscal autonomy	804,909	0.346	0.108	0.162	0.619
9	Financial responsibility	731,864	2.265	1.201	1	14
10	City: unemployment	804,909	9.669	2.465	4.978	15.302
11	City: exports diversification	804,909	0.275	0.258	0.018	0.990
12	Educational level	521,306	0.381	0.486	0	1
13	Potential know-how	804,805	27.094	19.929	–7	102
14	City: population	804,909	3073.255	2381.422	962.527	8264.020
15	City: murder rate	804,909	22.204	10.405	11.444	53.142
16	Agriculture activities	505,666	0.010	0.101	0	1
17	Fishing activities	505,666	0.000	0.021	0	1
18	Mining activities	505,666	0.002	0.048	0	1
19	Industries activities	505,666	0.141	0.349	0	1
20	Energy activities	505,666	0.007	0.082	0	1
21	Commerce activities	505,666	0.240	0.427	0	1
22	Education activities	505,666	0.049	0.217	0	1
23	Transport activities	505,666	0.094	0.291	0	1

24	Finances activities	505,666	0.018	0.134	0	1
25	Construction activities	505,666	0.070	0.256	0	1
26	Administration activities	505,666	0.037	0.188	0	1
27	Extraterritorial activities	505,666	0.000	0.013	0	1
28	Real estate activities	505,666	0.103	0.304	0	1
29	Health activities	505,666	0.056	0.230	0	1
30	Hotel activities	505,666	0.077	0.266	0	1
31	Community activities	505,666	0.061	0.240	0	1
32	GDP PC	390	5338.372	9304.161	13.452	67,301.59
33	Labor income—employer	354	3,468,594	1,811,644	900,000	16,000,000
34	Labor income—self-employed	376	783,205.9	268,408.8	111,108	1,790,237
35	Subsidies and transfers	320	999,940.5	744,716.5	120,000	8,174,323
36	Health affiliation expenses	390	79,899.66	29,865.27	0	263,311.3
37	Occupancy rate	390	5.726	6.814	0.03	27.83
38	Financial capital per year	377	3,501,747	4,081,232	217,742.7	67,600,000
39	Financial capital per month	372	1,139,853	694,663.8	277,345.7	9,791,897
40	Years of schooling	390	11.124	2.201	5.224	16.003
41	Reading and writing ability	390	0.983	0.027	0.804	1

Table 9.3 Correlation matrix: stage 1

Variables		1	2	3	4	5	6	7	8	9	10	11
1	Employer	1.000										
2	Self-employed	–0.100*	1.000									
3	Labor income	0.310*	–0.250*	1.000								
4	City: fiscal autonomy	0.014*	–0.064*	0.083*	1.000							
5	Computer possession	0.097*	–0.097*	0.234*	0.083*	1.000						
6	City: company taxes	0.001	0.000	0.003	–0.342*	0.004*	1.000					
7	Sex	0.080*	0.093*	0.077*	0.007*	–0.015*	–0.003*	1.000				
8	Age	0.023*	0.030*	0.037*	–0.002	–0.033*	0.012*	–0.051*	1.000			
9	Financial responsibility	–0.081*	–0.144*	–0.025*	–0.064*	–0.041*	0.017*	–0.058*	0.001	1.000		
10	City: unemployment	0.010*	–0.021*	0.042*	–0.084*	0.021*	0.604*	–0.003*	0.010*	–0.013*	1.000	
11	City: exports diversification	0.008*	0.034*	–0.035*	–0.622*	–0.030*	0.457*	–0.004*	–0.005*	0.019*	0.202*	1.000

Table 9.4 Correlation matrix: stage 2

Variables	1	2	3	4	5	6	7	8	9	10	11	12
1 Labor income	1.000											
2 Employer	0.310*	1.000										
3 Self-employed	–0.250*	–0.100*	1.000									
4 Educational level	0.303*	0.117*	–0.072*	1.000								
5 Potential know-how	–0.071*	–0.004*	0.052*	–0.001	1.000							
6 City: population	0.098*	0.021*	–0.063*	0.040*	–0.022*	1.000						
7 City: murder rate	–0.012*	–0.005*	–0.003*	–0.047*	0.015*	0.114*	1.000					
8 Agriculture activities	0.007*	0.044*	–0.026*	–0.001	0.044*	–0.030*	–0.015*	1.000				
9 Fishing activities	–0.002	0.003	0.011*	0.002	0.013*	–0.008*	0.001	–0.002	1.000			
10 Mining activities	0.049*	–0.004*	–0.011*	0.023*	–0.005*	–0.008*	–0.006*	–0.005*	–0.001	1.000		
11 Industries activities	–0.037*	–0.010*	–0.034*	–0.076*	0.015*	0.045*	0.032*	–0.042*	–0.009*	–0.020*	1.000	
12 Energy activities	0.045*	–0.013*	–0.052*	0.037*	–0.016*	–0.010*	0.001	–0.008*	–0.002	–0.004*	–0.034*	1.000
13 Commerce activities	–0.090*	–0.001	0.105*	–0.118*	0.060*	–0.028*	0.010*	–0.058*	–0.012*	–0.027*	–0.228*	–0.046*
14 Education activities	0.128*	–0.013*	–0.100*	0.199*	–0.048*	–0.006*	–0.019*	–0.023*	–0.005*	–0.011*	–0.092*	–0.019*
15 Transport activities	–0.029*	–0.039*	0.122*	–0.086*	0.025*	–0.013*	–0.005*	–0.033*	–0.007*	–0.016*	–0.130*	–0.027*
16 Finances activities	0.070*	–0.014*	–0.072*	0.074*	–0.069*	0.031*	–0.002	–0.014*	–0.003	–0.007*	–0.055*	–0.011*
17 Construction activities	–0.013*	0.024*	0.002	–0.043*	0.035*	–0.011*	–0.002	–0.028*	–0.006*	–0.013*	–0.112*	–0.023*
18 Administration activities	0.172*	0.046*	–0.091*	0.118*	–0.057*	–0.016*	–0.021*	–0.020*	–0.004*	–0.009*	–0.079*	–0.016*
19 Extraterritorial activities	0.027*	0.009*	–0.005*	0.013*	–0.004*	0.005*	–0.005*	–0.001	0.000	–0.001	–0.005*	–0.001

(*continued*)

Table 9.4 (continued)

Variables	1	2	3	4	5	6	7	8	9	10	11	12
20 Real estate activities	0.032*	0.021*	0.014*	0.082*	−0.032*	0.053*	−0.013*	−0.035*	−0.007*	−0.016*	−0.137*	−0.028*
21 Health activities	0.070*	0.004*	−0.079*	0.147*	−0.081*	−0.002	−0.004*	−0.025*	−0.005*	−0.012*	−0.099*	−0.020*
22 Hotel activities	−0.067*	0.021*	−0.023*	−0.097*	−0.001	−0.022*	0.000	−0.030*	−0.006*	−0.014*	−0.117*	−0.024*
23 Community activities	−0.047*	−0.011*	0.125*	−0.045*	−0.025*	−0.011*	0.012*	−0.026*	−0.005*	−0.012*	−0.104*	−0.021*
	13	**14**	**15**	**16**	**17**	**18**	**19**	**20**	**21**	**22**	**23**	
13 Commerce activities	1.000											
14 Education activities	−0.128*	1.000										
15 Transport activities	−0.180*	−0.073*	1.000									
16 Finances activities	−0.076*	−0.031*	−0.044*	1.000								
17 Construction activities	−0.154*	−0.063*	−0.088*	−0.037*	1.000							
18 Administration activities	−0.109*	−0.044*	−0.063*	−0.026*	−0.054*	1.000						
19 Extraterritorial activities	−0.007*	−0.003	−0.004*	−0.002	−0.004	−0.002	1.000					
20 Real estate activities	−0.190*	−0.077*	−0.109*	−0.046*	−0.093*	−0.066*	−0.004*	1.000				
21 Health activities	−0.137*	−0.055*	−0.078*	−0.033*	−0.067*	−0.047*	−0.003	−0.082*	1.000			
22 Hotel activities	−0.162*	−0.066*	−0.093*	−0.039*	−0.079*	−0.056*	−0.004*	−0.098*	−0.070*	1.000		
23 Community activities	−0.143*	−0.058*	−0.082*	−0.035*	−0.070*	−0.050*	−0.003	−0.086*	−0.062*	−0.074*	1.000	

Table 9.5 Correlation matrix: stage 3

Variable		1	2	3	4	5	6	7	8	9	10
1	GDP PC	1.000									
2	Labor income—employer	0.078	1.000								
3	Labor income—self-employed	−0.025	0.329*	1.000							
4	Subsidies and transfers	0.203*	0.097	0.062	1.000						
5	Health affiliation expenses	0.074	0.414*	0.106	0.202*	1.000					
6	Occupancy rate	0.362*	−0.282*	−0.257*	−0.007	−0.187*	1.000				
7	Financial capital per year	−0.090	0.199*	0.078	0.012	0.138*	−0.062	1.000			
8	Financial Capital per month	0.011	0.244*	0.152*	0.128	0.480*	−0.165*	0.135*	1.000		
9	Years of schooling	0.105	0.405*	0.635*	0.130	0.388*	−0.182*	0.030	0.306*	1.000	
10	Reading and writing ability	0.132*	0.032	0.414*	0.032	−0.012	0.101	0.038	0.080	0.601*	1.000

9.4.9 Empirical Strategy

To identify the effect of individual, household, and regional characteristics on entrepreneurial decisions and how income plays a fundamental role (from employer and self-employed) in linking entrepreneurial decision (micro) to economic growth (macro), we used a three-stage modeling. For the first stage, we sought to understand the individual, household, and regional characteristics that influence the probability of becoming an employer or self-employed (entrepreneurial choice). We used the following probit model:

$$P\left(E_i = 1\right) = f\left(IC_i, RC_i, C_i,\right) \quad (1)$$

where E_i corresponds to a person who is an employer or self-employed, IC_i refers to individual characteristics (gender and age), RC_i represents the regional characteristic factors, and C_i refers to controls at the individual, household, and city level. Looking at the technical side of the model, probit models use cumulative Gaussian normal distribution rather than the logistic function to calculate the probability of being in one category or not (Greene, 2003), so this model is appropriate to test hypothesis 1. In addition, this type of modeling has been used to examine the probability of being an entrepreneur considering determinants such as labor market experience and social connections, among others (Jagannathan et al., 2017).

Once we examined the effects that individual and regional characteristics have on the entrepreneurial choice, we proceed to use the same structure in a second stage (reusing the probability of being an employer or self-employed) to test the effect that the entrepreneurial decision has on labor income. To accomplish this, we used a two-stage probit least square (2SPLS) model, using the *cdsimeq* command developed by Keshk (2003) in Stata. Key research in entrepreneurship has used this estimation method to explain simultaneous effects on R&D, entrepreneurship, and social mobility (Aparicio et al., 2022; Urbano et al., 2017, 2020). Using the results of the first stage, we therefore employ a simultaneous econometric technique represented by the following equation:

$$LI_i = f\left(\widehat{E_\iota}, x_i\right) \quad (2)$$

where LI_i is labor income, E_i corresponds to either employer or self-employed (from the first stage), and x_i denotes the control variables for this equation. The estimation follows a two-stage simultaneous process with an additional step of standard error correction to avoid heteroscedastic results. In this estimation, equation (1) is estimated with probit, while equation (2) utilizes ordinary least squares (OLS), where the predicted values ($\widehat{E_i}$ and $\widehat{LI_\iota}$) from each model are obtained through the second stage. In this step, the original endogenous variable in equation (1) is replaced by $\widehat{E_i}$. Finally, the procedure ends with the correction of standard errors to guarantee the efficiency of the estimated equations.[1]

Finally, in the third stage, we check whether aggregated income among employers and the self-employed affects economic growth in Colombian cities. Thus, we propose the following linear econometric model:

$$GDP_{it} = \alpha + \beta_1 LI_{it} + \beta_2 X_{it} + U_{it} \quad (3)$$

where GDP_{it} is the production in period t in the city-economic activity i; LI_{it} refers to employers' and self-employed' labor income by city and economic activity i during period t; and X_{it} is the vector of control variables such as subsidies and transfers, health affiliation expenses, occupancy rate, financial capital per year, financial capital per year, and years of schooling. This econometric model was estimated through the pool (OLS) and fixed effect (by city, by economic sector, and by year) techniques.

[1] Using the *cdsimeq* command developed by Keshk (2003) in Stata, all these estimations were executed automatically.

9.5 Results

Table 9.2 provides a summary of the descriptive statistics for all variables. For stages 1 and 2, this table shows that in our sample, on average, 3.6% of adult persons are employers and 21.1% are self-employed. The labor income per individual during the period 2017–2019 was, on average, COP 1,143,936 (US $348). Regarding regional characteristics that influence the decision to become an employer or self-employed, 46.3% of individuals in our sample have access to a computer in their house; and the index of company taxes in cities was, on average, 6.018%. If we observe the individual characteristics that influence the entrepreneurial decision, 45.5% of the individuals are men, with a mean age of around 43.2 years old. For stage 3, and using the panel dataset, the average per capita GDP by city and economic activity was COP 5,338,372 (US $1624); the labor income was COP 3,468,594 (US $1055) for employers and COP 783,205.90 (US $238) for the self-employed. In addition, Table 9.3 shows several significant correlations at the 99% level for some of the variables in stage 1. This analysis shows that regional characteristics such as computer possession appears to be positively correlated with an employer, but negatively correlated with being self-employed. Table 9.4 also shows several significant correlations at the 99% level for some variables in stage 2. It is important to notice that the variables employer and labor income are positively correlated, while self-employed and labor income go in the opposite direction. Finally, Table 9.5 shows the same information for stage 3. The results show that per capita GDP is positively correlated with the employer's labor income and negatively correlated with self-employed labor income; however, these results are not significant.

Concerning the main results, Table 9.6 shows the results for stage 1. Models 1–4 show the results for employers, while models 5–8 show the results for self-employed people. Focusing on models 1–4, model 1 shows the results of the baseline model, while model 2 presents the partial effects of model 1. This is important because model 2 will facilitate the interpretation of our results (Cornelißen & Sonderhof, 2009). Models 3 and 4 have the same structure as models 1 and 2—that is, model 3 presents the

Table 9.6 Dichotomic model

	(1)	(2)	(3)	(4)	(5)	(6)	(7)	(8)
	Employer				Self-employed			
	Estimation	dy/dx	Estimation	dy/dx	Estimation	dy/dx	Estimation	dy/dx
Computer possession	0.491***	0.039***	0.347***	0.031***	–0.315***	–0.091***	–0.209***	–0.055***
	(0.006)	(0.000)	(0.008)	(0.001)	(0.003)	(0.001)	(0.004)	(0.001)
City: company taxes	–0.134***	–0.011***	–0.098***	–0.009***	–0.018	–0.005	–0.011	–0.003
	(0.023)	(0.002)	(0.027)	(0.002)	(0.014)	(0.004)	(0.017)	(0.005)
Sex	0.397***	0.032***	0.355***	0.031***	0.243***	0.070***	0.127***	0.033***
	(0.006)	(0.000)	(0.007)	(0.001)	(0.003)	(0.001)	(0.004)	(0.001)
Age	0.007***	0.001***	0.015***	0.001***	0.007***	0.002***	0.012***	0.003***
	(0.000)	(0.000)	(0.000)	(0.000)	(0.000)	(0.000)	(0.000)	(0.000)
City: fiscal autonomy	0.317***	0.025***	0.320***	0.028***	–1.006***	–0.291***	–1.019***	–0.266***
	(0.034)	(0.003)	(0.040)	(0.004)	(0.020)	(0.006)	(0.026)	(0.007)
Financial responsibility	–0.212***	–0.017***	–0.196***	–0.017***	–0.204***	–0.059***	–0.181***	–0.047***
	(0.003)	(0.000)	(0.004)	(0.000)	(0.002)	(0.000)	(0.002)	(0.001)
City: unemployment	0.013***	0.001***	0.018***	0.002***	–0.009***	–0.003***	–0.008***	–0.002***
	(0.001)	(0.000)	(0.002)	(0.000)	(0.001)	(0.000)	(0.001)	(0.000)
City: exports diversification	0.241***	0.019***	0.268***	0.024***	–0.010	–0.003	–0.049***	–0.013***
	(0.014)	(0.001)	(0.017)	(0.002)	(0.009)	(0.002)	(0.011)	(0.003)
Constant	–1.632***		–2.279***		–0.018		–0.270**	
	(0.131)		(0.157)		(0.078)		(0.100)	
Education FE	**NO**	**NO**	**YES**	**YES**	**NO**	**NO**	**YES**	**YES**
Observations	**731,864**	**731,864**	**483,246**	**483,246**	**731,864**	**731,864**	**483,246**	**483,246**
Pseudo R-squared	**0.081**		**0.112**		**0.052**		**0.046**	

Note = standard errors in parentheses: *p<0.05; **p<0.01; ***p<0.001

results of the probit model and model 4 their respective partial effects. However, these models contain the fixed effect by education. Model 4 offers the main results for our analysis, not only because it represents the partial effect of model 3, but also because, through the significance test of the education fixed effect ($p<0.001$), we realize the need to introduce this effect into the baseline model, which allows intra-educational analysis. The same holds true for models 5–8, but for the self-employed.

Models 4 and 8 in Table 9.6 allow us to interpret the results of the first stage. We can see that when regional characteristics such as computer possession and company taxes increase by 1%, the probability of being an employer increases by 0.031% and decreases by 0.009%, respectively; while the probability of being self-employed decreases by 0.055% and 0.003%, respectively (without significance, this may happen because self-employment in Colombia is strongly related to informality, thus avoiding taxes; Fiess et al., 2010), thus supporting hypotheses 1a and 1b. On the other hand, when individual characteristics such as gender and age increase by 1%, the probability of being an employer increases by 0.031% and 0.001%, respectively, while the probability of being self-employed increases by 0.033% and 0.003%, respectively. Hence, results support hypothesis 1c.

Focusing on the second stage, at the theoretical and technical level, we encounter a stumbling block. According to Aparicio et al. (2013), one of the determinants for being an entrepreneur lies in the fact that the expected profit from this activity exceeds the income from being employed (Sullivan, 2009; Trang Do & Duchene, 2008). Hörisch et al. (2017) suggest that the environmental orientation of entrepreneurial ventures is stronger if entrepreneurs have higher household incomes; we therefore face an endogeneity problem between our dependent and independent variables as our objective in the second stage is to check whether or not labor income depends on the decision to be an employer or self-employed. However, the specification and the chosen estimation method (2SPLS) allow us to work with an instrumental variable in the second estimation stage that eliminates the endogeneity problem. Table 9.7 shows the results of the second stage. Models 1 and 2 show the 2SPLS (stage 2) results for adults who are employers or self-employed, respectively. Model 1 shows

Table 9.7 The second stage of 2SPLS model

	(1)	(2)
	Labor income: employer	**Labor income: self-employment**
Employer instrumental variable	1.024***	
	(0.012)	
Self-employed instrumental variable		−1.924***
		(0.040)
Educational level	0.021***	0.040***
	(0.005)	(0.007)
Potential know-how	−0.207***	0.882***
	(0.008)	(0.016)
City: population	0.070***	−0.156***
	(0.004)	(0.007)
City: murder rate	0.003	0.045***
	(0.004)	(0.005)
Agriculture activities	−0.551***	0.382***
	(0.008)	(0.017)
Fishing activities	−0.111***	0.112***
	(0.005)	(0.008)
Mining activities	−0.158***	0.223***
	(0.005)	(0.010)
Industries activities	−1.762***	1.502***
	(0.022)	(0.056)
Energy activities	−0.335***	0.239***
	(0.006)	(0.013)
Commerce activities	−2.229***	2.126***
	(0.026)	(0.072)
Education activities	−0.960***	0.897***
	(0.013)	(0.034)
Transport activities	−1.424***	1.609***
	(0.018)	(0.051)
Finances activities	−0.580***	0.495***
	(0.009)	(0.021)
Construction activities	−1.338***	1.235***
	(0.017)	(0.043)
Administration activities	−0.884***	0.816***
	(0.013)	(0.029)
Extraterritorial activities	−0.052***	0.073***
	(0.002)	(0.005)
Real estate activities	−1.563***	1.511***
	(0.020)	(0.051)
Health activities	−1.109***	0.956***

(continued)

Table 9.7 (continued)

	(1) Labor income: employer	(2) Labor income: self-employment
	(0.015)	(0.036)
Hotel activities	−1.461***	1.155***
	(0.018)	(0.043)
Community activities	−1.252***	1.440***
	(0.015)	(0.044)
Constant	1.913***	−0.709***
	(0.020)	(0.019)
Observations	**316,855**	**316,855**
R-squared	**0.250**	**0.250**

Note = standard errors in parentheses: *p<0.05; **p<0.01; ***p<0.001

that when the probability of being an employer increases by 1%, labor income increases by 1.024%, while model 2 shows that when the probability of being self-employed increases by 1%, labor income decreases by 1.924%, supporting hypothesis 2. These results are in line with the findings of research such as Åstebro and Chen (2014), Baldwin and Chowhan (2003), and Soon and Lim (2016). An important effect to highlight is that the level of education increases the income of both population groups, because as a person's level of education increases, income increases by 0.021% if the individual is an employer and 0.040% if the individual is a self-employed.

Finally, transitioning to macroeconomic results, Table 9.8 presents the results of the third stage, which seeks to identify the effect of labor income on per capita GDP at the city and economy activity level, controlling for institutional factors. Models 1–6 present the results for employers and 7–12 present the results for the self-employed. The first aspect we can highlight from these results is that employers' income seems to positively affect cities' GDP regardless of the fixed effect we want to analyze. However, this is not the case for the self-employed group. The effects of income on GDP for this group seem to vary depending on the fixed effect analyzed. This may be due to the heterogeneity in the labor market of the self-employed generated by informality. Thus, model 6 indicates that

Table 9.8 Stage 3: labor income effects on economic growth (GDP)

	(1)	(2)	(3)	(4)	(5)	(6)	(7)	(8)	(9)	(10)	(11)	(12)
	Employer						**Self-employed**					
Labor income	0.196*	0.069	0.214**	0.192*	0.063	0.218**	0.001	–0.126*	0.158	–0.006	–0.135*	0.156
	(0.076)	(0.055)	(0.080)	(0.077)	(0.055)	(0.081)	(0.089)	(0.062)	(0.121)	(0.090)	(0.063)	(0.122)
Subsidies and transfers	0.172**	0.024	0.126*	0.176**	0.024	0.127*	0.176**	0.021	0.148**	0.179**	0.020	0.149**
	(0.056)	(0.040)	(0.055)	(0.056)	(0.040)	(0.055)	(0.055)	(0.039)	(0.055)	(0.056)	(0.040)	(0.055)
Health affiliation expenses	0.169	0.059	0.166	0.166	0.055	0.167	0.194*	0.058	0.195*	0.188*	0.050	0.194*
	(0.090)	(0.067)	(0.096)	(0.090)	(0.067)	(0.096)	(0.087)	(0.064)	(0.094)	(0.087)	(0.064)	(0.095)
Occupancy rate	0.410***	0.347***	0.853**	0.409***	0.345***	0.846**	0.376***	0.315***	0.878**	0.375***	0.313***	0.881**
	(0.056)	(0.039)	(0.271)	(0.056)	(0.039)	(0.274)	(0.055)	(0.038)	(0.272)	(0.056)	(0.038)	(0.275)
Financial capital	–0.156**	–0.145***	–0.143**	–0.158**	–0.148***	–0.142**	–0.126*	–0.126**	–0.128*	–0.130*	–0.130***	–0.129*
	(0.056)	(0.039)	(0.053)	(0.056)	(0.040)	(0.054)	(0.055)	(0.038)	(0.053)	(0.055)	(0.038)	(0.053)
Years of schooling	0.065	0.099	0.966***	0.066	0.101	0.973***	0.134	0.196**	0.777***	0.138	0.203**	0.773***
	(0.075)	(0.052)	(0.210)	(0.075)	(0.053)	(0.214)	(0.089)	(0.061)	(0.206)	(0.089)	(0.062)	(0.208)
Constant	0.046	–0.145	–1.612***	0.025	–0.189	–1.595***	0.049	–0.182	–1.403***	0.005	–0.249	–1.401***
	(0.057)	(0.136)	(0.326)	(0.098)	(0.147)	(0.331)	(0.056)	(0.135)	(0.308)	(0.097)	(0.145)	(0.315)
City FE	**NO**	**YES**	**NO**	**NO**	**YES**	**NO**	**NO**	**YES**	**NO**	**NO**	**YES**	**NO**
Sectors FE	**NO**	**NO**	**YES**	**NO**	**NO**	**YES**	**NO**	**NO**	**YES**	**NO**	**NO**	**YES**
Year FE	**NO**	**NO**	**NO**	**YES**	**YES**	**YES**	**NO**	**NO**	**NO**	**YES**	**YES**	**YES**
Observations	**309**	**309**	**309**	**309**	**309**	**309**	**316**	**316**	**316**	**316**	**316**	**316**
R-squared	**0.218**	**0.648**	**0.324**	**0.219**	**0.649**	**0.325**	**0.206**	**0.652**	**0.308**	**0.208**	**0.654**	**0.308**

Note = standard errors in parentheses: *p<0.05; **p<0.01; ***p<0.001

when there is a 1% increase in employers' income, the per capita GDP at the city level increases by 0.218%, supporting hypothesis 3. Because informality in Colombia seems to be rooted in structural problems across cities (Arango & Flórez, 2021), we analyze the results for the self-employed with city and year fixed effects (i.e., model 11). When there is a 1% increase in the labor income of the self-employed, per capita GDP at the city level decreases by 0.135%, also supporting hypothesis 3. This may be due to an interplay between employers and the self-employed, in addition to the heterogeneities generated by informality in the labor market.

9.6 Discussion and Conclusions

The literature studying the effects of entrepreneurship on economic growth is extensive (Acs et al., 2009; Aparicio et al., 2016; Audretsch et al., 2007; Wennekers & Thurik, 1999). However, determinants such as regional and individual characteristics on the entrepreneurial decision and the effect of entrepreneurship through labor income on regional economic growth in developing countries have been little explored. Attempting to fill this gap in the literature, this study has three main purposes: first, to examine the effects of individual and regional characteristics on the entrepreneurial choice; second, through the literature, to find a mechanism that connects the entrepreneurial decision and economic growth to identify the effect of the entrepreneurial decision on this mechanism; and third, to study the effects of entrepreneurship such as being an employer or self-employed (as a mechanism) on the economic growth (per capita GDP) of Colombian cities.

Using an empirical approach in three stages and separating the population into two categories—employers and self-employed (Mondragón-Vélez & Peña, 2010)—we arrived at three key findings. First, in stage 1, our results show that regional characteristics such as computer possession and company taxes are significant in the entrepreneurial decision for becoming an employer or self-employed. At the city level, cities with less support for entrepreneurship (high company taxes) reduce the probability of an individual becoming either an employer or self-employed. At the household level, access to ICTs (computer possession) increases the probability of an individual becoming an employer, while decreasing the probability of an individual becoming self-employed. According to Aparicio et al. (2013), access to and use of ICTs allow the systematized organization of information as well as searching and strategic management in favor of productive projects, going against the grain of self-employment conditions in Colombia. These results support research accepting the key role of regional characteristics on the entrepreneurial decision (Audretsch & Belitski, 2017; Mueller, 2006). The results also show, however, that individual characteristics such as gender and age show a positive and significant effect on the entrepreneurial decision for becoming an employer or self-employed, supporting what the literature has established about these effects (López-Núñez et al., 2020; Mas-Tur et al., 2015; Perez-Quintana et al., 2017).

Second, the results of stage 2 support that becoming an employer increases individual income, while becoming self-employed reduces it. This behavior is due to the structural informality at the city level in Colombia (Arango & Flórez, 2021; Fiess et al., 2010). This result is key to our research, as it supports the theoretical premise that economic incentives play a fundamental role (serving as a transmission mechanism) in the relationship between entrepreneurship and economic growth, because becoming an employer increases the labor income of individuals, who thus have great potential to trigger social development because they are generating employment and increasing their possible production and consumption frontiers (theoretically). Up to this point, the literature had been responsible for expanding the idea that knowledge spillover or innovation was the main mechanism or incentive for individuals to drive economic growth in their regions; however, the present result shows that economic incentives could also be a key mechanism.

Finally, in stage 3 the results show that employers' income positively affects economic growth in cities, while the income of the self-employed does not seem to have a consistent relation with economic growth in cities. These results suggest that employers are generating benefits for themselves and society, while the contrary occurs with the self-employed, who are not receiving individual benefits or generating societal benefits. In addition, the results follow the theory that supports the role of entrepreneurship spurring economic growth (Acs & Audretsch, 1993; Gómez 2005; Aparicio et al., 2013; Audretsch et al., 2015).

9.6.1 Theoretical Implications

The results presented in the previous section allow us to establish theoretical implications about entrepreneurship (i.e., employers and self-employed) and its relationship to economic growth in developing countries. Three important theoretical implications are derived from our findings. First, the literature shows that several determinants drive entrepreneurship (Freytag & Thurik, 2007; Ghani et al., 2014; Thai & Turkina, 2014), among which are regional (Audretsch et al., 2010; Ross et al., 2015) and individual (Cuervo, 2005; Krasniqi, 2009) characteristics; however, there is little research investigating the importance of both characteristics on the entrepreneurial decision in the regions of developing countries. It should be noted that regional characteristics are fundamental for this research, because Colombia is a regional country (Perobelli et al., 2010), in which each city adopts very different policies (Franz, 2019; Galvis & Meisel, 2013); for this reason, considering both characteristics is crucial for the understanding of the results under the regional context.

Second, labor income emerges as a transmission mechanism, because the entrepreneurial decision to become an employer increases the labor income of employers, while becoming self-employed decreases it, thus providing economic incentives. Employers not only receive individual benefits but also generate social ones, because they are generators of employment. The results of the second stage support the benefits that employers receive; however, can those individual benefits be converted into macro-level benefits?

Third, given that the results clearly show the effect of entrepreneurs' income on economic growth in Colombia, it is important to point out the underlying mechanism driving this relationship: labor income (Djido & Shiferaw, 2018). In economic theory, labor income is crucial for the economic growth of regions (Korkmaz & Korkmaz, 2017; Merkulova,

2019), but it is not highly appreciated as a transmission mechanism relating entrepreneurship to economic growth. This research thus opens the door to a more detailed study of the effects of labor income (e.g., employer and self-employed income) on per capita GDP in developing countries. The results show strong heterogeneity when we look at what happens with the self-employed, due to its strong correlation with informality (Arango & Flórez, 2021). We can therefore say that in developing countries such as Colombia, informality plays a fundamental role in labor market structures and is perhaps the greatest obstacle to entrepreneurship having a positive impact on the economy.

9.6.2 Policy Implications

Exciting challenges arise concerning recommendations to policymakers, applicable to the policy framework of developing and regional countries. We believe that our study allows policymakers to target policies on several specific points. First, they should direct special programs dedicated to facilitating access to ICTs (access to computers) for all regions of the country. It is also clear that regional characteristics are fundamental for the entrepreneurial decision, so it is also crucial to lower taxes on companies, as these taxes reduce the probability of becoming an entrepreneur (employer or self-employed). Second, the results lead to the need to rethink the political strategies of entrepreneurship, recognizing the differences between employers and the self-employed (e.g., individual characteristics such as sex and age), thus providing better structures for self-employed entrepreneurs to be productive, generating support channels, and monitoring in the initial stages of their projects for the creation of companies could be policies oriented toward better results for this type of entrepreneurship. Third, policymakers should seek to reduce informality by supporting productive projects, training small entrepreneurs, facilitating credit to small- and medium-sized enterprises, generating an educational movement focused on the creation of enterprises, and all kinds of policies aimed at reducing the high level of informality in Colombia. Another option to reduce informality could be the use of subsidies through companies, which would go directly to company payrolls, which would absorb informal workers without incurring high labor costs for health or pensions. Policymakers should perhaps focus their efforts on improving the structure of the labor market, which is the cause of many heterogeneities in labor outcomes.

9.6.3 Limitations and Future Research

When conducting this research, we encountered two main barriers: first, the identification and application of an empirical strategy that could bring together in an integrated way the whole process of entrepreneurship, as well as provide the effect that the entrepreneurial decision has on economic growth. We therefore decided to perform an integrated two-stage process and then to perform the last stage with a collapsed database. However, it would be interesting to be able to adapt this whole battery of data to a joint estimation strategy. Second, the literature studying the effects of labor income on economic growth is almost null, so it was a challenge to identify the niche to which the relationship between the labor income of entrepreneurs (employer and self-employed) on regional economic growth belonged. Finally, we believe that further studies are required to develop new datasets, perform alternative estimations, explore what kinds of firms are promoting economic growth, and what determinants are involved in the entrepreneurial phenomena. Further studies are required to construct theoretical models that explain the behavior of this group of agents (i.e., employers and the self-employed) in developing and regional countries.

References

Acs, Z. J., & Audretsch, D. B. (1993). *Small firms and entrepreneurship: an East-West perspective*. Cambridge University Press.

Acs, Z. J., & Szerb, L. (2007). Entrepreneurship, economic growth and public policy. *Small Business Economics, 28*(2–3), 109–122. https://doi.org/10.1007/s11187-006-9012-3

Acs, Z. J., Braunerhjelm, P., Audretsch, D. B., & Carlsson, B. (2009). The knowledge spillover theory of entrepreneurship. *Small Business Economics, 32*(1), 15–30. https://doi.org/10.1007/s11187-008-9157-3

Acs, Z. J., Audretsch, D. B., & Lehmann, E. E. (2013). The knowledge spillover theory of entrepreneurship. *Small Business Economics, 41*(4), 757–774. https://doi.org/10.1007/s11187-013-9505-9

Acs, Z. J., Estrin, S., Mickiewicz, T., & Szerb, L. (2018). Entrepreneurship, institutional economics, and economic growth: an ecosystem perspective. *Small Business Economics, 51*(2), 501–514. https://doi.org/10.1007/s11187-018-0013-9

Alm, J., & Erard, B. (2016). Using Public Information to Estimate Self-Employment Earnings of Informal Suppliers. *Public Budgeting & Finance, 36*(1), 22–46.

Aparicio, S., Hassan, A. R., & Sánchez, D. F. G. (2013). Elección de ocupaciones que generen empleo usando modelos de elección discreta: Medellín Área Metropolitana 2009. *Estudios Gerenciales, 29*(129), 476–484.

Aparicio, S., Urbano, D., & Audretsch, D. (2016). Institutional factors, opportunity entrepreneurship and economic growth: Panel data evidence. *Technological Forecasting and Social Change, 102*, 45–61. https://doi.org/10.1016/j.techfore.2015.04.006

Aparicio, S., Urbano, D., & Gomez, D. (2018). Entrepreneurship and regional economic growth in Antioquia: an empirical analysis. *Economics and business letters., 7*(2), 84–92.

Aparicio, S., Audretsch, D., Noguera, M., & Urbano, D. (2022). Can female entrepreneurs boost social mobility in developing countries? An institutional analysis. *Technological Forecasting and Social Change, 175*, 121401.

Arango, L. E., & Flórez, L. A. (2021). Regional Labour Informality in Colombia and a Proposal for a Differential Minimum Wage. *Journal of Development Studies, 57*(6), 1016–1037. https://doi.org/10.1080/00220388.2020.1841170

Åstebro, T. (2017). The private financial gains to entrepreneurship: Is it a good use of public money to encourage individuals to become entrepreneurs? *Small Business Economics, 48*(2), 323–329. https://doi.org/10.1007/s11187-016-9777-y

Åstebro, T., & Chen, J. (2014). The entrepreneurial earnings puzzle: Mismeasurement or real? *Journal of Business Venturing, 29*(1), 88–105.

Audretsch, D. B. (2005). The Knowledge Spillover Theory of Entrepreneurship and Economic Growth. *Research on Technological Innovation, Management and Policy*. JAI Press. https://doi.org/10.1016/S0737-1071(05)09003-7

Audretsch, D. B. (2009). The entrepreneurial society. *Journal of Technology Transfer, 34*(3), 245–254. https://doi.org/10.1007/s10961-008-9101-3

Audretsch, D. B., & Belitski, M. (2017). Entrepreneurial ecosystems in cities: establishing the framework conditions. *Journal of Technology Transfer, 42*(5), 1030–1051. https://doi.org/10.1007/s10961-016-9473-8

Audretsch, D. B., Keilbach, M. C., & Lehmann, E. E. (2007). *Entrepreneurship and Economic Growth. Entrepreneurship and Economic Growth* (pp. 1–236). Oxford University Press. 10.1093/acprof:oso/9780195183511.001.0001.

Audretsch, D., Dohse, D., & Niebuhr, A. (2010). Cultural diversity and entrepreneurship: A regional analysis for Germany. *Annals of Regional Science, 45*(1), 55–85. https://doi.org/10.1007/s00168-009-0291-x

Audretsch, D. B., Belitski, M., & Desai, S. (2015). Entrepreneurship and economic development in cities. *The Annals of Regional Science, 55*(1), 33–60.

Baldwin, J. R., & Chowhan, J. (2003). The impact of self-employment on labour-productivity growth: A Canada and United States comparison. *Available at SSRN 1387882.*

Baliamoune-Lutz, M. (2015). Taxes and entrepreneurship in OECD countries. *Contemporary Economic Policy, 33*(2), 369–380.

Baliamoune-Lutz, M., & Garello, P. (2014). Tax structure and entrepreneurship. *Small Business Economics, 42*(1), 165–190.

Baumol, W. J. (1996). Entrepreneurship: Productive, unproductive, and destructive. *Journal of Business Venturing, 11*(1), 3–22. https://doi.org/10.1016/0883-9026(94)00014-X

Baumol, W. J. (2010). *The microtheory of innovative entrepreneurship. The Microtheory of Innovative Entrepreneurship* (pp. 1–246). Princeton University Press. https://doi.org/10.1093/ajae/aar056

Bergmann, H., & Sternberg, R. (2007). The changing face of entrepreneurship in Germany. *Small Business Economics, 28*(2–3), 205–221. https://doi.org/10.1007/s11187-006-9016-z

Bernal, S. R. (2009). The Informal Labor Market in Colombia: identification and characterization. *Revista Desarrollo y Sociedad, 63*, 145–208. https://doi.org/10.13043/dys.63.4er

Bilan, Y., Mishchuk, H., Samoliuk, N., & Yurchyk, H. (2020). Impact of Income Distribution on Social and Economic Well-Being of the State. *Sustainability (Switzerland), 12*(1), 1. https://doi.org/10.3390/su12010429

Bol, T., Ciocca Eller, C., van de Werfhorst, H. G., & DiPrete, T. A. (2019). School-to-Work Linkages, Educational Mismatches, and Labor Market Outcomes. *American Sociological Review, 84*(2), 275–307. https://doi.org/10.1177/0003122419836081

Bosma, N., Content, J., Sanders, M., & Stam, E. (2018). Institutions, entrepreneurship, and economic growth in Europe. *Small Business Economics, 51*(2), 483–499. https://doi.org/10.1007/s11187-018-0012-x

Brixy, U., Sternberg, R., & Stüber, H. (2012). The selectiveness of the entrepreneurial process. *Journal of Small Business Management, 50*(1), 105–131. https://doi.org/10.1111/j.1540-627X.2011.00346.x

Bruton, G. D., Ahlstrom, D., & Obloj, K. (2008). *Entrepreneurship in emerging economies: Where are we today and where should the research go in the future.* Entrepreneurship: Theory and Practice. https://doi.org/10.1111/j.1540-6520.2007.00213.x

Budig, M. J. (2006). Gender, self-employment, and earnings: The interlocking structures of family and professional status. *Gender & society, 20*(6), 725–753.

Choi, Y. R., & Shepherd, D. A. (2004). Entrepreneurs' decisions to exploit opportunities. *Journal of Management, 30*(3), 377–395. https://doi.org/10.1016/j.jm.2003.04.002

Coduras, A., Velilla, J., & Ortega, R. (2018). Age of the entrepreneurial decision: Differences among developed, developing, and non-developed countries. *Economics and Business Letters, 7*(1), 36–46. https://doi.org/10.17811/ebl.7.1.2018.36-46

Cornelißen, T., & Sonderhof, K. (2009). Partial effects in probit and logit models with a triple dummy-variable interaction term. *Stata Journal, 9*(4), 571–583. https://doi.org/10.1177/1536867x0900900404

Cortés-Sánchez, J. D. (2018). Institutional strength, peacebuilding, and productive entrepreneurship-exploratory analysis in Colombia. *Business: Theory and Practice, 19*, 88–102. https://doi.org/10.3846/BTP.2018.10

Cuadros-Menaca, A., & Gaduh, A. (2020). Remittances, child labor, and schooling: Evidence from Colombia. *Economic Development and Cultural Change, 68*(4), 1257–1293.

Cuervo, A. (2005). Individual and Environmental Determinants of Entrepreneurship. *The International Entrepreneurship and Management Journal, 1*(3), 293–311. https://doi.org/10.1007/s11365-005-2591-7

Cuesta, J., & Bohorquez, C. (2014). Labor Market Transitions and Social Security in Colombia. *The Journal of Developing Areas, 48*(3), 149–174. https://doi.org/10.1353/jda.2014.0052

Darko, C. K., & Abrokwa, K. K. (2020). Do you really need it? Educational mismatch and earnings in Ghana. *Review of Development Economics, 24*(4), 1365–1392. https://doi.org/10.1111/rode.12681

Dew, N., Read, S., Sarasvathy, S. D., & Wiltbank, R. (2009). Effectual versus predictive logics in entrepreneurial decision-making: Differences between experts and novices. *Journal of Business Venturing, 24*(4), 287–309. https://doi.org/10.1016/j.jbusvent.2008.02.002

Dileo, I., & García Pereiro, T. (2019). Assessing the impact of individual and context factors on the entrepreneurial process. A cross-country multilevel approach. *International Entrepreneurship and Management Journal, 15*(4), 1393–1441. https://doi.org/10.1007/s11365-018-0528-1

Djido, A. I., & Shiferaw, B. A. (2018). Patterns of labor productivity and income diversification – Empirical evidence from Uganda and Nigeria. *World Development, 105*, 416–427. https://doi.org/10.1016/j.worlddev.2017.12.026

Eisenhauer, J. G. (1995). The Entrepreneurial Decision: Economic Theory and Empirical Evidence. *Entrepreneurship Theory and Practice, 19*(4), 67–79. https://doi.org/10.1177/104225879501900405

Elston, J. A., & Audretsch, D. B. (2011). Financing the entrepreneurial decision: An empirical approach using experimental data on risk attitudes. *Small Business Economics, 36*(2), 209–222. https://doi.org/10.1007/s11187-009-9210-x

Farné, S., & Vergara, C. A. (2015). Economic growth, labour flexibilization and employment quality in Colombia, 2002-11. *International Labour Review, 154*(2), 253–269. https://doi.org/10.1111/j.1564-913X.2015.00241.x

Feldman, M. P. (2001). The enterpreneurial event revisited: Firm formation in a regional context. *Industrial and Corporate Change, 10*(4), 861–891. https://doi.org/10.1093/icc/10.4.861

Ferreira, M. (2016). Informal versus precarious work in Colombia: Concept and operationalization. *Progress in Development Studies, 16*(2), 140–158.

Fiess, N. M., Fugazza, M., & Maloney, W. F. (2010). Informal self-employment and macroeconomic fluctuations. *Journal of Development Economics, 91*(2), 211–226. https://doi.org/10.1016/j.jdeveco.2009.09.009

Franz, T. (2019). Why 'Good Governance' Fails: Lessons from Regional Economic Development in Colombia. *International Journal of Urban and Regional Research, 43*(4), 776–785. https://doi.org/10.1111/1468-2427.12742

Freytag, A., & Thurik, R. (2007). Entrepreneurship and its determinants in a cross-country setting. *Journal of Evolutionary Economics, 17*(2), 117–131. https://doi.org/10.1007/s00191-006-0044-2

Galvis, L. A., & Meisel, A. (2013). Regional inequalities and regional policies in Colombia: The experience of the last two decades. In *Advances in Spatial Science* (Vol. 84, pp. 197–223). Springer International Publishing. https://doi.org/10.1007/978-3-642-39674-8_9

Gartner, W. B., & Shane, S. A. (1995). Measuring entrepreneurship over time. *Journal of Business Venturing, 10*(4), 283–301. https://doi.org/10.1016/0883-9026(94)00037-U

Garza-Rodríguez, J. (2016). Los determinantes de la pobreza en los estados mexicanos en la frontera con Estados Unidos. *Estudios fronterizos, 17*(33), 141–167.

Ghani, E., Kerr, W. R., & O'Connell, S. (2014). Spatial Determinants of Entrepreneurship in India. *Regional Studies, 48*(6), 1071–1089. https://doi.org/10.1080/00343404.2013.839869

Ghio, N., Guerini, M., Lehmann, E. E., & Rossi-Lamastra, C. (2015). The emergence of the knowledge spillover theory of entrepreneurship. *Small Business Economics, 44*(1), 1–18. https://doi.org/10.1007/s11187-014-9588-y

Ghosh, S. (2017). Regulation and entrepreneurial intention: cross-country evidence. *Journal of Entrepreneurship and Public Policy, 6*(2), 193–205. https://doi.org/10.1108/JEPP-02-2017-0004

Glaeser, E. L., Kerr, W. R., & Ponzetto, G. A. (2010). Clusters of entrepreneurship. *Journal of urban economics, 67*(1), 150–168.

Greene, W. H. (2003). *Econometric analysis.* Pearson Education India.

Grilo, I., & Thurik, R. (2008). Determinants of entrepreneurial engagement levels in Europe and the US. *Industrial and Corporate Change, 17*(6), 1113–1145. https://doi.org/10.1093/icc/dtn044

Guerrero, M., & Urbano, D. (2012). The development of an entrepreneurial university. *Journal of Technology Transfer, 37*(1), 43–74. https://doi.org/10.1007/s10961-010-9171-x

Hall, J., Matos, S., Sheehan, L., & Silvestre, B. (2012). Entrepreneurship and innovation at the base of the Pyramid: A recipe for inclusive growth or social exclusion? *Journal of Management Studies, 49*(4), 785–812. https://doi.org/10.1111/j.1467-6486.2012.01044.x

Henrekson, M., & Sanandaji, T. (2020). Measuring Entrepreneurship: Do Established Metrics Capture Schumpeterian Entrepreneurship? *Entrepreneurship: Theory and Practice, 44*(4), 733–760. https://doi.org/10.1177/1042258719844500

Hörisch, J., Kollat, J., & Brieger, S. A. (2017). What influences environmental entrepreneurship? A multilevel analysis of the determinants of entrepreneurs' environmental orientation. *Small Business Economics, 48*(1), 47–69.

Humphries, J., & Weisdorf, J. (2019). *Unreal Wages? Real Income and Economic Growth in England, 1260-1850.* Oxford University Press. https://doi.org/10.1093/ej/uez017

Iftikhar, M. N., Ahmad, M., & Audretsch, D. B. (2020). The knowledge spillover theory of entrepreneurship: the developing country context. *International Entrepreneurship and Management Journal, 16*(4), 1327–1346. https://doi.org/10.1007/s11365-020-00667-w

Išoraitė, M. (2014). ICT and entrepreneurship: social network marketing. *Entrepreneurship and Sustainability Issues, 2*(1), 19.

Jabeur, S. B., Ballouk, H., Mefteh-Wali, S., & Omri, A. (2022). Forecasting the macrolevel determinants of entrepreneurial opportunities using artificial intelligence models. *Technological Forecasting and Social Change, 175*, 1. https://doi.org/10.1016/j.techfore.2021.121353

Jagannathan, R., Camasso, M. J., Das, B., Tosun, J., & Iyengar, S. (2017). Family, society and the individual: determinants of entrepreneurial attitudes among youth in Chennai, South India. *Journal of Global Entrepreneurship Research, 7*(1), 1. https://doi.org/10.1186/s40497-017-0070-6

Keshk, O. M. (2003). CDSIMEQ: A program to implement two-stage probit least squares. *The Stata Journal, 3*, 1–11.

Kirchhoff, B. A. (1992). Entrepreneurship's Contribution to Economics. *Entrepreneurship Theory and Practice, 16*(2), 93–112. https://doi.org/10.1177/104225879201600207

Korkmaz, S., & Korkmaz, O. (2017). The Relationship between Labor Productivity and Economic Growth in OECD Countries. *International Journal of Economics and Finance, 9*(5), 71. https://doi.org/10.5539/ijef.v9n5p71

Krasniqi, B. A. (2009). Personal, household and business environmental determinants of entrepreneurship. *Journal of Small Business and Enterprise Development, 16*(1), 146–166. https://doi.org/10.1108/14626000910932935

Kritikos, A. S. (2015). Entrepreneurship and Economic Growth. In International Encyclopedia of the Social and Behavioral Sciences: Second Edition (pp. 675–680). 10.1016/B978-0-08-097086-8. 94004-2

Krueger, N. F., Reilly, M. D., & Carsrud, A. L. (2000). Competing models of entrepreneurial intentions. *Journal of Business Venturing, 15*(5), 411–432. https://doi.org/10.1016/S0883-9026(98)00033-0

Kuratko, D. F. (2005). The emergence of entrepreneurship education: Development, trends, and challenges. *Entrepreneurship: Theory and Practice*. Blackwell Publishing Inc. 10.1111/j.1540-6520.2005.00099.x

Lasch, F., Robert, F., & Le Roy, F. (2013). Regional determinants of ICT new firm formation. *Small Business Economics, 40*(3), 671–686. https://doi.org/10.1007/s11187-011-9382-z

Laukkanen, M. (2000). Exploring alternative approaches in high-level entrepreneurship education: Creating micromechanisms for endogenous regional growth. *Entrepreneurship and Regional Development, 12*(1), 25–47. https://doi.org/10.1080/089856200283072

Leibenstein, H. (1968). Entrepreneurship and development. *The American Economic Review, 58*(2), 72–83.

Lévesque, M., & Minniti, M. (2006). The effect of aging on entrepreneurial behavior. *Journal of Business Venturing, 21*(2), 177–194. https://doi.org/10.1016/j.jbusvent.2005.04.003

Liñán, F., & Chen, Y. W. (2009). Development and cross-cultural application of a specific instrument to measure entrepreneurial intentions. *Entrepreneurship: Theory and Practice, 33*(3), 593–617. https://doi.org/10.1111/j.1540-6520.2009.00318.x

Long, D., Wang, H., & Wang, P. (2021). Built to sustain: The effect of entrepreneurial decision-making logic on new venture sustainability. *Sustainability (Switzerland), 13*(4), 1–20. https://doi.org/10.3390/su13042170

López-Núñez, M. I., Rubio-Valdehita, S., Aparicio-García, M. E., & Díaz-Ramiro, E. M. (2020). Are entrepreneurs born or made? The influence of personality. *Personality and Individual Differences, 154*, 1. https://doi.org/10.1016/j.paid.2019.109699

Lucas, R. E. (1988). On the mechanics of economic development. *Journal of Monetary Economics, 22*(1), 3–42. https://doi.org/10.1016/0304-3932(88)90168-7

Markman, G. D., Gianiodis, P. T., Phan, P. H., & Balkin, D. B. (2004). Entrepreneurship from the Ivory Tower: Do incentive systems matter? *Journal of Technology Transfer, 29*(3–4), 353–364. https://doi.org/10.1023/b:jott.0000034127.01889.86

Marshall, M. I., & Flaig, A. (2014). Marriage, children, and self-employment earnings: An analysis of self-employed women in the US. *Journal of Family and Economic Issues, 35*(3), 313–322.

Mas-Tur, A., Pinazo, P., Tur-Porcar, A. M., & Sánchez-Masferrer, M. (2015). What to avoid to succeed as an entrepreneur. *Journal of Business Research, 68*(11), 2279–2284. https://doi.org/10.1016/j.jbusres.2015.06.011

Matos, S., & Hall, J. (2020). An exploratory study of entrepreneurs in impoverished communities: when institutional factors and individual characteristics result in non-productive entrepreneurship. *Entrepreneurship and Regional Development, 32*(1–2), 134–155. https://doi.org/10.1080/08985626.2019.1640476

Merkulova, E. Y. (2019). The effect of labor productivity on economic growth. *Statistics and Economics, 16*(2), 34–44. https://doi.org/10.21686/2500-3925-2019-2-34-44

Millán, J., Congregado, E., & Román, C. (2010). Determinants of Self-Employment dynamics and their Implications on Entrepreneurial Policy Effectiveness. *Lecturas de Economía, 72*, 45–76.

Minniti, M., & Naudé, W. (2010). What do we know about the patterns and determinants of female entrepreneurship across Countries? *European Journal of Development Research*. https://doi.org/10.1057/ejdr.2010.17

Mohamad, N. M. Masron, T. A., & Ibrahim, H. (2021). The Role of Entrepreneurship on Income Inequality in Developing Countries. *Journal of Poverty*. https://doi.org/10.1080/10875549.2020.1869662

Mondragón-Vélez, C., & Peña, X. (2010). Business ownership and self-employment in developing economies: The Colombian case. In *International differences in entrepreneurship* (pp. 89–127). University of Chicago Press.

Mondragón-Vélez, C., Peña, X., & Wills, D. (2010). Labor Market Rigidities and Informality in Colombia. *Economía, 11*(1), 65–95. https://doi.org/10.1353/eco.2010.0009

Mueller, P. (2006). Entrepreneurship in the region: Breeding ground for nascent entrepreneurs? *Small Business Economics, 27*(1), 41–58. https://doi.org/10.1007/s11187-006-6951-7

Mueller, S. L., & Thomas, A. S. (2001). Culture and entrepreneurial potential: A nine country study of locus of control and innovativeness. *Journal of Business Venturing, 16*(1), 51–75. https://doi.org/10.1016/S0883-9026(99)00039-7

Naudé, W. (2010). Entrepreneurship, developing countries, and development economics: New approaches and insights. *Small Business Economics, 34*(1), 1–12. https://doi.org/10.1007/s11187-009-9198-2

Naudé, W., Gries, T., Wood, E., & Meintjies, A. (2008). Regional determinants of entrepreneurial start-ups in a developing country. *Entrepreneurship and Regional Development, 20*(2), 111–124. https://doi.org/10.1080/08985620701631498

Ngwaba, C. A., & Azizi, S. (2020). Effectiveness of tax reform on entrepreneurship. *Journal of Entrepreneurship and Public Policy, 9*(1), 94–111. https://doi.org/10.1108/JEPP-07-2019-0060

Nkongolo-Bakenda, J. M., & Chrysostome, E. V. (2013). Engaging diasporas as international entrepreneurs in developing countries: In search of determinants. *Journal of International Entrepreneurship, 11*(1), 30–64. https://doi.org/10.1007/s10843-012-0098-1

Osiobe, E. U. (2019). A Literature Review of Human Capital and Economic Growth. *Business and Economic Research, 9*(4), 179. https://doi.org/10.5296/ber.v9i4.15624

Othman, N., & Tengku Muda, T. N. A. A. (2018). Emotional intelligence towards entrepreneurial career choice behaviours. *Education and Training, 60*(9), 953–970. https://doi.org/10.1108/ET-07-2017-0098

Perez-Quintana, A., Hormiga, E., Martori, J. C., & Madariaga, R. (2017). The influence of sex and gender-role orientation in the decision to become an entrepreneur. *International Journal of Gender and Entrepreneurship, 9*(1), 8–30. https://doi.org/10.1108/IJGE-12-2015-0047

Perobelli, F. S., Haddad, E. A., Moron, J. B., & Hewings, G. J. D. (2010). Structural interdependence among Colombian departments. *Economic Systems Research, 22*(3), 279–300. https://doi.org/10.1080/09535314.2010.510467

Rapp, D. J., & Olbrich, M. (2020). On entrepreneurial decision logics under conditions of uncertainty: an attempt to advance the current debate. *Journal of Innovation and Entrepreneurship, 9*(1). https://doi.org/10.1186/s13731-020-00131-7

Romano, C. A., Tanewski, G. A., & Smyrnios, K. X. (2001). Capital structure decision making: A model for family business. *Journal of Business Venturing, 16*(3), 285–310. https://doi.org/10.1016/S0883-9026(99)00053-1

Ross, A. G., Adams, J., & Crossan, K. (2015). Entrepreneurship and the spatial context: A panel data study into regional determinants of small growing firms in Scotland. *Local Economy, 30*(6), 672–688. https://doi.org/10.1177/0269094215600135

Schulz, M., Urbig, D., & Procher, V. (2017). The role of hybrid entrepreneurship in explaining multiple job holders' earnings structure. *Journal of business venturing insights, 7*, 9–14.

Sobel, R. S. (2008). Testing Baumol: Institutional quality and the productivity of entrepreneurship. *Journal of Business Venturing, 23*(6), 641–655. https://doi.org/10.1016/j.jbusvent.2008.01.004

Soon, J. J., & Lim, H. E. (2016). Be your own boss, anyone? Earnings, employment chances and job choice of fresh university graduates. *International Journal of Business and Society, 17*(3), 1.

Stam, E. (2014). The Dutch entrepreneurial ecosystem. *Available at* SSRN 2473475.

Stel, A. V., Carree, M., & Thurik, R. (2005). The effect of entrepreneurial activity on national economic growth. *Small Business Economics, 24*(3), 311–321. https://doi.org/10.1007/s11187-005-1996-6

Stenholm, P., Acs, Z. J., & Wuebker, R. (2013). Exploring country-level institutional arrangements on the rate and type of entrepreneurial activity. *Journal of Business Venturing, 28*(1), 176–193. https://doi.org/10.1016/j.jbusvent.2011.11.002

Sternberg, R., & Wagner, J. (2004). The Decision to Start a New Firm: Personal and Regional Determinants. Empirical Evidence from the Regional Entrepreneurship Monitor (REM) Germany. In *Gründungsprozess und Gründungserfolg* (pp. 19–38). Physica-Verlag HD. https://doi.org/10.1007/978-3-7908-2679-1_3

Sternberg, R., & Wennekers, S. (2005). Determinants and effects of new business creation using global entrepreneurship monitor data. *Small Business Economics, 24*(3), 193–203. https://doi.org/10.1007/s11187-005-1974-z

Stuetzer, M., Obschonka, M., Brixy, U., Sternberg, R., & Cantner, U. (2014). Regional characteristics, opportunity perception and entrepreneurial activities. *Small Business Economics, 42*(2), 221–244. https://doi.org/10.1007/s11187-013-9488-6

Stull, W. J. (2014). Taking the Plunge: Teaching the Microeconomics of Entrepreneurship. *International Advances in Economic Research, 20*(2), 139–150. https://doi.org/10.1007/s11294-013-9456-6

Sullivan, P. (2009). Estimation of an Occupational Choice Model when Occupations are Misclassified. *Journal of Human Resources, 44*(2), 495–535.

Thai, M. T. T., & Turkina, E. (2014). Macro-level determinants of formal entrepreneurship versus informal entrepreneurship. *Journal of Business Venturing, 29*(4), 490–510. https://doi.org/10.1016/j.jbusvent.2013.07.005

Trang Do, T. Q., & Duchene, G. (2008). Determinants of self-employment: the case in Vietnam. *CES Working Papers, 38*.

Urbano, D., & Aparicio, S. (2016). Entrepreneurship capital types and economic growth: International evidence. *Technological Forecasting and Social Change, 102*, 34–44.

Urbano, D., Turro, A., & Aparicio, S. (2017). Antecedents and Consequences of Corporate Manufacturing Entrepreneurship via R&D. *Academy of Management Proceedings, 2017*(1), 16838. https://doi.org/10.5465/ambpp.2017.16838abstract

Urbano, D., Turro, A., & Aparicio, S. (2020). Innovation through R&D activities in the European context: antecedents and consequences. *Journal of Technology Transfer, 45*(5), 1481–1504. https://doi.org/10.1007/s10961-019-09752-x

Valliere, D., & Peterson, R. (2009). Entrepreneurship and economic growth: Evidence from emerging and developed countries. *Entrepreneurship and Regional Development, 21*(5–6), 459–480. https://doi.org/10.1080/08985620802332723

Van Praag, C. M., & Ophem, H. V. (1995). Determinants of Willingness and Opportunity to Start as an Entrepreneur. *Kyklos, 48*(4), 513–540. https://doi.org/10.1111/j.1467-6435.1995.tb01282.x

Wennekers, S., & Thurik, R. (1999). Linking Entrepreneurship and Economic Growth. *Small Business Economics, 13*(1), 27–56. https://doi.org/10.1023/A:1008063200484

Wennekers, S., & Van Stel, A. (2017). Types and roles of productive entrepreneurship: A conceptual study. In *The Wiley Handbook of Entrepreneurship* (pp. 37–69). John Wiley and Sons Inc.. https://doi.org/10.1002/9781118970812

Wong, P. K., Ho, Y. P., & Autio, E. (2005). Entrepreneurship, innovation and economic growth: Evidence from GEM data. *Small Business Economics, 24*(3), 335–350. https://doi.org/10.1007/s11187-005-2000-1

Zhang, F., & Li, D. (2018). Regional ICT access and entrepreneurship: Evidence from China. *Information & Management, 55*(2), 188–198.

10

Does Company Size Matter for Economic Growth? An Analysis Across OECD, Latin American, and Caribbean Countries

Diego Gomez, Sebastian Aparicio, and David Urbano

10.1 Introduction

The Smithian question of why some nations are wealthier and have higher growth rates than others has leveraged a lot of research about growth antecedents, leading special attention to be paid to Solow's (1956) approach and subsequent advances made by Barro (1991) and Mankiw Gregory et al. (1992). Despite the large number of studies that have investigated the determinants of economic growth (Chirwa & Odhiambo, 2016; Spolaore & Wacziarg, 2013), there exists a key element that has

D. Gomez
Fundación ECSIM, Medellin, Colombia

S. Aparicio (✉) • D. Urbano
Department of Business, Universitat Autònoma de Barcelona, Cerdanyola del Vallés, Barcelona, Spain

Centre for Entrepreneurship and Social Innovation Research (CREIS), Universitat Autònoma de Barcelona, Sabadell, Barcelona, Spain
e-mail: Sebastian.Aparicio@uab.cat

D. Gomez et al. (eds.), *Driving Complexity in Economic Development*,
https://doi.org/10.1007/978-3-031-34386-5_10

not received enough attention yet: companies' size (Rothwell, 1977). This constitutes a research opportunity to bring together the separate literatures on firm growth and economic growth.

In this chapter, we analyze how companies are linked to economic growth according to their size. To achieve this, we draw on theories of endogenous economic growth (Sala-i-Martin et al., 2004) and the effects of company characteristics on such growth (Fuster et al., 2019; Vincett, 2010). Having set the theoretical basis, we proceed to propose a hypothesis that supports the fundamental role played by the companies' characteristics (size and growth—through annual sales) on economic growth (per capita gross domestic product [GDP]). To test this hypothesis, we used two sources of information. First, we used the World Bank Enterprise Surveys (WBES) to collect information about some companies' characteristics (e.g., industry, size, loans, legal status). Second, we used the World Development Indicators from the World Bank to create an unbalanced pseudo-panel. Thanks to this dataset, we were able to collect information for a maximum of 22,348 observations across Latin American and Caribbean countries over the period 2002–2018. Finally, we used full nested models (Allen, 1997) to develop the regression analysis and support the hypothesis.

The results showed that companies' size matters for economic growth in the analyzed region. As a robustness test, we performed the same regression for a group of Organisation for Economic Co-operation and Development (OECD) countries, showing that the hypothesis does not hold for economies that have reached a steady state. The importance of the economic structure of each of the groups of countries should be emphasized, because the full nested model results improve with the addition of the economic control variables. These findings strengthen the current knowledge level. This leads to theoretical and policy implications that allow us to propose some recommendations for scholars and policymakers about where to redirect efforts to obtain benefits in economic growth and to emphasize the fundamental role that companies play in a country's development.

This chapter is structured as follows. In the next section, we present the theoretical framework, whereby we establish economic growth and companies' characteristics as the main axis of the research. Next, we explain the methodology, including the source of the data and the empirical strategy. We then present the results. We conclude the chapter with a discussion of theoretical and policy implications.

10.2 Conceptual Framework

Economic growth has been extensively studied, as have its determinants and the effects they have on the economy (Jones, 1995; Sala-i-Martin et al., 2004). Some of the determinants of economic growth are productivity (Korkmaz & Korkmaz, 2017; Merkulova, 2019), innovation (Coe & Helpman, 1995; Thompson, 2018), education (Beine et al., 2001; Marquez-Ramos & Mourelle, 2019), savings (Atkinson & Hamilton, 2003; Sothan, 2014), exports (Feder, 1983; Indana & Mulyani, 2021), finance (Beck et al., 2000), entrepreneurship (Wennekers & Thurik, 1999), institutions (Glaeser et al., 2004), and the company's performance or characteristics (Laužikas & Krasauskas, 2013).

In regard to the last determinant, the literature on the effects of a company's performance on economic growth is not that extensive. Bykova and Coates (2020) studied how regional economic freedom drives the growth of a specific firm, which then transforms into economic growth for that region. Other studies have focused on observing the effects of academic spin-off companies. Vincett (2010) studied the impact of academic spin-off companies and their implications for public policy, finding that the spin-off impacts represent incremental contributions to GDP that are much larger than the government funding; governments will also receive more in additional tax than they spend. Fuster et al. (2019) examined the emerging role of university spin-off companies in the development of regional entrepreneurial university ecosystems, finding that university spin-off companies are the main actors in the entrepreneurial university ecosystem and strengthen knowledge transfer by relating with other businesses beyond this ecosystem. Fuster et al. (2019) emphasized the importance of this effect because universities play a strategic role as drivers of regional economic growth.

Two research studies are key to understanding the effect of companies on economic growth. First, Long Le et al. (2016) presented the outstanding postwar development of the Korean economy with a particular focus on the role played by Korean companies. The authors remarked on some key factors for this relationship. First, the market-led growth principle should be firmly established; public policies should be focused on the important industry, services, and finance; support for small and medium-size enterprises (SMEs) should be concentrated on start-up companies;

and the market competitive strength should be improved. Second, keeping in mind that the private sector is the main factor in national economic growth, the private sector should be encouraged to develop realistic policies, including tax policy, capital support, technology, employee training. Third, it is important to control and minimize macroeconomic risks by keeping inflation low, improving financial stability, and ensuring fiscal sustainability. The second key research project is Mahmud's (2003), which attempted to characterize capital structure on the basis of a country's economic factor, industry class, and firm-specific factors in three Asian countries: Japan, Malaysia, and Pakistan. Mahmud found that the results on firm factors were mixed but that there is a tendency for assets-related variables to be more important than sales-related variables in determining capital structure.

In this chapter, we search for a proxy of company size to help us understand the effect of this variable on economic growth in the Latin American and Caribbean region because this is an emerging field of study. Latin American firms have some interesting characteristics (Céspedes et al., 2010), including size (Herrera & Lora, 2005). According to Herrera and Lora (2005), Latin American firms are small because of trade openness, stock market capitalization, and physical infrastructure; nevertheless, little is known about the effect of company size on economic growth in that region.

10.3 Hypothesis Development

Companies play a fundamental role in the economic growth of regions including, among other ways, through their intermediation functions (Solomon & Marshal, 2015) and by attracting foreign direct investment (Mishra et al., 2017). However, the role of company size has not been specifically explored. Most studies related to company size focus on observing the effects of SMEs on economies, where literature is wide. Studying the effects of companies' sizes is crucial because, according to Verheyden and Goeman (2013), 99% of all companies in the European Union are SMEs. Four key investigations emphasize the importance of this phenomenon.

In the first investigation, Fanta (2015) provided a detailed account of the economic significance of SMEs by drawing on the extant empirical literature. The author stated that although modeling growth in the SME sector and its impact on economic development is a matter of ongoing scientific investigation, the most visible economic benefits of SMEs includes, among others, job creation, contribution to national output, and reducing income inequality and poverty. Second, Nguyen et al. (2020) explored the dynamic impacts of stock market development and innovation on key macroeconomic variables in Hong Kong, Singapore, Thailand, and Malaysia, using the propositions of Kaleckian–post-Keynesian macroeconomic framework. The authors found that SME stock market development and innovation have small but positive impacts on short-run economic stimulation. On the one hand, the SME stock market development spurs economic growth through the combination of private investment, savings, and productivity in Hong Kong, Singapore, and Thailand. Innovation, on the other hand, promotes growth through the combination of these channels and the employment channel in all four countries. Third, Gamidullaeva et al. (2020) tested an approach to measure SME institutional environment quality through the identification of regional-level determinants in Russia. The results suggested that governments should eliminate or reduce main obstacles (shadow economy, corruption, access to finance, high transportation fees, and instability in the political and economic field) at the country level, thus boosting the region's economic growth. Finally, Beck et al. (2005) used a new database on the share of SME labor in the total manufacturing labor force to explore the relationship between the relative size of the SME sector, economic growth, and alleviation of poverty alleviation. The authors found a strong, positive association between the importance of SMEs and GDP per capita growth. However, the data did not support the conclusion that SMEs have a causal impact on growth. Furthermore, we have found no evidence that SMEs alleviate poverty or decrease income inequality. These researches made clear the importance of analyzing the size of companies and trying to observe the possible transmission mechanism with economic growth.

Other research has attempted to analyze this relationship for some countries. Karadag (2016) developed a comparative analysis of the main indicators of SME sector performance in major advanced and emerging economies. She found that development of the SME sector and economic growth are linked in both developed and developing economies and that, in the post-crisis era (collapse of Lehman Brothers in 2008), new venture creation, employment, and value-added contributions of the SME sector to the economy significantly differ across different contexts. Cravo et al. (2012) examined this relationship for the Brazilian economy from 1985 to 2004. They investigated the importance of the relative size of the SME sector using the proportion of SME employment in total formal employment, finding that the relative importance of SMEs is negatively correlated with economic growth, a result that is consistent with those of previous studies that have examined developing countries. Roopchund (2020) analyzed the contribution of SMEs to the Mauritian economy, linking SME growth to macroeconomic variables such as economic growth and unemployment. He found a positive, but not significant, correlation between the growth of SME revenues and economic growth over a ten-year period, supporting the literature on this topic. Tambunan (2008) stated that government development expenditures are crucial for this relationship but argued that SMEs in less developed countries can survive, and even grow in the long run, spurring economic growth in, for example, Indonesia. This happens for three reasons: (1) the SMEs create a niche market for themselves, (2) they act as a last resort for the poor, and (3) they will grow along with large enterprises. Finally, in a study of Ghana and South Africa, Tsatsenko (2020) explored the nature of SME development, the nature of structural change, and the process of economic growth, finding that SMEs are very likely to contribute to these economies.

After reviewing this literature, we realized that SMEs are fundamental for economic growth. However, most of these studies analyzed this (sometimes-causal) relationship through the number of companies, and not through a specific company characteristic. Some limited research has focused on the importance of characteristics such as company size and growth, and analyzing both the size and growth of companies as a single characteristic will broaden our scope of inquiry. In regard to company size, Redlichová et al. (2019) investigated socioeconomic development drivers (which includes the companies' size and structure) of Nomenclature of Territorial Units for Statistics (NUTS) 3 regions in the Czech Republic.

They found that a higher number of small firms lead to improved regional GDP. These findings support the fact that small firms spur economic growth while playing a role of a social stabilizer in Czech regions. Dozier and Chang (2006) used 1992 and 1997 manufacturing data for the Los Angeles metropolitan area, stratified according to company size, to examine the impact of information technology investment. They found results suggesting that the change in productivity in the manufacturing sector is driven by the size of the companies in conjunction with information technology investment. In regard to company growth, Mishra et al. (2017) studied company growth, such as the total number of industries and the total number of positions approved for foreign investment and its effect on economic growth; however, the appropriate use of firm growth as a dependent variable was not consistent. It is for this reason that in this chapter we analyze the size and growth of companies as a single characteristic.

Two key pieces of research have investigated the close relationship between a company's size/growth and economic growth. First, Hart and Oulton (1996) used a dataset of 87,000 independent UK companies to investigate the relationship between company size and economic growth. Using a Galton–Markov model, the authors found that a positive and significant relationship occurs for the smallest firms (e.g., those with eight or fewer employees), but the opposite was the case for larger firms. The authors emphasized that, even for the smallest firm, the results may be due to transitory factors. This indicates that it is necessary to conduct research that takes into account not only transitory but also permanent macroeconomic factors. Second, Aastveit and Trovik (2012) found that asset prices on the Oslo stock exchange are the single most important block of data to improve estimates of the current quarter GDP in Norway. They explained that the high informational content in asset prices is explained by reference to the small size of companies and the small, open nature of the Norwegian economy. In this case, the relationship is indirect but strongly related.

Despite the limited literature on the use of company size/growth to observe macroeconomic effects, the question arises as to which measure to use. Buzby (1975) mentioned that an approach could be made through the use of companies' annual sales; however, there are risks due to the reliability of the reports provided by the companies. Here we find a gap in the literature: the use of annual sales as company size to observe the effects on the economic growth of nations. Salam et al. (2018) analyzed the possibility of using sales and tax data of public listed companies to measure the economy. They found a positive relationship between sales and GDP and no relationship between tax and GDP. Siegel et al. (1993) analyzed many characteristics of companies and concluded that an appropriate way to identify the size/growth of companies is through their sales. Although the literature regarding this relationship using company sales is almost null, it allows us to establish two hypotheses:

Hypothesis 1: Companies' size, such as sales, spurs the economic growth (GDP) of Latin American and Caribbean countries.

Hypothesis 2: Having reached a steady state of growth (as in most OECD countries), companies' size, such as sales, does not significantly contribute to economic growth (GDP).

10.4 Methodology

10.4.1 Data

One of the challenges we faced when we did the analysis for this chapter was how to choose a reliable data collection method. Among our options were the micro-company database of Forbes and carrying out the web-scrapping method of some web pages that collected preliminary information, among others. However, we considered that, in this case, it is essential to have reliable information because companies can hide or modify their data. For this reason, to examine the hypotheses, we used two data sources. First, we used the WBES, which uses standard survey instruments to collect firm-level data on the business environment from business owners and top managers and covers a broad range of topics, including access to finance, corruption, infrastructure, crime, competition, labor, obstacles to growth, and performance measures. The WBES is a reliable database that has been used in important research, such as Mthimkhulu and Aziakpono (2016), Williams et al. (2017), and

Mohammed and Bunyaminu (2021). Our sample is based on data from 12 countries in Latin America and the Caribbean: Argentina, Bolivia, Colombia, Dominican Republic, Ecuador, El Salvador, Guatemala, Honduras, Nicaragua, Paraguay, Peru, and Uruguay. Although 135 countries are covered by the WBES, and data are available from 2002 to 2018 (by waves), we restricted the sample to 12 countries that had information corresponding to companies' annual sales (not all countries met this criterion). Second, we used the World Development Indicators from the World Bank to create an unbalanced (due to the fact that data in developing countries is often remarkably poor and frequently missing) pseudo-panel (one for each country group) data with a maximum of 22,348 observations from 2002 to 2018 for Latin American and the Caribbean countries.

This unbalanced pseudo-panel data allowed us to identify some key variables for the research. As the dependent variable, we used the per capita GDP to capture the economic growth of countries. As the principal independent variable, the annual sales in the last fiscal year of the companies were used as a proxy of the company's size. Several variable groups were used for the control variables. First, the micro information of the companies was used to establish some main characteristics, such as industry variables, that correspond to dummy variables that assume a value of 1 depending on the sector to which they belong, including manufacturing, retail, and other service industries. Second, dummy variables assume a value of 1 when a company matches its legal status. Examples of legal statuses are a shareholding company with shares traded in the stock market, a shareholding company with non-traded shares or shares traded privately, sole proprietorship, partnership, limited partnership, and others. Third, we screened companies by size in the form of the number of employees: 5–19 (small), 20–99 (medium), and 100+ employees (large). Some research has used the number of employees as a proxy to measure the size of companies; however, we believe that it is not sufficiently adequate because some small companies dedicated to technological services can generate large sales with few employees. Fourth, we used a dummy variable that assumes a value of 1 when a company has a line of credit or a loan from a financial institution. Finally, there was a group of control variables focused on the countries' economic characteristics. These included total taxes and contribution rate, imports, and exports. These variables allowed us to develop an appropriate econometric model to support the hypotheses.

10.4.2 Empirical Strategy

We used the following full nested econometric model to observe the direct effect that companies' size (companies' annual sales) had on economic growth (GDP per capita) in company *i* in a specific country *c*, through years *y*:

$$GDPpc_{icy} = \alpha + \beta_1 CZ_{icy} + \beta_2 I_{icy} + \beta_3 LS_{icy} + \beta_5 C_{icy} + \beta_5 SS_{icy} + \beta_5 E_{cy} + \varepsilon_{icy} \quad (6)$$

The outcome $GDPpc_{icy}$ is related to economic growth (i.e., per capita GDP). The effect of the company's size (i.e., annual sales) is captured through CZ_{icy}. We control by I_{icy}, LS_{icy}, C_{icy}, SS_{icy}, and E_{cy}, which contain the effects of the company and country characteristics. Standard errors were robust, to account for the arbitrary correlation of outcomes between countries.

In nested models, "nested" means that one model is a subset of another. This type of model is used for several statistical tests and analyses, including multiple regression, conjoint analysis, and others (Allen, 1997). Nested models allow one to identify a full model that explains digital entrepreneurship through individual- and country-level variables and compare it with other models, which contain additional restrictions. In our particular case, we are in an identification world, in which it is important not to discard any variable that could be significant (i.e., issues of omitted variables), so the nested models fit our intentions. Thus, we applied the fixed-effects method to estimate several nested models, which are controlled by company and country characteristics. It is important to clarify that, with these models and the proposed hypotheses, we seek to delve into a world of directly correlated relationships, leaving aside possible endogeneity and other problems related to the estimations.

10.5 Results

10.5.1 Main Results

Tables 10.1 and 10.2 show the descriptive statistics of the variables used (Table 10.1 contains the descriptive statistics of the variables for the OECD countries used to perform a robustness check). The first thing to observe is the statistics of our dependent variable: For the OECD

Table 10.1 Descriptive statistics (OECD countries)

Variables	Mean	SD	Min	Max	P50	p99	N
GDPpc*	23.521	4.590	15.016	33.790	24.309	33.790	9685
Company's size (sales)**	9.782	23.231	0.000	101.500	0.784	101.500	8707
Manufacturing	0.283	0.451	0.000	1.000	0.000	1.000	9685
Retail	0.104	0.306	0.000	1.000	0.000	1.000	9685
Other_services	0.104	0.306	0.000	1.000	0.000	1.000	9685
A shareholding firm with shares traded in the stock market	0.023	0.150	0.000	1.000	0.000	1.000	9685
A shareholding firm with non-traded shares	0.495	0.500	0.000	1.000	0.000	1.000	9685
Sole proprietorship firm	0.209	0.407	0.000	1.000	0.000	1.000	9685
Partnership firm	0.179	0.383	0.000	1.000	0.000	1.000	9685
Limited partnership, and others	0.031	0.173	0.000	1.000	0.000	1.000	9685
Small firm	0.223	0.417	0.000	1.000	0.000	1.000	9685
Medium firm	0.159	0.366	0.000	1.000	0.000	1.000	9685
Large firm	0.098	0.297	0.000	1.000	0.000	1.000	9685
Loan services	0.223	0.416	0.000	1.000	0.000	1.000	9685
Unemployment	10.850	3.995	5.608	19.895	9.710	19.895	9685
Gross capital formation***	88.204	95.740	4.003	278.187	51.052	278.187	9685
Government effectiveness	0.645	0.247	0.269	1.051	0.655	1.051	9685

Note: ***values in billions; **values in millions *values in thousand N is equal to the observations

Table 10.2 Descriptive statistics (Latin American and the Caribbean countries)

Variables	Mean	SD	Min	Max	P50	p99	N
GDPpc*	11.401	5.713	4.043	23.597	10.066	23.597	22,348
Company's size (sales)**	2.509	4.006	0.000	12.520	0.510	12.520	21,878
Manufacturing	0.572	0.495	0.000	1.000	1.000	1.000	22,348
Retail	0.194	0.395	0.000	1.000	0.000	1.000	22,348
Other_services	0.214	0.410	0.000	1.000	0.000	1.000	22,348
A shareholding firm with shares traded in the stock market	0.080	0.272	0.000	1.000	0.000	1.000	22,348
A shareholding firm with non-traded shares	0.513	0.500	0.000	1.000	1.000	1.000	22,348
Sole proprietorship firm	0.153	0.360	0.000	1.000	0.000	1.000	22,348
Partnership firm	0.082	0.275	0.000	1.000	0.000	1.000	22,348
Limited partnership, and others	0.121	0.326	0.000	1.000	0.000	1.000	22,348
Small firm	0.356	0.479	0.000	1.000	0.000	1.000	22,348
Medium firm	0.299	0.458	0.000	1.000	0.000	1.000	22,348
Large firm	0.187	0.390	0.000	1.000	0.000	1.000	22,348
Loan services	0.581	0.493	0.000	1.000	1.000	1.000	22,348
Total taxes and contribution rate	59.644	26.641	32.500	107.400	41.900	107.400	20,538
Imports	10.933	9.127	−4.060	35.915	9.995	35.915	22,348
Exports	6.382	5.133	−4.975	24.612	6.100	24.612	22,348

Note: **values in millions *values in thousand N is equal to the observations

countries, the mean per capita GDP is around US $23,500 per year, and the mean GDP of the Latin America and the Caribbean countries is around US $11,400 per year. Thus, the purchasing power of OECD countries is nearly double that of Latin American and Caribbean countries. Looking at the statistics of our independent variable, for OECD countries the mean annual sales reach US $9.78 million, and for Latin American and Caribbean countries it reaches US $2.5 million. We should mention that the OECD countries considered in our database are not the countries with the largest economies, and this group of countries is smaller than the Latin America and the Caribbean countries considered. Concerning the industry to which the OECD companies belonged, we found that 28% of the companies belonged to the manufacturing industry, 10% to retail services, and 10% to other services (the other 52% of the companies did not disclose this information). For Latin American and Caribbean countries, these figures were 57%, 19%, and 21%, respectively (the other 3% of the companies did not disclose this information).

When we examined the legal status of the companies, we noted that for both OECD and Latin American and Caribbean countries, the majority of companies are joint-stock entities with non-negotiable shares or privately traded shares, 49.5% and 51.3%, respectively. In regard to the size of companies by the number of employees (small, medium, and large), for OECD countries 22% were small, 15.9% were medium, and 9.8% were large; for Latin America and the Caribbean countries these numbers were 35.6%, 30%, and 18.7%, respectively. In addition, Tables 10A1 and 10A2 show the correlation matrices between the variables for each group of countries. Here it is key to highlight that, without carrying out any estimation, the company's size variables, such as annual sales, showed a positive correlation with economic growth, such as per capita GDP.

In regard to the main results, Table 10.3 shows our models through fixed-effects estimation, reporting the relationships outlined in the hypotheses development for Latin American and Caribbean countries. Models 1 through 6 present fixed-effects estimates, although Model 6 is the full nested model with all control variables and fixed effects. Therefore, to explain the results, we focus on explaining Model 6. Regarding the hypotheses, we suggested in Hypothesis 1 that companies' size, such as annual sales, spurs the economic growth (per capita GDP) of Latin American and Caribbean countries. All models in Table 10.3 support this hypothesis; when companies' size, such as annual sales, increase by 1%, this spurs the economic growth of Latin American and Caribbean countries (i.e., per capita GDP) by 0.061% (approximately $6.84 [relative to the mean]). In addition, for all models (1–6) we have a positive and significant effect (at 0.01%), and both R^2 and the Akaike Information

Table 10.3 Companies' size effect on economic growth (per capita GDP) in Latin American and Caribbean countries

	(1)	(2)	(3)	(4)	(5)	(6)
	GDP per capita	GDP per capita	GDP per capita	GDP per capita	GDP per capita	GDP per capita
Company's size	0.095***	0.092***	0.090***	0.089***	0.085***	0.061***
	(0.008)	(0.008)	(0.008)	(0.008)	(0.008)	(0.007)
Constant	0.025***	0.025***	0.024***	0.024***	0.029***	0.090***
	(0.000)	(0.000)	(0.000)	(0.000)	(0.001)	(0.001)
Company industry FE	**NO**	**YES**	**YES**	**YES**	**YES**	**YES**
Company legal status FE	**NO**	**NO**	**YES**	**YES**	**YES**	**YES**
Company magnitude FE	**NO**	**NO**	**NO**	**YES**	**YES**	**YES**
Company loan services FE	**NO**	**NO**	**NO**	**NO**	**YES**	**YES**
Economy FE	**NO**	**NO**	**NO**	**NO**	**NO**	**YES**
Observations	**21,878**	**21,878**	**21,878**	**21,878**	**21,878**	**20,538**
R-squared	**0.034**	**0.058**	**0.068**	**0.069**	**0.086**	**0.448**
AIC	**−27,786.440**	**−28,331.581**	**−28,558.258**	**−28,568.340**	**−28,985.137**	**−36,632.268**
BIC	**−27,778.447**	**−28,299.608**	**−28,486.319**	**−28,488.407**	**−28,881.225**	**−36,513.318**

Note: standard errors in parentheses: *p<0.05; **p<0.01; ***p<0.001

Criterion (AIC) and Bayesian Information Criterion (BIC) improved considerably in the full nested model (Model 6). We should note that, once the economic fixed effect is added, the R^2 increased (to 44.8%); this is supported by the results of the AIC and BIC, because they are increasingly lower (Akaike, 1974).

10.5.2 Robustness Check

Robustness checks involve reporting alternative specifications that test the same hypothesis; in our case, companies from Latin American and Caribbean countries and companies from some OECD countries have different characteristics, and even a different composition, as can be seen in Tables 10.1 and 10.2. Therefore, we sought to test Hypothesis 1 through Hypothesis 2. In our sample, we used nine OECD countries (Czech Republic, Estonia, Hungary, Latvia, Lithuania, Poland, Slovakia, Slovenia, and Turkey), excluding some important countries, such as Germany, Korea, France, and Ireland because of a lack of information.

In regard to the OECD countries, the data in Table 10.4 also support Hypothesis 2: When companies' size, such as annual sales, increased by 1%, the economic growth (i.e., per capita GDP) raised by 0.078% (approximately $18.35 [relative to the mean]), but with a low level of significance ($p < .05$); this is due to the low growth margin of the OECD countries. In this case, individual company characteristics were insufficient to reveal the relationship between economic growth and company size, from Model 1 to Model 5 we noted a negative but insignificant effect; however, both R^2 (63.6%) and the AIC and BIC improved considerably in the full nested model (Model 6). It is important to note that from Models 1 through 5 the effect is negative, indicating that if we concentrate on observing this relationship taking into account only individual company characteristics, we would be omitting key economic variables that reveal the true relationship.

Table 10.4 Companies' size affects economic growth (per capita GDP) in OECD countries

	(1)	(2)	(3)	(4)	(5)	(6)
	GDP per capita	GDP per capita	GDP per capita	GDP per capita	GDP per capita	GDP per capita
Company's size	–0.084	–0.083	–0.088	–0.071	–0.067	0.078*
	(0.048)	(0.048)	(0.050)	(0.047)	(0.047)	(0.031)
Constant	0.051***	0.033***	0.027**	0.037***	0.088***	–0.079***
	(0.000)	(0.005)	(0.009)	(0.009)	(0.013)	(0.008)
Company industry FE	**NO**	**YES**	**YES**	**YES**	**YES**	**YES**
Company legal status FE	**NO**	**NO**	**YES**	**YES**	**YES**	**YES**
Company magnitude FE	**NO**	**NO**	**NO**	**YES**	**YES**	**YES**
Company loan services FE	**NO**	**NO**	**NO**	**NO**	**YES**	**YES**
Economy FE	**NO**	**NO**	**NO**	**NO**	**NO**	**YES**
Observations	**8707**	**8707**	**8707**	**8707**	**8707**	**8707**
R-squared	**0.004**	**0.013**	**0.061**	**0.080**	**0.087**	**0.636**
AIC	**–7526.578**	**–7600.554**	**–8023.131**	**–8202.185**	**–8263.596**	**–16,254.990**
BIC	**–7519.506**	**–7579.338**	**–7966.556**	**–8138.538**	**–8178.733**	**–16,148.912**

Note: standard errors in parentheses: *p<0.05; **p<0.01; ***p<0.001

10.6 Discussion and Conclusions

The literature on the relationship between companies' size, such as annual sales, and economic growth (per capita GDP) is almost null. Therefore, this chapter is crucial because it fills this gap in the literature, especially in regard to Latin American and Caribbean countries. We relied on key research (Salam et al., 2018) that sought to measure the economy through annual sales, thus marking a possible relationship between this variable and economic growth. Using unbalanced pseudo-panel data and nested models as the main empirical strategy, we arrived at two important findings.

First, the results support the hypothesis that companies' size (i.e., annual sales) spurs the economic growth of countries, not only countries with a high level of development (e.g., some OECD countries) but also developing countries in Latin America and the Caribbean. However, one should take into account that, perhaps because of the level of development of the OECD countries, the effect of company size/growth on economic growth is much greater than that in Latin American and Caribbean countries, $123 higher (however, being less significant). Even so, one must considered that the number of observations and the information from Latin American and Caribbean companies is much more complete than that of the OECD countries, not to mention that key countries, such as Germany, Korea, France, and Ireland, were left out of the estimates because of lack of information. Thus, we can conclude that the effect of companies' size, in the form as sales, on the economic growth of countries depends to a large extent on how far the economy of that country is from its steady state, because the further away it is from the steady state, the greater the effect of the size of companies is.

Second, the inclusion of the behavior of key economic variables (taxes, imports, exports, government effectiveness, unemployment, gross fixed capital formation, etc.) is crucial to reveal the true effect of company size/growth on the economic growth of countries because of possible transitory effects and the economic composition of each country. For this reason, it was crucial to choose an empirical strategy that allowed us to operate in a world of identification because the full nested model allowed us to make comparisons against other models that do not contain the entire structure.

10.6.1 Theoretical Implications

The results of our analyses allow us to deduce two important theoretical implications about the importance of company characteristics (e.g., size) on economic growth (per capita GDP).

First, filling the gap in the literature on the relationship between company size and economic growth is fundamental to economic theory. Company characteristics, such as size, allowed us to identify new relationships and the effects on the economic growth of countries. Because of the economic crisis generated by the COVID-19 pandemic and the consequent shortage of fundamental products and services, it is crucial to establish new forms of economic growth. Second, it supports the fundamental role of companies in countries' economic, institutional, and social frameworks. The literature has positioned companies as one of the fundamental engines of economic growth (Audretsch & Fritsch, 2002; Buckley & Casson, 1998; Ilegbinosa & Jumbo, 2015; Szarzec et al., 2021) but has not yet evaluated in depth the effects of their characteristics on macroeconomic variables, such as GDP. That is why in this research we tried to mark a path in the study of these characteristics and their effects.

10.6.2 Policy Implications

A big challenge in writing this chapter was to generate a discussion about policy decisions that would help spur economic growth from companies' characteristics, specifically, companies' size, such as the annual sales. In this chapter, we have generated important policy implications.

First, we sought to make policymakers understand the fundamental role of companies in economies and the positive effect that the growth of these companies, through their sales, generates on economic growth, under favorable institutional and social conditions. Second, some policies, such as tax reductions, that allow companies to reduce their costs have a positive effect on the studied relationship because they will generate a boost not only at the micro level but also at the macro level, to boost employment. In addition, tax reduction policy can be accompanied by economic benefits, such as pension and health subsidies, with the possibility of promoting an increase in formal employment, especially in Latin American and Caribbean countries. Third, to carry out institutional improvements that reduce the barriers to market entry, and allow the creation of new companies, in addition to generating policies that boost the exports of these companies and help their sales grow, policies may encourage entrepreneurs and businessmen to carry out innovation and technical processes in their companies, aiming not only at personal benefits but also the generation of formal employment.

10.6.3 Limitations and Future Research

Finally, although this chapter has some limitations in terms of the collection of information, it makes clear that researchers have a long way to go in seeking to highlight the effect companies have on nations' economic growth. Future research could focus on identifying other types of company characteristics, such as level of innovation, whether they are public or private, their sector, and their effects on economic growth, perhaps taking into account external factors, such as COVID-19, the increase in prices of raw materials and the shortage of these materials, among others. Another approach that could generate a wide field of research is a focus on the role that institutions play in this relationship given that they are the ones that determine the rules of the game within societies (North, 1990, 2005).

References

Aastveit, K. A., & Trovik, T. (2012). Nowcasting norwegian GDP: The role of asset prices in a small open economy. *Empirical Economics, 42*(1), 95–119. https://doi.org/10.1007/s00181-010-0429-9

Akaike, H. (1974). A New Look at the Statistical Model Identification. *IEEE Transactions on Automatic Control, 19*(6), 716–723.

Allen, M. P. (1997). Testing hypotheses in nested regression models. In *Understanding Regression Analysis*. Springer. https://doi.org/10.1007/978-0-585-25657-3_24

Atkinson, G., & Hamilton, K. (2003). Savings, growth and the resource curse hypothesis. *World Development, 31*(11), 1793–1807. https://doi.org/10.1016/j.worlddev.2003.05.001

Audretsch, D. B., & Fritsch, M. (2002). Growth regimes over time and space. *Regional Studies, 36*(2), 113–124. https://doi.org/10.1080/00343400220121909

Barro, R. J. (1991). Economic growth in a cross section of countries. *Quarterly Journal of Economics, 106*(2), 407–443. https://doi.org/10.2307/2937943

Beck, T., Levine, R., & Loayza, N. (2000). Finance and the sources of growth. *Journal of Financial Economics, 58*(1–2), 261–300. https://doi.org/10.1016/s0304-405x(00)00072-6

Beck, T., Demirguc-Kunt, A., & Levine, R. (2005). SMEs, growth, and poverty: Cross-country evidence. *Journal of Economic Growth, 10*(3), 199–229. https://doi.org/10.1007/s10887-005-3533-5

Beine, M., Docquier, F., & Rapoport, H. (2001). Brain drain and economic growth: Theory and evidence. *Journal of Development Economics, 64*(1), 275–289. https://doi.org/10.1016/S0304-3878(00)00133-4

Buckley, P. J., & Casson, M. C. (1998). Models of the Multinational Enterprise. *Journal of International Business Studies, 29*(1), 21–44. https://doi.org/10.1057/palgrave.jibs.8490023

Buzby, S. L. (1975). Company Size, Listed Versus Unlisted Stocks, and the Extent of Financial Disclosure. *Journal of Accounting Research, 13*(1), 16. https://doi.org/10.2307/2490647

Bykova, A., & Coates, D. (2020). Firm performance and regional economic freedom: the case of Russia. *Post-Soviet Affairs, 36*(5–6), 395–415. https://doi.org/10.1080/1060586X.2020.1785239

Céspedes, J., González, M., & Molina, C. A. (2010). Ownership and capital structure in Latin America. *Journal of Business Research, 63*(3), 248–254. https://doi.org/10.1016/j.jbusres.2009.03.010

Chirwa, T. G., & Odhiambo, N. M. (2016). Macroeconomic determinants of economic growth: A review of international literature. *South East European Journal of Economics and Business*. School of Economics and Business in Sarajevo. https://doi.org/10.1515/jeb-2016-0009

Coe, D. T., & Helpman, E. (1995). International R&D spillovers. *European Economic Review, 39*(5), 859–887. https://doi.org/10.1016/0014-2921(94)00100-E

Cravo, T. A., Gourlay, A., & Becker, B. (2012). SMEs and regional economic growth in Brazil. *Small Business Economics, 38*(2), 217–230. https://doi.org/10.1007/s11187-010-9261-z

Dozier, K., & Chang, D. (2006). The effect of company size on the productivity impact of information technology investments. *Journal of information technology theory and application., 8*(1), 33–47.

Fanta, A. B. (2015). Exploring the economic significance of small and medium enterprises. *Journal of Governance and Regulation, 4*(1), 27–34. https://doi.org/10.22495/jgr_v4_i4_p3

Feder, G. (1983). On exports and economic growth. *Journal of Development Economics, 12*(1–2), 59–73. https://doi.org/10.1016/0304-3878(83)90031-7

Fuster, E., Padilla-Meléndez, A., Lockett, N., & del-Águila-Obra, A. R. (2019). The emerging role of university spin-off companies in developing regional entrepreneurial university ecosystems: The case of Andalusia. *Technological Forecasting and Social Change, 141*, 219–231. https://doi.org/10.1016/j.techfore.2018.10.020

Gamidullaeva, L. A., Vasin, S. M., & Wise, N. (2020). Increasing small- and medium-enterprise contribution to local and regional economic growth by assessing the institutional environment. *Journal of Small Business and Enterprise Development, 27*(2), 259–280. https://doi.org/10.1108/JSBED-07-2019-0219

Glaeser, E. L., La Porta, R., Lopez-de-Silanes, F., & Shleifer, A. (2004). Do institutions cause growth? *Journal of Economic Growth, 9*(3), 271–303. https://doi.org/10.1023/B:JOEG.0000038933.16398.ed

Hart, P. E., & Oulton, N. (1996). Growth and size of firms. *Economic Journal, 106*(438), 1242–1252. https://doi.org/10.2307/2235518

Herrera, A. M., & Lora, E. (2005). Why so small? Explaining the size of firms in Latin America. World Economy. https://doi.org/10.1111/j.1467-9701.2005.00718.x

Ilegbinosa, I. A., & Jumbo, E. (2015). Small and Medium Scale Enterprises and Economic Growth in Nigeria: 1975-2012. *International Journal of Business and Management, 10*(3), 1. https://doi.org/10.5539/ijbm.v10n3p203

Indana, Z., & Mulyani, E. (2021). The Effect of Labor, Export, and Government Expenditure on Economic Growth. *Journal of Economics and Business, 4*(3), 1. https://doi.org/10.31014/aior.1992.04.03.368

Jones, C. I. (1995). Time series tests of endogenous growth models. *Quarterly Journal of Economics, 110*(2), 495–525. https://doi.org/10.2307/2118448

Karadag, H. (2016). The Role of SMEs and Entrepreneurship on Economic Growth in Emerging Economies within the Post-Crisis Era: an Analysis from

Turkey. *Journal of Small Business and Entrepreneurship Development, 4*(1). https://doi.org/10.15640/jsbed.v4n1a3

Korkmaz, S., & Korkmaz, O. (2017). The Relationship between Labor Productivity and Economic Growth in OECD Countries. *International Journal of Economics and Finance, 9*(5), 71. https://doi.org/10.5539/ijef.v9n5p71

Laužikas, M., & Krasauskas, A. (2013). Impacts of sustainable structural growth on the economic performance of listed companies. *Entrepreneurship and Sustainability Issues, 1*(2), 81–91. https://doi.org/10.9770/jesi.2013.1.2(2)

Long Le, P. C., Kim, J. I., & Kim, K. (2016). The growth of Korean companies and their contributions to the miracle of the han river. *International Journal of Multimedia and Ubiquitous Engineering, 11*(5), 253. https://doi.org/10.14257/ijmue.2016.11.5.23

Mahmud, M. (2003). The relationship between economic growth and capital structure of listed companies: Evidence of Japan, Malaysia, and Pakistan. *Pakistan Development Review, 42*(4 II), 727–748. https://doi.org/10.30541/v42i4ii

Mankiw Gregory, N., Romer, D., & Weil, D. N. (1992). A contribution to the empirics of economic growth. *Quarterly Journal of Economics, 107*(2), 407–437. https://doi.org/10.2307/2118477

Marquez-Ramos, L., & Mourelle, E. (2019). Education and economic growth: an empirical analysis of nonlinearities. *Applied Economic Analysis, 27*(79), 21–45. https://doi.org/10.1108/AEA-06-2019-0005

Merkulova, E. Y. (2019). The effect of labor productivity on economic growth. *Statistics and Economics, 16*(2), 34–44. https://doi.org/10.21686/2500-3925-2019-2-34-44

Mishra, S., Degtereva, E. A., & Paneru, K. (2017). Role of Foreign Direct Investment by Multinational Companies in Economic Growth of Nepal. *Journal of Economics and Development Studies, 5*(1). https://doi.org/10.15640/jeds.v5n1a9

Mohammed, I., & Bunyaminu, A. (2021). Major obstacles facing business enterprises in an emerging economy: The case of Ghana using the World Bank Enterprise Survey. *Journal of Small Business and Enterprise Development, 28*(3), 475–487. https://doi.org/10.1108/JSBED-04-2020-0110

Mthimkhulu, A., & Aziakpono, M. (2016). What characterises high-growth firms in South Africa? Evidence from World Bank Enterprise Survey. *South African Journal of Business Management, 47*(4), 71–81. https://doi.org/10.4102/sajbm.v47i4.76

Nguyen, T., Chaiechi, T., Eagle, L., & Low, D. (2020). Dynamic impacts of SME stock market development and innovation on macroeconomic indicators: A Post-Keynesian approach. *Economic Analysis and Policy, 68*, 327–347. https://doi.org/10.1016/j.eap.2020.10.002

North, D. C. (1990). *Institutions, institutional change and economic performance.* Cambridge University Press.

North, D. C. (2005). *Understanding the process of economic change.* Princeton University Press.

Redlichová, R., Chmelíková, G., Blažková, I., & Tamáš, V. (2019). Role of companies' size in socio-economic development of regions in the Czech Republic. *Ekonomski Pregled, 70*(6), 833–848. https://doi.org/10.32910/ep.70.6.2

Roopchund, R. (2020). SMEs in Mauritius: Economic growth, employment and entrepreneurial culture. *International Journal of Entrepreneurship and Small Business, 39*(4), 585–596. https://doi.org/10.1504/IJESB.2020.106475

Rothwell, R. (1977). The characteristics of successful innovators and technically progressive firms (with some comments on innovation research). *R&D Management, 7*(3), 191–206. https://doi.org/10.1111/j.1467-9310.1977.tb01334.x

Sala-i-Martin, X., Doppelhofer, G., & Miller, R. I. (2004). Determinants of long-term growth: A Bayesian averaging of classical estimates (BACE) approach. *American Economic Review*. https://doi.org/10.1257/0002828042002570

Salam, Z. A., Zakaria, Z., Rizal, A. M., Mahadi, N., Jamil, R., Hussin, N., et al. (2018). Sales and Tax to Measure Economy? *Advanced Science Letters, 24*(12), 9376–9378. https://doi.org/10.1166/asl.2018.12278

Siegel, R., Siegel, E., & Macmillan, I. C. (1993). Characteristics distinguishing high-growth ventures. *Journal of Business Venturing, 8*(2), 169–180. https://doi.org/10.1016/0883-9026(93)90018-Z

Solomon, I. D., & Marshal, I. (2015). The Intermediation Functions of Finance Companies and Economic Growth: Issues, Theory and Empirical Evidence from Nigeria. *Journal of Finance and Accounting, Vol. 3, 2015, Pages 47-56, 3*(3), 47–56. Retrieved from http://pubs.sciepub.com/jfa/3/3/2/index.html

Solow, R. M. (1956). A contribution to the theory of economic growth. *Quarterly Journal of Economics, 70*(1), 65–94. https://doi.org/10.2307/1884513

Sothan, S. (2014). Causal Relationship between Domestic Saving and Economic Growth: Evidence from Cambodia. *International. Journal of Economics and Finance, 6*(9), 1. https://doi.org/10.5539/ijef.v6n9p213

Spolaore, E., & Wacziarg, R. (2013). How deep are the roots of economic development? *Journal of Economic Literature, 51*(2), 325–369. https://doi.org/10.1257/jel.51.2.325

Szarzec, K., Dombi, Á., & Matuszak, P. (2021). State-owned enterprises and economic growth: Evidence from the post-Lehman period. *Economic Modelling, 99*, 1. https://doi.org/10.1016/j.econmod.2021.03.009

Tambunan, T. (2008). SME development, economic growth, and government intervention in a developing country: The Indonesian story. *Journal of International Entrepreneurship, 6*(4), 147–167. https://doi.org/10.1007/s10843-008-0025-7

Thompson, M. (2018). Social capital, innovation and economic growth. *Journal of Behavioral and Experimental Economics, 73*, 46–52. https://doi.org/10.1016/j.socec.2018.01.005

Tsatsenko, N. (2020). SME development, economic growth and structural change: evidence from Ghana and South Africa. Journal of agriculture and environment, *2*(2 (14)), 2020. Retrieved from http://jae.cifra.science/index.php/jae/article/view/55

Verheyden, M., & Goeman, K. (2013). Does (company) size matter? Differences in social media usage for business purposes. *Journal of Applied Quantitative Methods, 8*(4), 3–16. Retrieved from http://search.ebscohost.com/login.aspx?direct=true&db=a9h&AN=94825329&site=ehost-live

Vincett, P. S. (2010). The economic impacts of academic spin-off companies, and their implications for public policy. *Research Policy, 39*(6), 736–747. https://doi.org/10.1016/j.respol.2010.02.001

Wennekers, S., & Thurik, R. (1999). Linking Entrepreneurship and Economic Growth. *Small Business Economics, 13*(1), 27–56. https://doi.org/10.1023/A:1008063200484

Williams, C. C., Martinez-Perez, A., & Kedir, A. M. (2017). Informal Entrepreneurship in Developing Economies: The Impacts of Starting Up Unregistered on Firm Performance. *Entrepreneurship: Theory and Practice, 41*(5), 773–799. https://doi.org/10.1111/etap.12238

11

Understating (Under)Development Through Inequality and Poverty: A Principal Component Analysis

Diego Gomez, Sebastian Aparicio, and David Urbano

11.1 Introduction

Study of the behavior of GDP as a measure of the growth of countries is broad, helping the development of theories and schools of thought (Coe & Helpman, 1995; Lucas, 1988). Even so, in recent decades, there has been a call not only to study growth in terms of the total value of products, goods, and services produced by a country but also to observe how these goods can help improve the quality of life of the agents that are part of the socioeconomic system. This is known as economic development,

D. Gomez
Fundación ECSIM, Medellin, Colombia

S. Aparicio (✉) • D. Urbano
Department of Business, Universitat Autònoma de Barcelona, Cerdanyola del Vallés, Barcelona, Spain

Centre for Entrepreneurship and Social Innovation Research (CREIS), Universitat Autònoma de Barcelona, Sabadell, Barcelona, Spain
e-mail: Sebastian.Aparicio@uab.cat

D. Gomez et al. (eds.), *Driving Complexity in Economic Development*,
https://doi.org/10.1007/978-3-031-34386-5_11

which is based on taking advantage of national production to generate something indispensable for the agents, that is, welfare (Costantini & Monni, 2008; Ravallion, 2001).

Although some countries have focused on promoting welfare, many others have only focused on the production of goods, in the pursuit of GDP growth rather than development. Thus, the accumulation of wealth and the uneven distribution of income under schemes of little economic freedom have created problems such as poverty, which affects people including those who are excluded from the socioeconomic system. Extensive literature analyzes and investigates poverty and income distribution (Apergis & Cooray, 2020; Dao, 2008). However, it focuses only on observing causal effects, often neglecting to make clear policy recommendations that would help identify mechanisms to be promoted.

Hence, this chapter has a twofold purpose: first, to carry out a Principal Component Analysis (PCA), a methodology that has been little used to discover the factors that explain poverty and income distribution (Gini index); second, to use this methodology to identify which factors have the most influence on these two variables and be able to make direct policy recommendations. To this end, the literature on poverty and income distribution helps us embrace a variety of elements, which are subsequently assessed through data reduction techniques such as factor analysis. World Development Indicators (WDIs) covering 15 years are used. Thanks to this information, 343 observations between 2004 and 2019 were collected for our purposes. However, given the reduction of indicators through Ordinary Least Square (OLS) estimation, we used data from 2007 as this is the year in which most of the indicators have information for a larger pool of countries.

The results show that institutional, economic, and social factors are key to determining poverty and income distribution. Thus, government entities must provide the necessary conditions for free exchange between agents through pro-institutional policies. However, these results show a key point when we focus on poverty: that it is not sufficient only to encourage favorable economic and social environments—institutions also play a fundamental role (Mehlum et al., 2006) in the creation of firms (entrepreneurship), which, in the literature, has been presented as the main engine of economic development through innovation (Aparicio et al., 2016; Audretsch & Keilbach, 2008).

11.2 Literature on Inequality and Poverty

Since Williamson's (1977, 1980) works on prices and wages, more attention has been paid to income inequality generated by the natural course of capitalism. Much research has focused on analyzing different types of inequalities (regional, gender, ethnic, etc.) and their relationship with economic development. Tirado et al. (2016) investigate the long-term evolution of regional income inequality in Spain, and using a novel dataset covering 150 years, the authors describe per capita GDP disparities across Spanish provinces (NUTS3) from 1860 to 2010, confirming the existence of an inverted U-shaped pattern. Two key pieces of research address the issue of gender inequality and economic development. On the one hand, Carlsen (2020) establishes that education plays a significant role in reducing gender inequality and improving economic development. On the other hand, Forgues-Puccio and Lauw (2021) investigate the effect of bureaucratic corruption on economic development when women are discriminated against (gender inequality) in the labor market. The authors find three interesting results: first, when the public sector is a more gender-equal employer than the private sector, female bureaucrats are less corrupt than males; second, corruption and development are jointly determined, allowing the possibility of a poverty trap; and third, a policy to increase female participation in the public sector potentially reduces corruption and fosters economic development. However, for our purposes, we focus on income inequality.

Regarding income inequality, Castells-Quintana et al. (2019) estimate the association between income inequality and the Human Development Index and its components in a panel of 117 countries from 1970 to 2010. The authors find two key pieces of evidence: first, a negative long-run association between inequality and human development; and second, different short-run associations between inequality and different dimensions of human development: a positive one with economic development but a negative one with educational outcomes, hinting at particular transmission channels. Malinen (2012) uses a new measure of income distribution and panel data cointegration methods to test for the existing relationship between income inequality and the economic development steady-state equilibrium relation. The author finds that there is a long-run equilibrium relationship between the variables and that this relationship is negative, especially in developed economies. Through extensive literature, the importance of income inequality in economic development has been evidenced, but undoubtedly, another important force that emerges as a result of the economic model used by the vast majority of countries is poverty.

The World Bank describes poverty as hunger and lack of shelter. It is therefore not only a question of money, although this also has an influence. The literature analyzing the concept of poverty is extensive, from its causes and effects to its interaction with other key variables for the socioeconomic system such as economic development. Whitfield (2012) reviewed new and old literature explaining why some countries are rich and others are poor, supporting the assertion that building up capabilities in manufacturing and improving the productivity of agriculture are the keys to wealth creation and sustained long-term poverty reduction. The author also emphasizes that the discussion about ending world poverty needs to be shifted back to consideration of economic transformation. In a more empirical analysis, Zhu et al. (2022) use various econometric estimations to measure the effect of inequality and poverty on economic development from 1990 to 2016 in Vietnam, finding a long-run association between inequality, poverty, and economic growth in the matter of the poverty headcount ratio. In research that is fundamental to this literature, Škare and Družeta (2016) review and synthesize relevant literature on growth versus poverty, analyzing the causal link between the two phenomena. The authors conclude that growth is good for poverty alleviation but is not enough. The extent to which growth reduces poverty depends upon how we measure poverty, the absorptive capacity of the poor, and the pace and pattern of growth.

Other high-quality research emphasizes the role of population, innovation, and sustainable economic development. Sinding (2009) examines recent trends in demographic change and economic development and argues that the countries representing the last development frontier, those of Sub-Saharan Africa, would be well advised to incorporate policies and programs to reduce high fertility rates in their economic development strategies, as this could reduce poverty. While Hall and Howell-Moroney (2012) explore the effects of poverty in two ways: first, they study the relationship between poverty and capacity for innovation in the US states; second, they study the combined effects of poverty and innovation capacity on economic output and employment across US states. The results reveal a negative indirect effect of socioeconomic need (poverty) on humans, US states and local financial innovation capacity. They also find non-statistically significant evidence of the contemporaneous effect of poverty on economic performance, holding innovation capacity constant. Thus, the authors support the claim that poverty primarily affects US states' economic performance indirectly through the reduction of innovation capacity.

Two other studies are relevant, as they go further and investigate what the main determinants or factors of poverty are and why it is a difficult problem to solve. First, Mansi et al. (2020) analyze the factors that impact poverty and compare these results between countries such as Albania, Bosnia and Herzegovina, Montenegro, North Macedonia, and Serbia (European Union and post-communist countries that include the Western Balkans [WB]). The authors show that income inequality does indeed impact the further progress of poverty for both the EU and WB countries. However, factors such as education, investment environment, unemployment, and economic development in terms of GDP are also shown to have a significant impact. Second, Mehanna (2004) reports that the relationships among various subsets of economic development, poverty, crime, and/or income inequality have been separately investigated in several theoretical and empirical studies. The author therefore examines the causality between economic development and poverty while incorporating crime and inequality, revealing a feedback loop mechanism between economic development, poverty, and crime. Interestingly, income inequality, measured as the Gini coefficient, has no important effects on any of the variables.

This brief review of the literature on inequality and poverty allows us to identify two gaps in the literature. First, many factors can determine the income distribution (Gini) and poverty, since they are indicators that establish socioeconomic conditions, so there is no discussion of specific factors based on which policy decisions can be made. Second, most of the research estimates causal effects, leaving the way open for other methodologies that allow us to detect other determinants of both variables. However, is it possible, through different methodologies such as PCA, to determine fundamental factors for poverty reduction and better income distribution? This question will be addressed in the next section.

11.3 Principal Component Analysis

PCA is a procedure (method) in its own right and is used to simplify the simultaneous interpretation of several related variables (Jackson, 1980). There is research that shows the appropriate use of this method in complex areas such as healthcare (Joliffe & Morgan, 1992). However, Fávero and Belfiore (2019) clarify the step-by-step process and the interpretation of the results obtained.

Fávero and Belfiore (2019) discuss the circumstances in which the principal component factor analysis technique can be used. The authors utilize several factor analysis concepts, calculations, and interpretations. For example, "the concept of factor (an evaluation of the factor analysis's overall adequacy through the KMO statistic); concepts of eigenvalues and eigenvectors in Pearson's correlation matrices; the calculation and interpretation of factor scores, and, from these, the definition of factors; the calculation and interpretation of factor loadings and commonalities; the construction of loading plots; concepts of factor rotation and preparation of the Varimax orthogonal rotation; construction of performance rankings from the joint behavior of variables" (Fávero & Belfiore, 2019, pp. 1). All these methodological concepts are key to our chapter.

Four investigations that make use of this methodology to observe socioeconomic factors can be highlighted. First, Zsarnóczai et al. (2021) use a PCA with varimax rotation and principal component scores to provide a case study in the field of ambitious agricultural and rural development programs of four neighboring EU member states, namely Czechia, Italy, Hungary, and Austria. The results show that the rural population was able to increase income (compensation payments, wages, and salaries) in the four member states during the period from 2010 to 2018. Second, Amiri et al. (2021) present a twofold objective: (a) to investigate how the socioeconomic characteristics of a specific area can influence the level of traffic safety in that area; (b) to evaluate and compare the capabilities of different modeling approaches in pursuit of the former goal. Thus, using a set of 365 cities in the state of California with their socioeconomic characteristics and the PCA, the authors find that the male population percentage has the most significant impact on the modeling process, followed by the unemployment rate and the education level, and conclude that evaluation of the correlation between socioeconomic factors and traffic collision occurrence can provide decision-makers with valuable insight into preventive policies in pursuing the goal of improving the overall level of traffic safety. Third, in recent research, Duarte and Riveros-Perez (2021) examine the cyclical properties of the incidence curves of coronavirus disease 19 (COVID-19) in various countries and use PCA to shed light on the underlying dynamics that are common to all countries. The authors find that the cyclical series of 37 countries can be summarized by four principal components which explain over 90% of the variation. Finally, Tsiouni et al. (2021) determine goat farm profitability by surveying goat farmers to find the revenues, variable costs, and fixed costs of their farms. Using the PCA method, they state that goat farms in Greece are not profitable, so farmers cannot survive without government subsidies. Even so, the number of studies that have analyzed the factors of income inequality and poverty through PCA is almost null. Therefore we develop this methodology to identify these factors.

11.3.1 Gini Index

We use the Gini index variable calculated by the World Bank to represent income distribution (inequality) at the country level. First, a linear regression is performed through Ordinary Least Square (OLS) estimation to identify the causal effects of some economic, social, institutional, and other indicators on the income distribution. Table 11.1 shows the results of this estimation.

Some interesting findings are the expected effects of variables such as gross domestic income, unemployment, ratio of waged and salaried workers, population growth, homicides, gross capital formation, government effectiveness, economic complexity index, and adolescent fertility rate, among others. Some effects have unusual behavior due to a lack of information, which leads to the creation of an unbalanced panel of data. However, these effects help us to understand which types of indicators are more significant for the reduction of the Gini index. With these results, we choose 21 indicators (the most significant ones) to perform a PCA,

Table 11.1 OLS estimation method for Gini index

Variables	Gini
Gross domestic income	-0.141***
	(0.0296)
GNI per capita	-0.0992
	(0.0910)
Labor force participation rate	-0.0337
	(0.0595)
Population total	3.043**
	(1.041)
Unemployment	0.305***
	(0.0334)
Government expenditure on education	0.123***
	(0.0346)
Wage and salaried workers	-2.824***
	(0.420)
Vulnerable employment	-2.947***
	(0.427)
Access to electricity	0.707***
	(0.159)
Inflation consumer price	-0.140
	(0.0715)
Control of corruption estimate	0.230*
	(0.0959)
Population growth	0.202***
	(0.0515)
Intentional homicides	0.0164
	(0.0242)
People using at least basic drinking water	-0.0719
	(0.159)
Individuals using the internet	-0.185**
	(0.0705)
Domestic general government health	-0.219**
	(0.0826)
Domestic credit to private sector by banks	-0.0739**
	(0.0270)
Total natural resources rents	-0.167*
	(0.0713)
Gross capital formation	-0.0721
	(0.0447)
Starting a business score	0.0644
	(0.0547)
Taxes on income, profits, and gain	0.111*

(*continued*)

Table 11.1 (continued)

Variables	Gini
	(0.0446)
Trade	-0.128**
	(0.0424)
Livestock production index	0.123**
	(0.0451)
Current health expenditure	-0.334***
	(0.0553)
Out-of-pocket expenditure	-0.221**
	(0.0723)
Export value index	-0.308*
	(0.122)
Import value index	0.243**
	(0.0784)
Government effectiveness estimate	0.0364
	(0.104)
Economic complexity index	-0.157*
	(0.0697)
Average total years of schooling	-0.0351
	(0.0726)
Adolescent fertility birth rate	0.946***
	(0.0989)
Constant	1.131***
	(0.308)
Observations	343
R-squared	0.855

Note: Standard errors in parentheses: * p<0.05; ** p<0.01; *** p<0.001

which helps us find factors (components) that we can group and interpret. It should be clarified that we choose 2017, given that it is the year with the highest number of observations for the selected indicators.

Through the following estimation of components, we can choose the number of factors that contain the highest percentage of information on the variables studied and their relationship with the income distribution (Gini). Table 11.2 and Fig. 11.1 make it clear that these five factors have the largest amount of information among the whole set of variables (eigenvalues above 1 in Table 11.1), and we use these factors to name specific aspects (of the information).

Using these five factors, we perform a rotation of the main matrix to assign variables to these factors and name them. Table 11.3 shows the

Table 11.2 Factor analysis (principal component factors)

Factor	Eigenvalue	Difference	Proportion	Cumulative
Factor1	8.21433	5.60468	0.3912	0.3912
Factor2	2.60966	0.36129	0.1243	0.5154
Factor3	2.24837	0.6998	0.1071	0.6225
Factor4	1.54857	0.53658	0.0737	0.6962
Factor5	1.01199	0.13402	0.0482	0.7444
Factor6	0.87798	0.07049	0.0418	0.7862
Factor7	0.80748	0.06157	0.0385	0.8247
Factor8	0.74592	0.15372	0.0355	0.8602
Factor9	0.59219	0.12759	0.0282	0.8884
Factor10	0.4646	0.09726	0.0221	0.9105
Factor11	0.36734	0.01407	0.0175	0.928
Factor12	0.35327	0.06349	0.0168	0.9448
Factor13	0.28978	0.06856	0.0138	0.9586
Factor14	0.22122	0.03789	0.0105	0.9692
Factor15	0.18333	0.0371	0.0087	0.9779
Factor16	0.14623	0.02137	0.007	0.9849
Factor17	0.12485	0.03745	0.0059	0.9908
Factor18	0.0874	0.02165	0.0042	0.995
Factor19	0.06575	0.02915	0.0031	0.9981
Factor20	0.0366	0.03345	0.0017	0.9999
Factor21	0.00315	.	0.0001	1.0000

Note: number of observations: 72; retained factors: 5; LR test: independent versus saturated: chi2(210) = 1432.18 prob>chi2 = 0.0000

results of the variables associated with each factor. This allows us to identify and organize the variables across these five factors. For example, for gross domestic income, the value closest to 1 is 0.93, which is part of factor 1, and therefore it belongs to this factor. Thus, we perform the analysis one variable at the time and reorganize the variables within the five resulting factors. However, three variables have been reorganized within the factors to give them an economic sense: population and population growth have been placed within factor 5 and taxes within factor 3. It should be noted that for these three variables, the values chosen from the rotation matrix are positive, which gives us some freedom when reorganizing them. Then, in Table 11.4 we organize all the variables within each of the factors and we proceed to name the factors depending on the characteristics of the grouped variables. This will facilitate the understanding of the factors obtained.

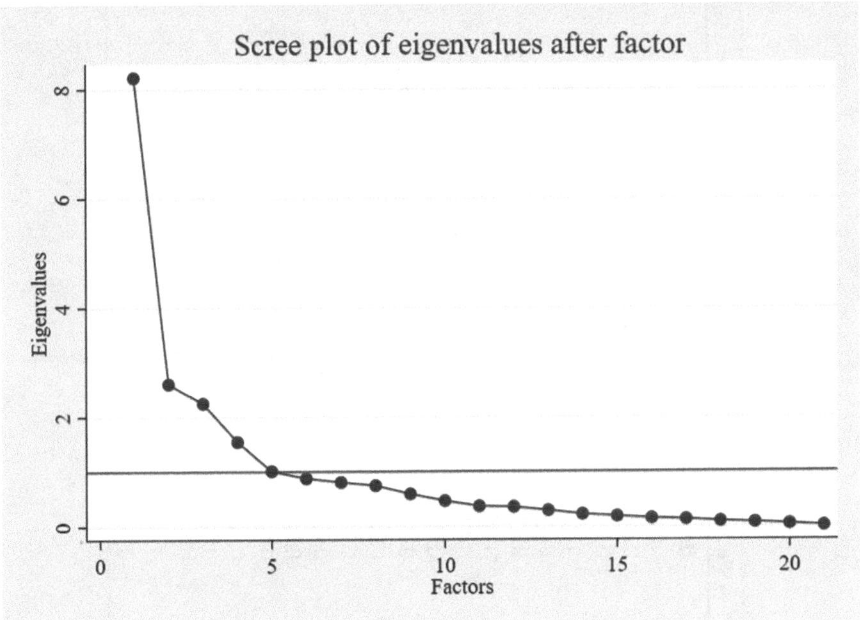

Fig. 11.1 Scree plot of eigenvalues (Gini)

We can identify factors associated with economic and institutional aspects (Factor 1), social aspects (Factor 2), private sector aspects (Factor 3), exchange aspects (Factor 4), and social and vulnerable aspects (Factor 5). This indicates that an effort on the part of the institutions related to economic, institutional, trade, and private sector aspects could considerably reduce the Gini index; that is, a better distribution of income would be obtained through good results for the indicators that make up these factors. Therefore, a good performance is expected through the control of corruption, greater effectiveness of governments, employment of a greater number of salaried workers under favorable conditions, an increase in credit through a reduction in interest rates, improvements in social indicators such as health, use of the Internet, and a greater effort to strengthen gross capital formation and exports. Therefore, the improvement in income distribution is not only an economic effort but also a governmental and institutional effort through the improvement of social, political, and economic indicators.

Table 11.3 Factor-variable rearrangement

Variable	Factor 1	Factor 2	Factor 3	Factor 4	Factor 5	Uniqueness
Gross domestic income	0.9368	0.1498	-0.0427	-0.0053	-0.0799	0.0918
Labor force participation	-0.0185	0.8511	-0.0614	0.0154	0.0712	0.2662
Population	-0.1022	-0.0904	0.8473	0.0877	0.3079	0.161
Unemployment	-0.0537	-0.7309	-0.2476	0.0281	0.1039	0.39
Waged and salaried workers	0.7888	-0.2729	-0.1734	-0.2226	-0.3175	0.1228
Vulnerable employment	-0.7909	0.2838	0.1954	0.2236	0.3045	0.113
Control of corruption estimate	0.9226	0.0979	-0.0722	-0.0029	0.1282	0.1176
Population growth	-0.3275	0.5653	-0.0885	0.1007	0.4909	0.3142
Intentional homicides	-0.3977	0.0296	-0.1105	-0.6819	0.064	0.3597
Individuals using the internet	0.8146	-0.19	-0.1807	0	-0.1434	0.2471
Domestic credit to private sector	0.7089	-0.0975	0.1261	0.0539	0.3804	0.3245
Gross capital formation	0.0366	0.197	0.7321	0.225	-0.1223	0.3583
Taxes on income, profits, and gain	0.2328	0.1331	0.1507	-0.3026	0.6339	0.4119
Trade	0.4746	0.1165	0.0325	0.1008	-0.6152	0.3715
Current health expenditure	0.5668	-0.3802	-0.3971	-0.1605	0.354	0.2254
Out-of-pocket expenditure	-0.6055	-0.0864	0.1127	0.2931	-0.0367	0.526
Export value index	-0.3809	0.0197	0.1395	0.7348	-0.0983	0.2854
Import value index	-0.4027	0.1021	0.3929	0.6333	-0.2	0.232
Government	0.9404	0.0967	0.012	-0.0382	0.0841	0.0975
Government effectiveness	0.751	-0.1498	0.2571	-0.3123	-0.1482	0.228
Adolescent fertility rate birth	-0.7609	0.4017	-0.2576	-0.1686	0.204	0.1232

Table 11.4 Organization and naming of factors

	Factor 1	Factor 2	Factor 3	Factor 4	Factor 5
Variables	Economic and institutional aspects	Social aspects	Private sector and input aspects	Trade aspects	Social aspects
1	Gross domestic income	Labor force participation	Taxes on income, profits, and gain	Export value index	Unemployment
2	Waged and salaried workers	Adolescent fertility rate birth	Gross capital formation	Import value index	Vulnerable employment
3	Control of corruption estimate				Intentional homicides
4	Individuals using the internet				Population
5	Domestic credit to private sector				Population growth
6	Trade				
7	Current health expenditure				
8	Government effectiveness				
9	ECI				

But, is it really necessary to develop this whole process to identify the factors influencing income distribution? The Kaiser-Meyer-Olkin (KMO) measure is a statistic that allows us to indicate the proportion of variance in our variables (indicators) that can be explained by underlying factors. A value close to 1 (above 0.5) indicates that factor analysis is generally necessary for a dataset. Thus, Table 11.5 confirms the need for this study, as the overall KMO is around 0.78, confirming the need to carry out this PCA and the importance of the grouped factors, especially the economic, institutional, and social factors.

Table 11.5 Kaiser-Meyer-Olkin measure

Variable	KMO
Gross domestic income	0.9166
Labor force participation	0.5158
Population	0.394
Unemployment	0.5056
Wage and salaried workers	0.796
Vulnerable employment	0.8019
Control of corruption estimate	0.8308
Population growth	0.7995
Intentional homicides	0.6553
Individuals using the internet	0.8913
Domestic credit to private sector	0.8891
Gross capital formation	0.5767
Taxes on income, profits, and gain	0.8237
Trade	0.6713
Current health expenditure	0.8228
Out-of-pocket expenditure	0.7806
Export value index	0.7061
Import value index	0.6494
Government	0.8465
Government effectiveness	0.7694
Adolescent fertility rate birth	0.8597
Overall	0.7839

11.3.2 Poverty

Using an analysis identical to that of the Gini index, we survey indices related to the incidence of poverty, that is, the percentage of the population that is poor. This is developed using the multidimensional poverty index calculated by the World Bank.

In this case, four factors are selected to group the set of variables (see Fig. 11.2), since they contain about 72% of the fundamental information of the selected variables (see Table 11.6).

In order to assign the variables to the determining factors, it can be seen in Table 11.7 that once the rotation of the orthogonal matrix has been performed, the great majority of the variables are assigned to Factors 1 and 3 since their loading factors are closest to 1 (Table 11.8).

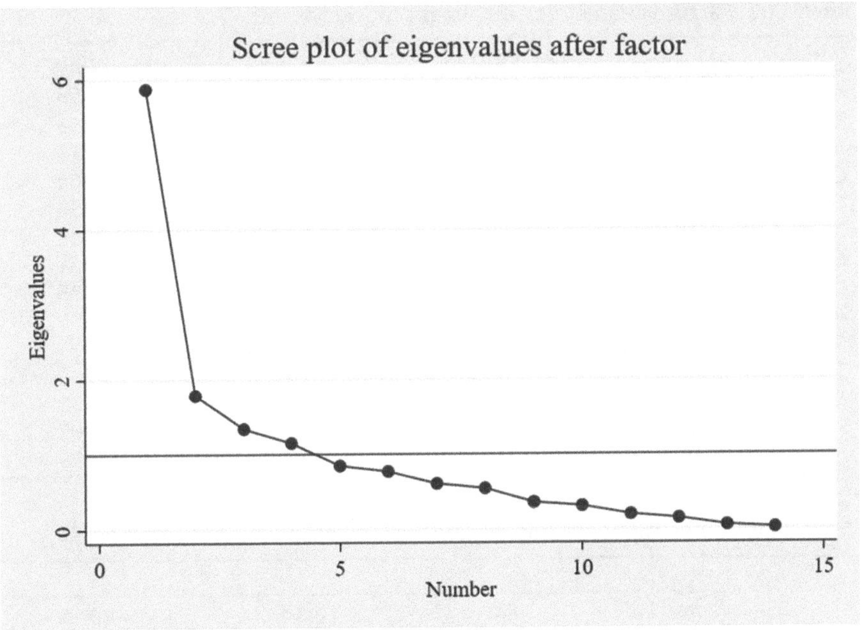

Fig. 11.2 Scree plot of eigenvalues (poverty)

Table 11.6 Factor analysis: poverty (principal component factors)

Factor	Eigenvalue	Difference	Proportion	Cumulative
Factor1	5.87619	4.08864	0.4197	0.4197
Factor2	1.78755	0.44669	0.1277	0.5474
Factor3	1.34086	0.1903	0.0958	0.6432
Factor4	1.15056	0.30419	0.0822	0.7254
Factor5	0.84638	0.07714	0.0605	0.7858
Factor6	0.76924	0.16298	0.0549	0.8408
Factor7	0.60627	0.06198	0.0433	0.8841
Factor8	0.54428	0.18734	0.0389	0.923
Factor9	0.35695	0.04848	0.0255	0.9484
Factor10	0.30846	0.11132	0.022	0.9705
Factor11	0.19714	0.05265	0.0141	0.9846
Factor12	0.14449	0.09308	0.0103	0.9949
Factor13	0.05141	0.0312	0.0037	0.9986
Factor14	0.02021	.	0.0014	1.0000

Table 11.7 Factor-variable rearrangement (poverty)

Variable	Factor1	Factor2	Factor3	Factor4	Uniqueness
Political stability and absence	0.7568	0.2014	-0.2452	-0.2999	0.2366
Rule of law estimate	0.9436	0.1676	-0.051	-0.1322	0.0615
Voice and accountability	0.8257	0.1178	0.0809	-0.2657	0.2273
Control of corruption	0.9069	0.1814	-0.1204	-0.1397	0.1106
Government effectiveness	0.9575	0.1042	-0.0536	-0.0631	0.0655
GDP constant 2010	0.3303	0.2364	0.6308	0.2494	0.3749
Labor force participation	-0.3088	0.7966	-0.2765	-0.0398	0.192
Unemployment	0.0255	-0.6401	0.2347	-0.2933	0.4485
Access to electricity	0.6582	-0.4853	0.0038	0.3103	0.235
Gross capital formation	-0.0447	0.14	-0.4404	0.6184	0.402
Starting a business score	0.677	-0.087	-0.2218	0.1199	0.4705
Taxes on income	0.2346	0.4262	0.6374	0.0398	0.3555
Subsidies and other transfers	0.4226	0.1282	0.2465	0.4978	0.4965
Adolescent fertility rate birth	-0.8123	0.3168	0.1206	-0.2382	0.1685

Table 11.8 Organization and naming of factors (poverty)

	Factors			
	Factor 1	Factor 2	Factor 3	Factor 4
Variables	Institutional and necessity aspects	Social aspects	Economic aspects	Labor and social private aspects
1	Political stability and absence of violence	Labor force participation	GDP constant 2010	Gross capital formation
2	Rule of law estimate	Adolescent fertility rate birth	Taxes on income	
3	Voice and accountability		Unemployment	
4	Control of corruption estimate			
5	Government effectiveness estimation			
6	Starting a business score			
7	Access to electricity			
8	Subsidies and other transfers			

Once again, the importance of the institutional, economic, and social aspects should be emphasized, with the institutional aspect having the greatest importance among the four factors found. In this case, policymakers should consider presenting good results for indicators such as political stability and absence of violence, rule of law, voice and accountability, control of corruption, and government effectiveness. However, there is an additional variable regarding which policymakers must make a huge effort, and that is the improvement of the business startup score. For this, policies must be aimed at decreasing the number of procedures, time, cost, and paid-in minimum capital requirement for a small to medium-size limited liability company to start up and formally operate in each economy's largest business city, thus proving the fundamental role that entrepreneurship plays in the development dynamics of societies. Finally, Table 11.9 serves again as a methodological validation, as an overall KMO score of around 0.81 demonstrates the need to obtain factors in this set of variables stack.

Table 11.9 KMO (poverty)

Variable	KMO
Political stability and absence	0.894
Rule of law estimate	0.8113
Voice and accountability	0.8777
Control of corruption	0.9012
Government effectiveness	0.8103
GDP constant 2010	0.8074
Labor force participation	0.5032
Unemployment	0.4719
Access to electricity	0.7516
Gross capital formation	0.1757
Starting a business score	0.9629
Taxes on income	0.6305
Subsidies and other transfers	0.6962
Adolescent fertility rate birth	0.8764
Overall	**0.8118**

11.4 Conclusions

The economic growth literature has evolved to encompass issues more related to sustainable economic development, as researchers have seen the need to promote such development through social, institutional, environmental, and other aspects (Aparicio et al., 2020; Espinosa et al., 2021; Jakšić & Jakšić, 2018). Two of the key variables in the literature that are used to measure the level of development of a society through a broader concept are poverty and income distribution (Allen & Thomas, 2000; Dutt & Tsetlin, 2021; Sobczak et al., 2021). Thus, the accumulation of capital by a small part of the population and how this generates great inequalities that drive a vicious circle of poverty began to concern thinkers from the end of the twentieth century.

In this chapter, through a review of the literature on how income distribution and poverty distribution are identified and analyzed, we find two fundamental gaps: first, the lack of use of alternative methodologies that shed light on the understanding of these concepts; second, a lack of clear policy recommendations based on concrete and consolidated factors that directly affect both poverty and income distribution. In this analysis, we try to fill both gaps, in order to open a path on mechanisms to incentivize development.

Using the PCA methodology, we find that for both poverty and income distribution, it is important to promote institutional and economic aspects without neglecting the concern about social vulnerability. Better government performance, protection of property rights, and providing a healthy environment for the free market through a perception of a low level of corruption are necessary to dissipate high rates of population poverty and a high Gini coefficient. However, it is worth highlighting an interesting result when we analyze the specific case of poverty, which is that facilitating the creation of businesses seems to be crucial in the institutional factor that explains a large part of the population living in poverty. But, why can this happen? What is the mechanism? Recent literature has been clear on the fundamental role of entrepreneurship in the economic growth of nations (Bosma et al., 2018; Wennekers & Thurik, 1999) but also on how it can promote sustainable development in which economic agents that had not been taken into account in the generation of value are included. It is entrepreneurship or firms that generate value and innovate, so incentive for the creation of firms generates not only employment but also a better welfare state for the entire population, offering more and better products. This makes it possible to provide clear policy recommendations on where to direct efforts, that is, improving the institutional framework to encourage business creation.

References

Allen, T., & Thomas, A. (2000). Poverty and development into the 21st century. Oxford: Oxford University Press.

Amiri, A. M., Naderi, K., Cooper, J. F., & Nadimi, N. (2021). Evaluating the impact of socio-economic contributing factors of cities in California on their traffic safety condition. *Journal of Transport and Health, 20*. https://doi.org/10.1016/j.jth.2021.101010

Aparicio, S., Urbano, D., & Audretsch, D. (2016). Institutional factors, opportunity entrepreneurship and economic growth: Panel data evidence. *Technological Forecasting and Social Change, 102*, 45–61.

Aparicio, S. Turro, A., & Noguera, M. (2020). Entrepreneurship and intrapreneurship in social, sustainable, and economic development: Opportunities and challenges for future research. *Sustainability* (Switzerland). MDPI. https://doi.org/10.3390/su12218958

Apergis, N., & Cooray, A. (2020). How do human rights violations affect poverty and income distribution? *International Economics, 161*, 56–65. https://doi.org/10.1016/j.inteco.2019.11.003

Audretsch, D. B., & Keilbach, M. (2008). Resolving the knowledge paradox: Knowledge-spillover entrepreneurship and economic growth. *Research Policy, 37*(10), 1697–1705.

Bosma, N., Content, J., Sanders, M., & Stam, E. (2018). Institutions, entrepreneurship, and economic growth in Europe. *Small Business Economics, 51*(2), 483–499. https://doi.org/10.1007/s11187-018-0012-x

Carlsen, L. (2020). Gender inequality and development. *Sustainability Science, 15*(3), 759–780. https://doi.org/10.1007/s11625-019-00767-9

Castells-Quintana, D., Royuela, V., & Thiel, F. (2019). Inequality and sustainable development: Insights from an analysis of the human development index. *Sustainable Development, 27*(3), 448–460. https://doi.org/10.1002/sd.1917

Coe, D. T., & Helpman, E. (1995). International R&D spillovers. *European Economic Review, 39*(5), 859–887. https://doi.org/10.1016/0014-2921(94)00100-E

Costantini, V., & Monni, S. (2008). Environment, human development and economic growth. *Ecological Economics, 64*(4), 867–880. https://doi.org/10.1016/j.ecolecon.2007.05.011

Dao, M. Q. (2008). Human capital, poverty, and income distribution in developing countries. *Journal of Economic Studies*. https://doi.org/10.1108/01443580810895590

Duarte, P., & Riveros-Perez, E. (2021). Understanding the cycles of COVID-19 incidence: Principal Component Analysis and interaction of biological and socio-economic factors. *Annals of Medicine and Surgery, 66*. https://doi.org/10.1016/j.amsu.2021.102437

Dutt, P., & Tsetlin, I. (2021). Income distribution and economic development: Insights from machine learning. *Economics and Politics, 33*(1), 1–36. https://doi.org/10.1111/ecpo.12157

Espinosa, V. I. Neira, M. A. A., & de Soto, J. H. (2021). Principles of sustainable economic growth and development: A call to action in a post-covid-19 world. *Sustainability* (Switzerland). MDPI. https://doi.org/10.3390/su132313126

Fávero, L. P., & Belfiore, P. (2019). Principal component factor analysis. In *Data science for business and decision making* (pp. 383–438). Elsevier. https://doi.org/10.1016/b978-0-12-811216-8.00012-4

Forgues-Puccio, G. F., & Lauw, E. (2021). Gender inequality, corruption, and economic development. *Review of Development Economics, 25*(4), 2133–2156. https://doi.org/10.1111/rode.12793

Hall, J. L., & Howell-Moroney, M. E. (2012). Poverty, innovation capacity, and state economic development in the knowledge economy: Evidence from the U.S. *Growth and Change, 43*(2), 228–251. https://doi.org/10.1111/j.1468-2257.2012.00584.x

Jackson, J. E. (1980). Principal components and factor analysis: Part I—Principal components. *Journal of Quality Technology, 12*(4), 201–213. https://doi.org/10.1080/00224065.1980.11980967

Jakšić, M., & Jakšić, M. (2018). Inclusive institutions for sustainable economic development. *Journal of Central Banking Theory and Practice, 7*(1), 5–16. https://doi.org/10.2478/jcbtp-2018-0001

Joliffe, I. T., & Morgan, B. (1992). Principal component analysis and exploratory factor analysis. *Statistical Methods in Medical Research, 1*(1), 69–95. https://doi.org/10.1177/096228029200100105

Lucas, R. E. (1988). On the mechanics of economic development. *Journal of Monetary Economics, 22*(1), 3–42. https://doi.org/10.1016/0304-3932(88)90168-7

Malinen, T. (2012). Estimating the long-run relationship between income inequality and economic development. *Empirical Economics, 42*(1), 209–233. https://doi.org/10.1007/s00181-010-0432-1

Mansi, E., Hysa, E., Panait, M., & Voica, M. C. (2020). Poverty—A challenge for economic development? Evidences from Western Balkan countries and the European union. *Sustainability (Switzerland), 12*(18). https://doi.org/10.3390/SU12187754

Mehanna, R. A. (2004). Poverty and economic development: Not as direct as it may seem. *Journal of Socio-Economics, 33*(2), 217–228. https://doi.org/10.1016/j.socec.2003.12.013

Mehlum, H., Moene, K., & Torvik, R. (2006). Institutions and the resource curse. *Economic Journal, 116*(508), 1–20. https://doi.org/10.1111/j.1468-0297.2006.01045.x

Ravallion, M. (2001). Growth, inequality and poverty: Looking beyond averages. *World Development, 29*(11), 1803–1815. https://doi.org/10.1016/S0305-750X(01)00072-9

Sinding, S. W. (2009). Population, poverty and economic development. *Philosophical Transactions of the Royal Society B: Biological Sciences*. Royal Society. https://doi.org/10.1098/rstb.2009.0145

Škare, M., & Družeta, R. P. (2016). Poverty and economic growth: A review. *Technological and Economic Development of Economy, 22*(1), 156–175. https://doi.org/10.3846/20294913.2015.1125965

Sobczak, E., Bartniczak, B., & Raszkowski, A. (2021). Implementation of the no poverty sustainable development goal (SDG) in Visegrad group (v4). *Sustainability (Switzerland), 13*(3), 1–21. https://doi.org/10.3390/su13031030

Tirado, D. A., Díez-Minguela, A., & Martinez-Galarraga, J. (2016). Regional inequality and economic development in Spain, 1860–2010. *Journal of Historical Geography, 54*, 87–98. https://doi.org/10.1016/j.jhg.2016.09.005

Tsiouni, M., Aggelopoulos, S., Pavloudi, A., & Siggia, D. (2021). Economic and financial sustainability dependency on subsidies: The case of goat farms in Greece. *Sustainability (Switzerland), 13*(13). https://doi.org/10.3390/su13137441

Wennekers, S., & Thurik, R. (1999). Linking entrepreneurship and economic growth. *Small Business Economics, 13*(1), 27–56. https://doi.org/10.1023/A:1008063200484

Whitfield, L. (2012). How countries become rich and reduce poverty: A review of heterodox explanations of economic development. *Development Policy Review, 30*(3), 239–260. https://doi.org/10.1111/j.1467-7679.2012.00575.x

Williamson, J. G. (1977). "Strategic" wage goods, prices, and inequality. *The American Economic Review, 67*(2), 29–41.

Williamson, J. G. (1980). Earnings inequality in nineteenth-century Britain. *The Journal of Economic History, 40*(3), 457–475. https://doi.org/10.1017/S0022050700085181

Zhu, Y., Bashir, S., & Marie, M. (2022). Assessing the relationship between poverty and economic growth: Does Sustainable development goal can be achieved? *Environmental Science and Pollution Research, 29*(19), 27613–27623. https://doi.org/10.1007/s11356-021-18240-5

Zsarnóczai, S., Popp, J., Belás, J., & Kovács, S. (2021). Developments in the income situation of the agricultural sector in the selected EU member states. *Economics and Sociology, 14*(1), 232–248. https://doi.org/10.14254/2071-789X.2021/14-1/15

12

A Sociotechnical Approach to Economic Development: The Role of Entrepreneurship and Innovation

Diego Gomez, Sebastian Aparicio, David Urbano, and Diego Martinez-Moya

12.1 Introduction

The literature on economic development has focused on studying its determinants through endogenous models (Aghion, 2002; Kosempel, 2004; Madsen & Murtin, 2017), due to the better understanding of its mathematical development. Two of the key determinants to spur economic development have been entrepreneurship and innovation (Audretsch, 2004; Bouchouicha & Vieider, 2019; Cinnirella & Streb, 2017; Kogan et al.,

D. Gomez • D. Martinez-Moya
Fundación ECSIM, Medellin, Colombia

S. Aparicio (✉) • D. Urbano
Department of Business, Universitat Autònoma de Barcelona, Cerdanyola del Vallés, Barcelona, Spain

Centre for Entrepreneurship and Social Innovation Research (CREIS), Universitat Autònoma de Barcelona, Sabadell, Barcelona, Spain
e-mail: Sebastian.Aparicio@uab.cat

D. Gomez et al. (eds.), *Driving Complexity in Economic Development*,
https://doi.org/10.1007/978-3-031-34386-5_12

2017; Segerstrom, 2000). However, studying economic development from an endogenous approach has led to stagnation in the understanding of this phenomenon from a social perspective (Fine, 2000; Kerekes, 2012). Furthermore, some of the results are ambiguous concerning the empirical facts (Minniti & Venturini, 2017). Given the criticisms of the endogenous growth model, research has been carried out inviting us to rethink economic development (Shaffer et al., 2006). Hausmann et al. (2007) and Milenkovic et al. (2014) state that there is a change in economic complexity that must be addressed with innovative methodologies (Cissé & Barrett, 2018) such as an asset-based approach (Carter & Barrett, 2006), a sociotechnical subsystems approach (Bertalanffy, 1968; Johnson & Wiener, 1949), and a relational approach (Mosse, 2010), among others.

Despite the sociotechnical approach suggested 50 years ago, it may be helpful to advance the stagnated tradition of understanding economic development from different dimensions (Savaget et al., 2019). Derived from systems theory to face the limitations of the classic analysis technique of analytic reduction, a sociotechnical subsystem is a combination of humans, machines, environments, work activities, organizational structures, and processes that comprise a given enterprise, and embraces complex systems in which many humans collaborate toward a common goal (Carayon et al., 2015). This approach has been used in different areas of knowledge (Bertalanffy, 1968; Carayon et al., 2015; Johnson & Wiener, 1949), more so in the organizational field, as it is an approach that allows an interdisciplinary combination to achieve objectives (Walker et al., 2008). However, some analyses have gone further and found that through this approach it is possible to understand the complexity of urban systems (Frank et al., 2015; Patorniti et al., 2018), while others try to consolidate a measurement that allows the boosting of regional economies (Kleiner & Drury, 1999). Here we find two gaps in the literature. First, the use of the sociotechnical approach to study, understand, and estimate economic development is almost nonexistent. Second, it shows us that although entrepreneurship and innovation are key drivers to spur economic development (Acs et al., 2008; Audretsch et al., 2015), these have not been analyzed from this approach yet.

Thus, this chapter explores entrepreneurship and innovation as key drivers to boost economic development in a sociotechnical subsystems approach. To achieve this, we use a structural equation model (SEM)

(Bagozzi & Yi, 2012; Evermann & Tate, 2016; Merkle & Rosseel, 2018) to estimate and understand economic development through three fundamental factors that the literature has highlighted, namely per capita GDP (Acemoglu & Johnson, 2007; Guerrero et al., 2015), the Human Development Index (HDI) (Roy & Mohanty, 2020; Viddy & Asniwati, 2019), and the GINI coefficient (Hartmann et al., 2017). In turn, these factors present linear causal relationships with a network of sociotechnical subsystems, necessary to more accurately estimate the complexity required for economic development. These subsystems, including social, environmental, generation (economic), governmental, and institutional, are socioeconomic indicators that express in an interdependent manner their importance for social well-being. We create unbalanced panel data with 1640 observations for 164 countries from 2004 to 2014, using the World Development Index (WDI), Doing Business (from the World Bank), the World Change data lab project (project supported by Oxford University), and the Human Development Reports as sources of information. This research unveils three fundamental results. First, that economic development can be estimated and analyzed from the sociotechnical subsystems approach using subsystems such as social, generation (economic), governmental, institutional, and environmental—generating a systemic balance where an integral evolution is created (Del Monte et al., 2020; Kast & Rosenzweig, 1981; Savaget et al., 2019). The second result indicates that economic development through a sociotechnical subsystems approach depends on three fundamental factors: GDP per capita, the HDI, and GINI The last and most important result indicates that the generation (economic) subsystem, such as the new business density index (NBD), has a positive and significant effect on GDP and the HDI and a negative and significant effect on GINI.

These results invite policymakers to support the creation of new ventures to lead an increase in the NBD, given that it has positive effects on the three fundamental factors of economic development, that is, GDP per capita (Fritsch, 2013; Meyer & Meyer, 2019), the HDI (Grant et al., 2019), and GINI (Boudreaux, 2014), and it helps to support previous literature. Challenges for policymakers are high because they not only have to focus on boosting the economic system but they also need to spur the indicators representing social, environmental, institutional, and governmental subsystems. Thus, this research not only fills literature gaps but may also open a path to study economic development using methodologies that represent greater difficulty at a theoretical, econometric, and practical level, empirically showing a better understanding of economic development based on indicators or systems that make up society, and analyzes the economy as a broad social concept (Bali Swain & Yang-Wallentin, 2020; Cristea et al., 2020).

This research is structured as follows. Section 2 presents the conceptual framework, where we establish the sociotechnical subsystems approach as the main axis of the research, which supports the analysis around the effects of the entrepreneurship and innovation subsystem and others through three key factors of economic development, namely GDP, the HDI, and GINI. Section 3 explains the methodology, including the source of the data and the empirical strategy. Results are presented in Section 4. Finally, in Section 5, we conclude and generate a discussion on policy and theoretical implications and future research lines.

12.2 Conceptual Framework

According to Helpman (2004), economists have been concerned with the growth of nations for centuries. The starting point came after Smith (1776), who proposed the hypothesis of the circular causation of income, which establishes that technological change and product diversification increase productivity and income, and therefore boost economic growth.

From this point on, a debate about the causes of the nation's wealth was opened. Leading economists have addressed this issue, each from different perspectives. Some argue that wealth is derived from optimal institutional structures (Modigliani, 1986; Rosenberg, 1960), while others support the idea that the economy should be divided into isolated local markets with limited specializations (Kelly, 1997), and some modern holdings associate wealth with social sustainability (Arrow et al., 2012; Diener & Diener, 1995). Yet, all these thoughts converge to the idea that specialization and technological progress are indispensable to achieving the wealth of nations, which is strongly related to economic growth.

In the last 60 years, there have been three phases of discussion on economic growth (Crafts, 1995; Klenow & Rodríguez-Clare, 1997; Kocherlakota & Yi, 1996). The first phase began with Solow's (1956) research, in which it is proposed that the accumulation of capital (exogenous growth) explains higher economic output. The second one came later when the concept of capital was broadened by introducing the accumulation of human capital. Mankiw et al. (1990) suggest a re-evaluation of the neoclassical growth model after the initial contributions of Lucas (1988) and Romer (1986, 1992), which began the second phase of the discussion, endogenous growth. From this arises a great current, assimilationism, which consists of the systematic adaptation of workers' skills leading to economic growth (Murton, 2015). And the third phase began in the second half of the 1990s when Bell and Pavitt (1993) consolidated the relationship between innovation, technological change, and development, which led not only to theoretical but also empirical advances such as that of Nelson and Pack (1999).

Solow (1956) established in his research the fundamental role of technological change on economic growth. However, technical progress was considered to be one of the fundamental variables in determining growth—neither its origin nor its dependence on decisions and the interaction between different agents was specified, that is, it was determined exogenously. Following this pioneering research, Lucas (1988) described models of capital accumulation and technological change, human capital through schooling, and specialized human capital through the learning-by-doing method. These models attempt to explain growth through agent learning and decision-making, which was called "endogenous growth" since the explanation of technological change was not due to external but internal forces. Although the differences between the approaches that seek to explain economic growth lie in identifying whether technological change occurs exogenously or endogenously, they agree that technological change is the way to achieve such growth.

Although technological change is identified as a key mechanism of growth, the dilemma about the determinants of economic growth is still present (Bernanke & Gürkaynak, 2001; Hausmann et al., 2005; Rodrik, 1999). Nonetheless, there seems to be a tendency toward endogenous growth models in the twenty-first century, because their mathematical procedure is more understandable than in the exogenous growth models (Bhaduri, 2006; Laincz & Peretto, 2006). In these endogenous growth models, there is a variety of determinants of growth, of which perhaps the most important are entrepreneurship (Bouchouicha & Vieider, 2019), innovation (Cinnirella & Streb, 2017; Kogan et al., 2017; Segerstrom, 2000), education (Madsen & Murtin, 2017), technological progress and human capital accumulation (Aghion, 2002; Kosempel, 2004), and institutions (Acemoglu, 2008; Acemoglu & Johnson, 2005), among others. However, Minniti and Lévesque (2010) reveal that some research focused on explaining economic growth through increased research and development (R&D) due to its ability to generate technological change has failed once the opposite behavior in countries such as China and Japan has been demonstrated. The statements of Minniti and Lévesque (2010) and Minniti and Venturini (2017) lead us to establish that although endogenous growth models have good results and are mathematically understandable, economic development is a complex process that may need other methodologies to be addressed, such as the asset-based approach (Carter & Barrett, 2006) or relational approach (Mosse, 2010), among others. Yet, complexity is not grasped within the core of these perspectives (Barrett & Carter, 2013) as it is in the sociotechnical subsystems approach (Bertalanffy, 1968; Johnson & Wiener, 1949; Kast & Rosenzweig, 1981; Savaget et al., 2019), incorporating innovation and entrepreneurship (Del Monte et al., 2020).

Drawing on Hammer and Pivo (2017), one might suggest that embracing complexity contributes to the third phase of the economic growth discussion, because the main difference with the second phase lies in the way society assimilates skills and learning (capital and human accumulation) and transforms it into innovation that serves to drive industries (through new products or processes) and spur development (Bell & Pavitt, 1993). Nelson and Pack (1999) present a clear example in their analysis by demonstrating that new production processes generated through the assimilation of learning (mainly the industrial sector) were present in the development process of countries such as Japan, Singapore, Korea, and Ireland.

12.2.1 Sociotechnical Subsystems

The rapid growth of Southeast Asian countries and Ireland shows that economic development depends on plenty of factors (which are interrelated at the same time), so a linear perspective might fall short. Instead, we need to understand economic development as a system composed of clear but complex structures. Thus, a sociotechnical subsystem is a combination of humans, machines, environments, work activities, organizational structures, and processes that comprise a given enterprise; it embraces complex systems, in which many humans collaborate toward a common goal (Carayon et al., 2015). Systems theory as a general framework to comprehend subsystems was formulated in the 1930s and 1940s to face the limitations of the classic analysis technique of analytic reduction or the process of dividing a system into separate elements for analysis purposes (Carayon et al., 2015). Johnson and Wiener (1949) applied this approach to control and communications engineering, while Bertalanffy (1968) developed similar ideas for biological systems. This approach was later used in different research areas to face situations involving different complex systems, for example, the sociotechnical system (STS) theory built at the Tavistock Institute of Human Relations in London (Mumford, 2006).

The Tavistock Institute tried to find the reasons why technological change that had been introduced in English coal mines had brought unexpected consequences—namely, after a strong mechanization process, productivity decreased (cf. Carayon et al., 2015; Mumford, 2006). The Institute's researchers found that the mechanization process had radically transformed the traditional structure of human groups of miners who carried out all the coal extraction tasks, being replaced by specialists who worked independently (Pasmore et al., 2019). The disruption of the social fabric changed the sociotechnical structures, and the resulting system was less efficient (Emery & Trist, 1965).

With the introduction of sociotechnical structures, ergonomics was born to improve organizational performance by blending systems within organizations (Walker et al., 2008). Thus, Carayon et al. (2015) and Walker et al. (2008) show that understanding the environmental, organizational, and work system factors that contribute to workplace safety helps develop more effective and integrated solutions to deal with persistent workplace safety problems. Some analyses have gone further (Arranz & Fernandez de Arroyabe, 2008; Frank et al., 2015) and have found that through this approach it is possible to understand the complexity of urban systems (Patorniti et al., 2018), while others try to strengthen the concept of ergonomics to consolidate a measurement that enables the increase of regional economic development (Kleiner & Drury, 1999).

Although the use of the sociotechnical subsystems approach as a theoretical basis for conducting economic research is not regularly explored, especially in research related to economic development (Savaget et al., 2019), a couple of works can be mentioned. On the one hand, Fagerberg and Srholec (2008) use the sociotechnical subsystems approach to identify the role of capabilities in economic development; on the other hand, Del Monte et al. (2020) utilize the concept of sociotechnical subsystems using entrepreneurship, innovation, and economic growth as subsystems to explain economic development. It is here that our research seeks to use the concept of sociotechnical subsystems as a theoretical basis to build an econometric apparatus that allows us to understand economic development more broadly.

12.2.2 Hypothesis Development

Due to the limited use of the sociotechnical subsystems approach in the study of economic development, this section will strengthen the foundations of this approach and then lay the preliminaries for the development of the hypotheses. Thus, the theoretical development of the hypotheses is divided into two blocks. The first block allows implementation of the idea that the economic development of a country is a sociotechnical systemic arrangement in which multiple subsystems associated with indicators of society are interdependent and express the level of development through the accumulation, assimilation, and adaptation of processes acquired through knowledge, skills, and learning. In the second block, hypotheses are established proposing that innovation and entrepreneurship are key tools in the process of dynamic evolution of the subsystems to spur a country's economy toward economic development.

With regard to the first block, since the pioneering theories on economic growth (Lucas, 1988; Solow, 1956), the literature seeking effects on economic growth has grown. Some research revolves around the effect of innovation and capital formation on economic growth. Segerstrom (1991) develops a dynamic general equilibrium model of economic growth, where innovation and imitation are endogenously determined based on the outcomes of R&D races between firms. Innovation subsidies are shown to unambiguously promote economic growth. Welfare is enhanced, however, only if the steady-state intensity of innovative effort exceeds a critical level. Malamud and Zucchi (2019) built an innovation-driven endogenous growth model in which innovative firms have costly access to outside financing and hoard cash reserves to maintain financial flexibility, showing that financing frictions slow down Schumpeterian creative destruction by discouraging entry, and finding that financing frictions significantly affect the composition of growth, by reducing the contribution of entrants but spurring the contribution of incumbents. Zeira (1998) analyzes a model of economic growth with technological innovations that reduce labor requirements but raise capital requirements. Something similar but with a different methodology is developed by Lentz and Mortensen (2008), who estimate the structure of an equilibrium model of growth through innovation designed to identify and quantify the role of resource reallocation in the growth process.

Other research has moved away from determinants such as capital formation and innovation to address variables with a social component. The explanatory variables of economic growth include women's schooling and home teaching (Behrman et al., 1999), bureaucratic corruption (Ehrlich & Francis, 1999), long-distance flights (Campante & Yanagizawa-Drott, 2018), religion (Campante & Yanagizawa-Drott, 2015), social capability (Temple & Johnson, 1998), human capital risk (Krebs, 2003), life expectancy (Acemoglu & Johnson, 2007), and health (Weil, 2007), among others. This shows the interest in the effects on economic growth, but also reveals that the aim is to analyze economic development from the perspective of product growth. As a result, the literature that tries to understand and explain economic development from a systems perspective started to become more common.

The literature on economic development and society as a system has been growing. Some key research shows how economic development can be understood from socioeconomic systems. Guerrero et al. (2015) try to contribute to a better understanding of the economic impact of entrepreneurial universities' teaching, research, and entrepreneurial activities on economic development. The authors find a positive and significant economic impact of teaching, research, and entrepreneurial activities; the higher economic impact of the United Kingdom's entrepreneurial universities is explained by entrepreneurial spin-offs. Fagerberg and Srholec (2008) used factor analysis on data for 25 indicators and 115 countries between 1992 and 2004 to identify the role of capabilities in economic development. The authors found four different types of "capabilities": the development of the "innovation system," the quality of "governance," the character of the "political system," and the degree of "openness" of the economy, where innovation systems and governance are shown to be of particular importance for economic development. Sutthichaimethee et al. (2019) aim to forecast future economic and environmental growth for the next 16 years (2020–2035) according to the government's strategic framework by applying the second-order autoregressive structural equation model (second-order autoregressive SEM). The authors find that the long-term analysis indicates that the current political policy will result in continuous economic growth, where the gross national product (GNP) growth rate will climb up to 6.45% per annum by 2035, while the environment is being negatively affected. In this research, the authors conclude that economic growth is positively and significantly affected by a system of effective policies accompanied by an environmental subsystem. Del Monte et al. (2020) propose a conceptual framework in which long-term regional entrepreneurship and innovation foster the growth of regions. They find that empirical evidence supports the conceptual framework and shows that the cultural environment has an indirect effect on regional growth through entrepreneurship and innovation, and regions with higher levels of entrepreneurship and innovation grow faster than other regions.

Other important researches that follow this path include those carried out by Bali Swain and Yang-Wallentin (2020), Cristea et al. (2020), Hall and Kanaan (2020), and Mansour et al. (2020). Bali Swain and Yang-Wallentin (2020) contribute by quantifying and prioritizing the United Nations Sustainable Development Goals (SDGs) and their impact on sustainable development. The authors employ structural equation models (SEMs) to investigate which of the underlying pillars of SDGs (economic, social, and environmental) are the most effective in achieving sustainable development and find that the developed countries benefit most by focusing on social and environmental factors, whereas the developing countries benefit most by retaining their focus on the economic and social factors. Cristea et al. (2020) seek to develop a general assessment framework for several shaping factors of bioeconomy fundamentals within the European Union under the decisive impact of the intellectual capital credentials, namely educational attainment, research and development activities, and innovation patterns, on sustainable development. The authors find that education, innovation, and research, along with the main bioeconomy credentials, are at the core of the economic development of both EU-13 (new member states) and EU-15 (old member states) countries, having distinctive dissimilarities between them, particularly enhanced for the new EU-13 MS. Hall and Kanaan (2020) use a structural equation model to estimate the effects of local tax choices on economic development performance. The authors find that municipalities implementing the 4a local option sales taxes LOST tax choice (traditional industry-related efforts) experienced a significant and positive effect on economic development as measured through a latent construct assessing five years of growth in population, property value, and new home construction. The phenomenon suggests that states and municipalities can influence economic development activity by permitting municipal choice in the allocation of tax revenues dedicated to economic development. In research for Saudi Arabia, Mansour et al. (2020) prioritize investment spending in the construction sector to meet sustainable development. Through a partial least squares structural equation modeling (PLS-SEM) method, the authors find that the influencing factors are five economic, five environmental, and three social sub-criteria in sustainable development. This literary support allows us to establish the following hypothesis:

Hypothesis 1: Economic development positively depends on sociotechnical subsystems.

Since economic development can be analyzed and measured through a sociotechnical subsystems approach (Bali Swain & Yang-Wallentin, 2020; Cristea et al., 2020; Hall & Kanaan, 2020; Mansour et al., 2020), it is now important to recognize which factors significantly influence this measure. The literature highlights three important factors for measuring development: per capita GDP (Acemoglu & Johnson, 2007; Bourguignon & Morrisson, 1998; Fagerberg, 1987; Guerrero et al., 2015; McCleary & Barro, 2006; Stel et al., 2005), the Human Development Index (HDI)

(Roy & Mohanty, 2020; Viddy & Asniwati, 2019), and the GINI coefficient (Barro, 2000; Hartmann et al., 2017; Kentor, 2001; Ram, 1997).

Therefore, for this research, we need to delve into sociotechnical subsystems that may have effects on these factors, without losing sight of the innovation and entrepreneurship subsystems. On the one hand, we'll observe what happens with the effects of some sociotechnical subsystems on GDP. First, Chiu (2016) and Glaeser et al. (2004) study the effects of an institutional subsystem such as government effectiveness index on GDP. Chiu (2016) uses a fixed-effects model to estimate the effect of governance indicators (government effectiveness, among others) on the GDP per capita growth rate, consumer inflation, and government expenditure, finding that each of these variables positively affects the economic growth. Similarly, Glaeser et al. (2004) revisit the debate over whether political institutions cause economic growth and find that most indicators of institutional quality used to establish the proposition that institutions cause growth are constructed to be conceptually unsuitable for that purpose; however, they found significance and a positive effect of government effectiveness on economic growth. In another study, the relationship between government performance and the quality of government institutions with economic development in Indonesia is analyzed; in this analysis, Ramadhan (2019) uses the generalized methods of moments (GMM) time series method and finds that government performance like government effectiveness has a fundamental role in driving economic growth. In a study for African countries, Olaoye et al. (2020) develop an overview of the effect of government effectiveness and R&D expenditure on economic growth. For this, four countries were chosen due to the availability of data from 2000 to 2016, analyzed through linear regression models. The authors find that both are key factors in predicting economic growth, leading African countries toward sustainable development. In contrast, Kacho and Dahmardeh (2018) find that financial development and institutional quality (including government effectiveness) have a negative and statistically significant effect on economic growth in the Middle East and North African MENA countries, which may be due to the high levels of corruption and political instability in these countries. This leads us to establish the following hypothesis:

Hypothesis 1.A: An institutional sociotechnical subsystem (represented by government effectiveness) has a positive effect on GDP (factor of economic development).

Second, the effect of government final consumption expenditure on economic growth is diverse and depends on many factors (Afonso, 2010; Sokolov Mladenović et al., 2019). However, Jermsittiparsert et al. (2019) study the importance of final government expenditure to spur GDP, examining the impact of public spending on ASEAN-5 countries' economic development and provide evidence on, reference, and contribute to the knowledge about government spending and economic growth. Finding positive results, the authors show that there is evidence that government expenditure has a positive and significant impact on economic growth. In a study for the Turkish economy, Şimşek et al. (2017) studies the same relationship through conditional dynamic and marginal models with a superexogeneity test and finds that government spending is exogenous and significant to GDP. This result goes beyond simple causality, as it implies that the policy regime shift for the period of the global financial crisis in Turkey did not cause structural variance in government expenditure. In a key study, Ghose and Das (2013) employed a panel cointegration test and estimated the parameters using the dynamic ordinary least squares method, finding a positive effect of government size, such as government final consumption expenditure, on economic growth such as GDP in the long run during the period 1970–2006 for a sample of 19 emerging economies. The big contribution of this research is that it proves that the effect of this relationship depends on the measures of the variables. This leads us to construct the following hypothesis:

Hypothesis 1.B: A governmental sociotechnical subsystem (represented by government final consumption expenditure) has a positive effect on GDP (factor of economic development).

Third, Park et al. (2019) demonstrate the importance of the differentiation between GDP and per capita GDP in measuring a country's economy. From a tautological analysis, economic theory has indicated the positive relationship between per capita GDP and labor force, but given the mathematical obviousness of the issue, few studies have analyzed this relationship (Loren et al., 2008). For example, Eren et al. (2014) examine the determinants of development, finding a causal relationship among per capita GDP, total labor force participation rate, and the HDI for 84 developed countries and support the idea that per capita GDP and labor force are positively correlated. In a similar study, Zayed et al. (2019) examine the impact of the labor force on GDP in advanced economies, and using data from 1870 to 2000 the authors use the augmented Dickey-Fuller test, the Johansen test, and the error correction model (ECM) to test the stability of the model. The authors find a positive and significant relationship between the labor force and GDP. In more specific studies, Ahmadov (2020) analyzes the impact of the labor force (science, technology, engineering, and math [STEM]) on GDP in European Union countries. Using data from 1992 to 2015 for 28 countries, the authors use estimated marginal effects to quantify the impact and find, as in previous research, a positive and significant effect of this relationship; and Han et al. (2018) conducts a similar study for the economy of Kazakhstan, finding consistency with classical theory, affirming the positive relationship between these two variables. The above invites us to propose that:

Hypothesis 1.C: A generation sociotechnical subsystem such as labor force has a positive effect on GDP (factor of economic development).

Fourth, as in the previous hypothesis, there is a mathematical and theoretical relationship between gross national income (GNI) and GDP. For example, Kohli (2003) develops a decomposition of GDP with a national income function approach, which allows the identification of microeconomic factors that spur GDP. In another key research, Diacon and Maha (2015) tried to investigate the cointegration relationship between consumption, income, and GDP per capita. The results show a positive and significant effect of income (GNI) on GDP, but more importantly, they find that in middle- and low-income countries the relationship between consumption, income (GNI), and GDP is closer because they do not have large capital flows. Supporting the relationship between these variables, Jannat et al. (2020) conducted an empirical analysis of factors influencing the economic growth rate in Bangladesh. Using data from 2000 to 2015, the bivariate analysis shows that gross national income, export merchandise, import merchandise, foreign direct investment, population, remittance paid, and remittance received are correlated with the gross domestic product. The authors find that gross national income and remittance received are the most significant factors, thereby supporting the literature. This leaves us to propose:

Hypothesis 1.D: A generation sociotechnical subsystem (represented by gross national income (GNI)) has a positive effect on GDP (factor of economic development).

On the other hand, in the literature, some sociotechnical subsystems can affect the HDI. First, some research has shown the importance of social determinants to spur the HDI (Apinran et al., 2018; Sofilda et al., 2015; Vettore et al., 2020). Ejemeyovwi and Osabuohien (2020) investigate the impact of mobile technology adoption on inclusive growth (HDI) in 15 West African countries and find a positive relationship between them, albeit statistically insignificant due to the high acquisition costs of cellphones in these countries, high inflationary rates, and low exchange rates. These results are in line with previous research, showing evidence of the relationship between mobile subscriptions and economic development, especially in developing countries (Kelly et al., 2012). In other research for African countries, Njoh (2018) analyzes the connection between the consumption of information and communications technologies (ICTs) and development in Africa. The author finds a positive link between cellphone subscription and development in Africa, thus supporting what Aker and Mbiti (2010) stated. In a study for a larger group of countries, Lee et al. (2017) pose the question of whether the diffusion of information and communications technology (ICT) in countries can affect human progress and find that mobile cellular subscriptions have positive and significant effects on economic freedom, political rights, and civil liberties. Thus, the following hypothesis can be proposed:

Hypothesis 1.E: A social sociotechnical subsystem (represented by mobile cellular subscriptions) has a positive effect on the HDI (factor of economic development).

Second, some research proposes that other social determinants can spur the development of societies (Roy & Goll, 2014; Sookias et al., 2018; Yong, 2020). HIV and its treatments are analyzed as a determinant for sociocultural measures (Fauk & Mwanri, 2015; Gari et al., 2013). On the one hand, Mansori et al. (2017) investigate and estimate the global HIV/AIDS mortality, prevalence, and incidence rates, and explore their associations with the HDI, finding that the prevalence and incidence rates of HIV/AIDS each had an inverse correlation with the HDI, which is similar to the findings of Lou et al. (2014), a research with a survey of 141 countries. On the other hand, Jha et al. (2018) make policy recommendations to countries with low levels of development (HDI), since the eradication of HIV will improve the quality of life of the population, while Sharp (2007) conducts a study for Russia and finds a negative relationship between new HIV-infected persons and major HDI indicators such as life expectancy and GDP. Thus, we establish the following hypothesis:

Hypothesis 1.F: A social sociotechnical subsystem represented by an indicator like people (aged 15–49) newly infected with HIV has a negative effect on the HDI (factor of economic development).

Third, a significant body of research has focused its effort on observing the effects of environmental variables on economic development (Bali Swain & Yang-Wallentin, 2020; Hammer & Pivo, 2017; Mansour et al., 2020), which leads us to use the environment as a sociotechnical subsystem to promote economic development. However, the relationship between forest areas and the HDI has not been studied in detail. In a first approach, Mather and Needle (1999) show us that a high level of development is beneficial rather than detrimental to the sustainability of forest areas; this raises the question of what happens in the opposite direction. On the one hand, Kauppi et al. (2018) reveal that the forest resources (forest areas, among others) trends of nations correlate positively with the

HDI. On the other hand, Wang et al. (2016) conducted a study to determine the forest transition in China, and using four regression models they found that there is a "U-shaped" relationship between changes in forest areas and per capita GDP (key variable for calculating the HDI). Therefore, the authors recommend strengthening the management of large-scale interconversions between forest and grassland. The above let us establish the following hypothesis:

Hypothesis 1.G: An environmental sociotechnical subsystem represented by forest area has a positive effect on the HDI (factor of economic development).

Finally, we proceed to review the literature to see if some sociotechnical subsystems might spur our last factor of economic development (GINI). First, a large literature has been concerned with explaining the positive and significant effect of corruption on inequality (Akkoyunlu & Ramella, 2020; Gupta et al., 2002; Sáenz-Castro & García-González, 2019). However, when the corruption control index is used as a proxy for corruption, the effects appear to be diverse (Adams & Klobodu, 2016; Yadav et al., 2020). While Yadav et al. (2020) find a significant and positive effect of the control of corruption index on GINI, Adams and Klobodu (2016) find significance but with a negative effect; this is apparently because a perception index depends on other sociocultural components of the countries being observed. This leads us to state that:

Hypothesis 1.H: An institutional sociotechnical subsystem represented by the control of corruption index has a positive effect on GINI (factor of economic development).

And second, some research is focused on studying the effects of economic variables on GINI (Brida et al., 2020; Caminada et al., 2019; Shahpari et al. 2014). Suganthi (2019) uses the analytical hierarchical process to determine the importance of the sustainable development indices. Among the results, the author found that per capita GNI reduces GINI, which leads us to believe that boosting per capita GNI allows us to maintain high levels of sustainable development. In support of the above, Bilan et al. (2020), in trying to improve methodological tools of income distribution analysis based on identifying the links between different structural indicators of income inequality and the most essential features of social and economic well-being, find a negative correlation between GNI and GINI. This leads us to state that:

Hypothesis 1.I: A generation sociotechnical subsystem such as per capita GNI has a negative effect on GINI (factor of economic development).

However, the literature has highlighted a key driver for economic development: innovation and entrepreneurship (Acs et al., 2008; Audretsch et al., 2015; King & Levine, 1993). Audretsch et al. (2015) examined the link between entrepreneurship and economic development using a panel of 127 European cities between 1994 and 2009 and found that the immediate economic development impact of new firm start-ups is positive for both small-/medium-sized cities and large cities. The relationship is U-shaped for large cities, with the indirect effect taking seven years, but the indirect effect does not occur in small-/medium-sized cities. Acs et al. (2008) state the importance of the three stages of economic development—the factor-driven stage, the efficiency-driven stage, and the innovation-driven stage—and examine the empirical evidence on the relationship between stages of economic development and entrepreneurship, finding that the stages have a positive effect on economic development, bearing in mind that the effects vary depending on the regions to which the countries belong. Although the effect of innovation on economic development has been little studied, key research about this was developed by King and Levine (1993). The authors construct an endogenous growth model in which financial systems evaluate prospective entrepreneurs, mobilize savings to finance the most promising productivity-enhancing activities, and diversify the risks associated with these innovative activities, and the results show that better financial systems improve the probability of successful innovation and thereby accelerate economic growth. Through this large literature review we can propose that:

Hypothesis 2: Entrepreneurship and innovation (represented by NBD) has a positive effect on economic development through a sociotechnical subsystem.

Trying to identify the importance of entrepreneurship and innovation for economic development through the sociotechnical subsystems approach, we review in the literature its possible effects on our three development factors (per capita GDP, the HDI, and GINI). Literature shows that entrepreneurship has a positive effect on economic development (Acs, 2010; Acs et al., 2008; Audretsch et al., 2015; Nepal, 2020). First, Fritsch and Mueller (2008) investigate the effects of new business formation on employment change in German regions and find that the different phases of the effects of new business formation on regional development (per capita GDP) are relatively pronounced in agglomerations as well as in regions with a high level of labor productivity. In support of the above, Fritsch (2013) provides an overview of the current state of knowledge about the positive and significant effect of new business formation on regional development (Fritsch, 2004). Also, Meyer and Meyer (2019) examine the impact of entrepreneurial activity on employment and economic growth and find that both established business ownership (EBO) and new business density (NBD) are positive significant predictors at 5% and 10% significance levels, respectively, of economic growth (GDP). This allows us to propose that:

Hypothesis 2.A: Entrepreneurship and innovation (represented by NBD) has a positive effect on GDP (factor of economic development).

Second, for effects on HDI, Grant et al. (2019) provide evidence on how entrepreneurial activity and entrepreneurship facilitators (government, incubators, and financial institutions) help in improving the business environment in all countries across the world and hence contribute to poverty alleviation (HDI). The authors found that there is a positive and significant relationship between entrepreneurial activity (creating business opportunity) and the changes in the Human Development Index (HDI) across all countries studied over the 12-year period. In the same sense, Lowrey (2011) attempts to relate economic well-being to business density, defined as the number of business firms per 1000 persons, and finds that the impact of business density on economic well-being is robust. This leads us to believe that:

Hypothesis 2.B: Entrepreneurship and innovation (represented by NBD) has a positive effect on the HDI (factor of economic development).

Lastly, Boudreaux (2014) analyzes the institutional determinants behind entrepreneurship and their effect on income mobility. For this purpose, the author uses the new business density (NBD) from the World Bank's Doing Business project as a proxy for entrepreneurship, and finds a positive and significant effect on income mobility (as measured with a vector of variables including the GINI coefficient), confirming that countries with a greater number of new businesses tend to also have higher income mobility and lower earnings persistence; however, this relationship erodes when controlling for the institutional framework and healthcare and education expenditures per person. This allows us to propose the following hypothesis

Hypothesis 2.C: Entrepreneurship and innovation (represented by NBD) have a negative effect on GINI (factor of economic development).

This theoretical development allows us to lay the foundations of our research and, together with the methodology that will be presented below, will allow us to reach our goals.

12.3 Methodology

12.3.1 Data

To examine the previous hypotheses, we create unbalanced (due to data in the developing countries often being remarkably poor and often missing) panel data with 1640 observations for 164 countries in a ten-year time series, using several sources of information. The bulk of the data used in this research is obtained from the World Development Indicator database (World Bank, 2016). The Economy Complexity Index (ECI) and the average years of schooling were obtained from the World Change data lab project (project supported by Oxford University). The ECI is a measure of the relative knowledge intensity of an economy (used as a proxy for innovation), and the average years of schooling represent the number of years of education received by people aged 25 and older. Converted from educational attainment levels using official durations of each level, this measure was developed by Barro and Lee (2013). Another fundamental variable in our research is the Human Development Index (HDI), which was obtained from the Human Development Reports. This index was created to emphasize that people and their capabilities should be the ultimate criterion for assessing the development of a country, not economic growth alone.

To determine economic development through a connection of sociotechnical subsystems, the following observed variables are used as variables that determine these subsystems. Total labor force (as the number of people) represents the generation (economic) subsystem since it is accepted in the literature as a variable to measure human input to carry out production. The new business entry density is defined as the number of newly registered corporations per 1000 working-age people (those aged 15–64) (this measure is developed by the World Bank in doing the business project). This variable is important in this research because it supports innovation and entrepreneurship, which are key drivers of economic development, therefore we can name it as one of the determinants of the generation (economic) subsystem. The gross national income (GNI) is used as another generation (economic) subsystem since it determines the overall income level of the economy. For the government subsystem, we use the government final consumption variable, since it is a measure that allows us to establish the degree of incidence and participation of the government within a socioeconomic system. To measure the institutional system, we use the government effectiveness index (from the World Bank), since this index captures perceptions of the quality of public services, the quality of the civil service and the degree of its independence from political pressures, the quality of policy formulation and implementation, and the credibility of the government's commitment to such policies. Then, to capture the social subsystem, we use mobile cellular subscriptions (from the World Bank's World Development Index data), since this makes it possible to establish the degree of development at the social level through telecommunications. Another variable that composes the social subsystem is HIV, which represents the quality of health systems as an important part of their social subsystem. Through literature it is known that measuring this variable is complex because it depends on human behaviors; however, on this occasion, we use the number of people infected with HIV to determine this subsystem. The explanation for this decision is based on being able to integrate the health system, which is so important to measure the development of the welfare of society. The variable that captures the environmental subsystem is the forest area because it serves to establish the environmental framework in which a population is involved. Finally, to make sense of the GINI measure, we use the control of corruption to observe the perceptions of the extent to which public power is exercised for private gain, including both petty and grand forms of corruption, as well as "capture" of the state by elites and private interests. This variable is a determinant of the institutional subsystem.

Other variables (right side of Fig. 12.1) are included in the measurement of economic development; however, due to the extension that could generate conclusions on these variables, we will focus on showing in the following section the fundamental variables (variables that are proxies for the subsystems) to fulfill the objective of the research. Table 12.1 shows the descriptive statistics of the variables used to examine the hypotheses proposed above (for more detailed information on the variables, refer to Online Supplementary Material).

We employ factor and path analysis in a structural equation model (SEM) in our analyses. The path diagram of the model of interest is explained in Fig. 12.1. The measurement model is captured by the rectangles, and arrows connect the observed and the latent variable (economic development) on the left-hand side of Fig. 12.1. The middle part of Fig. 12.1 shows the causal relationship between the development factors (HDI, GINI, and GDP) and the sociotechnical subsystems of economic development (social, environmental, generation (economic), institutional, and government), thus forming the structural model. In this way, the causal impact of the development factors on the latent economic development variable is estimated in the structural model. Tarka

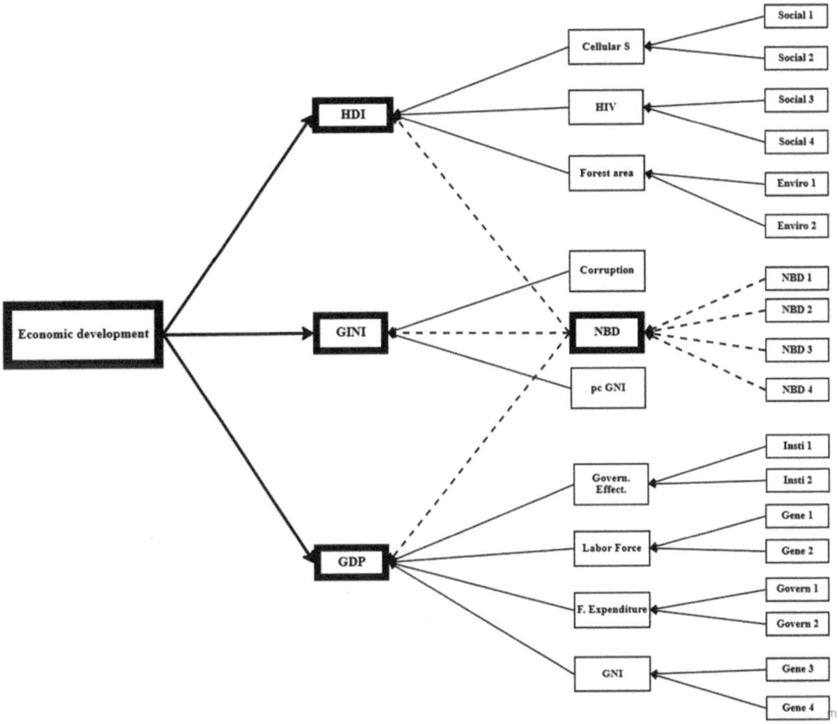

Fig. 12.1 Path diagram for structural equation model (SEM) of economic development

(2018) developed a literature review where he unveils the importance of SEM models and their wide use in economics. Also, literature presents the SEM as the pioneer language of causal analysis for both linear and nonlinear analyses (Bollen & Pearl, 2013; Pearl, 2012).

12.3.2 The Structural Equation Models

The use of path analysis is associated with different areas of research. Wright (1918) developed research on animal genetics and was the developer of such a methodology. Later, using path analysis as a basis, many economists studied the use of simultaneous equations to introduce a variety of research methods and identification problems (Haavelmo, 1943;

Table 12.1 Descriptive statistics

Variables	Mean	SD	Min	Max	P50	p99	N
Per capita GDP	12,299.93	17,224.97	221.096	91,565.73	4405.409	74,984.14	1598
HDI	0.684	0.165	0.294	0.946	0.72	0.937	1359
GINI	37.191	8.182	23.7	61	35.4	56.2	705
Labor force*	30.521	119.950	0.147	1203.246	4.569	773.615	1637
New business density	3.145	4.601	0.006	39.039	1.348	24.562	907
GNI**	521.559	1669.241	0.706	16,412.14	44.274	8484.893	1417
Government final consumption	15.736	8.125	2.047	115.932	14.710	39.548	1531
Government effectiveness	–0.115	1	–2.445	2.436	–0.317	2.166	1610
Mobile cellular subscriptions	78.435	45.178	0	239.437	81.463	181.773	1640
Infected HIV	8848.739	18,448.87	100	130,000	2000	84,000	1110
Forest areas	35,9974.1	1,187,874	0	8,151,356	36,244	7,357,653	1624
Control of corruption	–0.155	1	–1.868	2.469	–0.410	2.325	1610
Per capita GNI	11,942.08	16,485.69	217.622	92,187.5	4500.884	61,172.45	1417
Self-employment	44.586	27.906	.447	94.792	39.891	93.625	1640
ECI	0.026	0.969	–2.791	2.648	–0.084	2.141	1180
Years of schooling	7.839	3.282	1.3	14	8	13.3	1406
Scientific journal	12,506.72	44,305	0	433,192.3	413.855	254,574.4	1630
Time required to start a business	34.341	34.492	0.5	260.5	25	158.5	1489
Starting a business score	69.470	19.668	2.205	99.957	73.939	97.217	1412
Gross capital formation	6.760	19.787	–137.635	231.418	5.511	67.389	1416
Inflation	5.870	6.097	–10.067	62.168	4.407	31.373	1516
Access to electricity	76.182	31.395	1.243	100	97.846	100	1604
Imports	46.001	27.201	0.064	236.391	39.012	175.737	1547
Domestic private health expenditure	43.613	18.370	5.955	84.602	41.546	81.195	1570
Political stability	–0.240	.961	–3.314	1.595	–0.179	1.368	1609
CO_2 emissions	4.610	6.450	0.020	62.066	2.253	33.773	1626
People using drinking water	83.253	18.959	26.234	100	91.913	100	1639

Note: * Value expressed in millions of people. **Value expressed in billions of dollars

Koopmans, 1945). Later still, Jöreskog (1970) developed a general model fitting systems of linear equations including latent variables. This author also developed the methodology for fitting these models using maximum likelihood estimation. Thus, structural equation modeling is not just an estimation method for a particular model; it is a way of thinking and estimating.

Structural equation models (SEMs) allow the use of a set of latent observable variables, which could be dichotomous, ordinal, or nominal variables. In this research, we use this methodology due to its flexibility to estimate sets of independently related variables, given that economic development is a complex concept that requires analysis from different indicators.

The structural model in Fig. 12.1 shows us the paths of the causal relationship between the development factors and the economic development (confirmatory factor analysis [a tool that is used to confirm or reject the measurement theory]). This model can be expressed in matrix form as follows:

$$\alpha = \theta_o o + \vartheta \tag{1}$$

$$\varphi = \theta_f \alpha + \varepsilon \tag{2}$$

$$d = \omega \varphi + \gamma \tag{3}$$

where o and α are the indicator vectors of development factors, o includes the observed variables on the right-hand side of the path diagram, and α includes the observed variables in the middle of the path diagram. φ represents the matrix of measures of economic development. The parameter d is the latent economic development depending on φ matrix. θ_o and θ_f are factor loadings that connect the development factors and the observed indicators. The ω coefficients indicate the causal relations between the economic development latent variable and the development factors, whereas ϑ, ε, and γ are the error terms associated with the measurements.

The SEM models have three estimation methods: maximum likelihood (ML), maximum likelihood with missing values (MLMV), and the asymptotically distribution-free (ADF). In this case, the model is estimated by the maximum likelihood estimation method, because in this methodology estimates are obtained by maximizing the likelihood function derived from the multivariate normal distribution (in our case, most of the indexes used have a normal distribution), and we discard the MLMV and ADF methods because they lead to saturated models and violate the normality assumption, respectively (Hayashi et al., 2007). The maximum likelihood (ML) approach estimates the unknown parameters in the model by minimizing the fit function:

$$F(\varnothing) = \ln\|\Sigma\| + tr\left(s\Sigma^{-1}\right) - \log\|s\| - k + \left(\overline{z} - \mu\right)' \Sigma^{-1}\left(\overline{z} - \mu\right) \quad (4)$$

where k is the number of indicators, s and Σ are the sample and model implied variance and covariance matrix, respectively. This fit function assumes that the observed indicators have a multinormal distribution.

12.4 Results

The SEM model of economic development through sociotechnical subsystems determines the latent economic development using factors such as GINI, the HDI, and per capita GDP. Table 12.1 shows the linear causal relationship between economic development as a measure of the three factors mentioned above and presents the causal relationship between these development factors and sociotechnical subsystems such as generation (economic), social, environmental, governance, and institutional.

For the measure of economic development, we find that all three factors are significant (bearing in mind that Stata uses per capita GDP as a restricted variable to adequately measure development) and show an expected effect, that is, the HDI and GDP per capita have positive effects while GINI has a negative effect. On the one hand, the variable that has the greatest impact on development is GINI, therefore as inequality measured by the GINI index increases by 1%, economic development through factors determined by subsystems decreases by 5.064% (significant at 1%). On the other hand, when the HDI increases by 1%, the measure of development increases by 2.677% with a significance of 0.1%. This allows us to support results like those obtained by Acemoglu and Johnson (2007), Barro (2000), Guerrero et al. (2015), Hartmann et al. (2017), Kentor (2001), Roy and Mohanty (2020), Stel et al. (2005), and Viddy and Asniwati (2019).

Looking at what happens with each of the factors that determine economic development, we can see that there is a high significance of the sociotechnical subsystems, confirming the existing causal relationships between these subsystems and the three factors that determine economic development, thus supporting the interdependence of these subsystems. As regards the HDI, the social subsystem has a positive and significant effect, so when the number of mobile cellular subscriptions increases by 1%, the HDI increases by 0.267% (in row 4 and column 3 of Table 12.2), supporting results like those revealed by Ejemeyovwi and Osabuohien (2020) and Lee et al. (2017). Also, for this subsystem the HIV has a negative and significant effect on the HDI due to the variable used as a proxy, that is, when the number of people infected with HIV increases by 1%, the HDI decreases by 0.239% with a significance of 0.1%, so that reductions in this variable would lead to positive effects on the HDI, which goes hand in hand with the results presented by Lou et al. (2014) and Mansori et al. (2017). The environmental subsystem, with a significance of 0.1%, has a positive effect, so that when forest areas (measured in square kilometers) increase by 1%, the HDI increases by 0.513%, supporting results like those obtained by Kauppi et al. (2018) and Needle (1999). Therefore, it can be affirmed that the social and environmental subsystems have significance for the HDI factor, supporting Hypotheses 1.E-G. In regard to the GINI, the results show that an increase in per capita GNI as the generation (economic) subsystem by 1% decreases the GINI index by 0.530%, supporting what literature has stated about the importance of GNI in the control and good results of GINI (Bilan et al., 2020; Suganthi, 2019). When we look at what happens with the institutional subsystem, results seem to bear out research like Yadav et al. (2020), since when the corruption control index increases by 1%, the GINI increases by 0.971%, results that also appear to be ambiguous at the theoretical level. This may be due to the availability of data and also the fact that the mean of this variable is -0.155, which indicates that most countries have not been able to prevent public power from being provided for

Table 12.2 Estimated parameters of the measurement model for economic development

	Factors			
Variables	Economic development	HDI	GINI	pcGDP
HDI	2.677*** (0.846)			
GINI	–5.064** (1.618)			
Social—mobile cellular subscription		0.267*** (0.042)		
Social—HIV		–0.239*** (0.056)		
Environmental—forest area		0.513*** (0.156)		
Institutional—corruption			0.971*** (0.126)	
Generation—NBD		0.282*** (0.057)	-0.450*** (0.126)	0.093+ (0.048)
Generation—pcGNI			–0.530*** (0.149)	
Institution—gov. effectiveness				0.414*** (0.046)
Generation—labor force				3.333*** (0.929)
Government—final government expenditure				0.207*** (0.062)
Generation—GNI				0.901*** (0.084)

Note: Observation is 184. Standard errors in parentheses: + p<0.1, *p<0.05, **p<0.01, ***p<0.001. The result of the effect of GDP per capita on the development measure is not reported because the indicator is fixed at a value of 1. By doing this, we are essentially specifying a reference point from which the rest of the indicators (which would be GINI and HDI) can be estimated in terms of their relation to the latent factor (development)

private benefit, and any positive impact on this index will cause imbalances in the measurement of inequality given bureaucratic dependency. In this way, we can support what was stated in Hypotheses 1.H-I. As per the per capita GDP, the government effectiveness index as the institutional subsystem shows a positive and significant effect at 0.1%; thus, when this index increases by 1%, the GDP undergoes an increase of 0.414%, supporting what is stated by Chiu (2016) and Glaeser et al. (2004). Something similar happens with the generation (economic) subsystem, since when the GNI increases by 1%, GDP increases by 0.901%, reinforcing results presented by Diacon and Maha (2015) and Kohli (2003). The government subsystem, like the previous two, has a positive and significant effect on GDP, since when government spending increases by 1%, the GDP increases by 0.207%; however, the level of significance is 1%, supporting what Jermsittiparsert et al. (2019) state. And finally, the other generation (economic) subsystem, the labor force, has a positive and significant expected effect: When the labor force increases by 1%, the GDP increases by 3.333%, in the same direction that Loren et al. (2008) proposed. This allows us to uphold Hypotheses 1.A-D.

LINK Excel.Sheet.8 "https://eafit-my.sharepoint.com/personal/dam-artine1_eafit_edu_co/Documents/Trabajo/ECSIM/Proyecto%20Libro/Paper1/Resultados/SEM_3_factors_new.xls" "Labor force^2 reported!F1C1:F28C5" \a \f 4 \h * MERGEFORMAT

Due to the impossibility of finding how well the model fits data through a chi-square test (because the fitted model is not full rank), Table 12.3 shows equation-level goodness of fit for the factors that determine economic development and the sociotechnical subsystems that affect economic development factors. In general, positive results are obtained on the construction of the equations that give life to the structural model. The above allows us to assume that economic development can be measured and analyzed from a sociotechnical subsystem approach, confirming what was assumed in Hypothesis 1.

Finally, a generation (economic) subsystem such as NBD has positive and significant expected effects on per capita GDP and the HDI, and negative and significant effects on GINI. When the new business density index (NBD) increases by 1%, per capita GDP and the HDI increase by 0.093% and 0.282%, respectively, with a significance of 10% and 0.1%,

Table 12.3 Equation-level goodness of fit

Dep. Variables	Fitted	R-squared	mc	mc2
pcGDP	0.629	0.872	0.934	0.872
HDI	0.309	0.795	0.892	0.795
GINI	1.051	0.689	0.830	0.689
Human	0.009	0.999	0.999	0.999
Entrepreneurship	0.360	0.370	0.608	0.370
Economic	0.200	0.999	0.999	0.999
Government	0.275	0.923	0.961	0.923
Social	0.454	0.911	0.954	0.911
Cultural	0.220	0.998	0.999	0.998
Institution	0.608	0.980	0.990	0.980
Environment	0.035	0.999	0.999	0.999

Note: mc = correlation between depvar and its prediction; mc2 = mc^2 is the Bentler-Raykov squared multiple correlation coefficient

respectively, reinforcing results presented by Fritsch and Mueller (2008), Fritsch (2013), Grant et al. (2019), Lowrey (2011), and Meyer and Meyer (2019), while when this index increases by 1%, the GINI decreases by 0.450% with a significance of 0.1%, supporting results like those presented by Boudreaux (2014). This indicates that economic development can be analyzed and measured from a sociotechnical subsystems approach with drivers related to innovation and entrepreneurship, thereby supporting Hypotheses 2 and 2.A-C.

12.5 Discussion and Conclusions

The bulk of the literature has tried to explain economic development from a simplistic perspective as required by economic models (Meramveliotakis & Manioudis, 2021; Saunders, 2021); however, time and in-depth research have shown that development is somewhat more complex, not only in its structure but also in its measurement, given that it depends on many factors that are interrelated in society (Dam and Van Dam & Frenken, 2020; Sbardella et al., 2017).

Using the SEM model (Tarka, 2018) to measure economic development as a latent variable across three key factors, we found three important results of great value to fill literature gaps. The first result supports the belief that economic development can be measured and analyzed from a sociotechnical subsystems approach such as generation (economic), social, governance, institutional, and environmental (Mansour et al., 2020). This result also reveals the importance of beginning to study economic development as a system that depends not only on economic relations and results but also on social results (Dam and Van Dam & Frenken, 2020), which in most cases are difficult to measure, given that the meaning of classical economic theory is to show results from a simplified world to arrive at the general. The second result supports the hypothesis that economic development through a sociotechnical subsystems approach depends on three fundamental factors: GDP per capita, the HDI, and GINI. Per capita GDP and the HDI have a positive linear causal effect on the measure of economic development, and GINI has a negative effect due to the construction of its definition. Therefore, the measurement of economic development must begin to consider indicators that consider the impact of social and welfare results on the population. The last result indicates that a generation (economic) subsystem such as NBD has a positive and significant effect on the key factors of economic development (Nguyen et al., 2021). NBD not only has a positive and significant effect on the per capita GDP (Fritsch, 2013; Meyer & Meyer, 2019), which is an intuitive effect, but also shows the same behavior on the HDI (Lowrey, 2011), which is an indicator that measures economic development through a broader concept than just the economy, health, and education variables that come into play that allows us to measure the welfare of society. Both effects are congruent with the effect that NBD has on the GINI, given that an increase in NBD decreases the GINI; that is, the greater the number of new businesses and enterprises, the lower the inequality.

12.5.1 Theoretical Implications

This research, besides focusing on encouraging new methodologies for the analysis of economic development, covers a wide theoretical field, touching on topics such as economic development, innovation and entrepreneurship, socioeconomic indicators, sociotechnical subsystems, and SEM approach, among others. Thus, after a discussion based on the results, this segment seeks to present three fundamental theoretical implications obtained from this research.

First, the results strengthen the use of approaches different from those normally used such as classical and neoclassical theories aimed at analyzing development from endogenous and exogenous growth models (Lucas, 1988; Mankiw et al. 1990; Romer 1986, 1992; Solow, 1956). The sociotechnical subsystems approach is little explored in economic development research, although some researchers make approximations intending to analyze what is called "sustainable development" (Cristea et al., 2020; Mansour et al., 2020). This approach is used in several research fields (Carayon et al., 2015; Wiener 1949), and this chapter shows that it is an appropriate approach for studying economic development due to its flexibility in implementing independently dynamic socioeconomic indicators. For this reason, our research seeks to put forward the idea that development is a complex concept that depends on many socioeconomic factors and needs to be addressed from more flexible approaches such as sociotechnical subsystems.

Second, the use of more flexible approaches requires more flexible statistical and econometric methodologies. In this research, we use structural equation modeling (SEM), which allows us to estimate latent variables related to aspects outside the economic study (Hayashi et al., 2007). Our results support modern econometric methodologies that allow the relaxation of some strict economic assumptions. And the last theoretical implication is related to innovation and entrepreneurship. Although relatively modern approaches and methodologies are used to analyze economic development, the results support the literature that holds up the strong effect of innovation and entrepreneurship on economic development (Aparicio et al., 2016; Audretsch et al., 2015; Urbano et al., 2019). Therefore, we conclude that innovation and entrepreneurship can be observed as a driver of economic development; this goes hand in hand with assimilationist thinking, which supports the idea that workers and agents of society assimilate knowledge and skills and transform them into productive activity to drive development (Murton, 2015; Thornton et al., 2011).

12.5.2 Policy Implications

The results presented in this research invite policymakers to support the creation of new enterprises to lead to an increase in NBD, given that this variable has positive effects on the fundamental factors of economic development. Innovation and entrepreneurship are factors that have been adopted by countries such as Korea, Germany, and Ireland to achieve economic development based on the technification and innovation of companies. However, not only are innovation and entrepreneurship important for achieving economic development, but this research allows us to recommend to policymakers that they provide support for socio-technical subsystems such as those analyzed in the results, since in this approach not only are economic indicators important but also social indicators to achieve sustainable development.

Based on the results, it is recommended that to achieve sustainable development, the labor force must be increased by supporting self-employment with support for entrepreneurs; GNI must be increased by reinforcing the physical capital through which companies produce and take advantage of the increase in the labor force; the final government expenditure must be increased in a controlled way while monitoring inflation; the technological communication of society must be increased as they promote mobile cellphone subscriptions, providing access to electricity and a variety of imported products to be used; HIV cases should be reduced through sex education that reduces cases in minors, as this would lead to a society with more self-care and public health awareness, which are fundamental to economic development; the government's effectiveness index that provides reliability in government institutions should be increased; and finally, the forest areas must be increased by reducing CO_2 emissions. Therefore, achieving economic development depends on many factors. It is not enough to focus efforts on a single system—an effort must be made to promote the subsystems proposed to achieve sustained development; however, the dynamics of entrepreneurship and the progressive improvement of the new business density index generate a continuous learning process for society through the advancement of fundamental factors for development such as GDP, the HDI, and GINI.

12.5.3 Limitations and Future Research

It should be noted that the results, as well as policy implications obtained in this research, play an important role in the literature on economic development and entrepreneurship/innovation, but undoubtedly future lines of research emerge from the limitations observed in this chapter. A first limitation is linked to the data because one of the main development factors, the GINI, has limited information at the data panel level, therefore the results are biased toward countries with high-quality information, not only in the GINI but also in the institutional, corruption, government, and business creation indices, therefore future investigations are necessary to strengthen the information used in this type of investigation. A second limitation goes hand in hand with the first, and that is that the most accepted econometric methodologies depend on variables that meet certain characteristics, and therefore the use of indicators is scarce due to the complexity of their constraints. However, it is necessary to implement the idea that economic development is something complex to calculate and interpret given that it depends on sociotechnical subsystems.

Although most of the limitations are related to the lack of information on the observable variables used, at the theoretical level there is a major limitation, and that is the limited exploration of the sociotechnical subsystems approach for the analysis of economic development. This allows us to ensure that it is necessary to develop future research that observes the behavior of economic development under flexible approaches such as the one used in this research. Therefore, future research is also needed to develop mathematical models to establish entrepreneurship and innovation as the main driver of economic development, which can be estimated using more complex statistical and econometric methodologies.

References

Acemoglu, D. (2008). *Introduction to modern economic growth. Introduction to Modern Economic Growth*. Princeton University Press. https://doi.org/10.1111/j.1475-4932.2011.00816.x

Acemoglu, D., & Johnson, S. (2005). Unbundling institutions. *Journal of Political Economy, 113*(5), 949–995. https://doi.org/10.1086/432166

Acemoglu, D., & Johnson, S. (2007). Disease and development: The effect of life expectancy on economic growth. *Journal of Political Economy, 115*(6), 925–985. https://doi.org/10.1086/529000

Acs, Z. J. (2010). Entrepreneurship and economic development: the valley of backwardness. *Annals of Innovation & Entrepreneurship, 1*(1), 5641. https://doi.org/10.3402/aie.v1i1.5602

Acs, Z. J., Desai, S., & Hessels, J. (2008). Entrepreneurship, economic development and institutions. *Small Business Economics, 31*(3), 219–234. https://doi.org/10.1007/s11187-008-9135-9

Adams, S., & Klobodu, E. K. M. (2016). Financial development, control of corruption and income inequality. *International Review of Applied Economics, 30*(6), 790–808. https://doi.org/10.1080/02692171.2016.1208740

Afonso, A. (2010). Expansionary fiscal consolidations in Europe: New evidence. *Applied Economics Letters, 17*(2), 105–109. https://doi.org/10.1080/13504850701719892

Aghion, P. (2002). Schumpeterian growth theory and the dynamics of income inequality. *Econometrica, 70*(3), 855–882. https://doi.org/10.1111/1468-0262.00312

Ahmadov, D. (2020). Stem effect on GDP in EU countries: Labor force perspective. *Journal of Eastern European and Central Asian Research, 7*(1), 114–121. https://doi.org/10.15549/jeecar.v7i1.236

Aker, J. C., & Mbiti, I. M. (2010). Mobile phones and economic development in Africa. *Journal of Economic Perspectives, 24*(3), 207–232. https://doi.org/10.1257/jep.24.3.207

Akkoyunlu, S., & Ramella, D. (2020). Corruption and economic development. *Journal of Economic Development, 45*(2), 63–94. https://doi.org/10.21113/iir.v2i1.164

Aparicio, S., Urbano, D., & Audretsch, D. (2016). Institutional factors, opportunity entrepreneurship and economic growth: Panel data evidence. *Technological Forecasting and Social Change, 102*, 45–61. https://doi.org/10.1016/j.techfore.2015.04.006

Apinran, M. O., Taşpınar, N., & Gökmenoğlu, K. K. (2018). Impact of Foreign Direct Investment on Human Development Index in Nigeria. *Business and Economics Research Journal, 9*(1), 1–13. https://doi.org/10.20409/berj.2018.90

Arranz, N., & Fernandez de Arroyabe, J. C. (2008). Joint R&D projects as complex systems: A framework of analysis. *IEEE Transactions on Engineering Management, 55*(4), 552–565. https://doi.org/10.1109/TEM.2008.927816

Arrow, K. J., Dasgupta, P., Goulder, L. H., Mumford, K. J., & Oleson, K. (2012). Sustainability and the measurement of wealth. *Environment and Development Economics, 17*(3), 317–353. https://doi.org/10.1017/S1355770X12000137

Audretsch, D. B. (2004). Sustaining innovation and growth: Public policy support for entrepreneurship. *Industry and Innovation, 11*(3), 167–191. https://doi.org/10.1080/1366271042000265366

Audretsch, D. B., Belitski, M., & Desai, S. (2015). Entrepreneurship and economic development in cities. *Annals of Regional Science, 55*(1), 33–60. https://doi.org/10.1007/s00168-015-0685-x

Bagozzi, R. P., & Yi, Y. (2012). Specification, evaluation, and interpretation of structural equation models. *Journal of the Academy of Marketing Science, 40*(1), 8–34. https://doi.org/10.1007/s11747-011-0278-x

Bali Swain, R., & Yang-Wallentin, F. (2020). Achieving sustainable development goals: predicaments and strategies. *International Journal of Sustainable Development and World Ecology, 27*(2), 96–106. https://doi.org/10.1080/13504509.2019.1692316

Barrett, C. B., & Carter, M. R. (2013). The Economics of Poverty Traps and Persistent Poverty: Empirical and Policy Implications. *Journal of Development Studies, 49*(7), 976–990. https://doi.org/10.1080/00220388.2013.785527

Barro, R. J. (2000). Inequality and growth in a panel of countries. *Journal of Economic Growth, 5*(1), 5–32. https://doi.org/10.1023/A:1009850119329

Barro, R. J., & Lee, J. W. (2013). A new data set of educational attainment in the world, 1950-2010. *Journal of Development Economics, 104*, 184–198. https://doi.org/10.1016/j.jdeveco.2012.10.001

Behrman, J. R., Foster, A. D., & Rosenzweig, M. R. (1999). Women's Schooling, Home Teaching, and Economic Growth. *Journal of Political Economy, 107*(4), 682–714. https://doi.org/10.1086/250075

Bell, M., & Pavitt, K. (1993). Technological accumulation and industrial growth: Contrasts between developed and developing countries. *Industrial and Corporate Change, 2*(1), 157–210. https://doi.org/10.1093/icc/2.2.157

Bernanke, B. S., & Gürkaynak, R. S. (2001). Is Growth Exogenous? Taking Mankiw, Romer, and Weil Seriously. *NBER Macroeconomics Annual, 16*(1), 1. https://doi.org/10.1162/088933601320224829

Bertalanffy, L. V. (1968). General Systems Theory: Foundations, Development and Applications. *Human Behavior Theory and Social Work Practice*, 215–249.

Bhaduri, A. (2006). Endogenous economic growth: A new approach. *Cambridge Journal of Economics, 30*(1), 69–83. https://doi.org/10.1093/cje/bei047

Bilan, Y., Mishchuk, H., Samoliuk, N., & Yurchyk, H. (2020). Impact of Income Distribution on Social and Economic Well-Being of the State. *Sustainability (Switzerland), 12*(1). https://doi.org/10.3390/su12010429

Bollen, K. A., & Pearl, J. (2013). Eight Myths About Causality and Structural Equation Models (pp. 301–328). 10.1007/978-94-007-6094-3_15

Bouchouicha, R., & Vieider, F. M. (2019). Growth, entrepreneurship, and risk-tolerance: a risk-income paradox. *Journal of Economic Growth, 24*(3), 257–282. https://doi.org/10.1007/s10887-019-09168-0

Boudreaux, C. J. (2014). Jumping off of the great gatsby curve: How institutions facilitate entrepreneurship and intergenerational mobility. *Journal of Institutional Economics, 10*(2), 231–255. https://doi.org/10.1017/S1744137414000034

Bourguignon, F., & Morrisson, C. (1998). Inequality and development: The role of dualism. *Journal of Development Economics, 57*(2), 233–257. https://doi.org/10.1016/S0304-3878(98)00089-3

Brida, J. G., Carrera, E. J. S., & Segarra, V. (2020). Clustering and regime dynamics for economic growth and income inequality. *Structural Change and Economic Dynamics, 52*, 99–108. https://doi.org/10.1016/j.strueco.2019.09.010

Caminada, K., Goudswaard, K., Wang, C., & Wang, J. (2019). Income Inequality and Fiscal Redistribution in 31 Countries After the Crisis. *Comparative Economic Studies, 61*(1), 119–148. https://doi.org/10.1057/s41294-018-0079-z

Campante, F., & Yanagizawa-Drott, D. (2015). Does religion affect economic growth and happiness? Evidence from Ramadan. *Quarterly Journal of Economics, 130*(2), 615–658. https://doi.org/10.1093/qje/qjv002

Campante, F., & Yanagizawa-Drott, D. (2018). Long-range growth: Economic development in the global network of air links. *Quarterly Journal of Economics, 133*(3), 1395–1458. https://doi.org/10.1093/QJE/QJX050

Carayon, P., Hancock, P., Leveson, N., Noy, I., Sznelwar, L., & van Hootegem, G. (2015). Advancing a sociotechnical systems approach to workplace safety – developing the conceptual framework. *Ergonomics, 58*(4), 548–564. https://doi.org/10.1080/00140139.2015.1015623

Carter, M. R., & Barrett, C. B. (2006). The economics of poverty traps and persistent poverty: An asset-based approach. *Journal of Development Studies, 42*(2), 178–199. https://doi.org/10.1080/00220380500405261

Chiu, W. H. (2016). Political governance and economic growth: Evidence from emerging economies. *International Journal of Economic Perspectives, 10*(4), 376–394.

Cinnirella, F., & Streb, J. (2017). The role of human capital and innovation in economic development: evidence from post-Malthusian Prussia. *Journal of Economic Growth, 22*(2), 193–227. https://doi.org/10.1007/s10887-017-9141-3

Cissé, J. D., & Barrett, C. B. (2018). Estimating development resilience: A conditional moments-based approach. *Journal of Development Economics, 135*, 272–284. https://doi.org/10.1016/j.jdeveco.2018.04.002

Crafts, N. F. R. (1995). Exogenous or Endogenous Growth? The Industrial Revolution Reconsidered. *The Journal of Economic History, 55*(4), 745–772. https://doi.org/10.1017/S0022050700042145

Cristea, M., Noja, G. G., Marcu, N., Siminică, M., & Ţîrcă, D. M. (2020). Modelling EU bioeconomy credentials in the economic development framework: The role of intellectual capital. *Technological and Economic Development of Economy, 26*(6), 1139–1164.

Del Monte, A. Moccia, S., & Pennacchio, L. (2020). Regional entrepreneurship and innovation: historical roots and the impact on the growth of regions. Small Business Economics. 10.1007/s11187-020-00425-w

Diacon, P. E., & Maha, L. G. (2015). The Relationship between Income, Consumption and GDP: A Time Series, Cross-Country Analysis. *Procedia Economics and Finance, 23*, 1535–1543. https://doi.org/10.1016/s2212-5671(15)00374-3

Diener, E. D., & Diener, C. (1995). The wealth of nations revisited: Income and quality of life. *Social Indicators Research, 36*(3), 275–286. https://doi.org/10.1007/BF01078817

Ehrlich, I., & Francis, T. L. (1999). Bureaucratic corruption and endogenous economic growth. In. *Journal of Political Economy, 107*. https://doi.org/10.1086/250111

Ejemeyovwi, J. O., & Osabuohien, E. S. (2020). Investigating the relevance of mobile technology adoption on inclusive growth in West Africa. *Contemporary Social Science, 15*(1), 48–61. https://doi.org/10.1080/21582041.2018.1503320

Emery, F. E., & Trist, E. L. (1965). The Causal Texture of Organizational Environments. *Human Relations, 18*(1), 21–32. https://doi.org/10.1177/001872676501800103

Eren, M., Çelik, A. K., & Kubat, A. (2014). Determinants of the levels of development based on the human development index: A comparison of regression models for limited dependent variables. *Review of European Studies, 6*(1), 10–22. https://doi.org/10.5539/res.v6n1p10

Evermann, J., & Tate, M. (2016). Assessing the predictive performance of structural equation model estimators. *Journal of Business Research, 69*(10), 4565–4582. https://doi.org/10.1016/j.jbusres.2016.03.050

Fagerberg, J. (1987). A technology gap approach to why growth rates differ. *Research Policy, 16*(2–4), 87–99. https://doi.org/10.1016/0048-7333(87)90025-4

Fagerberg, J., & Srholec, M. (2008). National innovation systems, capabilities and economic development. *Research Policy, 37*(9), 1417–1435. https://doi.org/10.1016/j.respol.2008.06.003

Fauk, N. K., & Mwanri, L. (2015). Inequalities in addressing the HIV epidemic: the story of the Indonesian Ojek community. *International Journal of Human Rights in Healthcare, 8*(3), 144–159. https://doi.org/10.1108/IJHRH-10-2014-0028

Fine, B. (2000). Endogenous growth theory: A critical assessment. *Cambridge Journal of Economics, 24*(2), 245–265. https://doi.org/10.1093/cje/24.2.245

Frank, A. G., Ribeiro, J. L. D., & Echeveste, M. E. (2015). Factors influencing knowledge transfer between NPD teams: A taxonomic analysis based on a sociotechnical approach. *R and D Management, 45*(1), 1–22. https://doi.org/10.1111/radm.12046

Fritsch, M. (2004). Entrepreneurship, entry and performance of new business compared in two growth regimes: East and West Germany. In. *Journal of Evolutionary Economics, 14*, 525–542. https://doi.org/10.1007/s00191-004-0230-z

Fritsch, M. (2013). The Effect of New Business Formation on Regional Employment: Empirical Evidence, Interpretation, and Avenues for Further Research. In Handbook of Research on Entrepreneurship and Regional Development. Edward Elgar Publishing. 10.4337/9780857936493.00008

Fritsch, M., & Mueller, P. (2008). The effect of new business formation on regional development over time: The case of Germany. *Small Business Economics, 30*(1), 15 29. https://doi.org/10.1007/s11187-007-9067-9

Gari, S. Doig-Acuña, C. Smail, T. Malungo, J. R. Martin-Hilber, A., & Merten, S. (2013). Access to HIV/AIDS care: A systematic review of socio-cultural determinants in low and high income countries. BMC Health Services Research. 10.1186/1472-6963-13-198

Ghose, A., & Das, S. (2013). Government size and economic growth in emerging market economies: a panel co-integration approach. *Macroeconomics and Finance in Emerging Market Economies, 6*(1), 14–38. https://doi.org/10.1080/17520843.2012.697075

Grant, K. A. Aziz, O., & Arshed, N. (2019). The impact of entrepreneurial activity on poverty alleviation. In DaSilva, AL and Tomic, D and Grilec, A (Ed.), Economic and social development (ESD): 39th International scientific conference on economic and social development – sustainability from and economic and social perspective (pp. 215–224).

Guerrero, M., Cunningham, J. A., & Urbano, D. (2015). Economic impact of entrepreneurial universities' activities: An exploratory study of the United Kingdom. *Research Policy, 44*(3), 748–764. https://doi.org/10.1016/j.respol.2014.10.008

Gupta, S., Davoodi, H., & Alonso-Terme, R. (2002). Does corruption affect income inequality and poverty? *Economics of Governance, 3*(1), 23–45. https://doi.org/10.1007/s101010100039

Haavelmo, T. (1943). The Statistical Implications of a System of Simultaneous Equations. *Econometrica, 11*(1), 1. https://doi.org/10.2307/1905714

Hall, J. L., & Kanaan, D. Z. (2020). State Tax Policy, Municipal Choice, and Local Economic Development Outcomes: A Structural Equation Modeling Approach to Performance Assessment. Public Administration Review. https://doi.org/10.1111/puar.13165

Hammer, J., & Pivo, G. (2017). The Triple Bottom Line and Sustainable Economic Development Theory and Practice. *Economic Development Quarterly, 31*(1), 25–36. https://doi.org/10.1177/0891242416674808

Han, S. T., Arefin, S., & Swe, K. M. (2018). The Impact of Service Sectors on Kazakhstan's Economy. *Business and Economic Research, 8*(4), 45. https://doi.org/10.5296/ber.v8i4.13808

Hartmann, D., Guevara, M. R., Jara-Figueroa, C., Aristarán, M., & Hidalgo, C. A. (2017). Linking Economic Complexity, Institutions, and Income Inequality. *World Development, 93*, 75–93. https://doi.org/10.1016/j.worlddev.2016.12.020

Hausmann, R., Pritchett, L., & Rodrik, D. (2005). Growth accelerations. *Journal of Economic Growth, 10*(4), 303–329. https://doi.org/10.1007/s10887-005-4712-0

Hausmann, R., Hwang, J., & Rodrik, D. (2007). What you export matters. *Journal of Economic Growth, 12*(1), 1–25. https://doi.org/10.1007/s10887-006-9009-4

Hayashi, K. Bentler, P. M., & Yuan, K. H. (2007). Structural Equation Modeling. Handbook of Statistics. 10.1016/S0169-7161(07)27013-0

Jannat, F. R., Miah, M. O., Faruk, M., & Alam, S. (2020). Empirical Analysis of Factors Influencing Economic Growth Rate in Bangladesh. *International Journal of Business and Economics Research, 9*(2), 78. https://doi.org/10.11648/j.ijber.20200902.14

Jermsittiparsert, K., Saengchai, S., Boonrattanakittibhumi, C., & Chankoson, T. (2019). The impact of government expenditures, gross capital formation, trade, and portfolio investment on the economic growth of ASEAN economies. *Journal of Security and Sustainability Issues, 9*(2), 571–584. https://doi.org/10.9770/jssi.2019.9.2(16)

Jha, R. P., Bhattacharyya, K., Mishra, R. N., & Mishra, A. (2018). Incidence, prevalence and mortality of HIV/AIDS across different levels of human development index: A global perspective. *Indian Journal of Public Health Research and Development, 9*(12), 1. https://doi.org/10.5958/0976-5506.2018.01801.6

Johnson, H. G., & Wiener, N. (1949). Cybernetics: Control and Communication in the Animal and the Machine. *The Economic Journal, 59*(236), 573. https://doi.org/10.2307/2226579

Jöreskog, K. G. (1970). A general method for estimating a linear structural equation system. *ETS Research Bulletin Series, 1970*(2), 1–41.

Kacho, A. A., & Dahmardeh, N. (2018). The role of institutional quality on the effectiveness of economic growth from financial development. *Journal of Advanced Research in Dynamical and Control Systems, 10*(7 Special Issue), 166–172.

Kast, F. E., & Rosenzweig, J. E. (1981). General systems theory: Applications for organization and management. *Journal of Nursing Administration, 11*(7), 32–41. https://doi.org/10.5465/255141

Kauppi, P. E., Sandström, V., & Lipponen, A. (2018). Forest resources of nations in relation to human well-being. *PLoS ONE, 13*(5), 1. https://doi.org/10.1371/journal.pone.0196248

Kelly, M. (1997). The dynamics of Smithian growth. *Quarterly Journal of Economics, 112*(3), 938–964. https://doi.org/10.1162/003355397555398

Kelly, T. Friederici, N. Minges, M., & Yamamichi, M. (2012). Information and communications for development 2012: maximizing mobile (English). Washington, D.C. : World Bank Group. http://documents.worldbank.org/curated/en/727791468337814878/Information-and-communications-for-development-2012-maximizing-mobile

Kentor, J. (2001). The long term effects of globalization on income inequality, population growth, and economic development. *Social Problems, 48*(4), 435–455. https://doi.org/10.1525/sp.2001.48.4.435

Kerekes, M. (2012). Growth miracles and failures in a Markov switching classification model of growth. *Journal of Development Economics, 98*(2), 167–177. https://doi.org/10.1016/j.jdeveco.2011.06.012

King, R. G., & Levine, R. (1993). Finance, entrepreneurship and growth. *Journal of Monetary Economics, 32*(3), 513–542. https://doi.org/10.1016/0304-3932(93)90028-E

Kleiner, B. M., & Drury, C. G. (1999). Large-scale regional economic development: Macroergonomics in theory and practice. *Human Factors and Ergonomics In Manufacturing, 9*(2), 151–163. 10.1002/(SICI)1520-6564(199921)9:2<151::AID-HFM2>3.0.CO;2-G.

Klenow, P. J., & Rodríguez-Clare, A. (1997). Economic growth: A review essay. *Journal of Monetary Economics, 40*(3), 597–617. https://doi.org/10.1016/S0304-3932(97)00050-0

Kocherlakota, N. R., & Yi, K. M. (1996). A simple time series test of endogenous vs. Exogenous growth models: An application to the United States. *Review of Economics and Statistics, 78*(1), 126–134. https://doi.org/10.2307/2109852

Kogan, L., Papanikolaou, D., Seru, A., & Stoffman, N. (2017). Technological innovation, resource allocation, and growth. *Quarterly Journal of Economics, 132*(2), 665–712. https://doi.org/10.1093/qje/qjw040

Kohli, U. (2003). GDP growth accounting: A national income function approach. *Review of Income and Wealth, 49*(1), 23–34. https://doi.org/10.1111/1475-4991.00072

Koopmans, T. (1945). Statistical Estimation of Simultaneous Economic Relations. *Journal of the American Statistical Association, 40*(232), 448–466. https://doi.org/10.1080/01621459.1945.10500746

Kosempel, S. (2004). A theory of development and long run growth. *Journal of Development Economics, 75*(1), 201–220. https://doi.org/10.1016/j.jdeveco.2003.08.004

Krebs, T. (2003). Human capital risk and economic growth. *Quarterly Journal of Economics, 118*(2), 709–744. https://doi.org/10.1162/003355303321675491

Laincz, C. A., & Peretto, P. F. (2006). Scale effects in endogenous growth theory: An error of aggregation not specification. *Journal of Economic Growth, 11*(3), 263–288. https://doi.org/10.1007/s10887-006-9004-9

Lee, S. O., Hong, A., & Hwang, J. (2017). ICT diffusion as a determinant of human progress*. *Information Technology for Development, 23*(4), 687–705. https://doi.org/10.1080/02681102.2017.1383874

Lentz, R., & Mortensen, D. T. (2008). An Empirical Model of Growth Through Product Innovation. *Econometrica, 76*(6), 1317–1373. https://doi.org/10.3982/ecta5997

Loren, B., Hsieh, C. T., & Zhu, X. (2008). Growth and structural transformation in China. In *China's Great Economic Transformation* (pp. 683–728). Cambridge University Press. https://doi.org/10.1017/CBO9780511754234.018

Lou, L. X., Chen, Y., Yu, C. H., Li, Y. M., & Ye, J. (2014). National HIV/AIDS mortality, prevalence, and incidence rates are associated with the Human Development Index. *American Journal of Infection Control, 42*(10), 1044–1048. https://doi.org/10.1016/j.ajic.2014.06.029

Lowrey, Y. L. (2011). Business Density, Entrepreneurship and Economic Well-Being. SSRN Electronic Journal. 10.2139/ssrn.744804

Lucas, R. E. (1988). On the mechanics of economic development. *Journal of Monetary Economics, 22*(1), 3–42. https://doi.org/10.1016/0304-3932(88)90168-7

Madsen, J. B., & Murtin, F. (2017). British economic growth since 1270: the role of education. *Journal of Economic Growth, 22*(3), 229–272. https://doi.org/10.1007/s10887-017-9145-z

Malamud, S., & Zucchi, F. (2019). Liquidity, innovation, and endogenous growth. *Journal of Financial Economics, 132*(2), 519–541. https://doi.org/10.1016/j.jfineco.2018.11.002

Mansori, K., Ayubi, E., Shadmani, F. K., Hanis, S. M., Khazaei, S., Sani, M., et al. (2017). Estimates of global HIV/AIDS mortality, prevalence and incidence rates, and their association with the Human Development Index. *Biomedical Research and Therapy, 4*(06), 1399. https://doi.org/10.15419/bmrat.v4i06.181

Mansour, M., Dawood, S., & Falqi, I. (2020). An integrated structural equation modeling and analytic hierarchy process approach to prioritize investment in the construction industry to achieve sustainable development in Saudi Arabia. *Polish Journal of Environmental Studies, 29*(3), 2285–2302. https://doi.org/10.15244/pjoes/110516

Mather, A. S., & Needle, C. L. (1999). Development, democracy and forest trends. *Global Environmental Change, 9*(2), 105–118. https://doi.org/10.1016/S0959-3780(98)00035-1

McCleary, R. M., & Barro, R. J. (2006). Religion and political economy in an international panel. *Journal for the Scientific Study of Religion, 45*(2), 149–175. https://doi.org/10.1111/j.1468-5906.2006.00299.x

Meramveliotakis, G., & Manioudis, M. (2021). History, knowledge, and sustainable economic development: The contribution of John Stuart Mill's grand stage theory. *Sustainability (Switzerland), 13*(3), 1–17. https://doi.org/10.3390/su13031468

Merkle, E. C., & Rosseel, Y. (2018). Blavaan: Bayesian structural equation models via parameter expansion. *Journal of Statistical Software, 85*, 1. https://doi.org/10.18637/jss.v085.i04

Meyer, N., & Meyer, D. F. (2019). Examining the impact of entrepreneurial activity on employment and economic growth: The case of the visegrÁd countries. *Polish Journal of Management Studies, 20*(1), 277–292. https://doi.org/10.17512/pjms.2019.20.1.25

Milenkovic, N., Vukmirovic, J., Bulajic, M., & Radojicic, Z. (2014). A multivariate approach in measuring socio-economic development of MENA countries. *Economic Modelling, 38*, 604–608. https://doi.org/10.1016/j.econmod.2014.02.011

Minniti, M., & Lévesque, M. (2010). Entrepreneurial types and economic growth. *Journal of Business Venturing, 25*(3), 305–314. https://doi.org/10.1016/j.jbusvent.2008.10.002

Minniti, A., & Venturini, F. (2017). The long-run growth effects of R&D policy. *Research Policy, 46*(1), 316–326. https://doi.org/10.1016/j.respol.2016.11.006

Modigliani, F. (1986). Life cycle, individual thrift, and the wealth of nations. Science. 10.1126/science.234.4777.704

Mosse, D. (2010). A relational approach to durable poverty, inequality and power. *Journal of Development Studies, 46*(7), 1156–1178. https://doi.org/10.1080/00220388.2010.487095

Mumford, E. (2006). The story of socio-technical design: Reflections on its successes, failures and potential. Information Systems Journal. 10.1111/j.1365-2575.2006.00221.x

Murton, G. (2015). The disempowered development of Tibet in China: a study in the economics of marginalization. *Contemporary South Asia, 23*(1), 92–94. https://doi.org/10.1080/09584935.2014.1001126

Nelson, R. R., & Pack, H. (1999). The Asian miracle and modern growth theory. *Economic Journal, 109*(457), 416–436. https://doi.org/10.1111/1468-0297.00455

Nepal, A. (2020). Entrepreneurship and Economic Development. Modern. *Economics, 19*(1), 143–148. https://doi.org/10.31521/modecon.v19(2020)-23

Nguyen, P. C. Nguyen, B. Bui, T., & Su, T. (2021). Economic Complexity and Entrepreneurship Density: A Non-Linear Effect Study. Technological Forecasting and Social Change. https://doi.org/10.1016/j.techfore.2021.121107

Njoh, A. J. (2018). The relationship between modern Information and Communications Technologies (ICTs) and development in Africa. *Utilities Policy, 50*, 83–90. https://doi.org/10.1016/j.jup.2017.10.005

Olaoye, I. J. Ayinde, O. E. Ajewole, O. O., & Adebisi, L. O. (2020). The role of research and development (R&D) expenditure and governance on economic growth in selected African countries. African Journal of Science, Technology, Innovation and Development. https://doi.org/10.1080/20421338.2020.1799300

Park, J. k., Ryu, D., & Lee, K. (2019). What determines the economic size of a nation in the world: Determinants of a nation's share in world GDP vs. per capita GDP. *Structural Change and Economic Dynamics, 51*, 203–214. https://doi.org/10.1016/j.strueco.2019.09.001

Pasmore, W., Winby, S., Mohrman, S. A., & Vanasse, R. (2019). Reflections: Sociotechnical Systems Design and Organization Change. *Journal of Change Management, 19*(2), 67–85. https://doi.org/10.1080/14697017.2018.1553761

Patorniti, N. P., Stevens, N. J., & Salmon, P. M. (2018). A sociotechnical systems approach to understand complex urban systems: A global transdisciplinary perspective. *Human Factors and Ergonomics In Manufacturing, 28*(6), 281–296. https://doi.org/10.1002/hfm.20742

Pearl, J. (2012). The causal foundations of structural equation modeling. Handbook of Structural Equation Modeling (pp. 68–91).

Glaeser, E. L. La Porta, R. Lopez-de-Silanes, F. and Shleifer, A. 2004. Do institutions cause growth? Journal of Economic Growth, 9(3), 271–303. https://doi.org/10.1023/B:JOEG.0000038933.16398.ed

Ram, R. (1997). Level of Economic Development and Income Inequality: Evidence from the Postwar Developed World. *Southern Economic Journal, 64*(2), 576. https://doi.org/10.2307/1060869

Ramadhan, M. (2019). Assessing of the impact of good governance and institutions on economic growth in Indonesia. *International Journal of Scientific and Technology Research, 8*(11), 2594–2598.

Rodrik, D. (1999). Where did all the growth go? External shocks, social conflict, and growth collapses. *Journal of Economic Growth, 4*(4), 385–412. https://doi.org/10.1023/A:1009863208706

Rosenberg, N. (1960). Some Institutional Aspects of the Wealth of Nations. *Journal of Political Economy, 68*(6), 557–570. https://doi.org/10.1086/258392

Roy, A., & Goll, I. (2014). Predictors of various facets of sustainability of nations: The role of cultural and economic factors. *International Business Review, 23*(5), 849–861. https://doi.org/10.1016/j.ibusrev.2014.01.003

Roy, S., & Mohanty, R. P. (2020). Microfinance models in improving "quality of life": Empirical analysis on Indian perspective. International Journal of Business Innovation and Research. Inderscience Publishers. 10.1504/IJBIR.2020.104031

Sáenz-Castro, J. E., & García-González, J. D. (2019). The relationship between corruption and inequality in Colombia: Empirical evidence using panel data for the period 2008-2017. Iberoamerican. *Journal of Development Studies, 8*(2), 28–43. https://doi.org/10.26754/ojs_ried/ijds.359

Saunders, N. (2021). Classical Economic Theory and the Modern Economy. *History of Economics Review, 79*(1), 78–79. https://doi.org/10.1080/10370196.2021.1877931

Savaget, P. Geissdoerfer, M., Kharrazi, A., & Evans, S. (2019). The theoretical foundations of sociotechnical systems change for sustainability: A systematic literature review. Journal of Cleaner Production. Elsevier Ltd. 10.1016/j.jclepro.2018.09.208

Sbardella, A., Pugliese, E., & Pietronero, L. (2017). Economic development and wage inequality: A complex system analysis. *PLoS ONE, 12*(9), 1. https://doi.org/10.1371/journal.pone.0182774

Segerstrom, P. S. (1991). Innovation, Imitation, and Economic Growth. *Journal of Political Economy, 99*(4), 807–827. https://doi.org/10.1086/261779

Segerstrom, P. S. (2000). The long-run growth effects of R & D subsidies. *Journal of Economic Growth, 5*(3), 277–305. https://doi.org/10.1023/A:1009881717993

Shaffer, R., Deller, S., & Marcouiller, D. (2006). Rethinking community economic development. *Economic Development Quarterly, 20*(1), 59–74. https://doi.org/10.1177/0891242405283106

Sharp, S. (2007). The economic impact of HIV/AIDS in Russia: Current trends and perspectives. In *HIV/AIDS in Russia and Eurasia: Volume I* (pp. 77–102). Palgrave Macmillan. https://doi.org/10.1057/9780230603394_5

Şimşek, E., Orhan, M., & Macit, F. (2017). Effect of Government Expenditure on GDP in the Turkish Economy. *International Econometric Review, 9*(2), 69–76. https://doi.org/10.33818/ier.336791

Smith, A. (1776). *An inquiry into the nature and causes of the wealth of nations* (p. 1910). J.M. and Sons Ltd..

Sofilda, E., Hermiyanti, P., & Hamzah, M. Z. (2015). Determinant Variable Analysis of Human Development Index in Indonesia (Case for High and Low Index at Period 2004-2013). *OIDA International Journal of Sustainable Development, 08*(09), 11–28.

Sokolov Mladenović, S., Mladenović, I., & Ćuzović, D. (2019). Distributive trade and economic growth: Eu28 evidence for the period 2008–2015. *Journal of Business Economics and Management, 20*(3), 489–506. https://doi.org/10.3846/jbem.2019.9857

Solow, R. M. (1956). A contribution to the theory of economic growth. *Quarterly Journal of Economics, 70*(1), 65–94. https://doi.org/10.2307/1884513

Sookias, R. B., Passmore, S., & Atkinson, Q. D. (2018). Deep cultural ancestry and human development indicators across nation states. *Royal Society Open Science, 5*(4), 1. https://doi.org/10.1098/rsos.171411

Stel, A. V., Carree, M., & Thurik, R. (2005). The effect of entrepreneurial activity on national economic growth. *Small Business Economics, 24*(3), 311–321. https://doi.org/10.1007/s11187-005-1996-6

Suganthi, L. (2019). Sustainable development index: A dashboard to measure a country's resilience. *Journal of Sociology and Social Anthropology, 10*(1–3), 12–21. https://doi.org/10.31901/24566764.2019/10-1-3.292

Sutthichaimethee, P., Chatchorfa, A., & Suyaprom, S. (2019). A forecasting model for economic growth and CO_2 emission based on industry 4.0 political policy under the government power: Adapting a second-order autoregressive-SEM. *Journal of Open Innovation: Technology, Market, and Complexity, 5*(3), 1. https://doi.org/10.3390/joitmc5030069

Tarka, P. (2018). An overview of structural equation modeling: its beginnings, historical development, usefulness and controversies in the social sciences. *Quality and Quantity, 52*(1), 313–354. https://doi.org/10.1007/s11135-017-0469-8

Temple, J., & Johnson, P. A. (1998). Social capability and economic growth. *Quarterly Journal of Economics, 113*(3), 964–990. https://doi.org/10.1162/003355398555711

Thornton, P. H., Ribeiro-Soriano, D., & Urbano, D. (2011). Socio-cultural factors and entrepreneurial activity: An overview. *International Small Business Journal, 29*(2), 105–118. https://doi.org/10.1177/0266242610391930

Urbano, D., Aparicio, S., & Audretsch, D. (2019). Twenty-five years of research on institutions, entrepreneurship, and economic growth: what has been learned? *Small Business Economics, 53*(1), 21–49. https://doi.org/10.1007/s11187-018-0038-0

Dam, A. Van, & Frenken, K. (2020). Variety, complexity and economic development. Research Policy. https://doi.org/10.1016/j.respol.2020.103949

Vettore, M. V., Vieira, J. M. R., Gomes, J. F. F., Martins, N. M. O., Freitas, Y. N. L., Lamarca, G. D. A., & Rebelo, M. A. B. (2020). Individual- and city-level socioeconomic factors and tooth loss among elderly people: A cross-level multilevel analysis. *International Journal of Environmental Research and Public Health, 17*(7), 1. https://doi.org/10.3390/ijerph17072345

Viddy, A. R., & Asniwati, B. (2019). The determinants of human development index and economic growth in Indonesia. *International Journal of Scientific and Technology Research, 8*(12), 661–665.

Walker, G. H., Stanton, N. A., Salmon, P. M., & Jenkins, D. P. (2008). A review of sociotechnical systems theory: A classic concept for new command and control paradigms. *Theoretical Issues in Ergonomics Science, 9*(6), 479–499. https://doi.org/10.1080/14639220701635470

Wang, J., Xin, L., Tan, M., & Wang, Y. (2016). Spatial heterogeneity in Chinese forest area change in the early 21st century. *Forests, 7*(10), 1. https://doi.org/10.3390/f7100232

Weil, D. N. (2007). Accounting for the effect of health on economic growth. Quarterly Journal of Economics. https://doi.org/10.1162/qjec.122.3.1265

World Bank. (2016). World development indicators. The World Bank. [accessed 2021 Feb 15]. http://data.worldbank.org/products/wdi.

Wright, S. (1918). On the nature of size factors. *Genetics, 3*(4), 367–374. https://doi.org/10.1093/genetics/3.4.367

Yadav, S., Antil, N., Gupta, D., & Kandpal, V. (2020). A panel data examination of income inequality in 24 African countries. *Journal of Public Affairs.* https://doi.org/10.1002/pa.2563

Yong, E. L. (2020). Understanding Cultural Determinants of Scientific-Knowledge Development: Empirical Conceptualization from a Cross-Country Investigation. *Journal of the Knowledge Economy, 11*(4), 1646–1662. https://doi.org/10.1007/s13132-020-00626-4

Zayed, N. M., Kamruzzaman, M., Chowdhury, S., Tasneem, S., & Islam, M. S. (2019). A strategic analysis of patterns of growth in advanced countries during 1870-2006. *Academy of Strategic Management Journal, 18*(4), 1.

Zeira, J. (1998). Workers, machines, and economic growth. *Quarterly Journal of Economics, 113*(4), 1091–1117. https://doi.org/10.1162/003355398555847

13

General Conclusions

Diego Gomez, Sebastian Aparicio, and David Urbano

13.1 Main Conclusions

Economic development has been an objective (Cypher, 2014; Hammer & Pivo, 2017; Nafziger, 2012) and a success story for some countries (Kim, 2011), but a mystery (Christensen, 2009; Helpman, 2009) and a failure for others (Hausmann & Rodrik, 2003). If the right development path were so clear, all countries would be very close to their steady state (Daly, 1974; Kohlscheen & Nakajima, 2021). However, the evidence shows different paths for different types of countries (Helpman, 2009), so the literature has come to conclude that there is a missing piece to the

D. Gomez
Fundación ECSIM, Medellin, Colombia

S. Aparicio (✉) • D. Urbano
Department of Business, Universitat Autònoma de Barcelona, Cerdanyola del Vallés, Barcelona, Spain

Centre for Entrepreneurship and Social Innovation Research (CREIS), Universitat Autònoma de Barcelona, Sabadell, Barcelona, Spain
e-mail: Sebastian.Aparicio@uab.cat

D. Gomez et al. (eds.), *Driving Complexity in Economic Development*,
https://doi.org/10.1007/978-3-031-34386-5_13

development puzzle. What then is the missing link? Is there just one? What kinds of methodologies should be used to address this link? Can this link be used to formulate development policies? Throughout the chapters of this book, we seek to answer these questions and arrive at a successful conclusion.

The history of economic growth theories has focused on the endogenous aspect (Hunt, 2012), that is, mechanisms determined within the economic model itself that can be drivers of growth (Howitt, 2010), such as human capital (Bucci et al., 2019; Ehrlich & Kim, 2015) or physical capital (Li et al., 2020). These theories were developed due to the impossibility of explaining economic growth through exogenous growth theories from a mathematical perspective, initially exposed by Solow (1956). However, the number of determinants extracted through endogenous models has led to a theoretical funnel that has stalled the new theories of development capable of becoming mainstream.

Although some currents derived from Schumpeterianism emerged, where economic growth through entrepreneurs' capacity to innovate was established, giving birth to new terms such as "creative destruction," among others. Thus was born the assimilationist approach, where theories were developed that go beyond human capital, where such human capital is capable of learning, innovating, and venturing (entrepreneurship). The literature then turned to explain economic growth through education (Maneejuk & Yamaka, 2021; Marquez-Ramos & Mourelle, 2019), innovation (Coe & Helpman, 1995; Maradana et al., 2019), and entrepreneurship (Acs et al., 2009; Audretsch et al., 2007; Urbano & Aparicio, 2016; Wennekers & Thurik, 1999); the latter two being conditioned by the institutional environment as a fundamental factor (North, 1990). However, despite identifying key determinants such as entrepreneurship, the same endogenous growth methodologies based on general equilibrium conditions were still used. For this reason, at the end of Chap. 3 ("A Review of Economic Development Thinking and the Role of Innovative Entrepreneurship: Past, Present, and Future"), the concept of social capability is introduced: it is all the products and services that are made or rendered in a given period, determined by a production flow (PF) and a demand (FS), with the difference that this model is considered a dynamic one through differential equations capable of replicating the s-shaped behavior of some successful economies such as Singapore.

This leads us to carry out a diagnosis of growth capable of delving into the concept of social capacity. The entire mathematical construction of the social capacity function is carried out, which depends mainly on two fundamental agents: families and firms. A dynamic process of supply and demand of goods, services, and labor is then generated, with the capacity to produce an economic flow model that considers payments, benefits, inventories, and investment. But although both agents are fundamental to the economic flow model, we focus on firms since they are capable of generating new processes through investment. In the chapter on growth diagnosis (Chap. 5), we highlight the role of the firms within the dynamic process. Firms take into account not only internal aspects but also external variables that modify their profit and loss account, such as taxes, interest rates, logistics, wages, and inputs, among others. All these variables influence the calculation of the Internal Rate of Return (IRR), which represents the profitability offered by an investment or a new project. This IRR filters the viable projects that come from innovation and entrepreneurial decisions, thus leading to the emergence of new ventures capable of generating economic development.

Therefore, starting with the chapter on growth diagnosis, we developed chapters capable of explaining the effect of some key variables for firms or ventures, such as taxes, entrepreneurial decisions, company size, and company expansion through exports. From these chapters, we can draw some conclusions. First, government performance reflected by indicators such as total central government debt (as a percentage of GDP) and claims on central government (annual growth as a percentage of broad money) has a significant and positive effect on taxes (total taxes and contribution rate), which in turn has a negative and significant effect on indicators of economic growth such as Gross National Income (GNI), New Business Density (NBD), and Gross Fixed Capital Formation. Second, country risk factors such as the lending interest rate, taxes and contribution rates, the cost of construction permits, electricity costs, and exporting costs harm investment decision measures such as IRR and Return On Equity (ROE), which are investment decision measures that spur economic growth. Third, institutional barriers (at firm, city, and country level) such as financial access, telecommunications notion, and cost of business start-up procedures affect the international business (direct exports) of firms (specifically formal firms). Fourth, individual (gender and age), household (computer possession), and city (taxes) characteristics are key in the entrepreneurial choice (employer or self-employed), which is significant in the generation of income (labor income), which drives GDP per capita at the city level (for employers only). Fifth, firm size (sales) has a positive and significant effect on GDP per capita of Latin American and Caribbean countries; however, as countries' economies become closer to their steady state, the effect becomes less significant (OECD countries). Thus, all the effects presented in these chapters make clear the role of entrepreneurship in economic growth but also the importance of what lies behind entrepreneurship and innovation, namely the profitability of investment decision measures such as IRR and ROE, as these measures are the mechanism by which entrepreneurship, innovation, and investment by households and firms can take place.

But given the complexity of economic development (Helpman, 2009), its engine cannot be single-cylinder, since entrepreneurship alone cannot work miracles. Thus, two fundamental chapters are developed in the book: on inequality and poverty (a component analysis) and socio-technical subsystems. Both chapters make it clear that economic development is complex because many actors must be considered: economic, social, and institutional. Institutions also play an important role in all this theoretical and practical development, since it is they that establish the rules of the game for the agents (households and firms), playing the role of facilitators or barriers that allow the development or stagnation of the economy. We therefore conclude that economic development, in addition to being complex due to the number of actors involved, must consider new methodologies capable of taking into account the dynamic decision-making processes of the agents. Theories such as system dynamics and socio-technical subsystems may be an option when generating literature capable of generating fresh air for the understanding of economic development.

13.2 Implications

This book puts forward both theoretical and public policy implications. From a theoretical point of view, this research may contribute to advances of the current knowledge in an area in which there is a space to keep working (new methods of analyzing and estimating economic development through entrepreneurship as the backbone of economic development), as some aspects remain underexplored. Some implications are mentioned below.

First, the search to solve the mystery of economic development has been tireless (Helpman, 2009), mainly based on theories tied to the general equilibrium proposed by Walras, from exogenous models to endogenous ones that involve external and internal factors as the main drivers of development, respectively. However, there seems to be a theoretical stagnation, since the research field has discovered an important accumulation of determinants that affect development but has not yet traced a route that leads to such a state. Thus, in Chap. 3 we propose system dynamics as an alternative way to create a scheme that is capable of involving the decisions of economic agents (households and firms), resulting in different scenarios of economic growth that depend on the investment decisions of these agents, where the economy is capable of generating a greater social capacity if it reinvests its profits.

Second, although entrepreneurship has been approached through different variables (e.g., self-employment, business owners, and total early-stage entrepreneurial activity), Chap. 2 has shown, through a systematic literature review and meta-regression analysis, that new ventures contribute significantly to economic growth. Existing nuances such as type and quality of entrepreneurship have motivated scholars to talk about the optimal level of entrepreneurial activity to achieve higher national productivity (Carree et al., 2002). More importantly, extant literature has also opened the possibility of exploring other socioeconomic outcomes, in which inclusive growth and poverty alleviation are obtained thanks to the existence of entrepreneurs (Aparicio et al., 2021).

Chapters 4 and 5 help us not only to analyze some evidence about why some countries have succeeded and others have failed but also to propose the mathematical scheme based on system dynamics that allows us to calculate the "social capacity"; furthermore, Chap. 5 allows us to make our third contribution: the proposal of a route by which countries can stimulate their economies through conditioning a closed pool of indicators such as taxes, measures of investment decisions such as IRR and ROE, institutional barriers (at the firm, city, and country level) such as financial access, telecommunications notion and cost of business start-up procedures, entrepreneurial choice to be an employer or self-employed, and company size such as firm sales. Thus, each of the above-mentioned indicators will allow us to derive some implications.

Fourth, some results of this research allow us to establish theoretical implications about tax structure and its relationship to economic growth and government institutions. On the one hand, there is bulk literature on the various effects of taxes on economic growth (Easterly & Rebelo, 1993; Stokey & Rebelo, 1995). Key research like Sabir (2019) and Denaux (2007) examines the impact of fiscal policy (tax structure) on the growth process of economies. However, these studies support the direct effects of taxes on economic growth such as GDP. This research addresses the gap in the literature, in which the tax structure has direct effects on the determinants of economic growth such as GNI, NBD, and capital formation. These determinants have effects on economic growth (Diacon & Maha, 2015; Meyer & Meyer, 2019), but they also play a key role in the process of economic development. On the other hand, taxes are the main source of distortion of economic growth, but the magnitude of this tax structure can be controlled by government policy. The results help reinforce the ideas put forward by Bassetto and Kocherlakota (2004) for understanding the relationship between government performance and taxation. These authors consider a government that can only raise funds by levying distortionary taxes. They allow the government to collect taxes in each period that are based on incomes earned in previous periods. The results show that once they do so, given any debt path, the government can adjust its tax policy to attain that debt path without affecting equilibrium allocations or prices. This indicates the importance of fiscal policies and policymakers' decisions, as they can positively or negatively influence the country's economic growth.

We believe that Chap. 6 will encourage policymakers to pay greater attention to their performance on debt, support for the creation of new businesses, and the way tax revenues are used. Ghourchian and Yilmazkuday (2020) compare the effects of government consumption and government debt on economic growth using data from 83 countries, including both developed and developing markets, over the period from 1960 to 2014. These authors suggest that the restrictions on government expenditure to prevent negative growth are more important for countries with lower trade openness, lower inflation, or greater financial depth, whereas the restrictions on government debt are shown to be more important for countries with higher trade openness, lower inflation, or greater financial depth. Although this research presents direct effects of government performance on economic growth, it shows us the importance of policy decisions. An interesting point to consider is how the revenues from this type of tax are used, given that if they are used in the wrong way, it not only discourages the creation of companies but also produces a huge fiscal gap for the country's finances. This indicates that the best option is to try to reduce taxes on income, profits, and gains and replace them with sales taxes, which have positive effects on growth in some regions (Hall & Kanaan, 2020).

Fifth, the chapter on IRR (Chap. 7) allows us to establish theoretical implications about the importance of measures of investment decisions such as IRR and ROE and their effect on economic growth. Four important theoretical implications will be shown below. The first implication concerns the relationship between IRR and economic growth, as GDP per capita is unexplored. Only a little research, such as Yassin and Derar (2014), has been concerned with unveiling the macroeconomic effects of IRR. This is because IRR is a measure of corporate and project investment decisions, that is, at the firm level. With this research we hope to fill this gap in the literature, raising interest in studying this relationship in depth, after having demonstrated the positive and significant effect of IRR and ROE on GDP per capita. The second implication is tied to the first; this research encourages the use of investment decision variables not only for the analysis of foreign investment or capital inflows but also for the study of their macroeconomic effects. The third implication is that the use of country risk factors should be used to study measures of investment decisions such as IRR and ROE. This implication is of significant importance, given that these country risk factors are variables that directly affect the decisions of a country's firms. Companies play a fundamental role in society since they are responsible for combining knowledge with innovation, and if variables such as lending interest rates, taxes they have to pay, and the increase in some operational costs affect them, then the economy of a country will be indirectly affected. The last theoretical implication focuses on highlighting that our measure of ROE showed a greater significance in the expected relationships and a greater effect on the variables. Although Feenstra et al. (2015) did an outstanding job in obtaining an IRR at the country level, we believe that there is still a long way to go to create a consistent variable that can be used to observe its effects on macroeconomic variables.

With regard to the policy implications of Chap. 7, we present two. On the one hand, the first implication is that policymakers should be encouraged to generate improvements in country risk factors. For example, interest rates should be decreased so that companies will have borrowing facilities to be able to carry out their operations and market expansions; tax rates for companies should be decreased, since in some countries there are high rates that hinder the profitability of projects or businesses; the costs derived from the construction permit process (warehouse costs) should be reduced, as this will promote the interest of foreign investors in investing in countries that implement such policies; the cost of electricity should be reduced, as it is one of the highest operational costs among the cost items of companies; and finally, export costs should be reduced, as these prevent companies from deciding to expand worldwide. On the other hand, we propose the inclusion of companies in the macroeconomic decisions of countries, since they are responsible for creating value and innovation. Policymakers should at least take into account the effects of some decisions on variables that affect companies' operating costs and investment decisions. Finally, these implications indicate the importance of companies within society. Therefore, policymakers should also make an effort to lower the barriers or costs in the creation of new businesses. The literature showing the positive and significant effect of the creation of new businesses on economic growth and development is extensive.

Sixth, in the international business chapter (Chap. 8), on one hand, we provide fresh insight into how institutional obstacles harm international businesses such as exports of formal or new firms (start-ups); although some research claims that institutional barriers drive exports, in this research we find that firms need not feel threatened by financial access and competition from the informal sector or services such as electricity and telecommunications or by national taxes or related costs of entrepreneurship. In addition, perhaps those investigations that support a positive effect of institutional obstacles on the firm's exports do not take into account the fundamental role of informality in the countries; thus, our research points to differences in the effects that these obstacles have on both informal and formal start-ups. This allows us to understand that the ability of initially informal firms to evade some institutional barriers may allow them to do better locally than abroad. Also, this chapter develops a micro- and macro-level analysis of the relationship between institutions, entrepreneurship, and international business, accompanied by informality bias, a methodology never before used to analyze this set of literature. Scholars have long called for deeper analysis and research into institutional economics and entrepreneurship (Ha et al., 2021), but until now, research has never been accompanied by international business and an important bias such as informality.

On the other hand, we focus on the policy implications by providing recommendations to the policymakers of the countries and cities considered in this chapter. First, it is necessary to reduce taxes on company profits, which will generate a more accelerated growth of firms, leading them to international markets, in addition to reducing the costs of procedures related to business start-ups. Second, the policymakers of the cities must provide adequate electrical and telecommunications services, so that companies do not worry about power outages or failures in the Internet or satellite signal, as this can affect productivity, leading to decreases in exports. Third, policymakers must provide easy access to credit and guarantees of competition in the sector in which these companies operate. Finally, it is necessary to generate programs for the formalization of companies, as this will lead them to generate high growth rates and possible international expansion.

Seventh, focusing on the chapter on entrepreneurial decisions (Chap. 9), three important theoretical implications are derived from our findings. First, the literature shows that several determinants drive entrepreneurship (Ghani et al., 2014), among which are institutional (Urbano et al., 2019), regional (Ross et al., 2015), and individual (Krasniqi, 2009) characteristics; however, there is little literature investigating the importance of both characteristics for entrepreneurial decisions in the regions of developing countries. It should be noted that regional characteristics are fundamental for the research, since Colombia is a regional country (Perobelli et al., 2010) where each city adopts very different policies (Franz, 2019), which is why the consideration of both characteristics is crucial for an understanding of the results under the regional context. Second, labor income emerges as a transmission mechanism, since the entrepreneurial decision to become an employer increases the labor income of employers, while becoming self-employed decreases it, and thus these factors play the role of economic incentives. Employers not only receive individual benefits but also generate social ones since they are generators of employment. The results of the second stage support the benefits that employers receive, but can those individual benefits be converted into macro-level benefits? Third, given that the results clearly show the effect of entrepreneurs' income on economic growth in Colombia, it is important to point out the underlying mechanism driving this relationship: labor income (Djido & Shiferaw, 2018). In economic theory, labor income is crucial for the economic growth of regions (Merkulova, 2019), but it is not highly appreciated as a transmission mechanism to relate entrepreneurship to economic growth. That is why this research opens the door to a more detailed study of the effects of labor income such as employer and self-employed income on per capita GDP in developing countries. The results show a strong heterogeneity when we look at what happens with self-employment, due to its strong correlation with informality (Arango & Flórez, 2021). Therefore, we can say that in developing countries such as Colombia, informality plays a fundamental role in labor market structures and is perhaps the greatest obstacle to entrepreneurship having a positive impact on the economy.

However, exciting challenges arise concerning recommendations to policymakers, applicable to the policy framework of developing and regional countries. We believe that this specific chapter ("Entrepreneurial Decision," Chap. 9) allows policymakers to target policies on several specific points. First, policies should direct special programs dedicated to facilitating access to ICTs (access to computers) in all regions of the country. In addition, it is clear that regional characteristics are fundamental for the entrepreneurial decision, and therefore it is also crucial to lower taxes on companies, as these taxes reduce the probability of becoming an entrepreneur (employer or self-employed). Second, the results lead to rethinking of the political strategies regarding entrepreneurship, recognizing the differences between employers and the self-employed (individual characteristics such as sex and age). Thus, providing better structures for self-employed entrepreneurs to be productive, generating support channels, and monitoring in the initial stages of their projects for the creation of companies could be policies oriented toward better results for this type of entrepreneurship. Third, the high level of informality in Columbia should be reduced by supporting productive projects, training small entrepreneurs, facilitating credit for small- and medium-sized enterprises, generating an educational movement focused on the creation of enterprises, and other policies. Another option to reduce informality could be the use of subsidies through the companies; thus, subsidies would go directly to the payrolls of the companies, which would absorb informal workers and would not have to incur high labor costs in health or pensions. Perhaps policymakers should focus their efforts on improving the structure of the labor market, which is the cause of many heterogeneities in labor outcomes.

Eighth, the results of the chapter on company size (Chap. 10) allow us to establish theoretical implications about the importance of company characteristics like company size for economic growth (per capita GDP). First, filling the gap in the literature on this relationship is fundamental to economic theory. Company characteristics such as size allow us to identify new relationships and effects on the economic growth of countries. Due to the economic crisis generated by the COVID-19 pandemic and as a consequence of the shortage of fundamental products or services, it is crucial to establish new forms of economic growth. Second, this chapter strengthens the fundamental role of companies in the economic, institutional, and social framework of countries. The literature has positioned companies as one of the fundamental engines of economic growth (Szarzcc ct al., 2021) but has not yet evaluated in depth the effect of their characteristics on macroeconomic variables such as GDP. That is why our research tries to mark a path in the study of these characteristics and their effects.

Considering the big challenge of Chap. 10 ("Company Size") about generating a discussion on policy decisions that would help spur economic growth from companies' characteristics, specifically from their size, such as the annual sales, we generated important policy implications. First, we seek to make policymakers understand the fundamental role of companies in economies and the positive effect of the growth of these companies on economic growth through their sales under favorable institutional and social conditions. Second, some policies such as tax reductions that allow companies to reduce their costs have a positive effect on the studied relationship, since such a policy will generate a boost not only at the micro-level but also at the macro-level by spurring employment growth. In addition, this policy can be accompanied by economic benefits such as pension and health subsidies, with the possibility of promoting an increase in formal employment, especially in Latin American and Caribbean countries. Third, institutional improvements that reduce the barriers to entry to the markets and allow the creation of new companies should be implemented, in addition to the generation of policies that boost the exports of these companies and help their sales grow. These may be some policies that encourage entrepreneurs and businesspeople to carry out innovation and technical processes in their companies, aiming not only at personal benefits but also the generation of formal employment.

Finally, the theoretical and policy implications governing this book are aimed at the ability to identify new methodologies such as system dynamics and dynamic subsystems, capable of estimating and analyzing economic development from a more complex point of view; thus, policymakers should redirect efforts toward social inclusion and employment generation by supporting entrepreneurship, which is the main engine of the economic system, while taking into account investment decision measures such as IRR and ROE, which are the measures that allow the implementation of investment projects that lead to more entrepreneurship and innovation.

13.3 Limitations and Future Research Lines

Although in the book we were able to generate important theoretical and policy implications, some limitations (mostly data-related) did not allow us to carry out an extension of the results. However, this allows for new lines of research related to regional analysis of development theories, given that each region presents different institutional characteristics; research with proxy variables that test our results; and the development of a more advanced model capable of integrating not only economic but also institutional, environmental, and external agents. Thus, these are some of the lines of future research that could be boosted by our book, two of which are mentioned below.

First, studies could be performed that are capable of identifying causal relationships that consider the cities, countries, and regions where the dependent and independent variables are related, that is, taking into account multilevel relationships, since these relationships are determined by cultural, institutional, and social aspects. Although some causal relationships seem to be proven, such as the relationship between entrepreneurship and economic growth, an effect can be distorted by cultural or institutional heterogeneities in countries, such as Latin American countries. This not only gives transparency to the empirical development of research but also provides possibilities for new research related to the mobility of human capital between cities or regions.

The second and perhaps most important future line of research that this book opens is related to the analysis of measures of investment decisions such as IRR and ROE at the macroeconomic level. Although it has been difficult for researchers to carry out macroeconomic calculations of microeconomic measures such as these, this book emphasizes the importance of knowing the returns of investment projects at the macroeconomic level, since it is these returns that determine whether the projects are carried out or not, leading to more entrepreneurship and innovation, the main cornerstone of economic development.

References

Acs, Z. J., Braunerhjelm, P., Audretsch, D. B., & Carlsson, B. (2009). The knowledge spillover theory of entrepreneurship. *Small Business Economics, 32*(1), 15–30. https://doi.org/10.1007/s11187-008-9157-3

Aparicio, S., Audretsch, D., & Urbano, D. (2021). Does entrepreneurship matter for inclusive growth? The role of social progress orientation. *Entrepreneurship Research Journal 11*(4), 20190308.

Arango, L. E., & Flórez, L. A. (2021). Regional labour informality in Colombia and a proposal for a differential minimum wage. *Journal of Development Studies, 57*(6), 1016–1037. https://doi.org/10.1080/00220388.2020.1841170

Audretsch, D. B., Keilbach, M. C., & Lehmann, E. E. (2007). *Entrepreneurship and economic growth*. Oxford University Press, pp. 1–236. https://doi.org/10.1093/acprof:oso/9780195183511.001.0001

Bassetto, M., & Kocherlakota, N. (2004). On the irrelevance of government debt when taxes are distortionary. *Statistics and Probability Letters, 66*(4), 299–304. https://doi.org/10.1016/j.jmoneco.2002.12.001

Bucci, A., Eraydın, L., & Müller, M. (2019). Dilution effects, population growth and economic growth under human capital accumulation and endogenous technological change. *Journal of Macroeconomics, 62*. https://doi.org/10.1016/j.jmacro.2018.08.003

Carree, M., Van Stel, A., Thurik, R., & Wennekers, S. (2002). Economic development and business ownership: An analysis using data of 23 OECD countries in the period 1976–1996. *Small Business Economics, 19*(3), 271–290.

Christensen, J. (2009). Reframing economic development: Thing or mystery? *International Review of Applied Economics, 23*(6), 723–741.

Coe, D. T., & Helpman, E. (1995). International R&D spillovers. *European Economic Review, 39*(5), 859–887. https://doi.org/10.1016/0014-2921(94)00100-E

Cypher, J. (2014). *The process of economic development* (4th ed.). Routledge. https://doi.org/10.4324/9780203080580

Daly, H. E. (1974). The economics of the steady state. *The American Economic Review, 64*(2), 15–21.

Denaux, Z. S. (2007). Endogenous growth, taxes and government spending: Theory and evidence. *Review of Development Economics, 11*(1), 124–138. https://doi.org/10.1111/j.1467-9361.2007.00377.x

Diacon, P.-E., & Maha, L.-G. (2015). The relationship between income, consumption and GDP: A time series, cross-country analysis. *Procedia Economics and Finance, 23*, 1535–1543. https://doi.org/10.1016/s2212-5671(15)00374-3

Djido, A. I., & Shiferaw, B. A. (2018). Patterns of labor productivity and income diversification—Empirical evidence from Uganda and Nigeria. *World Development, 105*, 416–427. https://doi.org/10.1016/j.worlddev.2017.12.026

Easterly, W., & Rebelo, S. (1993). Fiscal policy and economic growth. *Journal of Monetary Economics, 32*(3), 417–458. https://doi.org/10.1016/0304-3932(93)90025-B

Ehrlich, I., & Kim, J. (2015). Immigration, human capital formation, and endogenous economic growth. *Journal of Human Capital, 9*(4), 518–563. https://doi.org/10.1086/684717

Feenstra, R. C., Inklaar, R., & Timmer, M. P. (2015). The next generation of the Penn world table. *American Economic Review, 105*(10), 3150–3182. https://doi.org/10.1257/aer.20130954

Franz, T. (2019). Why 'good governance' fails: Lessons from regional economic development in Colombia. *International Journal of Urban and Regional Research, 43*(4), 776–785. https://doi.org/10.1111/1468-2427.12742

Ghani, E., Kerr, W. R., & O'Connell, S. (2014). Spatial determinants of entrepreneurship in India. *Regional Studies, 48*(6), 1071–1089. https://doi.org/10.1080/00343404.2013.839869

Ghourchian, S., & Yilmazkuday, H. (2020). Government consumption, government debt and economic growth. *Review of Development Economics, 24*(2), 589–605. https://doi.org/10.1111/rode.12661

Ha, L. T., Thanh, T. T., Thang, D. N., & Anh, P. T. H. (2021). Bribery, export decisions, and institutional constraints: Evidence from cross-country firm-level data. *Economic Analysis and Policy, 69*, 585–612. https://doi.org/10.1016/j.eap.2021.01.010

Hall, J. L., & Kanaan, D. Z. (2020). State tax policy, municipal choice, and local economic development outcomes: A structural equation modeling approach to performance assessment. *Public Administration Review.* https://doi.org/10.1111/puar.13165

Hammer, J., & Pivo, G. (2017). The triple bottom line and sustainable economic development theory and practice. *Economic Development Quarterly, 31*(1), 25–36. https://doi.org/10.1177/0891242416674808

Hausmann, R., & Rodrik, D. (2003). Economic development as self-discovery. *Journal of Development Economics, 72*(2), 603–633.

Helpman, E. (2009). *The mystery of economic growth.* Harvard University Press.

Howitt, P. (2010). Endogenous growth theory. In S. N. Durlauf & L. E. Blume (Eds.), *Economic growth* (The New Palgrave economics collection). Palgrave Macmillan. https://doi.org/10.1057/9780230280823_10

Hunt, S. D. (2012). Understanding the drivers of economic growth: Grounding endogenous economic growth models in resource-advantage theory. *Contemporary Economics, 6*(4), 4–8. https://doi.org/10.5709/ce.1897-9254.62

Kim, J. (2011). Foreign aid and economic development: The success story of South Korea. *Pacific Focus, 26*(2), 260–286.

Kohlscheen, E., & Nakajima, J. (2021). Steady-state growth. *International Finance, 24*(1), 40–52. https://doi.org/10.1111/infi.12386

Krasniqi, B. A. (2009). Personal, household and business environmental determinants of entrepreneurship. *Journal of Small Business and Enterprise Development, 16*(1), 146–166. https://doi.org/10.1108/14626000910932935

Li, Z., Chu, Y., & Gao, T. (2020). Economic growth with endogenous economic institutions. *Macroeconomic Dynamics, 24*(4), 920–934. https://doi.org/10.1017/S1365100518000536

Maneejuk, P., & Yamaka, W. (2021). The impact of higher education on economic growth in asean-5 countries. *Sustainability (Switzerland), 13*(2), 1–28. https://doi.org/10.3390/su13020520

Maradana, R. P., Pradhan, R. P., Dash, S., Zaki, D. B., Gaurav, K., Jayakumar, M., & Sarangi, A. K. (2019). Innovation and economic growth in European economic area countries: The Granger causality approach. *IIMB Management Review, 31*(3), 268–282. https://doi.org/10.1016/j.iimb.2019.03.002

Marquez-Ramos, L., & Mourelle, E. (2019). Education and economic growth: An empirical analysis of nonlinearities. *Applied Economic Analysis, 27*(79), 21–45. https://doi.org/10.1108/AEA-06-2019-0005

Merkulova, E. Y. (2019). The effect of labor productivity on economic growth. *Statistics and Economics, 16*(2), 34–44. https://doi.org/10.21686/2500-3925-2019-2-34-44

Meyer, N., & Meyer, D. F. (2019). Examining the impact of entrepreneurial activity on employment and economic growth: The case of the Visegrád countries. *Polish Journal of Management Studies, 20*(1), 277–292. https://doi.org/10.17512/pjms.2019.20.1.25

Nafziger, E. W. (2012). Theories of economic development. In *Economic development* (pp. 119–160). Cambridge University Press. https://doi.org/10.1017/cbo9781139028295.006

North, D. C. (1990). *Institutions, institutional change and economic performance*. Cambridge University Press.

Perobelli, F. S., Haddad, E. A., Moron, J. B., & Hewings, G. J. D. (2010). Structural interdependence among Colombian departments. *Economic Systems Research, 22*(3), 279–300. https://doi.org/10.1080/09535314.2010.510467

Ross, A. G., Adams, J., & Crossan, K. (2015). Entrepreneurship and the spatial context: A panel data study into regional determinants of small growing firms in Scotland. *Local Economy, 30*(6), 672–688. https://doi.org/10.1177/0269094215600135

Sabir, S. (2019). Fiscal policy, institutions and inclusive growth: Evidence from the developing Asian countries. *International Journal of Social Economics, 46*(6), 822–837. https://doi.org/10.1108/IJSE-08-2018-0419

Solow, R. M. (1956). A contribution to the theory of economic growth. *The Quarterly Journal of Economics, 70*(1), 65–94.

Stokey, N. L., & Rebelo, S. (1995). Growth effects of flat-rate taxes. *Journal of Political Economy, 103*(3), 519–550. https://doi.org/10.1086/261993

Szarzec, K., Dombi, Á., & Matuszak, P. (2021). State-owned enterprises and economic growth: Evidence from the post-Lehman period. *Economic Modelling*, 99. https://doi.org/10.1016/j.econmod.2021.03.009

Urbano, D., & Aparicio, S. (2016). Entrepreneurship capital types and economic growth: International evidence. *Technological Forecasting and Social Change, 102*, 34–44.

Urbano, D., Aparicio, S., & Audretsch, D. (2019). Twenty-five years of research on institutions, entrepreneurship, and economic growth: What has been learned? *Small Business Economics, 53*(1), 21–49.

Wennekers, S., & Thurik, R. (1999). Linking entrepreneurship and economic growth. *Small Business Economics, 13*(1), 27–56. https://doi.org/10.1023/A:1008063200484

Yassin, E.-T., & Derar, E.-O. (2014). Internal rate of return: A suggested alternative formula and its macro-economics implications. *Journal of American Science, 10*(11), 216–221.

Correction to: Driving Complexity in Economic Development

Diego Gomez, Sebastian Aparicio, and David Urbano

Correction to:

D. Gomez et al., *Driving Complexity in Economic Development*, https://doi.org/10.1007/978-3-031-34386-5

The original version of this book has been revised, the chapter author name Diego Martinez-Moya has been included in chapters 6, 7, 8 and 12.

The updated version of this book can be found at
https://doi.org/10.1007/978-3-031-34386-5

D. Gomez et al., *Driving Complexity in Economic Development*,
https://doi.org/10.1007/978-3-031-34386-5_14

Index

D. Gomez et al. (eds.), *Driving Complexity in Economic Development*,
https://doi.org/10.1007/978-3-031-34386-5

Y

FSC
www.fsc.org
MIX
Papier | Fördert gute Waldnutzung
FSC® C083411

Kolibri 360 GmbH
Ferdinand-Jühlke-Straße 7
99095 Erfurt, Deutschland
produktsicherheit@kolibri360.de